DATA

MODELING MADE SIMPLE

With PowerDesigner®

first edition

DATA

MODELING MADE SIMPLE

with PowerDesigner®

first edition

Steve Hoberman

George McGeachie

Technical Editor: David Dichmann

Technics Publications

New Jersey

Published by:

Technics Publications, LLC

966 Woodmere Drive
Westfield, NJ 07090 U.S.A.
www.technicspub.com

Edited by Carol Lehn
Cover design by Mark Brye
Cartoons by Abby Denson, www.abbycomix.com
Section III and V cartoons by George Brett McGeachie

ISBN, print ed.   978-0-9771400-9-1
First Printing 2011
Printed in the United States of America
Library of Congress Control Number: 2011933934

ATTENTION SCHOOLS AND BUSINESSES: Technics Publications books are available at quantity discounts with bulk purchase for educational, business, or sales promotional use. For information, please email Steve Hoberman, President of Technics Publications, at me@stevehoberman.com.

Contents at a Glance

Contents

From George

This may sound strange to some, but I need to say, "Thank goodness for software vendors!" Where would we professional data modelers be without software dedicated to helping us achieve our objectives, helping us to create and communicate our data models, and the associated extras we always need to define and integrate?

I thank Steve Hoberman for trusting me with his book and his words, and to Sybase for trusting me to bring out the best in their product. I am very grateful to them for allowing me to use material from their excellent PowerDesigner documentation.

Several individuals provided great assistance along the way: Steve, of course; and also the people from Sybase – David Dichmann, Matt Creason, and Laurie Barker, mainly, plus Jeff Giles and Jay Stevens from Team Sybase. I must also thank Alex Pratt and Ruairi Prendiville, my first PowerDesigner 'mentors'. Anthony Hill's patient responses to the many queries and issues I raised during the beta testing of PowerDesigner 16 were invaluable.

My old friend Ray Carroll found time during his busy retirement in France to chastise me for my hasty use of English.

Gabriel Tanase found time in his busy working life to review my work from the perspective of a PowerDesigner newbie.

Thanks also to David Hay for his helpful comments regarding the resolution of many-to-many relationships.

Without the help of all of the above people, this book would not be what it is today. Any errors or omissions that remain are purely mine.

Finally, thanks to my son George Brett for his amazing artwork; he calls these creatures "Koala Blobs".

From Steve

Thanks George for your precision and sense of humor. I'll think twice before consuming an *ice cream cup* in a *fast-paced class*. Thanks to Laurie Barker, David Dichmann, and Matt Creason for your guidance during this project. Thanks to all of the people who volunteer for our data management user groups, such as DAMA – you all help to advance our industry and keep us connected. Thanks Carol, for the superb editing job, Mark for the dynamite cover, and Abby for the great cartoons. Thanks to my family for tolerating my responses to "Dad, can you play with me?", "Honey, it's after midnight", and "Your dinner is getting cold", with "Just five more minutes on the computer and I'll be right there."

When Steve told me about his idea for this book, I thought it would be a book about data. I was wrong. In fact, it is a book about people, organizations, and relationships. OK, there's a lot about data in it, but the reason for modeling data is to make keeping track of things easier to manage. But it is more than that – it is also a book about how to make keeping track of things useful later on. Data modeling and data management is less about collecting than about using the collection to better our businesses. And this requires an understanding of data as it becomes information, and information as it is used to drive knowledge to make the best decisions possible.

The struggle to understand data as information, and information as knowledge, is rooted in context and perspective. What is the right context for this data? What is the right perspective to properly apply meaning and understanding to this information? It reminds me of the Aesop fable, "The Sheep and the Pig":

> One day a shepherd discovered a fat Pig in the meadow where his Sheep were pastured. He very quickly captured the porker, which squealed at the top of its voice the moment the Shepherd laid his hands on it. You would have thought, to hear the loud squealing, that the Pig was being cruelly hurt. But in spite of its squeals and struggles to escape, the Shepherd tucked his prize under his arm and started off to the butcher's in the market place. The Sheep in the pasture were much astonished and amused at the Pig's behavior, and followed the Shepherd and his charge to the pasture gate. "What makes you squeal like that?" asked one of the Sheep. "The Shepherd often catches and carries off one of us. But we should feel very much ashamed to make such a terrible fuss about it like you do." "That is all very well," replied the Pig, with a squeal and a frantic kick. "When he catches you he is only after your wool. But he wants my bacon! gree-ee-ee!" Aesop for Children (1919)

The fact that an animal is being taken away, by itself, does not tell us if there is danger or not; the facts surrounding the type of animal changes the context from safe (Sheep) to danger (Pig). The relationships between the action facts and the animal facts are what determine whether we should be scared or comfortable.

This concept is not limited to children's stories. In fact, I am seeing more and more organizations struggle with the need to transform data into "actionable" knowledge. I am not seeing them hampered as much by technical limitations in physically connecting systems together. Instead, I am seeing them hampered by conceptual barriers segregating business understanding of the information needed to arrive at critical decisions with the physical locations and makeup of the data elements themselves. This lack of defined relationship between business and IT creates greater "information problems" than any system, application, or project implementation ever has.

That is where this book comes in. Steve's approachable way of helping folks new to information architecture and data modeling leads us to understand why there are different levels of abstraction, and different ways of looking at data structures. Even for the more experienced,

Steve helps us see how these different viewpoints provide different understanding, a different model for each user, or stakeholder, so that we can achieve the right clarity for business without sacrificing the technologist's need for detail. With the addition of George's practical and applied use of Sybase PowerDesigner as more than just a modeling tool, George shows us how Steve's representations of data elements can be easily managed and transformed with PowerDesigner's Link and Sync technology to streamline the efforts needed to keep all the different levels and perspectives in sync.

So ultimately, this is not a book about creating drawings of these data "things". It really is a book about painting rich pictures of relationships. It is about the relationship between the data steward and the database administrator. It is about the relationship between the data management strategy of the IT department and the corporate strategy of the business. It is about the relationship between the diagrams, models and metadata needed to understand our systems, and the tools needed to accelerate and simplify it all.

Watching George and Steve working together on this book is an example of this. It is the relationship between Steve's insight into the challenges of representing data and information in an accessible format with George's years of experience as both a professional metadata specialist and a PowerDesigner user showing us how this incredible tool can be easily used to move theory into practice. If you are new to data modeling or new to PowerDesigner, this book provides easy to follow explanations and guidelines. If you are experienced, it is an excellent way to remind yourself what you can do with different model types, different modeling techniques, and a true information architecture tool like Sybase PowerDesigner.

Looking back over our 20 year history as a modeling tool, starting with the vision from PowerDesigner's inventor and current chief architect Xiao Wang, we have always recognized that this tie between conceptual and physical representations is key. We have always recognized that these models are loosely coupled to ensure they each represent the viewpoint they are intended for – business or technologist, but the relationship between them must be preserved, iteratively, as changes on both sides impact the other. Over the years, we extended this philosophy into application modeling, enabling platform independent and platform dependent models to synchronize together. We extended this into process modeling, linking data, application, and process together at all levels of abstraction. These empowering abilities helped thousands of customers in hundreds of countries worldwide, in all industries, realize the full business potential of well architected information, without all the manual effort it takes using multiple tools or multiple techniques. In our latest versions, we reached up into enterprise architecture and business architecture, arriving at V16, to uniquely position PowerDesigner as the world's first true information architecture tool, bridging business vision with technical implementation.

I hope you enjoy reading this book as much as I did, and I hope you enjoy using PowerDesigner as the enabling technology to help you realize your information architecture vision.

David Dichmann, Product Line Director, PowerDesigner
Sybase®, an SAP® company

If you are like me, you usually skip book introductions and jump straight into Chapter 1. By calling this section "Read me First" instead of "Introduction", I am hoping you will actually read this *first*. It will help you get the most out of this book by becoming familiar with the learning objectives and getting a glimpse of each section and chapter. You will also find out the meaning of the icons we've splashed liberally across the book – I'm sure you can guess most of them yourself, but good data modelers must ensure their meaning is clearly communicated to their audience.

This book has ten key objectives for you, the reader:

1. You will know when a data model is needed and which PowerDesigner models are the most appropriate for each situation
2. You will be able to read a data model of any size and complexity with the same confidence as reading a book
3. You will know when to apply and how to make use of all the key features of PowerDesigner
4. You will be able to build, step-by-step in PowerDesigner, a pyramid of linked data models, including a conceptual data model, a fully normalized relational data model, a physical data model, and an easily navigable dimensional model
5. You will be able to apply techniques such as indexing, transforms, and forward engineering to turn a logical data model into an efficient physical design
6. You will improve data governance and modeling consistency within your organization by leveraging features such as PowerDesigner's reference models, Glossary, domains, and model comparison and model mapping techniques
7. You will know how to utilize dependencies and traceability links to assess the impact of change
8. You will know how to integrate your PowerDesigner models with externally-managed files, including the import and export of data using Excel® and Requirements documents
9. You will know where you can take advantage of the entire PowerDesigner model set, to increase the success rate of corporate-wide initiatives such as business intelligence and enterprise resource planning (ERP)
10. You will understand the key differentiators between PowerDesigner and other data modeling tools you may have used before

This book contains seven sections:

Section I introduces data modeling, along with its purpose and variations.

Section II explains all of the components on a data model including entities, data elements, relationships, and keys. Also included is a discussion of the importance of quality names and definitions for your objects.

Section III explains the important role of data modeling tools, the key features required of any data modeling tool, and an introduction to the essential features of PowerDesigner. It also describes how to create and manage data modeling objects in PowerDesigner.

Section IV introduces the Data Model Pyramid, then dives into the relational and dimensional subject areas, logical, and physical data models, and describes how PowerDesigner supports these models and the connections between them.

Section V guides you through the creation of your own Data Model Pyramid.

Section VI focuses on additional PowerDesigner features (some of which have already been introduced) that make life easier for data modelers. Learn how to get information into and out of PowerDesigner, and improve the quality of your data models with a cross-reference of key PowerDesigner features with the Data Model Scorecard®.

Section VII discusses PowerDesigner topics beyond data modeling, including the XML physical model and the other types of model available in PowerDesigner.

To connect the book's content with the book's key objectives stated on the previous page: the following table shows the key sections that support each objective.

Section	Objective									
	1	2	3	4	5	6	7	8	9	10
I	✔	✔								
II	✔	✔								
III	✔	✔	✔	✔		✔	✔	✔		✔
IV	✔	✔	✔	✔	✔		✔			
V			✔	✔	✔		✔	✔		
VI			✔	✔		✔		✔	✔	✔
VII									✔	✔

Key points are included at the end of each chapter as a way to reinforce concepts. All of the key points are also summarized at the end of the text. Every chapter starts with a poem in the form of a haiku, which is a three-line poem containing five syllables in the first line, seven in the second, and five in the third.

As we introduce you to new PowerDesigner features, we use 'Your Turn' sessions to familiarize you with them. At the end of most chapters there are thought-provoking exercises, with answers provided in the Appendix. Also at the back of the book are two handy glossaries, a quick-reference guide to PowerDesigner, and a comprehensive index.

How to get the Most out of this Book

Data Modeling Experience	PowerDesigner Experience	Suggested Approach
Little or None	Little or None	Ignore the PowerDesigner-specific chapters at first. Read all the data modeling text and complete the exercises. Now work through the PowerDesigner-specific material. Before you tackle Chapter 19, review the exercises, and perhaps even do them again. Create at least one more Subject Area Model in PowerDesigner, and explore the Demo models provided with PowerDesigner. Work through Chapter 19.
Good or Great	Little or None	Read or skim through the data modeling text, taking note of all the PowerDesigner material, and complete the exercises. Work through Chapter 10 in detail. Before you tackle Chapter 19, create at least one more SAM in PowerDesigner, and explore the Demo models provided with PowerDesigner. Work through Chapter 19. Make sure that you cover at least the fundamental techniques – see "Fundamentals of PowerDesigner" in Chapter 10 to find out more.
Good or Great	Good or Great	Researching this book was a voyage of discovery for me. Please be patient, and work through Sections III, IV, V and VI. If you prefer, work from the PowerDesigner Glossary or the index to find topics of interest.

It is not possible to show you how to use all of PowerDesigner's features in the space available, so we tell you what features there are, introduce to you them, and refer you to the comprehensive PowerDesigner documentation for more information. Some features are especially important for all PowerDesigner users, or for data modelers in particular, so please bear with us, even if the detail is excruciating. There is always an end in sight. For the same reason, we may even repeat ourselves several times. In some areas, you may wish for more detail; sorry but this is not a PowerDesigner training manual.

It's important to know what you can expect to learn from a book, and it's equally important to know what you will NOT learn from a book. We make no attempt here to teach database design or SQL; PowerDesigner supports many different relational technologies as well as XML schemas, and it would take a much larger book to explain how best to utilize that support.

Icons Used in this Book

This book uses icons to focus your attention on PowerDesigner topics, helping you to identify what's really important to you.

Information
Generally useful information about PowerDesigner and how it can help you.

Gotcha
Pay attention, you really need to read this to avoid pain or upset.

Tips and Tricks
Pay attention, this is worth remembering, try to commit this to memory.

Fundamental Knowledge and Techniques
These sections provide fundamental information about PowerDesigner. You need to understand these sections, or you will never really get to grips with PowerDesigner. See "Fundamentals of PowerDesigner" in Chapter 10 to find out more.

YOUR TURN TO PLAY

Try it out for yourself; the experience will reinforce what you read. In some cases, new material is included.

Advanced
This is advanced stuff we're talking about here, beyond the scope of this book. Refer to the PowerDesigner documentation or more advanced data modeling and design texts for more information.

Help
We don't have space here to tell you everything about PowerDesigner: use this phrase to search for more information in the on-line help or documentation. For example,

◉ "business rules" (Core Features Guide)

This tells you to search for the phrase "business rules", and examine the topics in the location called "Core Features Guide".

Conventions Used in this Book

As you work through the book, you will see references to objects and symbols in data models, keys on the keyboard, and parts of the PowerDesigner environment, such as items on PowerDesigner menus, tools on the palette, and dialog buttons.

Sometimes we just enclose an entry in single quotes (like 'G') where the context makes it obvious what we mean. Otherwise, we make use of the following simple conventions.

Object and symbol names	e.g. **Ice Cream Flavor**
`menu options`	e.g. `Edit|Export in Color` refers to the 'Export in Color' option on the 'Edit' menu.
tool name	e.g. *Grabber, Export to Excel*
<keyboard keys>, including combinations of them	e.g. <F1> <Ctrl+A>
<dialog buttons>	e.g. <OK> <Cancel>

In Summary

PowerDesigner is a complex tool, providing support for a multitude of possible approaches. Sybase does not restrict you to any given methodology. We describe a methodology in this book, show you how to make it work in PowerDesigner, and describe some potential strategies for using PowerDesigner. By the way, every diagram in this book (except the cartoons and the pyramid in Section IV) was produced in PowerDesigner.

Data modeling is more than a job or a career - it is a mindset, an invaluable process, a healthy addiction, a way of life. Remember to Keep It Simple, and enjoy the ride!

Section I introduces data modeling along with its purpose and variations. At the completion of this section, the reader will be able to justify the need for a data model and know which type of model is most effective for each situation. The reader will also be able to perform a very high-level assessment of a data model by identifying certain characteristics of the data model and then determining how well these characteristics and the specific purpose of the model are aligned.

Chapter 1 introduces the data model and explains this powerful tool using two examples, both of which are used throughout the text. I love desserts and sweets, so one example will model ice cream (yes, ice cream!). The other example is modeling business cards. Both ice cream and business cards will illustrate modeling techniques so that the reader can appreciate the process of building a data model from requirements through to design.

Chapter 2 explains the two core characteristics of a data model that make it so valuable: communication and precision. You will learn where communication occurs and about the three situations that can weaken data model precision. This chapter then explores the areas within the business and application where the data model can be used.

How do I get there?
Maps, blueprints, data models
Please show me the way

I gave the steering wheel a heavy tap with my hands as I realized that once again, I was completely lost. It was about an hour before dawn, I was driving in France, and an important business meeting awaited me. I spotted a gas station up ahead that appeared to be open. I parked, went inside, and showed the attendant the address of my destination.

I don't speak French and the attendant didn't speak English. The attendant did, however, recognize the name of the company I needed to visit. Wanting to help and unable to communicate verbally, the attendant took out a pen and paper. He drew lines for streets, circles for roundabouts along with numbers for exit paths, and rectangles for his gas station and my destination, MFoods. The picture he drew resembled that which appears in Figure 1.1.

Figure 1.1 Simplification of geographic landscape

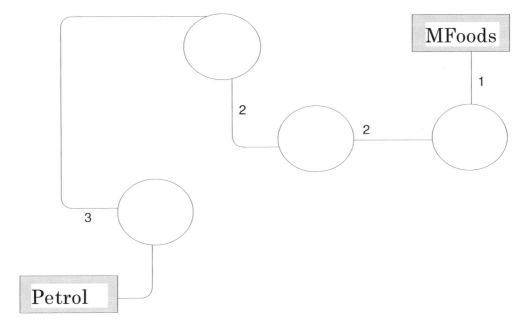

With this custom-made map, which contained only the information that was relevant to me, I arrived at my address without making a single wrong turn. This map was a model of the actual roads I needed to travel.

A map simplifies a complex *geographic* landscape in the same way that a data model simplifies a complex *information* landscape. In many cases, the complexities in the actual data can make those roundabouts in France look ridiculously simple. This chapter explains the data model and its role as an invaluable wayfinding tool. It also introduces the ice cream and business card examples which are carried throughout the text.

Wayfinding Explained

If the term 'data model' does not excite you or your business users, try the term 'wayfinding' instead. Wayfinding encompasses all of the techniques and tools used by people and animals to find their way from one site to another. If travelers navigate by the stars, for example, the stars are their wayfinding tools. Maps and compasses are also wayfinding tools.

All models are wayfinding tools. A model is a set of symbols and text used to make a complex concept easier to grasp. The world around us is full of obstacles that can overwhelm our senses and make it very challenging to focus only on the relevant information needed to make intelligent decisions. A map helps a visitor navigate a city. An organization chart helps an employee understand reporting relationships. A blueprint helps an architect communicate building plans. The map, organization chart, and blueprint are all types of models that represent a filtered, simplified view of something complex, with the goal of improving a wayfinding experience by helping people understand part of the real world.

It would probably have taken me hours of trial and error to reach my destination in France, whereas that simple map the gas station attendant drew provided me with an almost instantaneous broad understanding of how to reach my destination. A model makes use of standard symbols that allow one to grasp the content quickly. In the map he drew for me, the attendant used lines to symbolize streets, and circles to symbolize roundabouts. His skillful use of those symbols helped me visualize the streets and roundabouts.

Data Model Explained

When I was in college, the term 'information overload' was used to mean that my brain had reached the maximum number of words spoken by the professor, appearing on her flipcharts, and in the page of notes in front of me, that it could handle. It was time for a stroll around campus, a game of tennis, or a couple of quarters in Space Invaders to get my mind recharged and ready for more. Today however, it seems that we are creating and receiving more and more information, and taking fewer and fewer breaks. I have heard it quoted several times that the amount of information in the world is increasing by over 60% per year! I shudder to myself, wondering what very small portion of all of this information we really, truly understand.

Luckily, there is a tool that can help simplify all of this information - the data model. A data model is a wayfinding tool for both business and IT professionals, which uses a set of symbols and text to precisely explain a subset of real information to improve communication within the organization and thereby lead to a more flexible and stable application environment. A line represents a motorway on a map of France. A box with the word 'Customer' within it represents the concept of a real Customer such as Bob, IBM, or Walmart on a data model.

Our broad definition of a data model as "a set of symbols and text which precisely explain a subset of real information" encompasses models in many different forms. Data models can look like the box and line drawings which are the subject of this book, or they can take other forms, such as Unified Modeling Language (UML) Class Diagrams, spreadsheets, or State Transition Diagrams. All of these models are wayfinding tools designed with the single purpose of simplifying complex information in our real world

Fun with Ice Cream

Perhaps the most common form of data model we work with on a daily basis is the spreadsheet. A spreadsheet is a representation of a paper worksheet containing a grid defined by rows and columns, where each cell in the grid can contain text or numbers. The columns often contain different types of information. For example, I recently returned from a trip to Rome and I loved their ice cream (gelato). Upon entering a gelato store, you will see several spreadsheets. One example is shown in Table 1.1, which is a list of ice cream flavors. Table 1.2 contains the ice cream sizes along with prices.

Table 1.1 Sample ice cream flavors

Banana
Cappuccino
Chocolate
Chocolate Chip
Coffee
Kiwi
Marshmallow
Pistachio
Strawberry
Vanilla

Table 1.2 Ice cream sizes with prices

1 Scoop	1.75
2 Scoops	2.25
3 Scoops	2.60

This is a data model because it is a set of symbols (in this case, text) that are used to describe something real in our world (in this case, the yummy ice cream flavors along with prices). Guess how many scoops of chocolate gelato I purchased?

The data model format that is the subject of this book is very similar to a spreadsheet. (Although the definition of 'data model' is broader, going forward, when I use the term 'data model', I am referring to the format which is the subject of this book.) Unlike a spreadsheet, however, a data model:

- **Contains only types**. Data models don't usually display actual values such as 'Chocolate' and '3 Scoops'. Data models display concepts or types. So, a data model would display the type **Ice Cream Flavor**, instead of showing the actual values 'Chocolate' or 'Vanilla'. A data model would display the type **Ice Cream Size**, instead of showing the actual values '1 Scoop' or '2 Scoops'.
- **Contains interactions**. Data models capture how concepts interact with each other. For example, what is the interaction between **Ice Cream Flavor** and **Ice Cream Size**? If one orders three scoops, for example, must they all be the same flavor or could you have three different flavors? Interactions such as those between **Ice Cream Flavor** and **Ice Cream Size** are represented on a data model.
- **Provides a concise communication medium**. A single sheet of paper containing a data model communicates much more than a single piece of paper containing a spreadsheet. Data models display types, not actual values, and they use simple yet powerful symbols to communicate interactions. We can capture all of the types and interactions within the ice cream example in a much more concise format using a data model rather than in a spreadsheet.

Fun with Business Cards

Business cards contain a wealth of data about people and the companies for which they work. In this book, I illustrate many data modeling concepts by using business cards as the basis for a model. By building a business card data model, we see first-hand how much knowledge we gain from the actual values on a business card or, in a broader sense, the contact management area.

I opened the drawer in my nightstand (a scary proposition, as it had not been cleaned since the mid-1980s) and grabbed a handful of business cards. I laid them out and picked four that I thought would be the most fun to model. I chose my current business card, a business card from an internet business that my wife and I tried to start years ago when dot-com was hot, a business card from a magician who performed at one of our parties, and a business card from one of our favorite restaurants. I changed the names and contact information to protect the innocent, and reproduced them here, in Figure 1.2.

Figure 1.2 Four business cards from my nightstand

What information do you see on these business cards?

Assuming our objective with this exercise is to understand the information on the business cards, with an end goal of building a successful contact management application, let's begin by listing some of this information:

Steve Hoberman & Associates, LLC	BILL SMITH	212-555-1212
MAGIC FOR ALL OCCASIONS	President	Jon Smith
Steve and Jenn	FINE FRESH SEAFOOD	58 Church Avenue

We quickly realize that even though we are dealing with only four business cards, listing all the data would do little to aid our understanding. Now, imagine that instead of limiting ourselves to just these four cards, we looked through all the cards in my nightstand—or worse yet, every business card that has ever been received! We would become overloaded with data quickly.

A data model groups data together to make them easier to understand. For example, we would examine the following set of data and realize that they fit in a group (or spreadsheet column heading) called **Company Name**:

> Steve Hoberman & Associates, LLC
> The Amazing Rolando
> findsonline.com
> Raritan River Club

Another spreadsheet column heading could be **Phone Number**. Table 1.3 captures this subset of the business card information in the form of a spreadsheet.

Table 1.3 Subset of business card information in a spreadsheet format

Card	Company	Phone number
Business card 1	Steve Hoberman & Associates, LLC	212-555-1212
Business card 2	findsonline.com	973-555-1212
Business card 3	The Amazing Rolando	732-555-1212
Business card 4	Raritan River Club	(908)333-1212 (908)555-1212 554-1212

Taking this exercise a step further, we can organize the data on the cards into the following groups:

> Person name
> Person title
> Company name
> Email address
> Web address
> Mailing address
> Phone number
> Logo (the image on the card)
> Specialties (such as "MAGIC FOR ALL OCCASIONS")

So, are we finished? Is this listing of groups a data model? Not yet. We are still missing a key ingredient: the interactions or relationships between these groups. For example, what is the interaction between **Company Name** and **Phone Number**? Can a Company have more than one **Phone Number**? Can a **Phone Number** belong to more than one Company? If so, is that a problem? Can a Company exist without a **Phone Number**? These questions, and others, need to be asked and answered during the process of building the data model.

In order to build any wayfinding tool, one must get lost enough times to know the right path. For example, the first person who builds a map of a region must have taken quite a bit of time and made quite a few wrong turns before completing the map. The process of building a map is both challenging and time-consuming.

The same is true for the process of completing a data model. There is the 'data model' and then there is 'data modeling'. Data modeling is the process of building a data model. More specifically, data modeling is the set of techniques and activities that enable us to capture the structure and operations of an organization, as well as the proposed information solution that will enable the organization to achieve its goals. The process requires many skills, such as listening ability, courage to ask lots of questions, and even patience. The data modeler needs to speak with individuals from many different departments with varying levels of technical and business experiences and skills. The data modeler not only needs to understand these individuals' views of their world, but also be able to demonstrate this understanding through feedback during the conversation and also as a final artifact in the form of the model. At the beginning of a project, it is rare that you, as the data modeler, are handed all of the information you need to complete the model. It will require reading through lots of documentation and asking hundreds of business questions.

EXERCISE 1: Educating Your Neighbor

Reinforce your own understanding of what a data model is by explaining the concept of a data model to someone completely outside the world of IT, such as to a neighbor, family member or friend.

Did they get it?

Refer to the Appendix to see how I explain the concept of a data model.

Key Points

- Wayfinding encompasses all of the techniques and tools used by people and animals to find their way from one site to another.

- A data model is a wayfinding tool, for both business and IT professionals, which uses a set of symbols and text to precisely explain a subset of real information to improve communication within the organization, and thereby lead to a more flexible and stable application environment.

- Data models come in many different forms. The most common and globally-understood form is a spreadsheet.

- The data model format that is the subject of this book is similar to the spreadsheet, yet is type-based, contains interactions, and is extensible.

- Data modeling is the process of building the data model. This process requires many non-technical skills, such as listening ability, courage to ask lots of questions, and patience.

Ambiguous talk
Data models are precise
Zero, one, many

Data modeling is an essential part of building an application. Communication and precision are the two key benefits that make a data model so important. This chapter explains these two core benefits, followed by a description of the areas within the business and application where the data model can be used. You will learn where communication occurs and about the three situations that can weaken data model precision.

Communication

People with different backgrounds and levels of experience across departments and functional areas need to speak with each other about business concerns and to make business decisions. In a conversation, therefore, there is a need to know how the other party views concepts such as Customer or Sales. The data model is an ideal tool for understanding, documenting, and eventually reconciling different perspectives.

When the spoken word failed to reach me, the model that the gas station attendant drew for me clearly explained how to get to my destination. Regardless of whether we are trying to understand how key concepts in a business relate to one another or the workings of a 20-year-old order-processing system, the model becomes an ideal mechanism for explaining information.

Data models allow us to communicate the same information at different levels of detail. For example, I recently built a data model to capture consumer interactions with snack food. So if someone called up a company and complained about one of the company's products, the model I built would store this complaint and related information about it. The key business user and I built a very high-level data model showing the subjects that are relevant for the project. The model helped with scoping the project, understanding key terms, and building a rapport with the business. This model became the mechanism we used to bridge our understandings of key terms such as Consumer, Product, and Interaction. Several months later, I used a much more detailed model of the same consumer-interaction information to inform the report developers of exactly what was expected to appear on each report, along with all the necessary selection criteria.

The communication we derive from modeling does not begin when the data modeling phase has ended. That is, much communication and knowledge is shared during the process of building the model. The means are just as valuable as the end. Let's look at the communication benefits derived both during and after the modeling process in more detail.

Communicating During the Modeling Process

During the process of building data models, we are forced to analyze data and data relationships. We have no choice but to acquire a strong understanding of the content of what is being modeled. A lot of knowledge is gained as the people involved in the modeling process challenge each other about terminology, assumptions, rules, and concepts.

During the process of modeling a recipe management system for a large manufacturing company, I was amazed to witness team members with years of experience debate whether the concept of an Ingredient differed from the concept of Raw Material. After a 30-minute discussion on ingredients and raw materials, everyone who participated in this modeling effort benefited from the debate and left the modeling session with a stronger understanding of recipe management.

When we model the business card example, you'll see that we can learn a lot about the person, company, and contact management, in general, during the modeling process.

Communicating After the Modeling Process

The completed data model is the basis for discussing what to build in an application, or more fundamentally, how something works. The data model becomes a reusable map to which analysts, modelers, and developers can refer to understand how things work. In much the same way as the first mapmaker painfully learned and documented a geographic landscape for others to use for navigation, the modeler goes through a similar exercise (often painful, but in a good way) so that others can understand an information landscape.

Before I started working at a large manufacturing company, my soon-to-be manager gave me a large book containing a set of data models for the company. I read this book several times, becoming familiar with the key concepts in the business and their business rules. On my first day on the job, I already knew much about how the business worked. When my colleagues mentioned terms specific to the company, I already knew what they meant.

In our example with the business cards, once we complete the model, others can read it to learn about contact management.

Precision

Precision, with respect to data modeling, means that there is a clear, unambiguous way of reading every symbol and term on the model. You might argue with others about whether the rule is accurate, but that is a different argument. In other words, it is not possible for you to view a symbol on a model and say, "I see A here" and for someone else to view the same symbol and respond, "I see B here."

Going back to the business card example, let's assume we define a 'contact' to be the person or company that is listed on a business card. Someone states that *a contact can have many phone numbers.* This statement is imprecise, as we do not know whether a contact can exist without a phone number, must have at least one phone number, or must have many phone numbers.

Similarly, we do not know whether a phone number can exist without a contact, must belong to only one contact, or can belong to many contacts. The data model introduces precision, such as converting this vague statement into these assertions:

- Each contact must be reached by one or many phone numbers.
- Each phone number must belong to one contact.

Because the data model introduces precision, valuable time is not wasted trying to interpret the model. Instead, time can be spent debating and then validating the concepts on the data model.

There are three situations however, that can degrade the precision of a data model:

- **Weak definitions**. If the definitions behind the terms on a data model are poor or nonexistent, multiple interpretations of terms become a strong possibility. Imagine a business rule on our model that states that an employee must have at least one benefits package. If the definition of Employee is something meaningless like "An Employee is a carbon-based life form", we may wrongly conclude that this business rule considers both job applicants and retired employees to be employees.
- **Dummy data**. The second situation occurs when we introduce data that are outside the normal set of data values we would expect in a particular data grouping. An old fashioned trick for getting around the rigor of a data model is to expand the set of values that a data grouping can contain. For example, if a contact must have at least one phone number and for some reason, a contact arrives in the application with no phone numbers, one can create a fake phone number such as 'Not Applicable' or '99' or 'other' and then the contact can be entered. In this case, adding the dummy data allows a contact to exist without a phone number, which violates, but circumvents our original business rule.
- **Vague or missing labels**. A model is read in much the same way as a book is read, with proper sentence structure. A very important part of the sentence is the verbs. On a data model, these verbs are captured when describing how concepts on the model relate to each other. Concepts like Customer and Order for example, may relate to each other through the verb 'place'. That is "A Customer can place one or many Orders." Vague verbs such as 'associate' or 'have', or missing verbs altogether, reduce the precision of the model, as we cannot accurately read the sentences.

In a data model, precision is also the result of applying a standard set of symbols. The traffic circles the gas station attendant drew for me were standard symbols that we both understood. There are also standard symbols used in data models, as we will discover shortly.

Data Model Uses

Traditionally, data models have been built during the analysis and design phases of a project to ensure that the requirements for a new application are fully understood and correctly captured before the actual database is created. There are, however, other uses for modeling than simply building databases. Among the uses are the following:

- **To understand an existing application.** The data model provides a simple and precise picture of the concepts within an application. We can derive a data model from an existing application by examining the application's database and building a data model of its structures. The technical term for the process of building data models from existing applications is 'reverse engineering'. The trend in many industries is to buy more packaged software and to build less internally; therefore our roles as modelers are expanding and changing. Instead of modeling a new application, the data modeler may capture the information in existing systems, such as packaged software. In fact, modeling of existing systems frequently takes place because originally, when the application was built, no modeling was done and therefore, the system is running with an inferior design that few people understand. Recently, a manufacturing organization needed to move a 25 year old application to a new database platform. This was a very large application, so to understand its structures, we built a data model of it.
- **To perform impact analysis.** A data model can capture the concepts and interactions that are impacted by a development project or program. What is the impact of adding or modifying structures for an application already in production? How many of an application's structures are needed for archival purposes? Many organizations today purchase software and then customize it. One example of impact analysis would be to use data modeling to determine what impact modifying its structures would have on the purchased software.
- **To understand a business area.** As a prerequisite to a large development effort, it usually is necessary to understand how the business works before you can understand how the applications that support the business will work. Before building an order entry system, for example, you need to understand the order entry business process. Data modeling provides a formal process for learning how part of the business works. The completed model will describe the business area. That is, the completed data model becomes a wayfinding tool for the order data entry area.
- **To educate team members.** When new team members need to come up to speed or developers need to understand requirements, a data model is an effective explanatory medium. A picture is worth a thousand words, and a data model is a picture that can convey information at different levels of detail. Whenever a new person joined our area, I spent some time walking through a series of high-level data models to educate the person on concepts and rules as quickly as possible.

EXERCISE 2: Converting the Non-Believer

Find someone in your organization who is a data model non-believer and try to convert him or her.

What obstacles did you run into? Did you overcome them?

Key Points

- The two main benefits of a data model are communication and precision.

- Communication occurs both during the building of the data model and after its completion.

- Data model precision can be compromised by weak definitions, dummy data, and vague or missing labels.

- Communication and precision make a data model an excellent tool for building new applications.

- Other uses for data models include understanding existing applications and business areas, performing impact analysis, and educating team members.

Section II explains all of the symbols and text on a data model. It contains the next five chapters, four of which describe different components of the data model. The remaining chapter describes the importance of quality names and definitions. By the time you finish this section, you will be able to 'read' a data model of any size or complexity.

Chapter 3 defines an entity and discusses the different categories of entities. Entity instances are also defined. The three different levels at which entities may exist, subject area, logical, and physical, are also explained, as well as the concepts of weak versus strong entities.

Chapter 4 defines a data element and discusses domains. Examples are provided for the three different types of domains.

Chapter 5 defines rules and relationships. Data rules are distinguished from action rules. Cardinality and labels are explained so that the reader can read any data model as easily as reading a book. Other types of relationships, such as recursive relationships, and subtyping are discussed, as well.

Chapter 6 expands on the statement that "Data can only be used effectively if it can be understood, and it can only be understood if the definitions are adequate", by focusing on the characteristics of definitions - clarity, completeness, accuracy, and lack of ambiguity.

Chapter 7 defines keys and distinguishes the terms candidate, primary, and alternate key. Surrogate keys and foreign keys are also defined, along with a discussion on their importance.

Concepts of interest
Who, What, When, Where, Why, and How
Entities abound

As I walked around the room to see if any students had questions, I noticed someone in the last row had already finished the exercise. I walked over to where she was sitting and, looking over her shoulder, noticed only a handful of boxes on the page. The large box in the center contained the word 'Manufacturing'. I asked her for her definition of 'Manufacturing'. "Manufacturing is the production process of how we turn raw materials into finished goods. All the manufacturing steps are in this box."

The data model boxes (also known as 'entities'), however, are not designed to represent or contain processes. Instead, they represent the concepts that are used *by* the processes. The Manufacturing entity on her model was eventually transformed into several other entities, including Raw Material, Finished Goods, Machinery, and Production Schedule.

This chapter defines the concept of an entity and discusses the different categories (Who, What, When, Where, Why, and How) of entities. Entity instances are also defined. The three different levels of entities, subject area, logical, and physical, are also explained, as well as the concepts of a weak versus a strong entity.

Entity Explained

An entity represents a collection of information about something that the business deems important and worthy of capture. A noun or noun phrase identifies a specific entity. It fits into one of several categories - who, what, when, where, why, or how. Table 3.1 contains a definition of each of these entity categories along with examples.

Entity instances are the occurrences or values of a particular entity. Think of a spreadsheet as being an entity, with the column headings representing the pieces of information about the entity. Each spreadsheet row containing the actual values represents an entity instance. The entity Customer may have multiple customer instances, with names Bob, Joe, Jane, and so forth. The entity Account can have instances of Bob's checking account, Bob's savings account, Joe's brokerage account, and so on.

Table 3.1 Definitions and examples of entity categories

Category	Definition	Examples
Who	Person or organization of interest to the enterprise. That is, "*Who* is important to the business?" Often a 'who' is associated with a role such as Customer or Vendor.	Employee, Patient, Gambler, Suspect, Customer, Vendor, Student, Passenger, Competitor
What	Product or service of interest to the enterprise. It often refers to what the organization makes that keeps it in business. That is, "*What* is important to the business?"	Product, Service, Raw Material, Finished Good, Course, Song, Photograph
When	Calendar or time interval of interest to the enterprise. That is, "*When* is the business in operation?"	Time, Date, Month, Quarter, Year, Calendar, Semester, Fiscal Period, Minute
Where	Location of interest to the enterprise. Location can refer to actual places as well as electronic places. That is, "*Where* is business conducted?"	Mailing Address, Distribution Point, Website URL, IP Address
Why	Event or transaction of interest to the enterprise. These events keep the business afloat. That is, "*Why* is the business in business?"	Order, Return, Complaint, Withdrawal, Deposit, Compliment, Inquiry, Trade, Claim
How	Documentation of the event of interest to the enterprise. Documents record the events, such as a Purchase Order recording an Order event. That is, "*How* does the business stay in business?"	Invoice, Contract, Agreement, Account, Purchase Order, Speeding Ticket

Careful consideration of the context and scope of a data model is required when identifying entities. For example, a data model created for an organization's Payroll department is very likely to have an entity called **Employee**; within the context of Payroll, this is likely to be acceptable. However, within the wider perspective of the organization, we recognize that an **Employee** is actually a **Person** fulfilling a particular role, one of perhaps many roles that are of interest. We only have to extend the context of the model from Payroll to Human Resources to introduce people who aren't employees. David Hay describes this issue very well in his book "Enterprise Model Patterns: Describing the World" (Hay, 2011, p. 25):

"There are problems with defining EMPLOYEE as an entity... - common trap for the unwary. What you have in the word "employee" is a common name for something including in its meaning not just the thing itself, but also its relationship to something else. A PERSON is a human being with specific characteristics, whether employed by anyone or not. An EMPLOYEE, on the other hand, is a PERSON who has established a relationship of employment with an ORGANIZATION."

Entity Types

The beauty of data modeling is that you can take the same information and show it at different levels of detail depending on the audience. In this book we discuss the three levels of detail: subject area, logical, and physical. Entities are components of all three levels.

For an entity to exist at a subject area level, it must be both basic and critical to the business. What is basic and critical depends very much on the concept of scope. At a universal level, there are certain subject areas common to all companies, such as Customer, Product, and Employee. Making the scope slightly narrower, a given industry may have certain unique subject areas. Phone Number, for example, will be a valid subject area for a telecommunications company, but perhaps not for other industries, such as manufacturing. Each company may have subject areas that are unique to its business or its way of doing business. For example, Complaint could be a subject area for a consumer affairs department. Person and Company could be valid subject areas in our business card example.

Entities at a logical level represent the business at a more detailed level than at the subject area level. In general, a subject area entity represents many logical model entities. Examining the subject area Address in more detail could produce a large number of logical entities, including Email Address, Web Address, and Mailing Address.

At a physical level, the entities correspond to database tables. The rigor applied to the logical model is reversed, at times, to make applications perform well or to manage space more efficiently. Web Address and Email Address could be logical entities that translate directly into physical tables. However, if there is a reporting requirement to view all virtual address information, we may decide to combine both Web Address and Email Address into the same physical entity. With very large volumes of data, we might also decide to break up Email Address into several physical entities, each of a more manageable size. So at times, one logical entity can break down into several physical tables, and even more frequently, one physical table can be created from many logical entities.

An entity is shown on diagrams as a rectangle with its name inside. Figure 3.1 contains several entities from our gelato store.

Figure 3.1 Sample entities

Ice Cream Flavor   Ice Cream Size   Ice Cream Order

Notice that there are two types of rectangles: those with straight corners, such as Ice Cream Flavor and Ice Cream Size, and those with rounded edges, such as Ice Cream Order. Without introducing archaic data modeling jargon, it is enough to know that in most tools, the rectangles with straight right angle corners are strong and those with rounded corners are weak.

Strong entities stand on their own. They represent one occurrence of a person, place, or thing, independent of any other entities. In order to find the information about a particular Customer, for example, its **Customer Identifier** could be used to retrieve it from the database. "This is Bob, Customer Identifier 123." An Ice Cream Flavor of 'Chocolate' might be retrieved with 'C'. An Ice Cream Size of '2 Scoops' might be retrieved with simply the number '2'.

Weak entities need to rely on at least one other entity. This means you *cannot* retrieve an entity instance without referring to an entity instance from another entity. For example, Ice Cream Order might be retrieved by an Ice Cream Flavor or Ice Cream Size, *in combination with* something within Ice Cream Order such as a **Sequence Number**.

In the 'Entity/relationship' notation that we're using in this book, PowerDesigner doesn't use the shape of the entity symbol to denote a weak entity. First, PowerDesigner refers to such entities as 'dependent', rather than 'weak'. Second, it is the individual relationships that cause an entity to be dependent, so dependency is shown in the relationship notation. An example appears in Figure 3.2.

Figure 3.2 Dependent entity in PowerDesigner

In this example, you cannot create or retrieve an **Ice Cream Order** without reference to the **Ice Cream Flavor**; the **Order** entity is dependent upon the **Flavor** entity. This is indicated by the triangular symbol on the relationship.

In the IDEF1X notation, round corners are used to indicate dependent entities, and there is no triangular symbol on the relationship. The Barker notation has no notation to indicate dependent entities.

See Chapter 9 for more information on the notation supported by PowerDesigner.

A data model is a communication tool. Distinguishing strong from weak entities on the model helps us understand the relationships and dependencies between entities. For example, a developer reading a data model showing that Ice Cream Order is a weak entity that depends on Ice Cream Flavor, would develop the application program to ensure that an ice cream flavor is present before orders for it are placed. That is, 'Chocolate' must be available as a flavor in the software system before an order for chocolate ice cream may be placed.

EXERCISE 3: Defining Subject Areas

List three subject areas in your organization. Does your organization have a single, agreed-upon definition for each of these subject areas? If not, why not? Can you achieve a single definition for each subject area?

Key Points

- An entity represents a collection of information about something that the business deems important and worthy of capture. An entity fits into one of several categories - who, what, when, where, why, or how.

- A noun or noun phrase identifies a specific entity.

- Entity instances are the occurrences or values of a particular entity.

- An entity can exist at the subject area, logical, or physical level of detail.

- An entity can be strong or weak; in PowerDesigner, weak entities are referred to as 'dependent' entities.

Spreadsheets have columns
Just like data elements
Models all around

This chapter defines the concept of a data element and the three different levels at which a data element can exist: subject area, logical, and physical. We also introduce domains and discuss the different types of domain.

Data Element Explained

A data element is an elementary piece of information of importance to the business, which represents a fact or a definition in an information system, and which may or may not have any eventual existence as a modeled object. In data models, they generally contribute to identifying, describing, or measuring instances of an entity. The data element **Claim Number** identifies each claim. The data element **Student Last Name** describes the last name of each student. The data element **Gross Sales Value Amount** measures the monetary value of a transaction.

Returning to our spreadsheet analogy, the column headings on a spreadsheet are data elements. The cells beneath each column heading are the values for that column heading. Data elements can be thought of as the column headings in a spreadsheet, the fields on a form, or the labels on a report. **Ice Cream Flavor Name** and **Ice Cream Size** are examples of data elements from our gelato store. **Company Name** and **Phone Number** are examples from my business cards.

Data Element Types

As with entities, data elements can exist at subject area, logical, and physical levels. A data element at the subject area level must be a concept both basic and critical to the business. We do not usually think of data elements as subject areas, but depending on the business need, they can be. When I worked for a telecommunications company, **Telephone Number** was a data element that was so important to the business that it was represented on a number of subject area models.

Within a PowerDesigner Conceptual Data Model, you would create **Telephone Number** as a Data Item. See Chapter 12 to find out more about PowerDesigner Data Items.

A data element on a logical data model represents a business property. Each data element shown contributes to the business solution and is independent of any technology, including software and hardware. For example, **Ice Cream Flavor Name** is a logical data element because it has business significance regardless of whether records are kept in a paper file or within the fastest database out there. A data element on a physical data model represents a database column. The logical data element **Ice Cream Flavor Name** might be represented as the physical data element ICE_CRM_FLVR_NAM or as FLVR_NAM within the table ICE_CRM.

I use the term *data element* throughout the text for consistency. However, I would recommend using the term that is most comfortable for your audience. For example, a business analyst might prefer the term 'entity attribute', 'attribute', or 'label', while a database administrator might prefer the term 'column' or 'field'.

In data modeling, PowerDesigner uses the term 'Attribute' as well as 'Entity Attribute'. For example, an entity property sheet has an 'Attributes' tab, and the property sheet for an attribute refers to 'Entity Attribute' (we will see this in Figure 12.12). For consistency, we use the term 'Attribute' in this book when referring to attributes in models.

PowerDesigner also uses the term 'Entity Attribute' on menus and in various dialogs, such as defining list reports or dependency matrices, and extending the underlying model.

Domain Explained

The complete set of all possible values that a data element may have is called a domain. A domain is a set of validation criteria that can be applied to more than one data element; it provides a means of standardizing the characteristics of the data elements. For example, the domain 'Date', which contains all possible valid dates, can be assigned to any of these data elements:

- Employee Hire Date
- Order Entry Date
- Claim Submit Date
- Course Start Date

A data element must never contain values outside of its assigned domain. The domain values are defined by specifying the actual list of values or a set of rules. **Employee Gender Code**, for example, may be limited to the domain of (*female, male*). **Employee Hire Date** may initially be assigned the rule that its domain contain only valid dates, for example. Therefore, this may include values such as:

- February 15th, 2005
- 25 January 1910
- 20030410
- March 10th, 2050

Because **Employee Hire Date** is limited to valid dates, it does not include February 30th, for example. We can restrict a domain with additional rules. For example, by restricting the **Employee Hire Date** domain to dates earlier than today's date, we would eliminate March 10th, 2050. By restricting **Employee Hire Date** to YYYYMMDD (that is, year, month, and day concatenated), we would eliminate all the examples given except for 20030410. Another way of refining this set of values is to restrict the domain of **Employee Hire Date** to dates that fall on a Monday, Tuesday, Wednesday, Thursday, or Friday (that is, the typical workweek).

In our example of the business card, **Contact Name** may have thousands or millions of values. The values from our four sample cards in Figure 1.2 are:
- Steve Hoberman
- Steve
- Jenn
- Bill Smith
- Jon Smith

This name domain may need a bit of refining. It may be necessary to clarify whether a valid domain value is composed of both a first and last name, such as 'Steve Hoberman', or just a first name, such as 'Steve'. Could this domain contain company names such as 'IBM', as well? Could this domain contain numbers instead of just letters, such as the name R2D2 from the movie Star Wars? Could this domain contain special characters, such as the name ♀®, representing "The Artist Formerly Known as Prince" (the musician Prince changed his name to this unpronounceable "Love Symbol" in 1993). If we decide that the 'First Name' and 'Last Name' of a person are separate data elements, we may decide to create two separate domains for them, called 'Person First Name', and 'Person Last Name'. We would probably then require more domains, such as 'Person Full Name'. Note that the domain names are qualified by 'Person', indicating that they do not apply to anything that is not a Person; more 'name' domains are required. There are three different types of domains:
- **Format.** Format domains specify the standard types of data one can have in a database. For example, Integer, Character(30), and Date are all format domains. The format domain for Ice Cream Size might be Character(15), meaning a particular Ice Cream Size can contain any sequence of characters and be at most 15 characters in length.
- **List.** List domains are similar to a drop-down list. They contain a finite set of values from which to choose. List domains are refinements of format domains. The format domain for **Order Status Code** might be Character(10). This domain can be further defined through a list domain of possible values {Open, Shipped, Closed, Returned}. The list domain for Ice Cream Size would be {one scoop, two scoops, three scoops}.
- **Range.** Range domains allow all values that are between a minimum and maximum value. For example, **Order Delivery Date** must be between Today's Date and three months in the future. As with list domains, range domains are a refined version of a format domain.

Data modeling tools generally regard a Domain as a single type of object, and a given Domain, such as 'Amount', could carry out the role of all three Domain types listed above. In addition, Domains in tools may provide the default optionality and description for data elements based on the domain. It is also common for the tool to allow you to prevent or allow data elements from diverging from the properties of the domain. For example, you could force data elements to have the same data type as their domain, and allow them to override the domain optionality and alter the default description. Domains are very useful for a number of reasons:

- **Improves data quality by checking against a domain before inserting data.** This is the primary reason for having a domain. By limiting the possible values of a data element, the chances of bad data getting into the database are reduced. For example, if every data element that represents money is assigned the Amount domain, consisting of all decimal numbers up to 15 digits in length including two digits after the decimal point, then there is a good chance that each of these data elements actually do contain currency. **Gross Sales Value Amount,** which is assigned the amount domain, would not allow the value 'R2D2' to be added.

- **The data model communicates even more.** When we display domains on a data model, the data model communicates that a particular data element has the properties of a particular domain, so the data model becomes a more comprehensive communication tool. We learn, for example, that **Gross Sales Value Amount**, **Net Sales Value Amount**, and **List Price Amount** all share the Amount domain and, therefore, share properties such that their valid values are limited to currency.

- **Greater efficiency in building new models and maintaining existing models.** When a data modeler embarks on a project, she can use a standard set of domains, thereby saving time by not reinventing the wheel. Any new data element that ends in Amount, for example, would be associated with the standard Amount domain, saving analysis and design time.

For an excellent introduction to and a detailed discussion of attribute domains, I suggest that you read Chapter 4 in "Data Quality Assessment" (Maydanchik, 2007).

EXERCISE 4: Assigning Domains

What is the most appropriate domain for each of the three data elements below?
- Email Address
- Gross Sales Value Amount
- Country Code

Key Points

- A data element is a property of importance to the business whose values contribute to identifying, describing or measuring instances of an entity.

- A domain is a set of validation criteria that can be applied to more than one data element.

- There are different types of domains, including format, list, and range domains.

Rules all around us
Relationships tell the tale
Connecting the dots

This chapter defines rules and relationships and the three different levels at which relationships can exist: subject area, logical, and physical. Data rules are distinguished from action rules. Cardinality and labels are explained so that you can read any data model as easily as reading a book. Other types of relationships, such as recursive relationships and subtyping, are discussed, as well.

Relationship Explained

In its most general sense, a rule is an instruction about how to behave in a specific situation. The following are familiar examples of rules:

- You must clean your room before you can go outside and play.
- If you get three strikes, you are out and it is the next batter's turn.
- The speed limit is 80 km/h (or 55 mph).

Many such rules can be visually captured on our data model through relationships. A relationship is displayed as a line connecting two entities. It captures the rules between these two entities. If the two entities are Employee and Department, the relationship may capture the rules "Each Employee must work for one Department" and "Each Department may contain many Employees."

Relationship Types

A rule can be either a data rule or an action rule. Data rules are instructions on *how* data relate to one another. Action rules are instructions on *what to do* when data elements contain certain values. Let's talk about data rules first. There are two types of data rules - structural and referential integrity (RI) data rules. Structural rules (also known as cardinality rules) define the quantity of each entity instance that can participate in a relationship. For example:

- Each product can appear on one or many order lines.
- Each order line must contain one and only one product.
- Each student must have a unique student number.

Referential Integrity rules focus on ensuring valid values:

- An order line cannot exist without a valid product.
- A claim cannot exist without a valid policy.
- A student cannot exist without a valid student number.

When we define a structural rule, we get the corresponding RI rule for free. For example, if we define this structural rule on our data model, "Each order line must contain one and only one product", it is automatically assumed and included that "An order line cannot exist without a valid product."

Action rules, on the other hand, are instructions on *what to do* when data elements contain certain values:

- Freshman students can register for at most 18 credits a semester.
- A policy must have at least three claims against it to be considered high-risk.
- Take 10% off an order if the order contains more than five products.

In our data models, we can represent the data and enforce data rules, but we cannot enforce action rules: the actions resulting from these rules would be within the scope of a process model, not a data model. A student data model can capture the level of student, such as Freshman or Senior, as well as the number of credits each student is taking each semester, but cannot enforce that a freshman student register for no more than 18 credits a semester.

Returning to our ice cream example, I eventually ordered a double scoop of gelato in a cone - one scoop of Chocolate and one scoop of Banana. Many relationships can describe the process of placing this order, such as:

- An ice cream container can be either a cone or a cup.
- Each ice cream container can contain many scoops of ice cream.
- Each ice cream scoop must reside in an ice cream container (or our hands would get really sticky holding that scoop of banana gelato).
- Each ice cream flavor can be chosen for one or many ice cream containers.
- Each ice cream container can contain many flavors.

The three levels of granularity that apply to entities and data elements, also apply to the relationships that connect entities. Subject area relationships are high level rules that connect key concepts. Logical relationships are more specific and enforce the rules between the logical entities. Physical relationships are also specific rules and apply to the physical entities that the relationship connects. These physical relationships eventually become database constraints, which ensure that data adheres to the rules. Therefore, in our ice cream example, "Each ice cream container can contain many scoops of ice cream", can be a subject area relationship. This high-level rule can be broken down into more detailed, logical relationships, such as defining the rule on the different types of containers: "An ice cream container can be either a cone or a cup." This logical relationship then translates into the physical relationship "An ice cream container must be of one ice cream container type, whose values are 'cone', 'cup', and 'not applicable'."

Cardinality Explained

Cardinality defines the number of instances of each entity that can participate in a relationship. It is represented by the symbols that appear on both ends of a relationship line. It is through cardinality that the data rules are specified and enforced. Without cardinality, the most we can say about a relationship is that two entities are connected in some way through a rule. For example, Person and Company have some kind of relationship, but we don't know much more than this.

The domain of values to choose from to represent cardinality on a relationship is limited to three values: zero, one, or many. *Many* (some people read it as *more*), means any number greater than one. Each side of a relationship can have any combination of zero, one, or many. Specifying zero or one allows us to capture whether or not an entity instance is "*required*" in a relationship. Specifying one or many allows us to capture "*how many*" of a particular instance participates in a given relationship.

Because we have only three cardinality symbols, we can't specify an exact number (other than through documentation), as in "A car has four tires." We can only say, "A car has many tires."

In PowerDesigner, we can record this information against the relationship, and display it on diagrams.

A data model represents something in the real world. In capturing this something, there is always a tradeoff between refinement and simplicity. The greater the variety of symbols we show on a model, the more we can communicate. But more symbols also means greater complexity. Data modeling (using the notation in this book), forfeits a certain amount of refinement for simplicity. The advantage is we can explain very complex ideas with a simple set of symbols. In fact, I taught my six-year-old cardinality and she can now read the business rules on a data model. She is the only person in her Kindergarten class who can read cardinality (I am so proud!).

Each of the cardinality symbols is illustrated in the following example of Ice Cream Flavor and Ice Cream Scoop. An ice cream flavor is a selection choice for an ice cream scoop. An ice cream scoop must be one of the available ice cream flavors. Formalizing the rules between flavor and scoop, we have:

- Each Ice Cream Flavor can be the selection choice for one or many Ice Cream Scoops.
- Each Ice Cream Scoop must contain one Ice Cream Flavor.

Figure 5.1 captures these business rules.

Figure 5.1 Ice Cream Flavor and Ice Cream Scoop, take 1

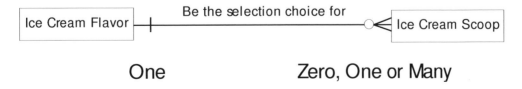

The small vertical line means "one." The circle means "zero." The triangle with a line through the middle means "many." Some people call the "many" symbol a *crow's foot*. Relationship lines are frequently labeled to clarify the relationship and express the rule that the relationship represents. Thus, the label "Be the selection choice for" on the line in this example, helps in reading the relationship and understanding the rule.

Having a zero in the cardinality makes us use optional-sounding words such as 'may' or 'can' when reading the relationship. Without the zero, we use mandatory-sounding terms such as 'must' or 'have to'. So instead of being redundant and saying:

- Each Ice Cream Flavor may be the selection choice for *zero*, one or many Ice Cream Scoops.

We take out the word 'zero' because it is expressed using the word 'can', which implies the zero:

- Each Ice Cream Flavor may be the selection choice for one or many Ice Cream Scoops.

Every relationship has a parent and a child. The parent entity appears on the "one" side of the relationship, and the child appears on the "many" side of the relationship. In Figure 5.1, the parent entity is 'Ice Cream Flavor', and the child entity is 'Ice Cream Scoop'. When I read a relationship, I always start with the entity on the "one" side of the relationship (the parent entity) first. "Each Ice Cream Flavor can be the selection choice for one or many Ice Cream Scoops." It's then followed by reading the relationship from the many side: "Each Ice Cream Scoop must contain one and only one Ice Cream Flavor." In truth, it doesn't matter which side you start from, as long as you are consistent. In Chapter 13 we'll see how PowerDesigner makes things easy for you with relationship role names.

I also always use the word 'each' in reading a relationship, starting with the parent side. The reason for the word 'each' is that you want to specify, on average how many instances of one entity relate to a different entity instance. 'Each' is a more user-friendly term to me than 'A'.

🖱 Fortunately, PowerDesigner also uses the word 'Each' within these phrases, which they call "Assertion Statements".

Let's change the cardinality slightly and see how this impacts the resulting business rule. Assume that because of the rough economy, this ice cream shop decides to allow consumers to select more than one flavor in a scoop. Figure 5.2 contains the updated cardinality.

Figure 5.2 Ice Cream Flavor and Ice Cream Scoop, take 2

This is known as a many-to-many relationship, in contrast to the previous example, which was a one-to-many relationship. The business rules here read as follows:

"Each Ice Cream Flavor must be the selection choice for one or many Ice Cream Scoops."

"Each Ice Cream Scoop must contain one or many Ice Cream Flavors."

Note the use of the word 'must' – the relationship is mandatory – there must be at least one child entity in each relationship.

Make sure the labels on relationship lines are as descriptive as possible. Here are some examples of good label names:

- contain
- work for
- own
- initiate
- categorize
- apply to

Always avoid the following words as label names, as they provide no additional information to the reader (you can use these words in combination with other words to make a meaningful label name; just avoid using these words by themselves):

- has
- have
- associate
- participate
- relate
- be

A useful technique for checking whether relationship names make sense is to read them out aloud to a colleague who's not directly involved in creating the model. If they don't understand what you mean, you may need to reconsider your choice of verb. For example, replace the relationship sentence:

A Person is *associated* with one Company.

with

A Person is *employed* by one Company.

Many modelers capture labels on both sides of the relationship line, instead of just one side, as shown in this chapter. In weighing simplicity versus precision, I chose simplicity. The other label can often be inferred from the label that appears on the model. For example, I assumed the label 'contain' in Figure 5.1 and read the rule from Ice Cream Scoop to Ice Cream Flavor this way: "Each Ice Cream Scoop must contain one Ice Cream Flavor."

Ron Ross (Ross, 2009, pp. 74, 77) makes some useful points regarding the role of verbs in describing facts. There are too many to repeat here, so we suggest you read his book to find out more.

Recursion Explained

A recursive relationship is a rule that exists between instances of the same entity. A one-to-many recursive relationship describes a hierarchy, whereas a many-to-many relationship describes a network. In a hierarchy, an entity instance has at most one parent. In a network, an entity instance can have more than one parent. PowerDesigner supports recursive relationships, but refers to them as 'reflexive' relationships; in this book, we'll use the word 'recursive' when discussing the concept, and 'reflexive' when discussing PowerDesigner specifically.

Let's illustrate both types of recursive relationships using Employee. See Figure 5.3 for a one-to-many recursive example and Figure 5.4 for a many-to-many example.

Figure 5.3 An Employee can work for one Manager

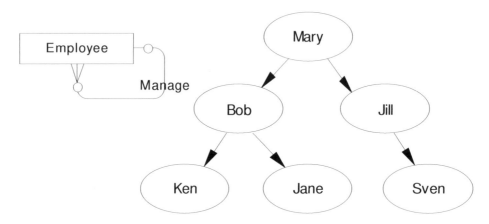

Each Employee may manage one or more other Employee
Each Employee may be managed by at most one other Employee

The two statements starting with 'Each Employee' were created by PowerDesigner, from the two role names given to the relationship. Without these role names, the statements would read:

"Each Employee may have one or more other Employee"
"Each Employee may have at most one other Employee".

These are known as 'Assertion' statements in PowerDesigner. You can see how much more meaningful the statements are in Figure 5.3, where the phrases 'manage' and 'be managed by' replace the default word 'have'.

Using sample values such as 'Bob' and 'Jill' and sketching a hierarchy or network can really help understand, and therefore validate, cardinality. In Figure 5.3, for example, where the one-to-many captures a hierarchy, each employee has at most one manager. Yet in Figure 5.4 where the many-to-many captures a network, each employee must have many managers, such as Jane working for Bob, Jill, Ken, and Sven. (I would definitely update my resume if I were Jane.)

Figure 5.4 An Employee must work for many Managers

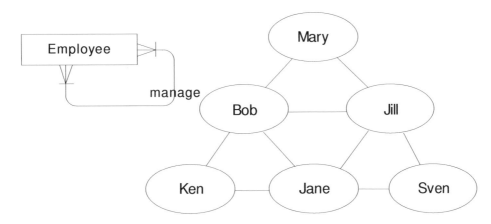

Each Employee must manage one or more other Employee
Each Employee must be managed by one or more other Employees

It is interesting to note that in Figure 5.3, there is optionality on both sides of the relationship. In this example, it implies we can have an Employee who has no boss (such as Mary) and an Employee who is not a manager (such as Ken, Jane, and Sven).

If you think about it, it makes sense for a recursive relationship to be optional; every hierarchy has to end somewhere – in the above example, Mary does not have a manager. If the relationship was mandatory, we would have to link Mary to another 'managing' employee, and that 'managing' employee would have to have a manager – where would we stop? We would have to create one or more dummy employees to implement the relationships, and this is definitely something we must avoid, if we value the quality of our data at all. Of course, this means that the mandatory recursive relationship shown in Figure 5.4 is invalid.

Data modelers have a love-hate relationship with recursion. On the one hand, recursion makes modeling a complex business idea very easy and leads to a very flexible modeling structure. We can have any number of levels in an organization hierarchy in Figure 5.3, for example. On the other hand, some consider using recursion to be taking the easy way out of a difficult modeling situation. There are many rules that can be obscured by recursion. For example, where is the Regional Management Level in Figure 5.4? It is hidden somewhere in the recursive relationship. Those in favor of recursion argue that you may not be aware of all the rules and that recursion protects you from having an incomplete model. The recursion adds a level of flexibility that ensures that any rules not previously considered are also handled by the model. It is therefore wise to consider recursion on a case-by-case basis, weighing obscurity against flexibility.

Relationship Descriptions

Many data modeling tools allow you to add a description to a relationship. In the majority of cases, the information provided by the relationship labels and cardinalities is sufficient to describe the rule, so the *Description* property is not required. Sometimes, however, you need to provide more information, perhaps regarding the circumstances that would cause the relationship to be created, in order for readers and users of the model to completely understand the relationship.

If you need to provide more information, remember that every PowerDesigner object has a *Description* property. Alternatively, you can document the information as a Business Rule, and link it to the relationship.

Subtyping Explained

Subtyping groups the common data elements and relationships of entities, while retaining what is unique within each entity. Subtyping is an excellent way of communicating that certain concepts are very similar.

In our ice cream example, we are told that an ice cream cone and ice cream cup can each contain many scoops of ice cream, as illustrated in Figure 5.5.

Figure 5.5 Ice cream example before subtyping

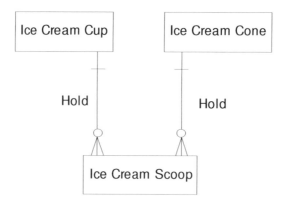

- Each Ice Cream Cone may hold one or many Ice Cream Scoops.
- Each Ice Cream Scoop must be held in one and only one Ice Cream Cone.
- Each Ice Cream Cup may hold one or many Ice Cream Scoops.
- Each Ice Cream Scoop must be held in one and only one Ice Cream Cup.

Rather than repeat the relationship to Ice Cream Scoop, we can introduce subtyping, as shown in Figure 5.6. The subtyping relationship implies that all of the properties from the supertype are inherited by the subtype. Therefore, there is an implied relationship from Ice Cream Cone to Ice Cream Scoop, as well as from Ice Cream Cup to Ice Cream Scoop. Not only does subtyping reduce redundancy on a data model, it makes it easier to communicate similarities across what otherwise would appear to be distinct and separate concepts.

Figure 5.6 Ice cream example after subtyping

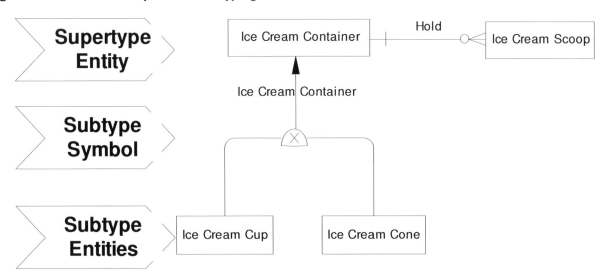

- Each Ice Cream Container may hold one or many Ice Cream Scoops.
- Each Ice Cream Scoop must be held in one and only one Ice Cream Container.
- Each Ice Cream Container must be either an Ice Cream Cone or an Ice Cream Cup.
- Each Ice Cream Cone is an Ice Cream Container.
- Each Ice Cream Cup is an Ice Cream Container.

EXERCISE 5: Reading a Model

Practice reading the relationships in this model. See the Appendix for my answers.

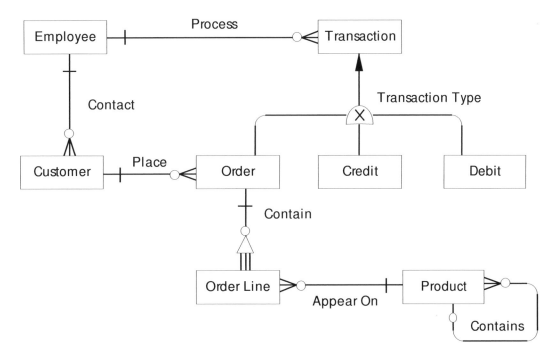

Note that I called one of the relationships 'Contains', as there is already a relationship called 'Contain', and I've decided to keep the relationship names and codes[1] unique within the model.

A better way to handle potentially duplicate names is to display 'Role Names' on the diagram instead. See Chapter 13.

In PowerDesigner, subtype symbols have names, and it's up to you what you call them. The most obvious choices are:
1. The name of the supertype entity (e.g. Transaction)
2. The name of the attribute we use to distinguish between the subtypes (e.g. Transaction Type)

In this model I used the name of the attribute. Either naming approach would be valid. Choose the one that's most meaningful to you.

Key Points

- A rule is visually captured on a data model by a line connecting two entities, called a relationship.

- Data rules are instructions on *how* data relate to one another. Action rules are instructions on *what to do* when data elements contain certain values.

- Cardinality is represented by the symbols on both ends of a relationship that define the number of instances of each entity that can participate in the relationship. The three simple choices are zero, one, or many.

- Labels are the verbs that appear on the relationship lines. Labels should be as descriptive as possible to retain data model precision.

- A recursive (reflexive) relationship is a rule that exists between instances of the same entity.

- Subtyping groups the common properties of entities while retaining what is unique within each entity.

---

[1] You'll find out about names and codes in Chapter 10

Disambiguated
Clear and complete and correct
Standards needed here

I was sitting at a table in a meeting room, listening to managers describing their projects. Although this meeting was part of a celebration of the success of a very large data warehouse project, this part of the meeting was dedicated to lessons learned. Each manager was talking about what he would like to have done if he had the opportunity to do it all over again. I jotted down the keywords from each of the presentations. Looking over my notes afterward, I noticed a common theme: each manager wished that he had put more effort into documenting the meanings behind the terms in his applications. They needed better definitions. They may also have needed better names.

Many data modeling objects have names that take the form of a noun or a phrase that involves a noun. Use the right noun or nouns in the name of an entity, and we'll all know what the entity is, surely? The same is true for attributes as well, isn't it? Perhaps not: Ron Ross quotes a practitioner who says "The more self-evident the meaning of a term is, the more trouble you can expect." (Ross, 2009, p. 12). How many different definitions of 'Product' or 'Customer' does your organization have?

Not all of your entity or attribute names will be quite so contentious, of course. That does not mean you have to pay less attention to them, though. Consider the simple entity shown in Figure 6.1.

Figure 6.1 Ambiguous or unclear attribute names

Order
Order Number
Date
Amount
Dispatch

Assume that you and your business experts have discussed what is meant by **Order**, and you agree on what the entity represents. Now you need to discuss the meaning of the data elements - their names currently lack meaning. For example, which of the many dates that could be associated with an order is the **Date** attribute meant to represent? Does the **Dispatch** attribute hold a dispatch date? If so, is that a requested, estimated, or actual dispatch date? Perhaps it tells us how many deliveries are needed, or whether or not the order has been fulfilled. The names in Figure 6.2 are more descriptive and answer more questions, but we still need to agree on their definitions.

Figure 6.2 Clearer attribute names

Order
Order Number
Estimated Completion Date
Total Value Amount
Customer Collection Indicator

As Ron Ross says, a "noun or noun phrase…represents merely the tip of an iceberg with respect to meaning" (Ross, 2009, p. 12). In Figure 6.2, what exactly is the **Total Value Amount** of an Order? Who estimated the **Completion Date**? When was the **Estimate** made? What does 'completion' mean?

It's vital that the definitions we provide for our data answer these questions. Data can only be used effectively if it can be understood, and it can only be understood if the definitions are adequate.

Definitions are important for three main reasons:

- **Assist business and IT with decision making**. If a business user has an interpretation of a concept that differs from the one actually implemented, it is easy for poor decisions to be made, compromising the entire application. For instance, if a business user would like to know how many products were ordered each month, imagine the poor judgments that could result if the user expected raw materials to be included with products, but they were not. Or, what if he or she assumed that raw materials were not included, but they were?
- **Help reveal, document, and resolve different perspectives on the same concept**. In Chapter 15, we discuss Subject Area Models, which are a great medium for resolving differences in opinion on the meaning of high-level terms. Folks in accounting and sales can both agree that Customer is an important concept. But can both groups agree on a common definition? If they can agree, you are one step closer to creating a holistic view of the business.
- **Support data model precision**. A data model needs to be precise, which requires that the subject area definitions are also precise. An Order Line cannot exist without a Product, for example. However, if the definition of Product is missing or vague, we have less confidence in the concept and its relationships. Is a Product, for example, raw materials and intermediate goods, or only a finished item ready for resale? Can we have an order for a service, or must a product be a tangible deliverable? The definition is needed to support the Product concept and its relationship to Order Line. When order data is spread across multiple systems, it is vital to understand the similarities and differences between the purpose and meaning of the data in each system, or we run the risk of counting apples and pears, and calling them all gooseberries.

There are several techniques for writing a good definition. One that Steve likes in particular is to write the definition as if you are explaining the term to a child. You wouldn't use many big words or restate the obvious. It also would not be too verbose, as a child may not have the same attention span as we do. Avoid defining a concept using only the terms in the name of the concept (e.g. "The Customer is our customer."); it's good practice to write the definition before naming a concept. Examine ways in which the definition could break down; these tend to be the result of exceptional business events, such as a customer filing for bankruptcy, or a container ship sinking with the loss of all cargo. Ensure that your proposed definitions are verified by as wide an audience as possible. Remember that your definitions will be read by people you don't know, and you cannot predict who those people will be, nor their background, nor what preconceptions they may have when they read your definitions.

Despite their importance, definitions are often omitted or written with minimal attention to their audience. Therefore, when writing definitions, we need to be aware of four characteristics that lead to a high-quality definition that the audience can understand. Those characteristics are clarity, completeness, accuracy, and lack of ambiguity; they're summarized in this section. Please refer also to another book of Steve's, *The Data Modeler's Workbench*, for an entire chapter dedicated to definitions.

Clarity

Clarity means that a reader can understand the meaning of a term by reading the definition only once. A clear definition does not require the reader to decipher how each sentence should be interpreted. A good way to make sure your definition is clear is to think about what makes a definition unclear. We need to avoid restating the obvious and using obscure technical terminology or abbreviations in our definitions. Just to restate the obvious, *restating the obvious* means that we are not providing any new information, we are merely describing something that already has been mentioned or that is easy to find elsewhere. Let's say, for example, that the definition of *associate identifier* is "Associate identifier" or "The identifier for the associate." Equally unclear is the use of synonyms, as in the pseudo definition "The identifier for an employee." As far as clarity is concerned, we also need to make sure our audience understands the terms in our definition. Using acronyms, abbreviations, and industry jargon in definitions without explaining them can cause one to lose some of one's audience.

Completeness

This category focuses on making sure the definition is at the appropriate level of detail and that it includes all the necessary components, such as derivations and examples. Having a definition at the appropriate level of detail means that it is not so general as to provide very little additional value, yet not so specific that it provides value to only one application or department—or that it adds value only at a certain point in time.

Sometimes, in order to meet the needs of the entire company (or even the entire industry), we create a very general definition so that all parties can agree on the meaning. It is usually a very short definition - one that does not offend any of the parties. It is a definition that leaves little to debate, because it meets everyone's needs at a high-level. General definitions may include dictionary quotations, ambiguous terminology, and omit detail such as units of measure or details of calculations.

An example of a dictionary quotation as a definition for *product* might be "something produced by human or mechanical effort or by a natural process." What value does this dictionary quotation provide to an organization? If this dictionary quotation is only *part* of the definition instead of *being* the definition, the definition may be considered complete.

An example of an ambiguous terminology definition for Social Security number might be "associated with an employee." We know the Social Security number is associated with an employee, but what does it mean?

An example of a definition containing an omission would be this hypothetical definition of *order weight*: "the total shipping weight of an order delivered to a destination, including packaging, used to ensure that the maximum carry weight on a truck is not exceeded." It is not clear from this definition whether the order weight is in pounds, hundredweights, tons, or tonnes (metric tons). Is *order weight* the same as *shipping weight*?

The opposite of making a definition too general is making it too specific. "Too specific" means that the definition is correct within a certain scope, but does not address the complete scope of the term being defined. Definitions that are too specific usually include references to certain departments, applications, or states. Sometimes they simply consist entirely of examples or derivations. For example, imagine if the definition of the term *party* included only examples. This is more common than you might think in draft data models, for instance this definition of "Party":

```
customer
supplier
competitor
employee
```

Examples alone make for an incomplete definition. For a definition to be complete, the broadness of the definition must match the broadness of the term. The examples listed don't tell us what a Party means to our organization, or why have we included it in our data model.

Accuracy

This category focuses on having a definition that completely matches what the term means and is consistent with the rest of the business. *Accuracy* means that an expert in the field would agree that the term matches the definition. One of the difficulties with this category is that as we define broader terms that cross departments, such as *product, customer*, and *employee*, we tend to get more than one accurate definition, depending on who we ask. A recruiting department, for example, may have a definition for *employee* that is accurate but nonetheless different from the definition offered by a benefits department. The problem is the state issue, discussed earlier. A good solution to this problem is to use subtypes on your model that contain each of the distinct states of an employee. Through the accurate definition of each subject, every state is captured.

Lack of Ambiguity

If your definition is ambiguous, then its accuracy is in doubt. One of the easiest ways to make a definition ambiguous is to insert the words 'may', 'should', or 'might'. When you use these words in conversation, the person you are talking to can interpret your meaning by your body language, tone of voice, and the context of the conversation. If the person is uncertain, they can ask for clarification. When they read your words on a page or a screen, those options are not available; the words used in the definition must prevent the question being asked, by being unambiguous.

George was flying home from a conference recently, the plane was rolling towards the gate, and a crew member was telling the passengers about the airport they were arriving at. In effect, she was describing business rules, including the rule about smoking in the airport terminal. She said, "Smoking may not be permitted in the terminal building". If you were a smoker, wanting to know when you'd be able to light your next cigarette, how would you interpret that rule? The words 'may not' make the rule ambiguous, implying that there are possibly some circumstances where you would be able to smoke. Perhaps there will be signs saying 'You may now smoke', or directing you to a special smoking area.

In fact, the airport is in a country where it is illegal to smoke in airport terminals; no ambiguity there at all. The airline wisely chose to avoid using the words 'illegal' or 'crime' in its announcements, but why did it choose to say 'may not be' instead of simply 'Smoking is not permitted in the terminal building'? Perhaps it was the author's cultural background, or the author wanted to avoid sounding like a parent laying down rules to their children. Whatever the reason, the airline failed to make an accurate statement of the business rule, which might lead a passenger to make a decision they later regret.

Not Only Entities and Data Elements

There are many objects in data models, most of which need to be provided with a name. The quality of the name you give a model or diagram is not as critical to the organization as the names of entities and data elements, but you must apply the same thought processes to choosing that name. If you're faced with four data models with similar names and no version numbers, how do you know which one you can rely on? The same is true for diagrams; it is essential to know what a diagram is meant to represent. If it helps (and it often does), consider providing definitions for models and diagrams that you expect others to re-use. PowerDesigner and other data modeling tools allow you to provide definitions for data models and diagrams, so take advantage of that.

Especially Relationships

Data modelers often overlook the need for quality, accurate relationship names – how many times have you looked at a relationship between two entities and had to ask the modeler what they mean by 'has associated'? What if the modeler is no longer available?

In Figure 6.3, none of the relationships have been named. At first sight, it appears that the relationship from **Contract** to **Contract Payment** would probably be called 'Results In'. However, on closer examination, we can see that **Contract Payment** includes *two* **Contract ID** attributes. They're both foreign keys, so there is at least one relationship missing from the diagram; Figure 6.1 is obviously not the complete model. The relationship that we *can* see is fully optional, so it cannot be the dependent relationship via which **Contract Payment** inherits the primary key attribute **Contract ID**. So what is this mysterious optional relationship? If the modeler is not available, do we have time to re-do the analysis that led the modeler to create this relationship? Should it even be there – perhaps it was created in error, and overlooked by whoever reviewed the model?

Figure 6.3 Unnamed relationships

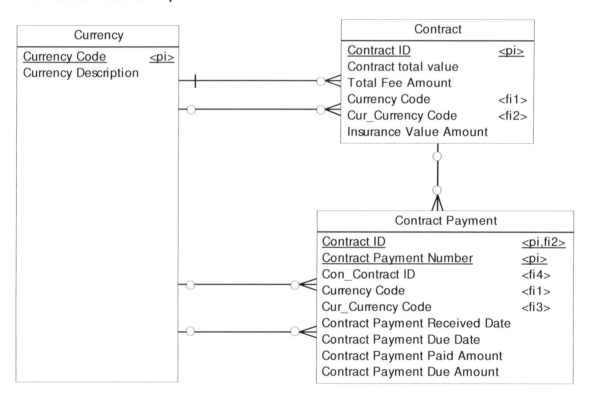

There is also uncertainty over the role of the four relationships involving **Currency**. Three of them are optional; what conditions would cause these relationships to exist? Why would a **Contract** or **Contract Payment** require a second **Currency Code**? Has the modeler made an assumption, valid or not, about standard industry practice? Will the potential audience for the model all make the same assumption, or a different one? To eliminate these uncertainties, provide meaningful relationship role names, and ensure that the descriptions of the foreign key attributes describe when and why they would exist. Don't be surprised if asking for more details about the relationships uncovers further changes you need to make to the model.

The Need for Naming Standards

Unless you're working in a very simple modeling and application environment, it's important to have naming standards for the key objects you're going to create. It's common to have naming standards for, say, Oracle databases, but you also need naming standards for conceptual and logical models.

For example, how do you structure the names of attributes in Logical Data Models, and how do they transform into database column names? Common considerations include the sequence of words in the name, and whether or not the entity name is included. I suggest you refer to "Data Modeling Essentials" (Simsion and Witt, 2005, pp. 166-171) for a discussion of the topic.

PowerDesigner provides support for naming standards, and helps you to achieve consistency of names across models, especially when you generate one model from another. See "Managing Names and Codes" in Chapter 20 for more on this topic.

The PowerDesigner Glossary allows you to manage the terminology you use in your object names. See "Deploying an Enterprise Glossary" in Chapter 20.

Key Points

- It's vital that the definitions we provide for our data answer the reader's questions.

- Three main functions that make definitions so important
    - Assist with decision making
    - Reveal, document and resolve different perspectives
    - Support data model precision.

- When writing definitions, remember your audience.

- Four characteristics of a high-quality definition
    - Clarity
    - Completeness
    - Accuracy
    - Lack of ambiguity.

- It's important to have naming standards for the key objects you're going to create
    - Not just entities and data elements
    - Relationships are especially important.

- PowerDesigner provides support for naming standards, and helps you to achieve consistency of names across models, especially when you generate one model from another.

- The PowerDesigner glossary allows you to manage the terminology you use in your names.

More than one John Doe
Which is the right Customer?
Recall by the key

There is a lot of data out there, but how do you sift through it all to find what you're looking for? That's where keys come in. Keys allow us to efficiently retrieve data, as well as navigate from one physical table to another. This chapter defines keys and distinguishes between the terms candidate, primary, and alternate keys. Surrogate keys, foreign keys and their importance are also explained.

Key Explained

Data elements identify, describe, or measure the entity instances in which they reside. There is often a need to find specific entity instances using one or more data elements. Those data element(s) that allow us to find specific entity instances are known as keys. The Library of Congress assigns an ISBN (International Standard Book Number) to every book. When the ISBN for this book, 9780977140091, is entered into many search engines and database systems, the book entity instance **Data Modeling Made Simple With PowerDesigner** will be returned (try it!). A particular tax identifier can help us find an organization. The key **Account Code** can help us find a particular account.

Candidate Key Explained

A candidate key is one or more data elements that uniquely identify an entity instance. Sometimes a single data element identifies an entity instance, such as ISBN for a book, or **Account Code** for an account. Sometimes it takes more than one data element to uniquely identify an entity instance. For example, both a **Promotion Type Code** and **Promotion Start Date** are necessary to identify a promotion. When more than one data element makes up a key, we use the term 'composite key'. Therefore, **Promotion Type Code** and **Promotion Start Date** together are a composite candidate key for a promotion.

A candidate key has three main characteristics:

- **Unique**. There cannot be duplicate values in the data in a candidate key and it cannot be empty (also known as 'nullable'). Therefore, the number of distinct values of a candidate key must be equal to the number of distinct entity instances. If the entity Book has ISBN as its candidate key, and if there are 500 book instances, there will also be 500 unique ISBNs.
- **Non-volatile**. A candidate key value on an entity instance should never change. Since a candidate key is used to find a unique entity instance, you would be unable to find that instance if you were still trying to use the value before it was changed. Changing a

candidate key would also mean changing it in every other entity in which it appears with the original value.

- **Minimal**. A candidate key should contain only those data elements that are needed to uniquely identify an entity instance. If four data elements are listed as the composite candidate key for an entity, but only three are really needed for uniqueness, then only those three should make up the candidate key.

Figure 7.1 contains a data model before candidate keys have been identified.

Figure 7.1 Data model before candidate keys have been identified

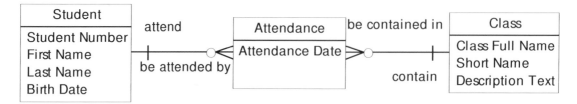

- Each Student may attend one or many Classes.
- Each Class may contain one or many Students.

Note that we have a many-to-many relationship between **Student** and **Class** that was replaced by the entity **Attendance** and two one-to-many relationships (more on this in our normalization section). In reading a many-to-many relationship, I have found it helpful to ignore the entity in the middle (Attendance, in this example) and just read the labels between the entities on either side. For example, each Student may attend one or many Classes and each Class may contain one or many Students. Table 7.1 contains sample values for each of these entities.

Table 7.1 Sample values for Figure 7.1

Student

Student Number	Student First Name	Student Last Name	Student Date Of Birth
SM385932	Steve	Martin	1/25/1958
EM584926	Eddie	Murphy	3/15/1971
HW742615	Henry	Winkler	2/14/1984
MM481526	Mickey	Mouse	5/10/1982
DD857111	Donald	Duck	5/10/1982
MM573483	Minnie	Mouse	4/1/1986
LR731511	Lone	Ranger	10/21/1949
EM876253	Eddie	Murphy	7/1/1992

Attendance

Attendance Date
5/10/2009
6/10/2009
7/10/2009

Class

Class Full Name	Class Short Name	Class Description Text
Data Modeling Fundamentals	Data Modeling 101	An introductory class covering basic data modeling concepts and principles.
Advanced Data Modeling	Data Modeling 301	A fast-paced class covering techniques such as advanced normalization and ragged hierarchies.
Tennis Basics	Tennis One	For those new to the game of tennis, learn the key aspects of the game.
Juggling		Learn how to keep three balls in the air at once!

Based on our definition of a candidate key and a candidate key's characteristics of being unique, non-volatile, and minimal, what would you choose as the candidate keys for each of these entities?

For Student, **Student Number** appears to be a valid candidate key. There are eight students and eight distinct values for **Student Number**. So unlike **Student First Name** and **Student Last Name**, which can contain duplicates like Eddie Murphy, **Student Number** appears to be unique. **Student Date Of Birth** can also contain duplicates such as '5/10/1982', which is the **Student Date Of Birth** for both Mickey Mouse and Donald Duck. However, the combination of **Student First Name**, **Student Last Name**, and **Student Date Of Birth** may make a valid candidate key.

For Attendance, we are currently missing a candidate key. Although the **Attendance Date** is unique in our sample data, we will probably need to know which student attended which class on this particular date.

For Class, on first glance it appears that any of its data elements are unique, and would therefore qualify as a candidate key. However, Juggling does not have a **Class Short Name**. Therefore, because **Class Short Name** can be empty, we cannot consider it a candidate key. In addition, one of the characteristics of a candidate key is that it is non-volatile. I know, based on my teaching experience, that class descriptions can change. Therefore, **Class Description**

Text also needs to be ruled out as a candidate key, leaving **Class Full Name** as the best option for a candidate key.

PowerDesigner reserves the term 'Key' for the Physical Data Model, and uses the term 'Identifier' in the Conceptual and Logical Data Models, hence the acronyms 'pi' (primary identifier), 'fi' (foreign identifier), and 'ai' (alternate identifier) in entity symbols. We'll discuss what these mean shortly.

Primary and Alternate Keys Explained

Even though an entity may contain more than one candidate key, we can only select one candidate key to be the primary key for an entity. A primary key is the candidate key that has been chosen to be *the* unique identifier for an entity. An alternate key is a candidate key that although unique, was not chosen as the primary key, but still can be used to find specific entity instances.

We have only one candidate key in the Class entity, so **Class Full Name** becomes our primary key. We have to make a choice in Student, however, because we have two candidate keys. Which Student candidate key would you choose as the primary key?

In selecting one candidate key over another as the primary key, consider succinctness and security. Succinctness means if there are several candidate keys, choose the one with the fewest data elements or shortest in length. In terms of security, it is possible that one or more data elements within a candidate key will contain sensitive data whose viewing should be restricted. We want to avoid having sensitive data in our entity's primary key because the primary key can propagate as a foreign key and therefore spread this sensitive data throughout our database.

Considering succinctness and security in our example, I would choose **Student Number** over the composite **Student First Name**, **Student Last Name**, and **Student Date Of Birth**. It is more succinct and contains less sensitive data.

Figure 7.2 shows our data model updated with primary and alternate keys. In PowerDesigner, primary key attributes are indicated by appending <pi> to their name in the entity symbol. Columns in alternate keys have <ai> appended to their name. If the entity has more than one alternate key, a number is appended to <ai> to differentiate between them. For example, <ai1> and <ai2>.

Attendance now has as its primary key **Student Number** and **Class Full Name**, which appear to make a valid primary key.

Figure 7.2 Data model updated with primary and alternate keys

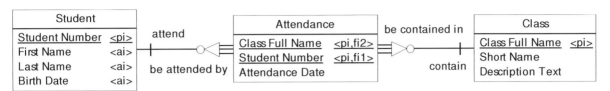

The primary key attributes in **Attendance** are both inherited from other entities; **Attendance** is dependent on and partially identified by the other entities. In PowerDesigner this is documented by marking the relationships as 'dependent'; this changes the relationship notation to include a triangular symbol:

attend

be attended by

So to summarize, a candidate key consists of one or more data elements that uniquely identify an entity instance. The candidate key that is selected as the best way to identify each unique record in the entity becomes the primary key. The other candidate keys become alternate keys. Keys containing more than one data element are known as composite keys.

Surrogate Key Explained

A surrogate key is a primary key that substitutes for a natural key, which is what the business sees as the unique identifier for an entity. It has no embedded intelligence and is used by IT (and not the business) for integration or performance reasons.

Surrogate keys are useful for integration, which is an effort to create a single, consistent version of the data. Applications such as data warehouses often house data from more than one application or system. Surrogate keys enable us to bring together information about the same entity instance that is identified differently in each source system. If the same concept, such as Student or Class, exists in more than one system, there is a good chance some amount of integration will be necessary. For example, Robert Jones in system XYZ and Renee Jane in system ABC might both be identified in their respective systems as RJ. But if we tried to bring them together using RJ to link them, the data would be incorrect – we'd have Robert and Renee identified as the same person. Instead, a different, non-overlapping, surrogate key could be assigned to each of them. Similarly, if Robert Jones is identified as RJ in system XYZ and BJ in system DEF, the information about him could be consolidated under a single surrogate key value. The fact that they're the same would need to be determined through a separate effort.

Surrogate keys are also efficient. You've seen that a primary key may be composed of one or more attributes of the entity. A single surrogate key is more efficient to use than having to specify three or four (or five or six) attributes to locate the single record you're looking for.

When using a surrogate key, always make an effort to determine the natural key, and then define an alternate key on this natural key. For example, assuming a surrogate key is a more efficient primary key than **Class Full Name**, we can create the surrogate key **Class Id** for Class and define an alternate key on **Class Full Name**, as shown in Figure 7.3. Table 7.2 contains the values in **Class**.

Figure 7.3 Data model updated with surrogate key

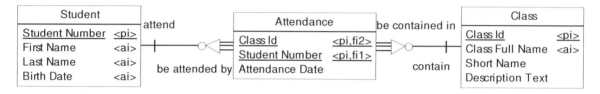

Table 7.2 Class values updated with surrogate key

Class Id	Class Full Name	Class Short Name	Class Description Text
1	Data Modeling Fundamentals	Data Modeling 101	An introductory class covering basic data modeling concepts and principles.
2	Advanced Data Modeling	Data Modeling 301	A fast-paced class covering techniques such as advanced normalization and ragged hierarchies.
3	Tennis Basics	Tennis One	For those new to the game of tennis, learn the key aspects of the game.
4	Juggling		Learn how to keep three balls in the air at once!

In this example, we are using **Class Full Name** as a candidate key, but in the real world, it is never a good idea to use a name as a key because names can change. It is often also difficult or impossible to make sure that names are unique.

Foreign Key Explained

A foreign key is a data element that provides a link to another entity. A foreign key allows a database management system to navigate from one entity to another. For example, we need to know who owns an Account, so we would want to include the identifier of the customer to whom it belongs in the entity. The **Customer Id** in Account is the primary key of that Customer in the Customer entity. Using this foreign key back to Customer enables the database management system to navigate from a particular account or accounts, to the customer or customers that own each account. Likewise, the database can navigate from a particular customer or customers, to find all of their accounts.

A foreign key is automatically created when we define a relationship between two entities. When a relationship is created between two entities, the entity on the "many" side of the relationship inherits the primary key from the entity on the "one" side of the relationship.

PowerDesigner Conceptual Data Models do not support Foreign Keys explicitly; Foreign Keys are not necessary when describing business concepts and the relationships between them. Indeed, Primary Keys are not mandatory in abstract Conceptual Data models.

Foreign Keys (Foreign Identifiers) are automatically included in any Logical or Physical Data Model you generate from a Conceptual Data Model.

PowerDesigner allows you to choose which attributes to migrate, and which identifier to migrate them from (if you have more than one, of course).

In Figure 7.3, there are two foreign keys in the Attendance entity. The **Student Number** foreign key points back to a particular student in the Student entity. The **Class Id** foreign key points back to a particular Class in the Class entity. Table 7.3 contains a few Attendance entity instances.

Table 7.3 Attendance entity instances

Student Number	Class Id	Attendance Date
SM385932	1	5/10/2009
EM584926	1	5/10/2009
EM584926	2	6/10/2009
MM481526	2	6/10/2009
MM573483	2	6/10/2009
LR731511	3	7/10/2009

By looking at these values and recalling the sample values from Tables 13.1 and 13.2, we learn that Steve Martin and Eddie Murphy both attended the Data Modeling Fundamentals class on 5/10/2009. Eddie Murphy also attended the Advanced Data Modeling Class with Mickey and Minnie Mouse on 6/10/2009. Lone Ranger took Tennis Basics (by himself, as usual) on 7/10/2009.

EXERCISE 6: Clarifying Customer Id

I was showing examples of both complete and incomplete definitions during a recent training class, when I shared the following incomplete definition for a **Customer Id**:

*A **Customer Id** is the unique identifier for a Customer.*

"What else can you say about **Customer Id** anyway?" a participant asked.

What else can you say about **Customer Id** (or any identifier) to add more meaning to its definition?

See the Appendix for my answers.

Key Points

- A key is a data element or set of data elements that helps us find entity instances.

- A candidate key is a set of one or more data elements that uniquely identify an entity instance.

- A candidate key becomes either a primary or alternate key.

- A primary key represents the one or more data elements that uniquely identify an instance of an entity and that is chosen to be *the* unique identifier everyone should use. In contrast, an alternate key also uniquely identifies entity occurrences, but is not chosen as *the* unique key.

- If a key contains more than one data element, it is known as a composite key.

- A surrogate key is a primary key with no embedded intelligence that is a substitute for a natural key. It is used by IT to facilitate integration and introduce database efficiencies.

- A foreign key points from one entity instance to another.

- The PowerDesigner CDM does not support foreign keys.

- PowerDesigner uses the word 'identifier' in the CDM and LDM, and 'key' in the PDM.

Section III explains the important role of data modeling tools, the key features required of any data modeling tool, and an introduction to the essential features of PowerDesigner. It also describes how to create and manage data modeling objects in PowerDesigner. By the time you finish this section, you will be able to create data models in PowerDesigner.

Chapter 8 explains why there is a need to model using a software tool instead of pencil and paper or drawing tools, and describes the key features required of a data modeling tool.

Chapter 9 provides a brief introduction to the features of PowerDesigner for data modelers, including a brief overview of the tool's features especially Linking and Syncing models.

Chapter 10 introduces you to the essential components and features of PowerDesigner for data modeling and general model management. After you have read this chapter, followed us in the 'Your Turn' sections, and finished the Exercise, you'll be ready to do some real work in PowerDesigner. If you only use PowerDesigner occasionally, or need to refresh your knowledge, come back to this chapter and work through it again.

Chapter 11 builds on the knowledge gained in Chapter 10, and shows you how to create and manage entities in PowerDesigner. It also expands on your knowledge of the properties of objects.

Chapter 12 describes the support provided for data elements by PowerDesigner Domains, Data Items, Attributes, and Columns. It outlines a simple strategy for how and when to use each of the types of data elements in PowerDesigner, and introduces you to the PowerDesigner

Glossary. More essential PowerDesigner features are introduced - dependency matrices, shortcuts and replicas, and generation links.

Chapter 13 shows you how to create and manage the different types of relationship introduced in Chapter 5, and discusses differences between the CDM and LDM in their support for relationships. The concept of graphical synonyms is discussed in more detail, and we show you how to route your relationships.

Chapter 14 shows you how to create and manage the different types of keys introduced in Chapter 7, and discusses differences between the CDM, LDM, and PDM in their support for keys.

A connected world
Integrated modeling
Needs specialized tools

From time to time, great debates arise in discussion forums about the pros and cons of various data modeling tools; inevitably, one or more people say that their favorite tools are the whiteboard and sticky notes. The whiteboard and sticky notes are great tools for workshop use, enabling rapid development of a model by a group of people without technical data modeling skills. Once a data model has been fleshed out on a whiteboard or a wall, it usually needs to be recorded in a more permanent fashion. Very often, the first choice is the old favorite analysis tool, the spreadsheet. Like the whiteboard and sticky notes, the spreadsheet is a great way of capturing information during and after a workshop, and doesn't require expensive software licenses or special skills. By itself, however, it only provides a fraction of the capabilities required to construct, validate, communicate and use a data model effectively.

Why not use a drawing tool for data modeling?

You may be tempted to use a drawing tool, such as Microsoft® PowerPoint® or Visio®, or Smart Draw®. These products allow you to draw lines and boxes, and add text to diagrams; they can create diagrams that communicate ideas visually, and maybe even capture some additional information about some of the symbols. However, each diagram stands alone: if an entity appears on five diagrams, there is no connection between those five entity symbols. There is no way to ensure that those five diagrams are consistent in how they depict that entity, nor is there a way of knowing whether or not the entity also appears on a sixth diagram that you haven't been told about. There is also no link from that entity to any database tables that were generated from it, and no link to the business processes that manage that entity. In short, the entities appear to live in a disconnected world. When it comes to managing change, that disconnected world gets very uncomfortable. As the models change, you have to manually change all the relevant diagrams and documents. Knowing which documents need to be changed and ensuring they remain consistent is a daunting task.

In Section III, you will see the different levels and types of data models, each with their own purposes and usage. There are dependencies between these different types of data models, between data models and other artifacts or models that represent other aspects of business and requirements, the enterprise and solutions architecture, and application design. The activities required to produce and manage data models are only part of a wider set of business and technology activities; integration with associated activities is key to the success of data modeling.

Without a tool that provides specialized support for data modeling, the data modeler cannot hope to work effectively in this environment.

Organizations take a variety of approaches to the enablement of data modeling, depending on the money available, and the perceived role of data models in their organization.

Key Features Needed in a Data Modeling Tool

With data modeling tools, you generally get what you pay for. The more you pay, the more features are provided by the product. The wider your use of data models within the organization, the more features you tend to need. If you're a data modeling novice, you should really read Sections I and II before reading this section.

In this section, we list some of the key features that we should expect a data modeling tool to provide. There is no hidden meaning in the order of the lists, other than to ensure that related features are close to each other. The features are grouped into five categories – Core Modeling, Usability, Interfaces and Integration, Tool Management and Communication, and Collaboration. Chapter 9 uses the same categories to analyze the features provided by PowerDesigner.

Core Modeling

- Construct different levels and types of data models, including any distinct notation and content required for each level
    - See section IV for details of the six types of data models
- Generate a new data model from selected content in an existing data model
    - create and maintain links between the original model and the generated model
    - includes transforming a logical data model into a physical data model, and vice versa
- Provide support for multiple data modeling notations, such as IDEF1X and Information Engineering
    - see Chapter 9 for more information about data modeling notation
- Create subsets of a data model using selected entities or tables
- Define validation and design rules, and use these to validate models
- Automatically correct validation errors, where appropriate
- Automatically enforce naming standards as model objects are created or modified
- View and edit multiple model objects in a single operation, similar to editing within a spreadsheet
- For physical data models, provide direct support for model objects specific to a technology, such as a given RDBMS or XML Schema Language
- Configurable support for technology objects (e.g. Creating generation capabilities for unsupported DBMS)
- Automated support for denormalization of physical data models, including rollback capabilities

- Record and manage the dependencies between objects in data models
    - o for example, "which diagrams does an entity appear in?", "which attributes are constrained by a given domain?"
    - o include the ability to traverse dependencies between model objects and filter the information provided; for example, starting with a given domain, extract details of the attributes constrained by the domain, any business rules referenced by those attributes, and also information about the owners of the business rules
- Support for multiple versions of models and model objects
- Automation of common modeling tasks, such as merging or splitting an entity, or converting a many-to-many relationship into an entity and two relationships
- Facilities for the re-use of modeling patterns and reference models within data models
- Record the vocabulary of the business as terms, and enforce naming standards based on those terms
- Replicate attributes between entities (ditto columns and tables)
- Replicate objects between models
- Create and manage shortcuts to objects in other models

Usability

- Control over the windows and toolbars displayed, and their position and size
- Auto-layout of selected parts of a diagram or a complete diagram
- Control of the placement of symbols on a diagram by the analyst
- Control over the style and content of symbols by the analyst
- A single editable view of any object
- Flexible editing capabilities
    - o allow the user to choose the properties to view and edit for a given type of object
    - o provide multiple ways of editing object properties, allowing the user to choose the method most appropriate for them
    - o include the ability to examine and define dependencies and links between model objects via a matrix
    - o include the ability to edit object properties within diagram symbols
- Flexible diagram printing capabilities
    - o visible page boundaries on canvas
    - o print whole diagram
    - o print specific pages
    - o fit to page
- Find objects in local models and in a repository by searching names or other properties
- Replace selected text in object names and other properties
- Save diagram images as graphics files in a variety of standard formats
- Group related models and other files that you need for a particular project in a container that can be shared with others and managed as a simple entity in a repository
- Defined browser workspaces to hold working sets of models and projects
- Annotate diagrams with additional symbols to improve communication
- Expert, timely support available

Interfaces and Integration

- Import existing data models created by other tools
- Reverse engineer existing data artifacts, such as XML schemas and database schemas, into physical data models
  - o includes the ability to reverse engineer database schemas from data definition language (DDL) files
- Generate or update an external data artifact, such as an XML or database schema, from a data model
  - o the combination of this feature and the previous feature is called 'round-trip engineering', and is *the* key capability when managing external data artifacts
  - o includes the ability to generate data definition language (DDL) files
- Create or update a model based upon information held in spreadsheets
- Compare two data models of the same or different types, and update one or both models as a result (this may also be referred to as merging models)
  - o include comparing two versions of a model
  - o preview, print, and save comparison results
- Compare a data model with an existing data artifact, such as an XML or database schema, and update the model and/or the data artifact as a result
- Export data models in a format that can be imported into other tools
- Generate test data to populate a test database or XML document
- Build cross-references or traceability links between data model objects and objects defined in other types of models, such as business process or enterprise architecture models
- Build cross-references or traceability links between data model objects and Business Requirement models
- Build cross-references or traceability links between data model objects and shared Business Rules
- Integration with popular development environments
- Integration with process and portfolio management workflows, and with IT configuration management
- Generate scripts to manage the movement of data through the archiving cycle, or data movements

Tool Management and Communication

- Extend the tool's underlying data model, allowing analysts to change the way in which model objects are defined and to define new types of model objects
- Extract information from model objects for publication in various formats, such as html and documents
- Provide access to the content of models via a programmable interface, to provide a mechanism for the automation of repetitive tasks, and to extend the functionality provided by the tool
- Integrate with LDAP/Active Directory for user authentication

Collaboration

- A shared location for the storage of and controlled access to data models
- Control access to models by multiple analysts
- Control access to subsets of a model, perhaps individual model objects
- Provide direct access to models and links between models via a portal designed for use by non-specialist users of data models
- Allow selected non-modelers to review or revise definitions via a portal
- Resolve potentially conflicting changes made by different analysts
- Share and apply a 'house style' for the appearance and content of data models
- Share reference models and common business rules via a repository
- Allow anyone to subscribe to a model to know when models are checked-in

EXERCISE 7: Examining Your Current Data Modeling Tool

Examine the list of tool features above, remove any that don't matter to you, and assess the priority of each of the remaining features. Now add more detail to the feature list, and convert it into a real list of tool requirements. Re-examine the features you decided weren't relevant for you; I'm sure you'll re-instate some of them.

Does your current toolset support your new requirements list? Read the rest of the book, and discover the key PowerDesigner features that provide support for your needs.

Key Points

- Whiteboards, sticky notes, and spreadsheets are great for capturing information during a workshop, but you need a specialized data modeling tool to capture and use data models effectively.

- The key features of a data modeling tool can be categorized as follows:
    - Core Modeling
    - Usability
    - Interfaces and Integration
    - Tool Management and Communication
    - Collaboration.

- Build your own list of features, and check them against PowerDesigner's feature list on the Sybase web site[2] or in Chapter 9.

---

[2] See the Quick Reference Guide for the link

Deep is the insight
That metadata provides
Models, Objects, Links

Using the tool features listed in Chapter 8, you will produce a lot of complex, interrelated information about data models, real-world data artifacts, and other types of models. We refer to all this 'about' information as 'metadata'. The *description* of an entity in a Logical Data Model is part of the entity's metadata, as is the *link* from the entity to a table in a Physical Data Model. The *description* of the table and the *link* from the table to a database view in another Physical Data Model are also metadata. The metadata underlying your data models is a key source of knowledge about your business, the data it requires to operate, and the way in which that data has been or will be implemented in your systems.

What is metadata?

If you ask us for our definition of metadata, before we can even think about what it really means, we hear ourselves say aloud, "Data about data." This is, however, a poor definition. As we will see from our discussion of definitions in Chapter 6, a good definition is clear, complete, and correct. Although the "Data about data" definition is correct, it is not clear or complete. It is not clear, since business people need to understand what metadata means and I have never found someone who responds with "Ah, I get it now" after hearing the "data about data" explanation. It is not a complete definition because it does not provide examples nor distinguish how metadata really differs from data. Therefore, we need a better definition for the term metadata.

Steve spoke on a metadata-related topic with several DAMA chapters and user groups. Collectively, they came up with the following definition for metadata:

Metadata is text, voice, or image that describes what the audience wants or needs to see or experience. The audience could be a person, group, or software program. Metadata is important because it aids in clarifying and finding the actual data.

A particular context or usage can turn what we traditionally consider data into metadata. For example, search engines allow users to enter keywords to retrieve web pages. These keywords are traditionally data, but in the context of search engines they play the role of metadata. Much the same way that a particular person can be an Employee in one role and a Customer in another role, text, voice or image can play different roles - sometimes playing 'data' and sometimes playing 'metadata', depending on what is important to a particular subject or activity.

There are at least six types of metadata: business (also known as 'semantic'), storage, process, display, project, and program.

Examples of business metadata are definitions, tags, and business terms. Examples of storage metadata are database column names, formats, and volumetrics. Examples of process metadata are source/target mappings, data load metrics, and transformation logic. Examples of display metadata are display format, screen colors, and screen type (e.g. tablet vs. laptop). Examples of project metadata are functional requirements, project plans, and weekly status reports. Examples of program metadata are the Zachman Framework, DAMA-DMBOK, and naming standards documentation.

PowerDesigner metadata scope

PowerDesigner provides a single modeling environment that brings together the techniques and notations of business process and requirements modeling, data modeling, enterprise architecture modeling, and UML application modeling. The scope of the metadata supported by PowerDesigner is therefore much wider than just the metadata required to describe and manage your data.

PowerDesigner enables you to integrate the design and maintenance of your organization's core data with your business requirements, business rules, business processes, Enterprise Architecture, Glossary of Terms, Object-Oriented code, XML vocabularies, and data movements. By providing you with a comprehensive set of models at all levels of abstraction, PowerDesigner helps you broaden the reach of your iterative design process to all aspects of your system architecture, from conception to deployment, and beyond.

PowerDesigner does not impose any particular software engineering methodology or process. Each organization can implement its own workflow, defining responsibilities and roles, describing what tools to use, what validations are required, and what documents to produce at each step in the process.

PowerDesigner Data Models

PowerDesigner provides support for eleven types of models, plus the Multi-Model Report. Which models are available to you depends upon the PowerDesigner edition you have licensed. Table 9.1 describes the models of most direct relevance to the data modeler; see Chapter 25 for information regarding the other types of model that are available.

The descriptions in Table 9.1 describe the broad characteristics of each type of model. In Section IV we will introduce six specific types of data models, each of which can be supported by one or more of the PowerDesigner models listed in the table.

Table 9.1 PowerDesigner Data Models

Conceptual Data Model (CDM)	A *Conceptual Data Model (CDM)* helps you identify the principal entities of importance to the business, their attributes, and the relationships between them. A CDM is more abstract than a logical (LDM) or a physical (PDM) data model.
Logical Data Model (LDM)	A *Logical Data Model (LDM)* helps you analyze the structure of an information system, independent of any specific physical database implementation. A LDM has migrated entity identifiers and is less abstract than a Conceptual Data Model (CDM), but does not allow you to model views, indexes, and other elements that are available in the more concrete Physical Data Model (PDM).
Physical Data Model (PDM)	A *Physical Data Model (PDM)* helps you analyze the tables, views, and other objects in a database, including the multidimensional objects necessary for data warehousing. A PDM is more concrete than a conceptual (CDM) or logical (LDM) data model. You can model, reverse-engineer, and generate for all of the most popular DBMSs.

When we refer to PowerDesigner models in this book, we use the three-letter codes shown above – CDM, LDM, and PDM. When we speak about the 'Logical Data Model' or the 'Physical Data Model', we're referring to the types of models described in Section IV.

Data Modeling Feature Comparison

PowerDesigner has a wide breadth, so it is useful to many people, but just how useful is it? Is it a jack-of-all-trades and master of none? If it was, then we wouldn't have written this book, you can be sure of that.

Using the tool feature categories that we introduced in Chapter 8, let us sell PowerDesigner's data modeling capabilities to you.

Core Modeling

PowerDesigner supports the majority of the features listed in Chapter 8. Here are just some of the ways in which this support is provided.

Support For Multiple Types Of Data-Related Models

PowerDesigner supports all six types of data models described in Section IV.

Linking and Syncing Models

One of the great features of PowerDesigner is the ability to take an existing model and generate another model of the same type, or a different type of model. A detailed record is kept of the links between models, and between objects in those models. This information is available for carrying out impact analysis, and is also used to ensure that models stay synchronized, where necessary. You can also import from or generate SQL files and database schemas. When generating a new model, you can be selective about which objects to generate from in the original model.

Sybase refers to these capabilities as 'Link and Sync'. Figure 9.1 shows a subset of the link and sync capabilities that are most relevant to a data modeler. For simplicity, it doesn't show the 'same model type' generation capabilities, which is supported for all these types of models; for example, you can generate a LDM from a LDM.

Figure 9.1 Data model generation links

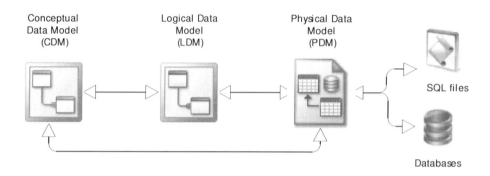

One File Per Model

In the real world, it's possible for the Logical and Physical views of data to be radically different, especially if the Physical view is based on one or more packages supplied by third party vendors. Supporting these views requires a loose coupling of Logical and Physical Data Models, or perhaps a loose coupling of Conceptual and Physical Data Models. In some other data modeling tools, achieving looser coupling between the Logical and Physical Data Models, or mapping any of those models to objects in models held in other files, can be difficult and cumbersome.

The way in which PowerDesigner manages models allows us to work flexibly. Each model is held in a separate file, and contains details of 'target models' that it is linked to. These target model entries are created automatically when you run standard PowerDesigner functions, such as generating a Logical Data Model from a Physical Data Model, creating mappings between models with the Mapping Editor, or creating shortcuts in a model to objects or diagrams in another model. The models can be as tightly or loosely coupled as you like. The model links can be interrogated and revised, and also shown graphically. There is no practical limit to the number and types of models you can generate and map together.

Multiple Notations Supported

PowerDesigner provides support for several different modeling notations, which you can vary from model to model. You can also change the notation in use in a model at any time, though you will have to be careful, as the types of model objects supported do vary somewhat, according to the notation.

You can change the notation for a model via the Model Options. If you click on <Set as Default>, the chosen notation becomes the default notation for new models of that type. PowerDesigner is supplied with a number of user profiles that allow you to ensure that your modelers use notation consistently.

For example, to create the notation samples in Table 9.2, I created a simple model using one notation, then generated additional models, each of which uses a different notation. This allowed me to create five models of the same type, identical except for notation differences. Using the PowerDesigner concept of a Project, I produced Figure 9.2, which shows you the generation links between the models. Each box in the diagram represents a model.

Figure 9.2 Example of generation links

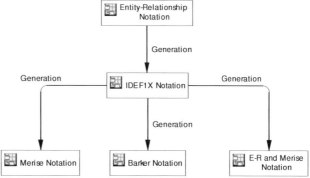

Table 9.2 describes the data modeling notations supported by PowerDesigner. All of the notations use rectangles to represent data objects (entities, tables or views); there are some exceptions – see Table 9.2. The notations all use lines to denote relationships or references, though the line style varies, as do the symbols used at the line endpoints. In the CDM/LDM examples, **Relationship_2** is a dependent relationship; see Chapter 7 for more information. For in-depth comparisons of modeling notation, you are advised to read David Hay's articles on the subject, available from www.essentialstrategies.com.

Table 9.2 Notations supported by PowerDesigner

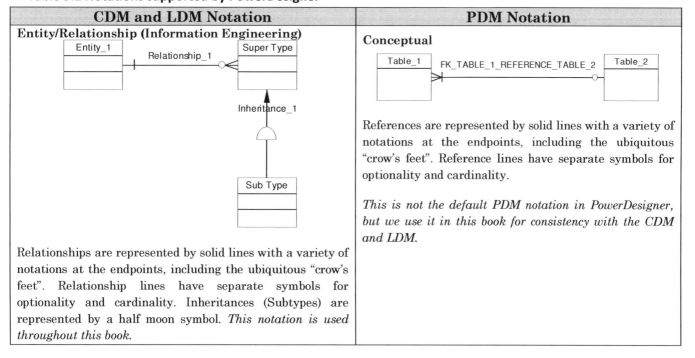

CDM and LDM Notation	PDM Notation
Entity/Relationship (Information Engineering)	**Conceptual**
Relationships are represented by solid lines with a variety of notations at the endpoints, including the ubiquitous "crow's feet". Relationship lines have separate symbols for optionality and cardinality. Inheritances (Subtypes) are represented by a half moon symbol. *This notation is used throughout this book.*	References are represented by solid lines with a variety of notations at the endpoints, including the ubiquitous "crow's feet". Reference lines have separate symbols for optionality and cardinality. *This is not the default PDM notation in PowerDesigner, but we use it in this book for consistency with the CDM and LDM.*

Table 9.2 Notations supported by PowerDesigner (continued)

CDM and LDM Notation	PDM Notation
IDEF1X (CDM and LDM)	**IDEF1X (PDM)**

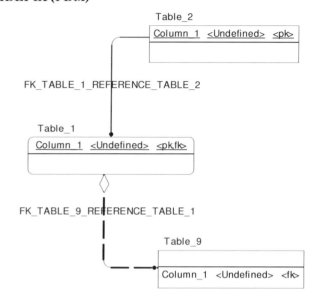

Round cornered rectangles represent "dependent" entities, whose unique identifier includes at least one relationship to another entity. On relationship lines, the endpoint symbols represent a combination of optionality and cardinality. If a relationship is part of an entity's unique identifier, it is shown as a solid line. Otherwise it is shown as a dashed line. Inheritances (Subtypes) are represented by a circle symbol with either one or two lines beneath.	Dependent tables are shown as rounded rectangles. On reference lines, the endpoint symbols represent a combination of optionality and cardinality. If a reference is part of a table's unique identifier, it is shown as a solid line. Otherwise it is shown as a dashed line.
Barker	**Relational**

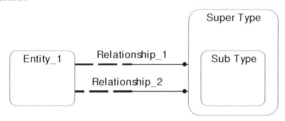

All entity symbols have rounded corners. Relationships are drawn in two parts, each reflecting the optionality of the associated entity role. In this example, the dashed portion of the relationship line tells us that **Entity_1** does not have to participate in the relationship; the solid part of the line means that **Super Type** <u>does</u> have to participate in the relationship. Inheritances (subtypes) are represented by placing the child entities inside the parent entity symbol.	All references are represented by a simple arrow, which points to the table from which a foreign key column is inherited. In the diagram above, the foreign key in **Table_1** is a primary key in **Table_2**. *This is the default PDM notation.*

Table 9.2 Notations supported by PowerDesigner (continued)

CDM and LDM Notation	PDM Notation
Merise 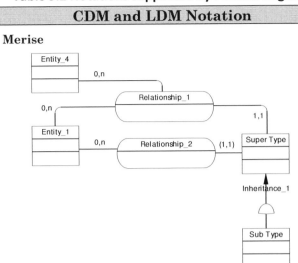	**CODASYL**  This notation pre-dates the relational database. In a reference, the arrow represents a set of objects. In the diagram above, the reference tells you that each row in **Table_2** can own a set of rows in **Table_1**. The simplest way to consider this is to view it as the opposite of Relational notation.

This notation uses multi-entity associations instead of relationships. In the example above, three entities participate in **Relationship_1**. In other notations, **Relationship_1** would be represented as an entity.

Inheritances (Subtypes) are identified via a half moon symbol.

E/R+Merise

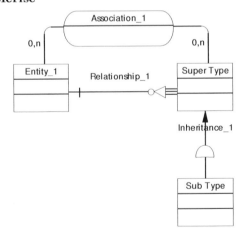

Both Entity/Relationship and Merise notation are used in the model.

 For consistency, we use the 'Entity/Relationship' notation in all CDM, LDM and PDM diagrams in this book.

 "Setting CDM/LDM Model Options" (Data Modeling)
"Setting PDM Model Options" (Data Modeling)

Subsets Of A Data Model

In a data model, you can have many diagrams, each containing a selected subset of the full model. If you like, you can select a load of symbols on one diagram, and create a new diagram with just those symbols in it. The layout of the new diagram will match the layout and display preferences of the original diagram.

For any diagram, you can choose the objects you wish to display, including objects from other models. For example, in an LDM, you can choose which entities and relationships are included on a diagram. You can also choose to hide selected attributes so they do not appear on entity symbols, though this applies to all the diagrams the entity appears in within the model.

In addition, PowerDesigner supports the UML package concept, and packages also contain diagrams - more on this later.

Model Validation

Press the <F4> key in any model and you'll be presented with a comprehensive list of checks that you can run against the model. You decide which checks to perform and how important each check is to you. PowerDesigner can automatically fix some errors for you. When you generate a new model, you can choose whether or not to check the original model for errors before generating the new one. Additional checks can be added using VBScript.

Naming Standards

You can define naming standards that apply when you create a model object or transform an object into a new object. There are different rules for creating different types of objects. For example, you can tell PowerDesigner how to convert an entity name into a table name. You can reuse naming standards via naming templates and provide lists of word conversions, such as replacing the word 'Account' with 'ACCT'.

The Glossary feature allows you to record the vocabulary of the business as Terms, and to use those Terms as the basis of a naming standard for data elements and other objects. Adherence to the Glossary is a standard part of the model validation capabilities.

Spreadsheet-like editing

PowerDesigner provides a grid-like editing mechanism within the properties of a single object, and also within a list of objects or a List Report. You can customize the properties displayed in the grid, and filter the objects or sub-objects listed.

Comprehensive Database Support

60+ RDBMS platforms are supported, including all the major platforms.

Dependencies Between Model Objects

Right-clicking a symbol on a diagram or an object in the Browser, and selecting 'Impact and Lineage Analysis', will show you the objects that the object depends on and the objects that depend on the selected object. You can change the analysis rules used, open up the definition of any object you come across, and view the analysis results as a diagram, which you can save as an audit trail.

Alternatively, look at the 'Dependencies' and 'Traceability Links' tabs when editing any object, or create a matrix showing the dependencies between any two types of object.

Internal and External Dependencies

Consider a shipping process, which depends on the order fulfillment process for accurate information. If the sales department decides to remove a field from an order fulfillment process on the company's web site, the shipping process may be affected.

That's a dependency. It's critical information for your enterprise architecture, which you can capture using PowerDesigner. In fact, simply using PowerDesigner in your day-to-day work will allow it to capture these dependencies automatically.

Dependencies can be internal (within models), or external (between models, or between models and external files). Figure 9.3 illustrates the key external dependencies supported out of the box for data-related models.

Figure 9.3 External dependencies

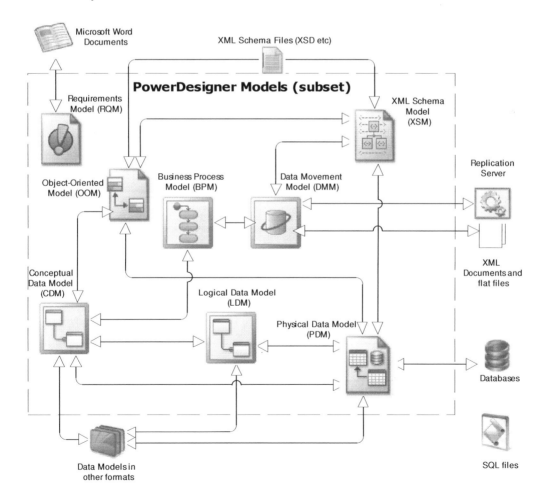

As you can see, PowerDesigner provides support for a complex network of interrelated models. The majority of these dependencies are out of scope for this book; we focus here on the CDM, LDM, and PDM. By the way, you may recognize the icons used in the diagram; they're the icons that PowerDesigner uses to represent those types of models. PowerDesigner allows you to change the image used for any model object, and the icons for model types are just a few of the images available. You're also able to link modeling objects to 'related diagrams'. For example, you could link a business process to a CDM or LDM diagram that shows the relevant entities.

The majority of model dependencies are created by generating one model from another, and further dependencies can be created using other standard functionality in PowerDesigner. For simplicity, Figure 9.3 does not show all generation possibilities. For example, it doesn't show the ability to generate a Physical Data Model from a Physical Data Model. In addition, Requirements documented in a Requirements model can be linked to model objects in any other type of model.

You can extend the capabilities of PowerDesigner to create additional dependencies, and add your own processes to manage them.

Versioning

The PowerDesigner repository allows you to store and share versioned copies of your models and non-PowerDesigner files. It also manages access security and provides check-in and check-out capabilities.

Automation

There is automation of some common modeling tasks, such as converting a many-to-many relationship into an entity. The main areas of automation are in the generation process, where a new model is created from an existing one, and in the realm of denormalization in the PDM - horizontal and vertical partitioning, table collapsing, and column denormalization are all supported, and can all be rolled back later. You can alter the supplied automation and create your own.

Assertion Statements

Whenever you create or update a relationship, PowerDesigner automatically produces assertion statements, converting the relationship and associated entity names into plain English sentences. For example, "Each Ice Cream Scoop must contain one and only one Ice Cream Flavor".

Reference Models

PowerDesigner allows you to create a library of reference models that are made available to all users of the repository. The objects in the reference models can be replicated in your data models, copied as new objects, or copied as shortcuts to the original objects.

Usability

I like the PowerDesigner interface. There is one working environment for all model types, and I have a lot of control over how much 'stuff' I can see on the screen and how it is arranged. Toolbars and other window panes can be docked along the edges of the work area, left floating, or hidden. If I'm working on several projects, I can set up a workspace for each one, containing just the models for the work I'm doing at the time, no matter where those models are located. The menus are sensibly organized, and can be customized by creating PowerDesigner add-ins.

Diagram Layout

In PowerDesigner, you decide where new symbols are placed in a diagram, using a 'snap-to' grid, if you so choose. You have fine control over which properties appear on symbols, you can display any property you like, and add custom properties generated on the fly. You also have fine control over the appearance of symbols on diagrams. For example, you can set a style that forces all attribute names to be displayed in a given font style, size, and color. You have control over the way relationship lines bend (or not), the color and width of the lines, and which properties are displayed on symbols.

PowerDesigner allows you to apply a variety of layout algorithms to arrange selected symbols or a complete diagram. You can choose between six algorithms, most of which have options allowing you to specify the direction in which relationships are oriented, such as a "Left to Right" hierarchy.

Flexible Facilities For Editing Objects

Every type of object can be modified by opening up its property sheet; the property sheet gives you access to practically anything you might want to do with that object. Within the property sheet, you can edit any sub-objects it contains, such as the attributes in an entity. You can sort and filter the list of sub-objects, choose which properties are displayed, and export the results to an Excel spreadsheet.

You can examine the object's dependencies, such as the relationships an entity participates in, open the property sheet for the dependent object, and examine the dependencies for that other object, even if it's in another model.

You can open the property sheet for the parent object, access the lineage and impact analysis, preview the code (e.g. table creation SQL) that would be generated from the object, access the object from which the current object was generated, access symbols on diagrams, or even add a new property of your own.

Lastly, you can rest assured, knowing that the property sheet will always contain all of the object's properties, even the properties you've created yourself, unless they've been deliberately hidden.

Role-based User Interface

In environments with a repository, administrators can define user profiles to customize and simplify the PowerDesigner interface for different kinds of users.

You can develop object permissions profiles to hide models, objects, and properties, or make models available in read-only form. In addition, you can develop User Interface and general preferences profiles to set defaults for menus, toolbars, toolboxes, options, and preferences.

These profiles are associated with users and groups in the repository and pushed to users to provide role-based customization of the PowerDesigner environment.

Interfaces And Integration

Importing Existing Data Models

If you're an ERwin user, you can migrate your existing models into a mix of Conceptual, Logical and Physical Data Models really easily. It's up to you to choose the types of models that are created.

If you're not an ERwin user, then you may have more work to do. Look at Chapter 21 to find out more.

Round-trip Engineering

If your DBMS is one of the 60+ supported, then you'll have no problem reverse-engineering your database schema from a script or via a database connection. If you choose to, you can automatically rebuild missing references and/or primary keys, and apply a naming template to convert names during the import. You can also reverse-engineer and generate XML Schemas, as long as the schema language is XSD, DTD, or XDR.

PowerDesigner supports round-trip engineering. See Figure 9.4. Reverse-engineer from a data artifact into a PDM or XML model, then generate a new data artifact, or apply model changes to a database.

Figure 9.4 Round-trip engineering

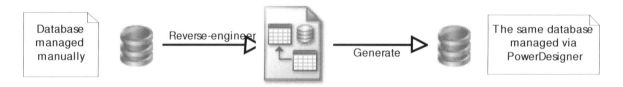

If your RDBMS is not supported, you can create your own reverse-engineering and generation capability.

Supporting Bulk Updates Via Excel

You can export spreadsheets from PowerDesigner in several ways. The simplest is to use a List Report, which creates a spreadsheet containing selected properties from one type of model object. You can ask your business or technical stakeholders to review and revise the content of the spreadsheet, and you can use the features of Excel to carry out bulk updates, such as populating a *Change History* property on all entities, using Excel to sort and filter the entities. The Excel Import facility allows you to import the revisions.

Generating New Models

For a data modeler, the generation facilities in PowerDesigner are unrivalled. It's a very simple task to generate another model from selected objects, and PowerDesigner automatically maintains the links between the original objects and the new objects.

Comparing and Merging Models

You can compare two models of the same type, and have complete control over which types of model objects and properties are compared. The comparison results are presented as side-by-side lists of objects, with icons indicating which objects are new, deleted, modified, or moved in the target model. You can filter the types of changes on view, and manually match objects to each other. You can open the property sheet for any object in either of the two models. The comparison results can be displayed in several different formats, and printed or saved to a text file.

The model merge function uses the same comparison facility to identify potential changes to the current model, based on the content of another model of the same type. The key difference here is that, by default, you only see the list of objects in the current model – you can click on a button to see the objects in the target model. You decide which changes to apply, right down to individual properties.

The model generation functions allow you to update one model from another, using the same dialog and selection mechanism as the model merge function. For example, you can update a Logical Data Model from a Conceptual Data Model, even if the two models have never been linked before.

Generating Test Data

PowerDesigner can generate random data to populate database tables for testing or to confirm estimated database sizing.

Displaying Data from a Database

You can connect to a database and display the data that corresponds to a PDM table, view, or reference.

Integration With Development Environments

Any PowerDesigner model can be created or updated within Microsoft Visual Studio, and integration with an existing Eclipse framework can be selected on installation. Both of these environments are especially useful for application developers.

Generate Data Replication Scripts

Using a Data Movement Model, you can generate SQL scripts to replicate data via a Sybase Replication Server®.

Tool Management And Communication

PowerDesigner supports all of the features listed in Chapter 8.

Extending PowerDesigner's Capabilities

PowerDesigner includes powerful tools to extend and customize your modeling objects. You can add new properties to objects, create entirely new objects, create new links between objects, customize object generation, and customize the toolbars and menus. You can also add completely new functionality like the Excel Import, which is a model extension.

Reporting Facilities

Reports can extract information from one or more models, and export the output in HTML, PDF, or RTF format. The report editor provides comprehensive options for the content, structure, and format of reports. Report definitions can be saved as templates for reuse in other models, or you can copy them to other models in the Browser. There are also a variety of ways in which selected parts of a model can be printed or exported to Excel.

Access via a Portal

The Repository Portal provides direct repository access to non-licensed users. Users who have access to the 'composer' license can edit comments, descriptions, and annotations via the portal. You can, of course, restrict the models and objects that a user can update via a combination of repository permissions and user roles.

Viewing Models for Free

The PowerDesigner Viewer software is essentially a read-only version of PowerDesigner, and can be downloaded for free, allowing anyone to read and extract information from models at any time.

Collaboration

PowerDesigner facilitates communication and collaboration by storing metadata and models in a central location, complete with documented histories and version control. Using this shared repository, teams can analyze and design the enterprise architecture using a single, common set of source materials. Without a repository, the models are still interrelated and some history is documented, which will suit some organizations, but the repository turns PowerDesigner into a true powerhouse of collaborative capability.

With a repository, if someone makes a change to the design of Database A, not only can PowerDesigner disseminate the change to every instance of Database A in your architecture, but it can communicate the change to people throughout your enterprise with visual cues in the user interface and email notifications.

Access Management

PowerDesigner provides several mechanisms for managing access to models managed via the repository. Essentially, you create users and groups and assign rights, permissions, and profiles to them. Within the repository, you can grant permissions on the repository root, folders, individual PowerDesigner models and model packages, and external application files, but not on individual model diagrams or objects. A repository administrator can delegate the authentication of repository users to an LDAP server.

Users with the necessary privileges can audit operations performed on repository documents, analyze user behavior patterns, and highlight activity sequences. Activities are actions that modify repository documents, such as check in, freezing, and deleting.

Sharing Best Practices

User profiles help you to standardize the look and feel of your models and to support standards, by sharing display preferences, model options. In addition, you can create your own template models, share report definitions, and share tool customizations.

Key Points

- The scope of PowerDesigner is wide enough and deep enough to support any data modeling environment.

- All the types of data models described in this book are well supported, complete with full model generation capabilities.

- One model per file enables flexible coupling of data models, providing robust, flexible linkages between models and between model objects.

- Link and Sync is a powerful tool to understand and manage the dependencies between models.

- Data models do not exist in a vacuum. PowerDesigner provides key facilities to integrate data models into your analysis and development environment, and to control the collaboration necessary to do that successfully.

- The import, export, and reporting capabilities of PowerDesigner keep your modelers in touch with reality.

- If you need to do something differently from what's supplied out of the box, the customization potential is amazing.

CHAPTER 10

How can we work within the PowerDesigner environment?

Objects, Symbols, Links
GUIDs, properties, methods
There's always a way

In this chapter, we introduce you to the essential components and features of PowerDesigner for data modeling and general model management. After you have read this chapter, followed us in the 'Your Turn' sections, and finished the Exercise, you'll be ready to do some real work in PowerDesigner.

If you only use PowerDesigner occasionally, or need to refresh your knowledge, come back to this chapter and work through it again. The PowerDesigner interface will look familiar if you've used other major data modeling tools before, but there are some important differences that may not be apparent at first.

Fundamentals of PowerDesigner

This book contains a lot of information about ways of doing things in PowerDesigner. In the exercise and 'Your Turn' sections, you may prefer to focus on the fundamental knowledge and techniques first. Please, feel free to practice the fundamental techniques in place of more advanced ones, and try out the advanced techniques when you have more experience with using PowerDesigner. The fundamental techniques are highlighted by the PowerDesigner symbol for a Requirements model ( ). Here is a list of sections containing fundamental information – each entry in the list is the relevant heading in the book. They are listed in the order in which you'll find them in the table of contents.

The building blocks	Renaming objects and symbols	Quickest way to create a primary id
Not just a load of symbols	Showing and hiding symbols	CDM settings
Names and codes in objects	Menus depend on models	LDM settings
Interface overview	Workspaces	Linking the LDM to other data models
Organizing views	Creating a model	PDM settings
The toolbox	Backup files	Approaches for creating a PDM
Contextual menus	Opening a model, project, or workspace	Creating a reference from the palette
Object property sheets	Finding things again	Creating a view
Common properties	Drawing new entities	Denormalization in PowerDesigner
Do not generate me	Creating entities in the browser	Reverse-engineering databases
Object lists	Object property sheets	Keeping model and database in synch
Moving, copying and deleting objects	Standard properties for data elements	Compare and merge
Undoing things	Data items in PowerDesigner	Checking a model
Working with diagrams	Attributes and columns in PowerDesigner	Impact and lineage analysis
Working with symbols	Creating candidate identifiers	

The Welcome Page

When you start the PowerDesigner application, you're presented with the Welcome Page (shown in Figure 10.1), which provides you with quick access to all your recent work, a range of helpful materials, and the ability to open or create models or projects. This screen will be presented every time you start PowerDesigner, unless you suppress it by selecting the 'Do not show this page again' checkbox. You can view the Welcome Screen any time you choose, via an option on the 'View' menu, or by pressing <Alt+3>.

Figure 10.1 The Welcome Page

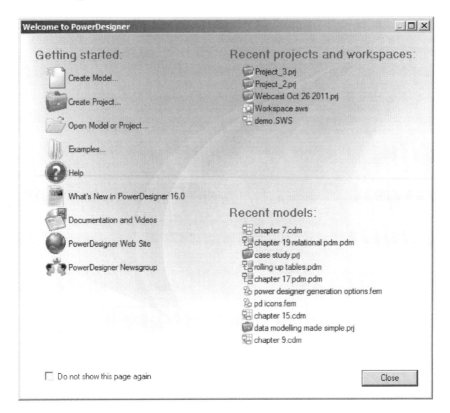

If you launch PowerDesigner by opening a model via Windows Explorer, you won't see the Welcome Page.

The Building Blocks

Model objects are the building blocks of your models. They are listed as items in the Browser and may also appear as symbols in your diagrams.

There are two main types of objects:

- Ordinary Objects – such as tables and entities, which are self-sufficient, and can be created in isolation from other objects
- Link Objects – such as relationships or references, which link two ordinary objects, and cannot be created in isolation

Some objects can only exist 'inside' another object. We call these 'sub objects'. For example, attributes within an entity, or columns within a table. The parent objects are called 'composite objects'.

You can create objects:

- Directly in your diagram using a Toolbox tool (only for objects that have symbols). See Chapter 11 for more information.
- From the Browser.
- From a list of objects.

Not Just a Load Of Symbols

In Chapter 8, we discussed the key differences between a drawing tool and a data modeling tool. If you've never used a data modeling tool before, you may not have encountered the distinction between a symbol on a diagram and the underlying definition of the object. In some drawing tools, the symbol does not have an underlying object definition: delete the symbol, and the object is lost forever.

Each type of PowerDesigner diagram supports certain specific types of objects, and each object created in a diagram is represented by a symbol. In fact, anything that appears on a diagram is a symbol. Most PowerDesigner objects can be represented on diagrams, so they have their own symbols. Links between objects also have symbols. The most common symbols you'll see in this book are Entities and Relationships. Some objects, such as Data Items and Domains, cannot appear on PowerDesigner diagrams, so they do not have symbols.

The majority of symbols on your diagrams will link to objects, the others are what we call 'decorative', though they may not be just for decoration. Notes, text boxes, and rectangles, for example, are very useful for providing additional information to the reader of a diagram.

In PowerDesigner, you can create a model by drawing symbols on diagrams, or by creating the object definitions first, and then drawing diagrams. For example, you can import a cartload of objects from Excel into a new model, and then create new diagrams containing symbols of those objects, manually. The Excel import can also create symbols on your current diagram for you.

An object can appear on many diagrams, and the object's symbol can look completely different on every diagram, if you want it to. The same object can be represented by many symbols. Objects can also appear as shortcuts or replicas in other models. So a symbol on a diagram in Model A could represent an object in Model B.

Names and Codes in PowerDesigner Objects

Every PowerDesigner object, including models and diagrams, has a *name* and a *code*. The *name* of an object identifies the object within the PowerDesigner model. The *code* is the 'technical' name for the object, automatically managed by PowerDesigner when you create or rename an object. The *code* is used when external objects are generated by PowerDesigner.

Put simply, the *name* is the 'business name' for an object, and the *code* is the name for the object when it is subject to constraints imposed by technology, such as a DBMS or XML Schema language.

This is a different approach from the other major data modeling tools, which generally have a 'logical' name (for entities and attributes, etc) and a separate 'physical' name (for tables and columns, etc). Table 10.1 demonstrates the differing approaches using a simple example, an entity called **Customer Address**.

Table 10.1 Alternative naming approaches

Object	PowerDesigner Object Name (and *Code*)	Object Name in other tools
Entity (Logical Data Model)	Customer Address *CUSTOMER_ADDRESS*	Customer Address
Table (Physical Data Model	Customer Address *CUSTOMER_ADDRESS*	CUSTOMER_ADDRESS
Table (SQL File)	CUSTOMER_ADDRESS	CUSTOMER_ADDRESS

PowerDesigner applies uniqueness checks on the names and codes of objects. The *namespace* defines an area in which the name and the code of an object of a given type must be unique. For all data models, the entire model is, by default, a single namespace - PowerDesigner applies checks on uniqueness at the model level. For Data Items and Relationships, the rules can be relaxed slightly, as we'll see later.

PowerDesigner allows you to partition your model using the Package concept, borrowed from the UML standard; see "Packages" later in this chapter to see how this can impact the uniqueness of names and codes.

By default, the object codes automatically mirror the object names. For example, the default code for an object called 'Ice Cream' could be 'ICE_CREAM' or 'IceCream'. The format of the name and code are determined by the naming conventions set for the model. The conventions also describe the way in which codes are generated from names. If you make changes to these conventions in the model options, names and codes will change accordingly.

You can override the mirroring process in several ways:

- To override the mirroring for a single object, deselect the 'equals sign' button, circled in Figure 10.2, in the 'General' tab on the object property sheet. This also works in a list of objects, if you have the code column displayed.

- To replace the mirrored code for an object, just overtype the code in an object property sheet or a list of objects. Mirroring will be automatically suspended when you do this, though you can (via the model options) re-impose the naming conventions.
- To reverse the Name to Code mirroring for a single object, select the 'equals sign' button to the right of the name field in the 'General' tab on the property sheet, or in a list of objects.

Figure 10.2 Name-Code mirroring buttons

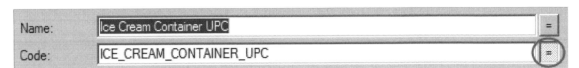

Within the General Options (on the 'Tools' menu), the 'Dialog' tab allows you to disable Name to Code Mirroring. If you do this, the code will mirror the name of the object given when it is created, and it will not subsequently be altered by PowerDesigner if you change the name of the object. You are strongly advised NOT to disable Name to Code mirroring in data models.

When you generate one model from another, you can influence the way in which codes are generated using conversion scripts. You do have the option to convert Codes into Names if you choose to - this would be appropriate when 'reverse-engineering' from a physical view of data to a business view.

See Chapter 20 for more on the topic of naming conventions.

"Naming Conventions" (Core Features Guide)

Interface Overview

The PowerDesigner interface contains panes that provide various views of your modeling project. Most of these panes can be closed or moved around the interface, so you can customize the interface to suit the way you work and the environment in which you're working. A typical view of the interface is shown in Figure 10.3. The user interface was re-written in Version 16, so expect it to look a little unfamiliar if you have experience with earlier versions of PowerDesigner.

In the upper part of Figure 10.3 you can see the PowerDesigner general title bar and the menu bar. Below the general menus, you can display any of eight customizable toolbars.

The labels in Figure 10.3 identify the key views available within PowerDesigner.

Figure 10.3 The PowerDesigner interface

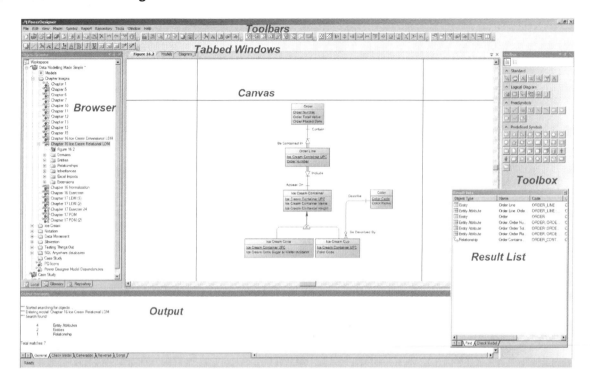

- The *Browser* view - displays your models and the objects belonging to them, and allows you to rapidly navigate between them. The Browser also has a tab that shows you the contents of your repository-based Glossary. The third tab gives you access to a PowerDesigner repository, where you can store all your models and associated files.

- The *Canvas* view - the primary pane that displays your current model diagram or report outline. Note the series of tabs that allow you to select which of the open diagrams you wish to view.

- The *Toolbox* view - provides graphical tools to help you quickly build model diagrams. The tools available will change depending on the type of diagram. The Toolbox provides a single location for all the tools you need to add content to your model diagrams. Introduced in PowerDesigner Version 16, the Toolbox replaces the old palette and predefined symbols toolbar.
  The Toolbox and Toolbars can be opened, closed, and moved in much the same way as the dockable views. In addition, you can customize toolbars and toolboxes, or create new ones.

- The *Output* view - shows the progress of any PowerDesigner process, such as checking in a model or generating or reverse engineering a database.

- The *Result List* view - displays the results of a search or a model check.

In addition, the bottom line of the PowerDesigner window is used to display information about current objects, such as:

- The file name and path for a model, when a model is selected in the Browser
- Progress messages when opening or saving a model
- The 'language' for a model, such as the DBMS for a PDM, the process language for a Business Process Model, or the XML Schema Language for an XML model

Toolbars

You can show, hide, organize, and customize the PowerDesigner toolbars to suit your workflow.

- To move a toolbar in the toolbar tray, click and hold on the four dots on the left edge of the toolbar and drag it to the desired position.
- To show a hidden toolbar or hide a visible toolbar, right-click the toolbar tray, select *Toolbars,* and check or uncheck the toolbar.
- To access tools on a toolbar that is not fully visible due to lack of space, click on the down arrow on the right edge of the toolbar.
- To lock all toolbars to protect them from accidental movements, right-click the toolbar tray and select `Toolbars|Lock Toolbars`.
- To add tools to or remove them from a toolbar, or to create new toolbars, right-click the toolbar tray and select `Toolbars|Customize Menus and Tools`.

"Organizing Toolbars" (Custom Features Guide)

Organizing Views

The views shown in Figure 10.3 can be moved, grouped, split, hidden, floated or auto-hidden. You can also carry out the same actions, in a more limited fashion, for diagram tabs in the Canvas.

There are two key techniques for manipulating views – mouse-clicking and dragging.

Mouse-clicking

All views, apart from the Canvas, have a set of icons on the title bar that can be used to change the view's behavior. Right-clicking the title bar, or left-clicking the drop-down arrow (circled in Figure 10.4) displays the menu shown in Figure 10.4.

Figure 10.4 A view menu

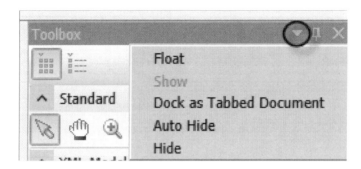

- Float - promote the view to an independent window.
- Show - disable auto-hiding (you can also click the sideways pin symbol to pin the view open).
- Dock as Tabbed Document - add the view to the Canvas as a new tab.
- Auto Hide - hide the view as a small tab on the side of the screen that re-expands when you hover over it (or click the vertical pin to unpin the view).
- Hide - remove the view from your window. To show a hidden view, select View|View Name on the menu bar.

If you click the pin symbol ![pin] in Figure 10.4, the view will auto-hide. The name of the view will appear on a tab, on the nearest edge of the PowerDesigner window. In Figure 10.5 all of the views have been auto-hidden, and the tabs for the views have been ringed. Hover the mouse over one of these tabs, and the view will appear; move the mouse away and the view will hide again. To stop the view from hiding away, use the Show option on the menu in Figure 10.4, or click the sideways pin symbol ![pin] to pin the view open.

Before we move on, take another look at the bottom right-hand corner of Figure 10.5. The current diagram is an XML diagram, so the XML Schema Language is displayed here.

Figure 10.5 All views auto-hidden

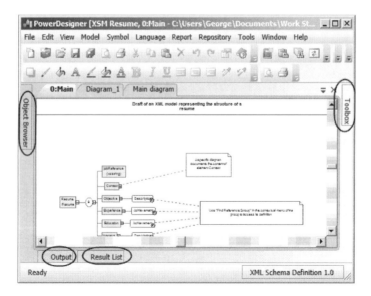

Dragging Views

You can move any view (as long as it isn't auto-hidden) to anywhere in the PowerDesigner window. Drag the title bar of any view with the mouse, and 'docking selectors' appear; release the view on one of these docking selectors to select the new location for the view. Figure 10.6 shows the docking selectors (circled) that appeared when the Output view was dragged away from the foot of the PowerDesigner window.

Note: The Browser is a single view with up to three sub-views (Local, Glossary, and Repository). These sub-views cannot be moved independently. The same applies to the tabs in the Output view.

There are two types of docking selectors shown in Figure 10.6, the four-way selector in the center, and one-way selectors on the edges of the window. Drop the Output view onto one of the one-way selectors, and it will extend the full height or breadth of the PowerDesigner window.

Figure 10.6 Docking selectors

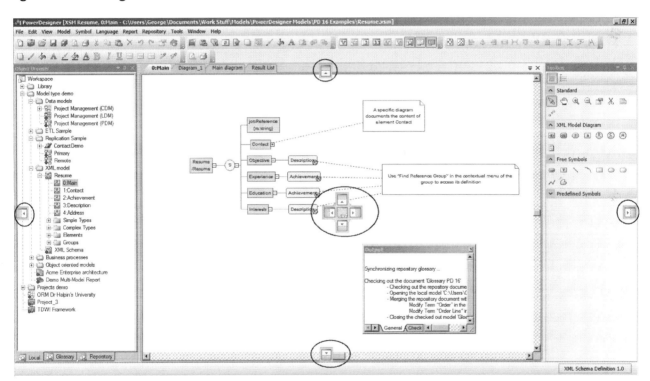

In Figure 10.7 you can see the result of docking the Output view at the foot of the PowerDesigner window, and docking the Result List on the right-hand side.

Figure 10.7 Docked at the foot and the side

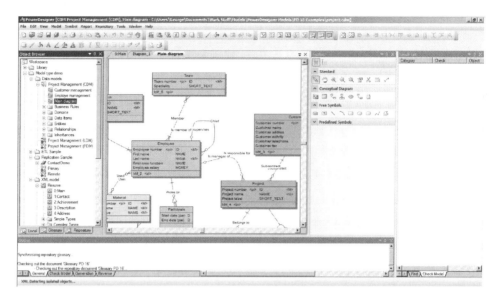

When you drag the Output view over any of the other views, the four-way selector appears; in Figure 10.6 it appears over the Canvas, but it could also appear over the Browser or the Toolbox. Drop the Output view over any of these selectors, and it will be grouped with that view.

Here's how it works - when you drag the Output view onto a docking selector, the new location for the view is highlighted. In Figure 10.8, the view has been dragged onto the circled docking selector; if the view is dropped here, it will occupy the shaded area in the Canvas.

Figure 10.8 Where the view would be dropped

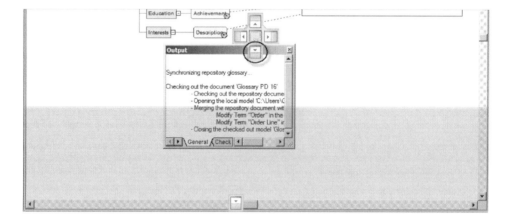

Figure 10.9 shows the result. The Output window is now in its own section of the Canvas.

Figure 10.9 The result

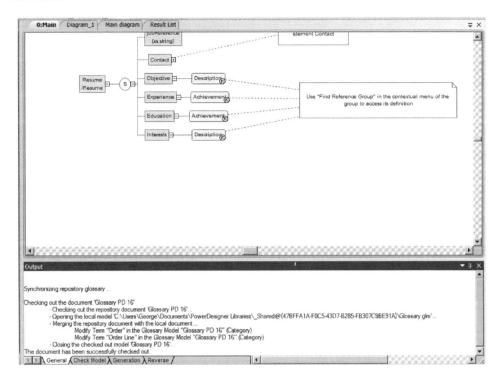

To group a view with another view – drag it over the view, then drop it on the central dock selector, shown on the right. For example, you could drag the output window into the Toolbox – see the result in Figure 10.10.

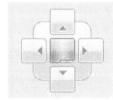

Figure 10.10 Grouping two views together

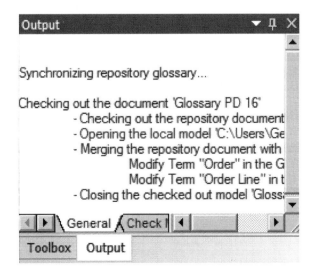

The dropped view is stacked on the other view, and each has a tab at the top of the group to select it. To separate the views, just drag one of the tabs to another location. To place the view next to, above, or below another view - drop it on the left, right, top, or bottom dock selector.

Promoting a View

To promote a view to an independent window, drop it anywhere *except* on a dock selector. You can move this window anywhere in your Windows real estate, even onto a different display.

Restoring a Window

You can restore a window that is no longer displayed via the menu. Select `View|window name` *(Browser, Output, Result List, Toolbox, or Welcome Page)*.

Windows are restored into their most recent position on the screen.

Resizing a Window

You can change the size of windows using the mouse pointer. Hover the mouse over the edge of the window; when the pointer changes into a double-headed arrow, you can drag the edge of the window to resize it. Other windows are adjusted to match. Figure 10.11 illustrates this.

Figure 10.11 Using the double-headed arrow to drag a window

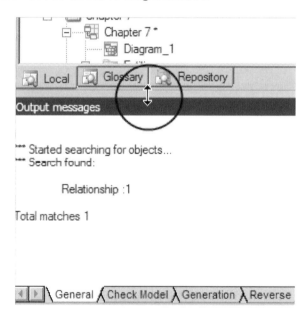

 "Organizing Views" (Custom Features Guide)

The View Toolbar

The 'View' Toolbar contains tools to show or hide some of the standard windows, and to change your view of the current diagram. See Figure 10.12.

Figure 10.12 The 'View' toolbar

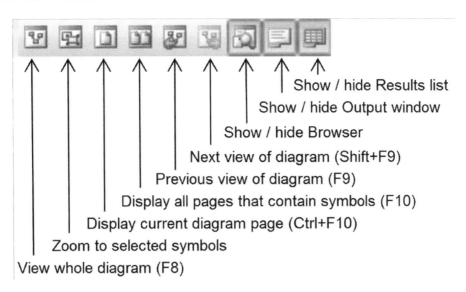

See also "Viewing Diagrams" later in this chapter.

Changing Focus

There are several ways to focus your attention on a given view. Usually, you will change focus by clicking on a tab or view title, but you don't have to do that. On the Window menu, the Windows option allows you to select any of the currently available views, or any of the currently-open diagrams. The selection is shown in Figure 10.13.

Figure 10.13 A list of windows

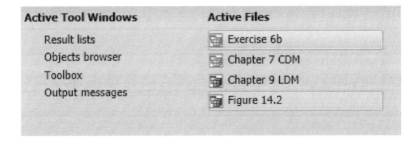

The list of open diagrams is also available on the Canvas tool bar, as shown in Figure 10.14.

Figure 10.14 Canvas toolbar

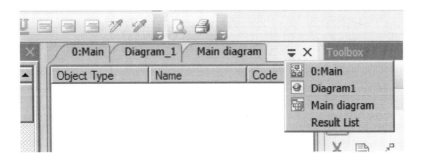

Re-arranging the Canvas

The Canvas is a special view that displays diagrams as tabbed documents. You can drag other views onto the Canvas, but you cannot drag Canvas diagrams elsewhere in the PowerDesigner window (though you can promote them to independent windows). Right-click a diagram tab to access a contextual menu that lets you close the diagram, close every diagram except this one, or split the canvas horizontally or vertically.

By default, the canvas is a single pane with a tab for each diagram that is currently open. When you open a new diagram, it opens in a new tab in the same pane. By default, all the diagrams you open will be within the same pane, and you will only see one diagram at a time,

I often want to have several diagrams visible at the same time, and PowerDesigner allows you to do just that. All you have to remember is that you can drag and dock a diagram tab in the same way as any other view, or leave them floating in independent windows. The caveat is that diagram tabs can only dock within the canvas, not in the Browser, Toolbox, or anywhere else.

When you drag a diagram tab, the four-way dock selector appears in the Canvas; hover over one of the selectors, and the potential position of the diagram is highlighted for you. In Figure 10.15, the diagram **0:Main** has been dragged onto the bottom selector.

Figure 10.15 Dragging a diagram

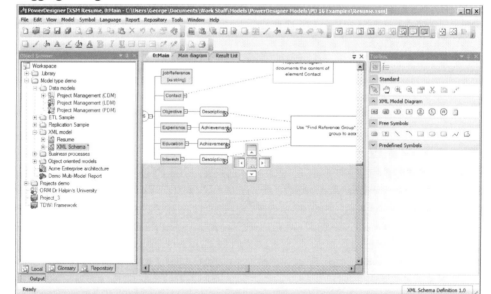

You can have more than one view of the same diagram. In Figure 10.16, there is one tab for the diagram **Chapter 7 CDM** and two tabs containing different views of the diagram **Figure 14.2**. Any changes you make to **Figure 14.2** will affect both tabs. To open a second or subsequent tab for a diagram, click the existing tab for that diagram, and then select New Window on the Window menu. The new tab may appear in the same pane as the existing tab, so you may need to drag one of them to another area of the canvas.

Figure 10.16 Two views of a diagram

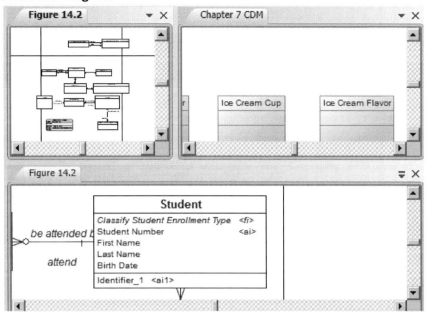

Working with Objects

Remember that an object is a 'thing' in a model. Entities, attributes, relationships, data items, domains etc, are all objects. You can examine and edit the properties of objects in several ways:

- *Object property sheets,* which permit you to view and edit the properties of objects in your models. You can access an object's property sheet by double-clicking its symbol or Browser entry, or right-clicking it and selecting **Properties**. In the section 'Many Ways of Doing Things', we present some of the other ways of accessing an object property sheet. Figure 10.17 shows a typical object property sheet. See "Object Property Sheets", later in this chapter, for more information.

Figure 10.17 A typical object property sheet

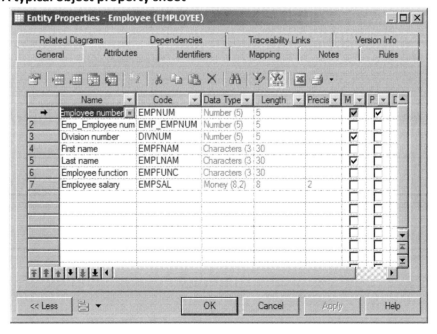

- *Object lists* - provide a spreadsheet-like presentation of, and allow for the easy creation and modification of one or more objects in your model. Lists are available under the `Model` menu, and on the property sheets of composite objects such as entities, tables, and classes, which contain sub-objects. Figure 10.18 shows a typical list. This list has been configured to show additional properties that the default list did not display. The tools in the Toolbar allow you to create or add, copy, or delete objects in the list, and open their property sheets. You can Ctrl-click to select multiple objects in the list and then edit their properties simultaneously. Other tools allow you to control the columns displayed in the list and to sort or filter the list. You can also print the contents of the list, and export the list to a spreadsheet or CSV[3] file. See "Object Lists", later in this chapter, for more information.

Figure 10.18 Typical object list

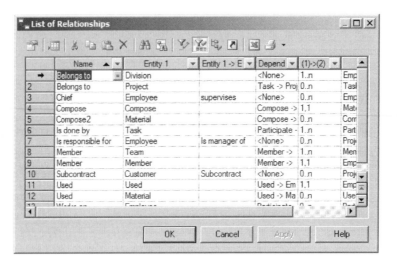

Looking at the Demo Workspace

Nothing reinforces learning better than doing the work yourself, so now it's time to start PowerDesigner. If you haven't installed it yet, you can download the evaluation version from www.sybase.com/powerdesigner. You will be able to use all of PowerDesigner's features for 15 days.

YOUR TURN TO PLAY

1. Start PowerDesigner, and then open the demo workspace supplied by Sybase. Click on the File menu, followed by 'Open Workspace'; the demo workspace is called 'demo.sws'; you can find it in the folder 'C:\Program Files\Sybase\PowerDesigner 16\Examples'. If you've installed PowerDesigner on a 64-bit system, choose the folder 'Program Files (x86)'.

---

[3] CSV – Comma-Separated Value – a textual format that can be edited in spreadsheet software such as Microsoft Excel. Other data modeling tools may be able to import these files.

The demo workspace contains a number of folders and models, and is a good place to play with PowerDesigner safely. Figure 10.19 shows the contents of the workspace.

Figure 10.19 The Demo Workspace

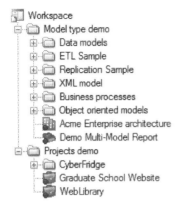

You can see that the workspace contains a mixture of folders, models, and projects. Folder names are shown in black, project and model names are shown in blue. The briefcase icon represents a project, which is a collection of folders, models, and other files. You'll find out more about workspaces, models, and projects later in this chapter.

Take note of the icons in front of each model name - the icon identifies the type of model. The same icons are used elsewhere in the book.

> 2. Now open the 'Data models' folder, and double-click the model called 'Project Management (CDM)'. PowerDesigner opens the model in the Browser, and also opens the default diagram on the Canvas, as shown in Figure 10.20.

Figure 10.20 The Project Management CDM

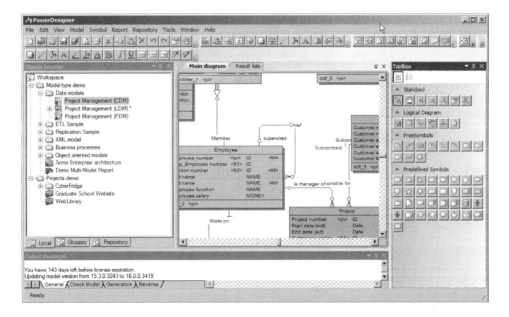

3. It's possible that PowerDesigner will tell you that you can only open the model read-only, because it's stored in the Program Files folder. That's not a problem for what we're looking at here, but you may wish to move the demo workspace to another folder. Here is what you need to do:

a. Move or copy the whole 'Examples' folder to another folder where you have update rights. Let's call this folder 'XX'

b. In PowerDesigner, click on `Tools|General Options`.

c. Select the <Named Paths> category, and then amend the entry for <_EXAMPLES_> to provide the full path to folder 'XX'

d. Open the Demo workspace in the new folder

In Figure 10.20, the Toolbox has been populated with buttons, some of which are specific to this type of diagram. The Output window is open; you can close it by clicking <X> in the window's title bar, or you can right-click the title bar, and select auto-hide. You can close the Browser and Toolbox in the same way.

The Toolbox

Figure 10.21 shows the Toolbox for a CDM, which contains four categories of tools. Each type of diagram has its own specific category - the 'Conceptual Diagram' category is specific to the current diagram.

Free Symbols and Predefined Symbols do not have an underlying object definition, they are purely graphical. We'll see how to make use of these later in this chapter – look for "Communicating Your Message".

Figure 10.21 Conceptual data model Toolbox

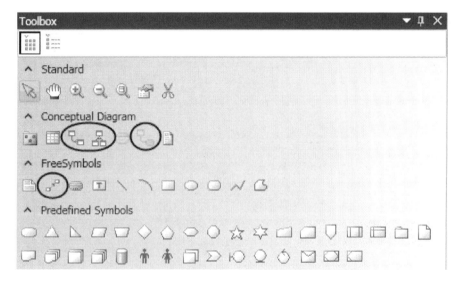

The Standard tools allow you to do things with symbols on a diagram; the remaining tools allow you to create or select objects on diagrams.

To create an object, click the appropriate tool, and then click in the diagram. When you release the mouse button, the object is created, and you can click again elsewhere to create a second object of the same type. To release the tool, simply select another tool or right-click in free space. To revert to a previously selected tool, hold down <Ctrl> and perform a double right-click.

To create a link, click the appropriate link tool, click in the object from which you want the link to begin and hold the mouse button as you drag the pointer to the object in which you want the link to end. When you release the mouse button, the link is created. The link tools are circled in Figure 10.21.

You will find out more about creating link objects in Chapter 13 – look for "Creating a Relationship from the Palette".

You can also use the Toolbox to select all symbols of a given type in the current diagram. For example, double-clicking the 'entity' tool will select all 'entity' symbols. To add another type of symbol to the selection, just hold down the <Shift> key and double-click another tool, such as 'relationship'. The standard tools are shown in Table 10.2.

Table 10.2 Standard tools

Icon	Icon Action
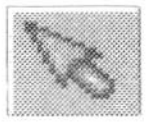	Pointer [default] – Selects, moves, and resizes individual symbols. Double-click to select all the objects in the diagram. To switch back to the Pointer from another tool, right-click anywhere in the diagram.
	Grabber – allows you to select, move and resize the entire diagram. Double-click to display the entire diagram, centered.
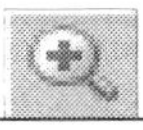	Zoom in
	Zoom out
	Open the diagram of a composite object or packages
	Open the property sheet of an object
	Delete a symbol and, optionally, its associated object.

We'll look at some of the diagram-specific tools later. Note that the availability of some tools may depend on your model options. For example, two of the tools in Figure 10.21 are unavailable because the model notation does not include support for 'Merise'. The standard free symbols are shown in Table 10.3.

Table 10.3 Free symbols

Icon	Icon Action	Example
	**Insert a symbol that can contain text** – this can be linked to other symbols (below). The standard RTF editor can be used.	 Note
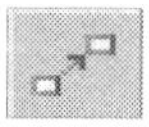	**Draw one of the following:** • **a graphical link between free symbols in the diagram** • **a note link between a note and an object** • **a traceability link between objects (where possible).** There are three points on the link for labels – double-click the line to edit text. The standard RTF editor can be used. The style of the corners can be changed – right-click the line and select Format from the contextual menu.	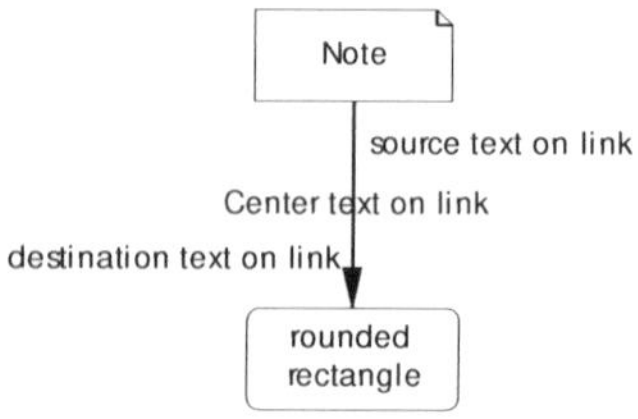 Note source text on link Center text on link destination text on link rounded rectangle
	**Insert a title box** – displays information such as: • **the model and the package to which the diagram belongs** • **the name of the diagram itself** • **the author and version of the model** • **the date of modification.** If no Author is specified in the model property sheet, the user name specified in the Version Info page is used. You can choose to display the repository version number of the model or a user-defined version number on the Title display preferences page. Double-click the title box to open the property sheet for the model.	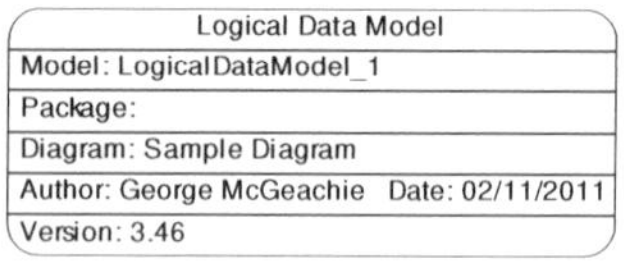 Logical Data Model Model: LogicalDataModel_1 Package: Diagram: Sample Diagram Author: George McGeachie Date: 02/11/2011 Version: 3.46
	**Insert free-standing text, without a symbol outline** – you can insert free text in your model independently of any shape, and can select and move it like any symbol. Click once to create the text symbol, then double-click it to edit the text.	<Default text>
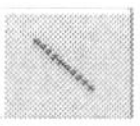	**Draw a line between two points** – depending on your display preferences, this line may have corners. This line cannot have any associated text.	
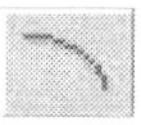	**Draw an arc between two points** – this line cannot have any associated text.	

Icon	Icon Action	Example
	Draw a rectangle by dragging the mouse, release the mouse button to complete - press \<Ctrl> while drawing to create a square. Double-click the symbol to edit text - the standard RTF editor can be used.	rectangular box
	Draw an ellipse by dragging the mouse, and release the mouse button to finish - press \<Ctrl> while drawing to create a circle. Double-click the symbol to edit text - the standard RTF editor can be used.	circle
	Draw a rounded rectangle by dragging the mouse, release the mouse button to complete - press \<Ctrl> while drawing to create a rounded square. Double-click the symbol to edit text - the standard RTF editor can be used.	rounded rectangle
	Draw a jagged line (polyline) by dragging the mouse - release the mouse button at each point where you want to create a corner. Right-click to finish. There are three points on the link for labels – double-click the line to edit text. The standard RTF editor can be used. The style of the corners can be changed – right-click the line and select Format from the contextual menu.	source center destination
	Draw a polygon by dragging the mouse - release the mouse button at each point where you want to create a corner. Right-click to finish and close the polygon. The style of corners will depend on your display preferences. The polygon cannot have any associated text – if you need to include text, follow these steps: 1. use the **T** tool to create free-standing text 2. use the Order options on the symbol contextual menu to bring the text in front of the polygon 3. select both the polygon and text symbols 4. select the Group Symbols option on the contextual menu (or on the Symbol menu) – the two symbols are combined into a single symbol. 5. To edit the text, ungroup the symbols first.	**Original symbol** **Grouped with free-standing text** \<Default text>

"Creating Objects from the Toolbox" (Core Features Guide)
"Decorative Symbols" (Core Features Guide)
"Text Editor Tools" (Core Features Guide)

If the Toolbox is not visible, it must have been hidden or closed. If it's closed, open it via the 'View' menu. If it's hidden, the Toolbox tab will be visible, probably on the right-hand side of the screen. Hover your mouse over the word 'Toolbox', and it'll appear.

Working in the Browser

The Browser displays hierarchical views of the contents of a local workspace, the glossary, and the repository, using three tabs called, unsurprisingly, *Local*, *Glossary*, and *Repository*. The best way to learn about the contents of these tabs is to use them, so we'll start with the 'Local' tab.

YOUR TURN TO PLAY

Expand the contents of the data model in the Browser, by clicking on the '+' to the left of the model name. The model contains three diagrams, and instances of the following types of object: Business Rule, Domain, Entity, Relationship, Inheritance, and Data Format. Later in the book we'll find out what these things are. For now, expand the list of entities by clicking on the '+' to the left of the word 'Entities', expanding the first entity, and then expanding the list of attributes that is displayed. Figure 10.22 shows the content of the model in the Browser.

Figure 10.22 The expanded model

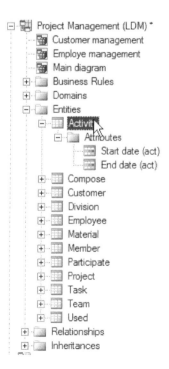

This Logical Data Model has three diagrams, shown immediately below the name of the model. The diagram called 'Main diagram' is the default diagram; this is the diagram that was automatically opened when you opened the model.

It is worth mentioning here that the name of the model and the name of the file it is contained in do not have to be the same. You can change the model name as many times as you like, and it'll still have the same file name.

YOUR TURN TO PLAY

1. In Figure 10.22 we expanded the list of attributes for the Activity entity; you'll see that it has two attributes. These are listed inside the entity because they're sub-objects. They cannot exist in their own right, they only have meaning in the context of the entity.
2. Now, right-click the name of the Activity entity in the Browser, and you'll see a contextual menu appear, shown in Figure 10.23.

Figure 10.23 Contextual menu for an entity object in the Browser

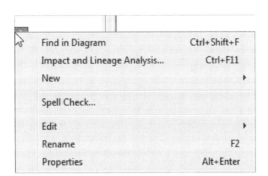

3. This is a good representation of the common options available on contextual menus, though these menus do differ slightly depending on the type of object. Now click on 'Properties', and you'll open the object property sheet for the entity. You can also open it by double-clicking the entity name in the Browser.

"The Browser" (Custom Features Guide)

Contextual Menus

If you right-click any symbol or reference to an object in PowerDesigner, a contextual menu will appear. References to objects can be found in the Browser, a list of objects, a list report, or a list of search results (called a result list – see "Object Lists" later in this chapter.

Figure 10.24 shows the contextual menu displayed when you right-click an entity symbol on a diagram. Notice the similarities between this and Figure 10.23, at the top and bottom of the menu. The entries from 'Related Diagram' down to 'Order' only apply to symbols – we'll come across all of these later.

The Browser menu shown in Figure 10.23 doesn't include access to the Entity's 'Attributes' and 'Identifiers'. These are easily accessible in the Browser, by expanding the entity node, as shown in Figure 10.22.

Figure 10.24 Contextual menu for an entity symbol

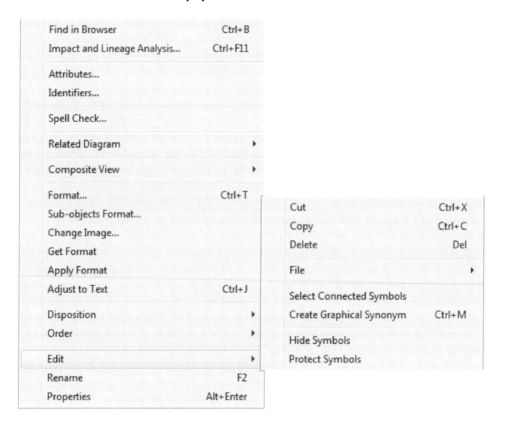

Object Property Sheets

Figure 10.25 shows the object property sheets for four entities, with each one displaying a different tab. All four sheets are open at the same time. Don't worry about the detail of each sheet just yet – we'll look at these later.

For the 'Compose' entity, we can see the 'General' Tab. Every object has one of these, which, by default, shows the object name, code, and a comment. The comment is where you may include a more descriptive name for the object. By default, the comment is one of the standard properties of an object that you can display on a diagram, but it would be better for most types of object to show the description, which is on the 'Notes' tab. Later we will show how to display the description on a diagram.

When you make changes to an object via the object property sheet, the changes are not applied until you click <OK> or <Apply>. Before pressing either of these buttons, you can prevent changes from being applied by clicking on <Cancel> or pressing <Esc>. If you want changes to be applied as soon as you make them, you can enable the 'auto commit' option in <General Options> (see Figure 11.4 in Chapter 11).

From this point on, we'll shorten 'Object Property Sheet' to 'Property Sheet' where it makes sense to do so without causing confusion.

Figure 10.25 Example object property sheets

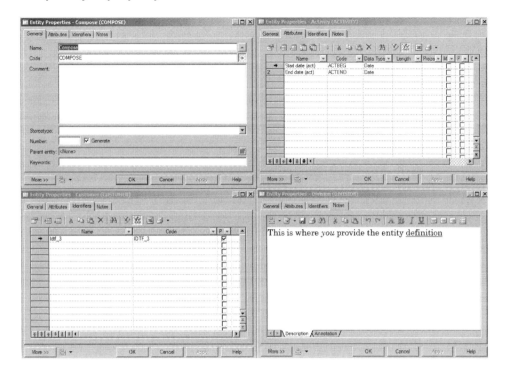

Hover the mouse over the edges of the property sheet, and you can use the standard Windows functions to stretch or shrink it to suit. You also have a 'Maximize' button in the top right corner, so you can make it fill the screen. Look out for these features on other PowerDesigner windows, such as when generating or comparing models.

❷ "Selecting, Editing and Resizing Symbols" (Core Features Guide)

> You can stretch or shrink a property sheet. You can even hit the 'Maximize' button so that it fills the screen. This also applies to some other PowerDesigner features, so look out for the 'Maximize' button; it's really useful on List reports and Dependency Matrices.

The content of the 'Attributes' and 'Identifiers' tabs in Figure 10.25 look very similar, because they both show a list of sub-objects, and the lists both show the default set of properties. The toolbars are almost identical.

Property Types

Object Property Sheets organize the properties of an object using tabs. Some tabs contain multiple properties, others contain only one property – this is more likely if the property is a Collection. Some tabs (such as *Traceability Links*) organize their content with sub-tabs.

PowerDesigner provides two types of properties – Attributes and Collections. See Table 10.4.

Table 10.4 Property types

Attribute*	Any property with a single value, such as 'Comment', 'Name', 'Stereotype', 'Data Type' and 'Description'.
Collection	A group of sub-objects such as 'Attributes', or other objects, such as the diagrams an entity appears in. When you add a Collection, you are able to limit the number of entries shown in the symbol, and also select the sub-object properties that can be displayed.

* In Table 10.4, the word 'Attribute' does not refer to an attribute on an entity (see Chapter 4). It refers to a type of property on a PowerDesigner object.

More Tabs for an Entity

YOUR TURN TO PLAY

1. In the property sheet for the 'Employee' entity, click on the 'Attributes' tab, double-click on the number to the left of any of the attribute names, and the property sheet for that attribute will open. Notice how different this is from the sheet for the entity. Now close the attribute property sheet. The simplest way to do this is to press <Esc> or click on <Cancel>.
2. On the entity property sheet, click on the button labeled 'More >>'; the number of tabs has increased, as shown in Figure 10.26.

The four tabs that were originally displayed are called your 'Favorite' tabs, and you can choose which ones to show via the menu option 'Customize Favorite Tabs' at the bottom of the property sheet. The menu also allows you to navigate to any of the symbols for the object on diagrams, or find the object in the Browser.

Figure 10.26 shows the 'Version' tab for an entity, which provides audit information, and also tells you which object this entity was generated from; let's call this the source entity. If you click on the (circled) tool to the right of the object name, you can open the property sheet for the source entity, even though it's in a different model and, therefore, in a different file. Now close the entity property sheet, it's time to see some more menus.

An object has only one definition, no matter how many diagrams it appears on. You can change the appearance and content of symbols on diagrams, so that they look very different, but they will still refer to the same underlying definition.

YOUR TURN TO PLAY

Right-click the name of the **Activity** entity in the Browser, and select Find in Diagram: PowerDesigner immediately focuses on the symbol in the 'Main diagram' and selects it. Now do the same for the **Employee** entity. This time a selection list appears, because the entity is included in more than one diagram. The selection list is shown in Figure 10.27.

Figure 10.26 More tabs for an entity

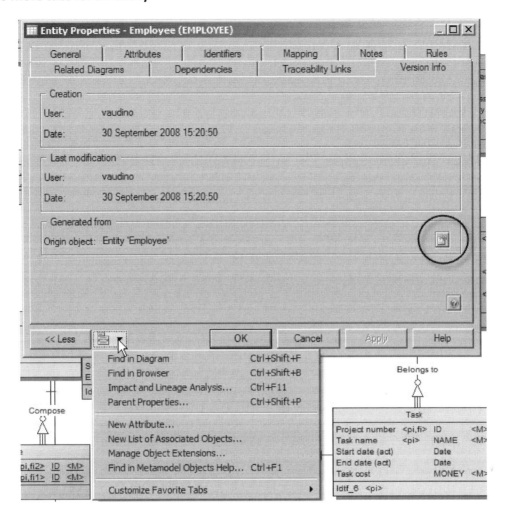

Figure 10.27 Choose your symbol

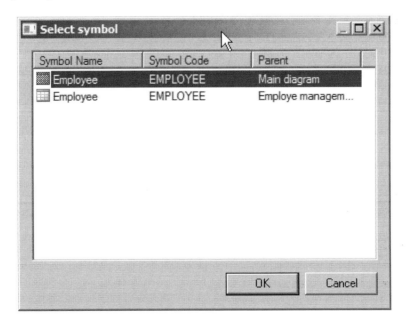

To go to a symbol, select one of the entries in the list and click on <OK>, or double-click one of the entries.

PowerDesigner allows you to include an object more than once on a given diagram, the symbols are known as Graphical Synonyms. If your object has graphical synonyms, you'll see more than one entry in the list for a given diagram. Don't worry if you choose the wrong graphical synonym. You can easily find the other graphical synonyms once you have the diagram in front of you. We will show you how later in this chapter.

Common Properties

As you open more property sheets, you'll see a pattern emerging - there is a standard set of properties common to all PowerDesigner objects. We have already discussed the *name* and *code*; the remaining properties are shown in Table 10.5, listed in the order in which you're likely to see them in a property sheet.

> Don't rely on the *Comment* property to hold a description or definition, use the *Description* property under the 'Notes' tab. The *Comment* property is purely text, whereas the *Description* provides much more flexible editing facilities, including the ability to use external word processing software, such as Microsoft Word. The *Comment* property is really only relevant for objects in a Physical Data Model. It provides a descriptive label for the object, which can be stored on the database for documentation.
>
> The Glossary Term is an exception – text in the 'comment' property of a Term can be displayed when the Glossary suggests terms for use in object names. See "The PowerDesigner Glossary" in Chapter 12.

"Object Properties" (Common Features Guide)

"Stereotypes (Profile)" (Customizing and Extending PowerDesigner)

 Do not generate me

The *Generate* property is common across most objects in PowerDesigner. You will find it on the 'General' tab of a property sheet, with a default value of 'True'. If an object has this property set to 'False', it will not be included in any generated models.

Table 10.5 Common properties

Tab Name[4]	Property	Description
General	*Comment*	A textual description of the object (see note below).
General	*Stereotype*	Keywords that can be used to classify an object. Can be used as a simple label on a symbol, or provide a means of extending and altering the standard behavior of PowerDesigner. You can enter a stereotype directly in this field, or add stereotypes to the list by specifying them as a model extension.
General	*Keywords*	Provide a way of loosely grouping objects through tagging. Separate multiple keywords with commas. You can use keywords as criteria for finding objects, and in impact and lineage analysis.
Notes	*Description*	A textual description of the object. The property can be edited directly in the tab with the internal PowerDesigner RTF editor.
Notes	*Annotation*	Notes regarding the implementation of a model or the objects it contains. For example, an annotation of the Employee entity might read: "Verify list of attributes with Director of Human Resources." The property can be edited directly in the tab with the internal PowerDesigner RTF editor.
Rules	*Rules*	Lists the business rules associated with the object. A business rule may be a government-imposed law, a customer requirement, or an internal guideline.
Requirements	*Requirements*	Lists the requirements that the object is intended to satisfy.
Related Diagrams	*Related Diagrams*	Diagrams that provide additional information about an object. You can associate any type of diagram open in the workspace with an object.
Dependencies	*Dependencies*	Links to other objects in the same model, or other objects managed by PowerDesigner.
Traceability Links	*Traceability Links*	User-defined documentary links between objects. Links can be stereotyped and classified by user-defined link types.
Version Info	*Creation Information*	The date and time that the object was created and the name of the user who created it. Provides details about the object owner, creation and modification dates, and allows you to access help for the PowerDesigner metamodel metaclass on which the object is based.
Version Info	*Modification Information*	The date and time that the object was last modified and the name of the user who modified it.
Version Info	*Generated From*	Information about the object that this object was generated from. Details are only available if the source model is open. The model can be opened by clicking on the 'Properties' button to the right of the object details.

---

[4] This is the name of the tab where you will usually find the property. It may vary for some types of objects. If your property sheets have been customized, properties may appear on different tabs.

Many Ways of Doing Things

PowerDesigner provides you with many ways to access the functionality provided. Here's a quick list.

- Options on the Main Menu at the top of the interface
- Contextual menus, obtained by clicking the right mouse button
  o On any symbol in a diagram
  o On a blank area of the diagram Canvas
  o On any item in the Browser window
- Drag and drop between different types of windows and different models
- Drag and drop between symbols on a diagram
- Buttons on Toolbars and Toolboxes
- Buttons in property sheets
- Keyboard Shortcuts
- Double-clicking
  o On any symbol in a diagram
  o On any item in the Browser window.

For example, here are all the ways you can access the property sheet for a model:

- Click on 'Model Properties' on the Model menu (if displayed)
- Double-click a Title box on a diagram (we'll see Title boxes later)
- Double-click the Model entry in the Browser window
- Right-click a blank area on a diagram, and then select 'Properties'
- Open the property sheet for a diagram, and then click on the 'Properties' button to the right of the *Parent* property in the 'General' tab
- Select the model in the Browser, and then press <Enter> or <Alt+Enter>.

Object Lists

Object lists provide a spreadsheet-like interface for manipulating large numbers of objects at the same time, including the ability to update multiple objects in the same way at the same time. Figure 10.28 shows a typical object list, in this case a list of entities.

Opening a List Of Objects

Lists of all the major objects in your model are available under the Model menu, or by right-clicking the name of a model in the Browser and selecting List of.... Either way, you'll see a list of all the types of objects your model could possibly include. Each list shows all the objects of that type in the currently selected package or model, including those that do not have symbols in the current diagram. If the list is empty, then your model does not contain any of that type of object.

Figure 10.28 List of entities

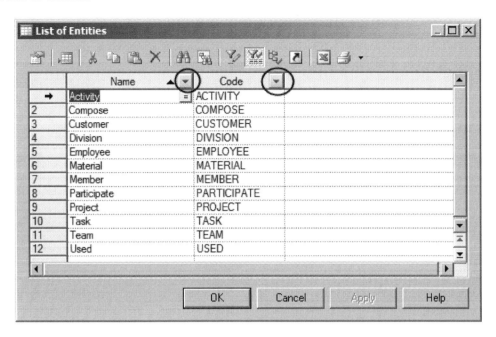

Organizing a List of Objects

The properties of the listed objects are organized in columns. You can order the list using the values in a particular column by clicking on the column header. Click again to reverse the sequence. You can also filter the list according to the content of a given column – just click on the filter arrow to the right of the column name (circled in Figure 10.28). This allows you to select individual objects, and to specify conditions, such as objects created between given dates. See Figure 10.29.

Figure 10.29 Filtering an object list

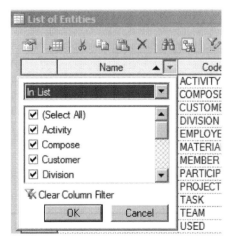

If some of your objects appear to be missing from the list, you may be showing a list of objects in a package. This happens if your current diagram is not a model-level diagram, but is a package diagram – remember what we said earlier, menus are based on the current diagram.

To fix this, view the model-level diagram and re-open the list. Later in this chapter you'll find out more about packages.

The Toolbar

Figure 10.30 shows the object list Toolbar; object lists provide a complete editing environment for objects.

Figure 10.30 Toolbar for object lists

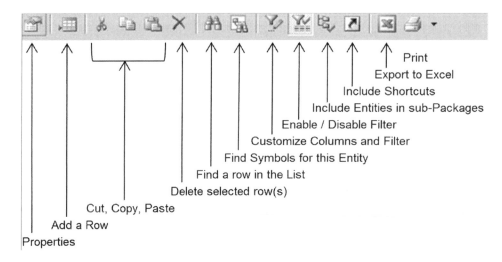

Customizing a List of Objects

By default, an object list shows only a few properties, but you can easily change that. Just click on the *Customize Columns and Filter* tool in the toolbar. You'll see a list of all the possible properties for objects in the list, as shown in Figure 10.31.

Figure 10.31 Customizing a list

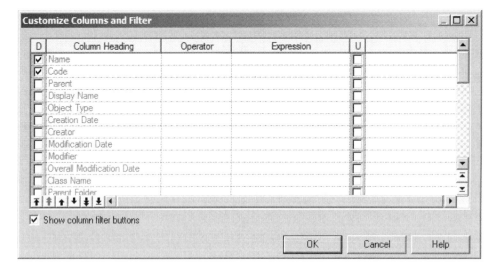

The columns to the right of 'Column Heading' allow you to specify conditions for filtering the items displayed. The arrow buttons just above 'Show column filter buttons' allow you to change the sequence of columns.

For now, assume we just want to change the list of properties to be displayed. We'll uncheck 'Code', and then select 'Modification Date', 'Parent Entity', and 'Has Symbol'. The result is shown in Figure 10.32.

 Short Description is a property calculated by PowerDesigner that shows a combination of the object type and name. It is not the 'Description' property.

 Description Text is also a calculated property, showing a non-editable copy of the object 'Description'.

The next time you open a list of entities in a Logical Data Model, PowerDesigner remembers your customizations, so you don't have to.

 The same customizing and filtering options are available elsewhere in PowerDesigner – wherever you see a grid-like presentation or a list of objects or sub-objects, such as the 'Attributes' tab in an entity property sheet.

Figure 10.32 Modified list of entities

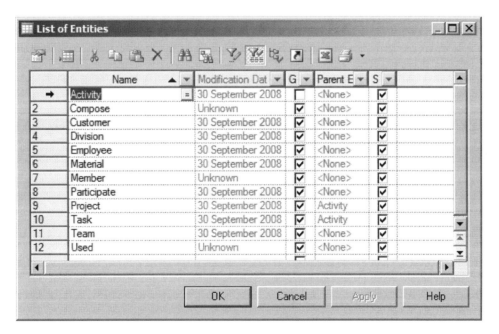

We can now see that two entities (**Project** and **Task**) have parent entities, and that every entity has at least one symbol on a diagram (column 'S').

The 'G' ('Generate') column tells you which entities would be included if you were to generate a new model from this one.

Working With a List of Objects

To select an item in an object list, click on the row number, or click directly on the property you want to change. You can select multiple individual items in a list by Ctrl-clicking them on the row number. You can also select a range of items by selecting an item at one end of the range, holding down the <Shift> key, and then selecting the item at the other end of the range.

To select all the items in a list, click the top-left corner box. When multiple items are selected, any edits you make to properties are applied to all the selected items.

Changes can be made in one row, and will be applied to all selected rows in the list.

Note: By default, you must click the <Apply> button to commit changes or the <OK> button to commit and close the list. If you prefer, you can have changes committed immediately when you enter them in a field, by enabling the 'Auto commit' option (via the menu `Tools|General Options` dialog).

If you click on a blank cell in the *name* column, you can create a new object. However, if you close the list without applying the changes, the new objects will not be created.

Remember, you can always use the *Undo* tool or press <Ctrl+Z> to cancel change(s).

Creating Objects in a List of Objects

Click the 'Add a Row' tool 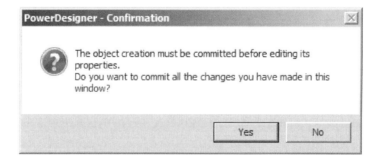 to add a new entity at the end of the list. You can also create a new entity by using the arrow keys. When you open a list, the name of the first entity is automatically highlighted for editing. Press the down arrow on your keyboard, and you select the second entry. Keep moving the arrow downwards and eventually you'll move to empty rows, which automatically become entities.

This works in any column in the list: move down the list of modified dates, and you'll eventually reach empty rows and start creating entities. If you have too many rows, select the rows you want to get rid of, and press <Delete>.

The new entities will not actually exist until you apply the changes via the <Apply> or <OK> buttons, or by double-clicking one of the new entities to access the property sheet. When you do this, you are asking PowerDesigner to edit an object that does not yet exist, so it will ask you to commit all the changes you have just made, first. That means ALL the changes, not just the entity you double-clicked. See Figure 10.33.

Figure 10.33 Commitment required

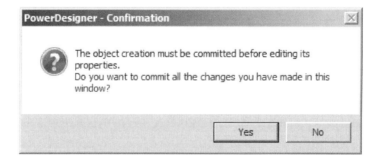

Click <Yes> to carry on, or <No> to go back to the list of objects without applying any changes.

In PowerDesigner 16.0, the *Description* property may appear empty in a list of objects, even though the Description exists. This will be obvious to you if you include both 'Description' and 'Description Text' in the same list. This appears to affect descriptions imported from Excel. The *Description* property will appear in the list (and in future lists) if you edit it, either via the property sheet or the object list.

- "Object Lists" (Core Features Guide)

- "Customizing Object List Columns and Filtering Lists" (Core Features Guide)

- "Defining a Filter Expression" (Core Features Guide)

- "Customizing Columns in Lists Containing Multiple Types of Objects" (Core Features Guide)

Moving, Copying and Deleting Objects

In PowerDesigner, you can drag and drop objects to copy, move, create a shortcut, or create a replica. You can also use menu options and the standard Windows keyboard shortcuts.

You can drag and drop objects

- **from** the
    - Browser
    - Diagram
    - Result list (showing the results of a search or model check)
- **to** the
    - Browser
    - Diagram window
    - **But NOT** to the Result list.

The default behavior when dragging with the left mouse button is to move the selected object or sub-object. You can modify this behavior by pressing one or more of the following keys while dragging with the left mouse button:

[no key]	Move (in the Browser) or paste as shortcut (between diagrams)
Shift	Move
Ctrl	Copy
Shift+Ctrl	Shortcut creation
Shift+Alt	Replica creation

If you drag with the right mouse button, when you release the mouse button a contextual menu opens, listing all the available options.

To modify the default Browser drag and drop behavior, select `Tools|General Options` and select the appropriate radio button.

We examine some of these options in more detail in Chapter 12.

⊘ "Dragging and Dropping Objects" (Core Features Guide)

When you copy an object, you copy not only its properties but also the properties of its related objects to the clipboard. For example, if you copy an entity between Logical Data Models, you also copy the attributes and business rules attached to that entity. You will also copy any domains or other objects attached to the attributes.

Be very careful when using Copy and Paste to include an existing object on a diagram. Use 'Paste as Shortcut' (Ctrl+K) to create a symbol for an existing object. If you use 'Paste' (Ctrl+V), PowerDesigner will create a new object that is identical to the original, apart from the name.

'Paste as Shortcut' is available on the Edit menu. Right-click on the drawing Canvas in the position where you'd like the symbol to appear, select 'Edit', and then 'Paste as Shortcut". If the object is already on the diagram, the symbol will be created, but the name will be suffixed with a number. If, for example, the object name is suffixed with ': 5', the object has at least four other symbols on the diagram. PowerDesigner refers to these duplicate symbols as 'Graphical Synonyms'. We will investigate these further later in this chapter and in Chapter 13.

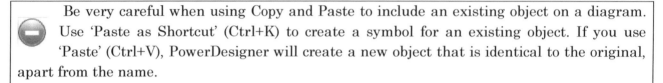

YOUR TURN TO PLAY

1. In the 'Project Management LDM', select the 'Activity' entity in the Browser window, and drag it onto the model name. Now press the <Ctrl> key, and you'll see the '+' symbol appear on the cursor, indicating that a new object will be created. Release the mouse button, and a new entity will be created, called 'Activity2'.
2. Select the 'Activity2' entity, and press <Ctrl+C>. Now select the 'Entities' heading above the list of entity names, and press <Ctrl+V>. Another copy will be created, this time called 'Activity3'. Note that the copy entities are not absolutely identical to the original – they don't participate in any relationships.

⊘ "Moving, Copying, and Deleting Objects" (Core Features Guide)

Undoing Things

PowerDesigner keeps track of changes you make, and allows you to rollback your edits, using the 'undo' facility. Even after you save a model, you can rollback changes you made before the model was saved. Once you close a model, that's it, no more undo.

Of course, you can also 'redo' edits you've previously undone.

PowerDesigner uses the standard Windows shortcuts for undo and redo, provides undo and redo options on the 'Edit' menu, and a couple of tools on the standard toolbar for you. See Table 10.6.

Table 10.6 Undo and redo

	Tool	Keyboard Shortcut	Menu Option
Undo	↺	<Ctrl+Z>	Edit|Undo
Redo	↻	<Ctrl+Y>	Edit|Redo

If you really mess things up, you can always close a model without saving it, and then open it again.

Working with Diagrams

A diagram is a graphical view of all or part of a model. All models have at least one diagram. You can add multiple diagrams to a model if you want to display different subsets of the model, or display the same objects in a different way for different audiences. To open a diagram, you must first open the model that contains it.

Dependency Matrices enable you to keep track of which objects appear on which diagrams. We will see one of these in Chapter 12.

Creating a Diagram

Every model (and package) has a default diagram that PowerDesigner creates for you. You can never delete the last diagram in a model (or package). You can create as many diagrams as you want in a model or in a package.

You can create a diagram in any of the following ways:

- In the View menu, select Diagram|New Diagram|Diagram type. If you have previously selected any object symbols, then the selected symbols are copied into the new diagram (see also "Creating a Diagram from a Selection" below).
- Right-click the background of your diagram and select Diagram|New Diagram|Diagam type. (see Figure 10.34).

Figure 10.34 Creating a diagram from a diagram

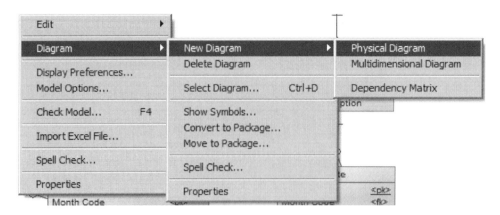

- Right-click the model node in the Browser and select New|*Diagram type*.

In each case, you will be invited to specify a name, code, and optional comment for the new diagram.

The default name for a diagram is 'Diagram_n'. It is definitely worth changing the name to something more meaningful – this makes it easier to distinguish between diagram tabs when you have more than one diagram open. See "Viewing Diagrams", later in this chapter.

"Creating a Diagram" (Core Features Guide)

Creating a Diagram from a Selection

If you have selected two or more symbols in a diagram, you can create a new diagram from your selection by right-clicking in the selection and choosing *Create Diagram from Selection* from the contextual menu.

- The selected objects will now be present in both the original and the new diagram
- The display preferences of the new diagram are identical to the display preferences of the original diagram
- The style and layout of the symbols will be identical in the two diagrams.

"Creating a Diagram from a Selection" (Core Features Guide)

Opening Diagrams

When you open a model, the default diagram opens in the canvas, in a new tab. Additional diagrams can be opened from the Browser or from the View menu.

- Double-click the diagram entry in the Browser.
  or
- To open another diagram in the same model
  o Press <Ctrl+D>, or select View|Diagram|Select Diagram to open the Select Diagram dialog box, select a diagram node in the tree, and click OK.

o On the contextual menu for an open diagram, select `Diagram|Select Diagram` to open the 'Select Diagram' dialog box.

"Opening and Viewing Diagrams" (Core Features Guide)

Viewing Diagrams

In PowerDesigner, you can choose how much of a diagram you want to view. The viewing options are supported by a combination of tools in the standard palette, the `View` menu, The 'View' toolbar, and keyboard shortcuts. Table 10.7 shows the options available. See also "The View Toolbar" earlier in this chapter.

Table 10.7 Diagram viewing tools

Tool	Keyboard Shortcut	Description
	F6	*Zoom In* Select the Zoom In tool and click anywhere in the diagram. The point clicked on is centered. Alternatively, you can select `View|Zoom In`, or turn your mouse scroll wheel away from you while holding the <Ctrl> key. To zoom in to a particular area, select the Zoom In tool and click and drag a rectangle around the area to be displayed. When you release the mouse button, the diagram zooms to the selected area.
	F7	*Zoom Out* Select the Zoom Out tool and click anywhere in the diagram. The point clicked on is centered. Alternatively, you can select `View|Zoom Out`, or turn your mouse scroll wheel towards from you while holding the <Ctrl> key.
	F8	*Global View* View the whole diagram - Double-click the *Global View* tool or select `View|Global View`.
[none]	F5	*View actual size* Select `View|Actual Size`.
[none]	Ctrl+F10	*View the current (printable) page* Select `View|Page View|Current Page`.
[none]	F10	*View all pages that contain symbols* Select `View|Page View|Used Pages`.
[none]		*View all pages in the diagram* Select `View|Page View|All Pages`.
[none]		*Center on selected symbols* Select `View|View Selection`.
[none]	F9	*Return to previous view* Select `View|Previous View`. Combined with the `Next View` option, this allows you to toggle back and forth between various selections and zooms you have used to navigate in your diagram, for example, between a limited view and a global view of the diagram.
[none]	Shift+F9	*Go to next view* Select `View|Next View`.
[none]	Shift+F5	*Refresh View* Select `View|Redisplay`. Scrolling the diagram will also cause the diagram to be refreshed.

Identifying Models

In Figure 10.35, there are several CDMs open in the Browser, and there are four diagram tabs in the canvas. One of the tabs is highlighted – this is the diagram we can see on the canvas. The name of the diagram is 'Diagram_1', but which model is it from?

Figure 10.35 Which diagram is which?

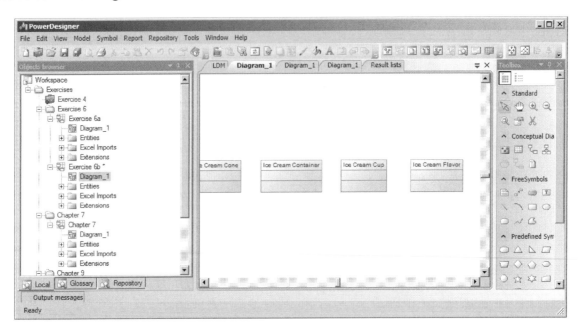

Before working on the diagram or accessing the menus, you need to be sure which model you're working in. There are several ways you can identify the model:

- Hover the mouse over the diagram tab, and a tooltip will appear. The tooltip will display the following information: Model Type, Model Name:Package Name (if relevant), Diagram Name, and the model path and filename.
- Right-click one of the entity symbols and select 'Find in Browser' from the contextual menu
- Right-click a blank area of the diagram and select 'Properties' from the Contextual menu – this opens the property sheet for the model
- Add a title box to the diagram (using the 'Title' tool on the 'Free Symbols' palette) – Figure 10.36 shows an example.

Figure 10.36 A diagram title box

Conceptual Data Model	
Model: Chapter 7	
Package:	
Diagram: Diagram_1	
Author: George McGeachie	Date: 05/07/2011
Version:	

If you double-click a title box, the model's property sheet will open.

The best way to distinguish your diagrams from each other is to give them a meaningful name, such as **Contact Subject Area - Fully Attributed**.

Changing the Default Diagram

Every model has a default diagram, which automatically opens when you open the model. Initially, this will be the diagram created for you by PowerDesigner when the model was created.

If your model has several diagrams, you can choose a different default diagram in three ways:

- Open the property sheet for the model, and change the 'Default Diagram' at the bottom of the 'General' tab
  - See 'Many Ways of Doing Things' to discover the many different ways you can access the model's property sheet
- Open the property sheet for the preferred default diagram, and then select 'Default Diagram' at the bottom of the 'General' tab
- Right-click the name of the diagram in the Browser, and select Set as Default.

The default diagram can be a Dependency Matrix.

Getting Ready To Print

By default, the Canvas shows vertical and horizontal lines in the background; these are the boundaries of the printed pages. The default orientation is portrait, and that doesn't suit every diagram. On the File menu, the Page Setup option allows you to change the diagram orientation, specify margins, and decide which information to include on printed pages. The <Apply To> button allows you to change the settings on several diagrams at the same time.

Once the page orientation is suitable, you can use the Fit to Page option on the Symbol menu to choose the way in which the diagram fits on the printed page. If the diagram is small enough, you can force it to fit onto a single page, using the options shown in Figure 10.37.

Figure 10.37 Fit to page

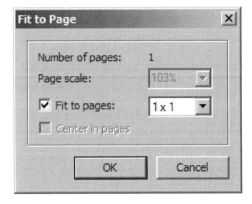

You can also use the 'Fit to Page' button ⊞ on the Layout toolbar.

After you 'Fit to Page', the cursor reverts to the last Toolbox tool you selected, such as drawing entities. Click the right mouse button to unset it.

Printing a Diagram

You can print the currently selected diagram at any time. You can print the whole diagram, a selection of pages, or a selection of objects.

1. [optional] Select certain symbols in the diagram in order to print them and exclude the others.
2. Select File|Print or click the *Print* tool to open the Print Diagram dialog (see Figure 10.38), which displays default print options and the number of printed pages needed for the diagram.

Figure 10.38 Diagram print options

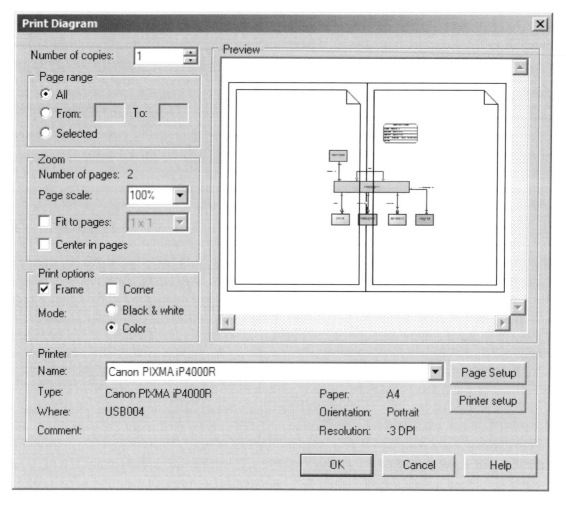

3. [optional] Specify the pages to print in the Page range groupbox or by clicking in the Preview pane. Only pages with an overlaid page frame will be printed.

4. [optional] Specify a page scale or set of pages to fit. By default, diagrams are printed at 100% scale on as many pages as necessary.

5. [optional] Click the <Page Setup> button to open the Page Setup dialog and specify your page layout.

     This allows you to alter the Page Setup for this print operation only. If you want to permanently change the Page Setup for the diagram, exit the Diagram print dialog, and access 'Page Setup' on the 'File' menu. See "Getting Ready To Print", earlier in this chapter.

6. Click OK to start printing.

 When you print a diagram, you do not print detailed information about the model objects. To do this, you need to create a model report.

 "Printing Diagrams" (Core Features Guide)

Deleting a Diagram

When you delete a diagram, you delete a view of a model or a package. This action does not affect the objects in the model or package. You cannot delete the last diagram in a model or package.

You can delete a diagram in any of the following ways:

- Select the diagram node in the Browser and press the <Del> key.
- Right-click the diagram window background and select Diagram|Delete from the contextual menu.
- Select View|Diagram|Delete.

 "Deleting a Diagram" (Core Features Guide)

Working with Symbols

 This section explains how to work with diagram symbols.

Creating and Drawing Symbols

PowerDesigner allows you to create symbols in several ways. The usual way is to draw new symbols and objects using the tools in the Toolbox (see "The Toolbox" earlier in this chapter). You can also create symbols by dragging objects from the Browser, copying and pasting existing symbols, and by creating a new diagram from an existing selection.

 "Creating Objects from the Toolbox" (Core Features Guide)
 "Copying and Pasting Objects" (Core Features Guide)
 "Dragging and Dropping Objects" (Core Features Guide)

Automatic Link Routing

PowerDesigner allows you to take complete control of the routing of your Link Symbols, and also offers to help manage the routing for you. To allow PowerDesigner to route your lines, ensure that your default corner style has right-angled corners, and select 'Automatic Link Routing' in the Display Preferences. It is also useful to select 'Show bridges at intersections' as well. See "Display Preferences for Relationships" in Chapter 13, to find out about the different line styles.

If 'Automatic Link Routing' is enabled in your diagram, then PowerDesigner decides on the route for any new link symbols you draw. If necessary, it will move other links and stretch symbols to accommodate the new link.

PowerDesigner doesn't take over completely - you're free to move the link yourself after PowerDesigner has routed it. See "Rerouting Link Symbols Manually" and "Bending and Straightening Link Symbols", later in this chapter.

Once you've manually moved a link, your preference overrides the algorithm, and the link is no longer controlled by auto-routing. By selecting the link, right-clicking it, and selecting reroute link, you make it subject again to auto-routing, your change is discarded, and the link is rerouted optimally according to the algorithm. If you don't like the result, remember 'Undo'.

Selecting, Editing, and Resizing Symbols

You can select symbols in a PowerDesigner diagram using standard Windows gestures. You can edit properties of the selected symbol's object or its sub-objects, or resize the symbol by clicking and dragging on its handles.

In Chapter 11, you'll see that you can select the 'Edit in place after creation' General option, to have the name of each object that you create immediately selected for editing.

To select a symbol, select the default Pointer tool ▨ from the standard palette, and click on the symbol. In the following example, the Division entity is selected, and can be moved by dragging the center of the symbol, or resized by dragging on one of its handles (the black boxes on the corners and along the sides), as shown in Figure 10.39.

Figure 10.39 An entity's handles

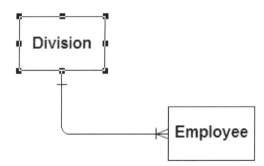

Note: To resize all the symbols in a diagram at once, click the Grabber tool and drag one of the handles.

Once a symbol is selected, clicking on one of its object properties lets you edit its value. In Figure 10.40, the entity name is selected for editing.

Figure 10.40 Editing the entity name

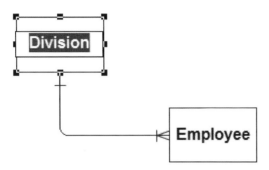

Once a symbol has been selected, you can also edit the name of a displayed sub-object by clicking on the name, as shown in Figure 10.41.

Figure 10.41 Editing a sub-object name

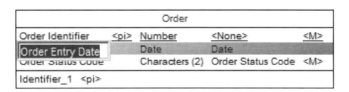

Once a sub-object is selected, you can move among its editable properties by pressing the <Tab> key. You can also move up and down the list of sub-objects using the arrow keys, as shown in Figure 10.42.

Figure 10.42 Editing further properties

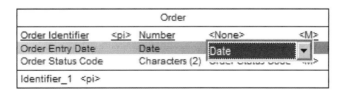

To open the property sheet for a sub-object, select it, and then double-click the highlighted entry (shown shaded gray in the figures above).

To select all the symbols in an area, click on the Canvas, hold down the mouse button, and drag the mouse. As you move the mouse, a selection box appears on the screen. When you release the mouse button, any symbol that lies *completely* inside the box will be included in the selection. The word *completely* is important – for a symbol to be included in the selection, *all* of the symbol's handles must be inside the box. For example, see the selection box shown as a dotted line in Figure 10.43. When the mouse button was released, the entities **Ice Cream Container**, **Order**, and the shortcut to **Division** were selected as shown in Figure 10.44; the **Division** and **Employee** entities and the relationship were not selected, as at least one of their handles was outside the selection box.

Figure 10.43 A selection box   **Figure 10.44 The resulting selection**

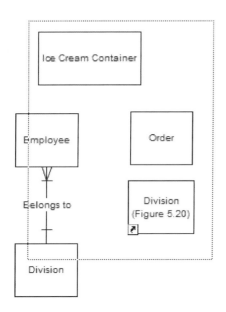
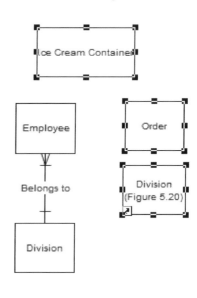

To include them in the selection, just hold down <Shift> and click on each symbol. Repeat the action to remove them from the selection.

Here's another trick for selecting multiple related objects – select any symbol, click the right mouse button, select `Edit`, and then select `Select Connected Symbols`. The same option is also available on the `Edit` menu. This also works if you have more than one object selected. Don't forget to use <Shift> and click to fine tune the selection, if you need to.

If you want to carry out a lot of actions on a set of selected symbols, use the `Group Symbols` command on the `Symbols` menu to make sure they're treated as a set. Ungroup them when you've finished.

Rerouting Link Symbols Manually

Whether or not you use auto-routing, you are able to exercise control over the positioning of individual relationships and groups of relationships.

The contextual (right-click) menu gives you a number of options for altering the layout of selected relationships. We have seen some of these before, so we do not describe them here – see "Contextual Menus", earlier in this chapter. Table 10.8 lists the remaining options.

Table 10.8 Relationship contextual menu options

Option	Description
Detail	Opens the Relationship property sheet.
Change to Entity	Runs a wizard to convert the relationship into an associative entity and two relationships.
Spell Check	Check the spelling in the relationship properties.
Related Diagram	Open or create a 'related diagram'. To create a link from an object to an existing diagram, do so via the 'Related Diagrams' tab on the property sheet.
Reroute Link	Re-applies automatic routing to the relationship.
Disposition	Automatically arranges selected symbols in the diagram. There are various forms of disposition: • Horizontal <Ctrl+H> – where possible, removes corners from selected link objects and converts them into horizontal lines. • Vertical <Ctrl+L> - where possible, removes corners from selected link objects and converts them into vertical lines. • Flip Horizontal – flips the selected symbols through the horizontal center of the group. Where appropriate, the orientation of an individual symbol may also be changed. For example, here is a line and three entities before applying 'Flip Horizontal': 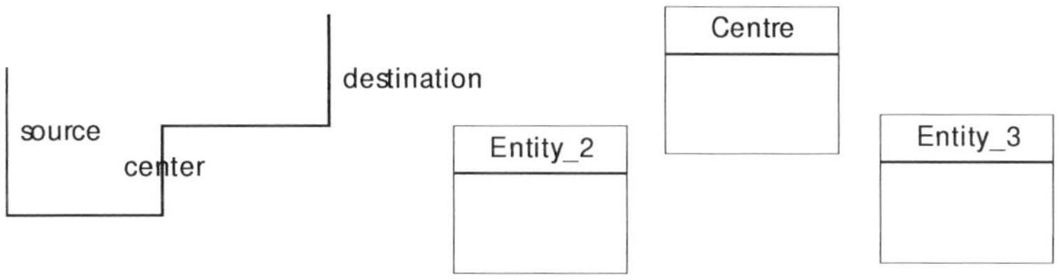 and after: 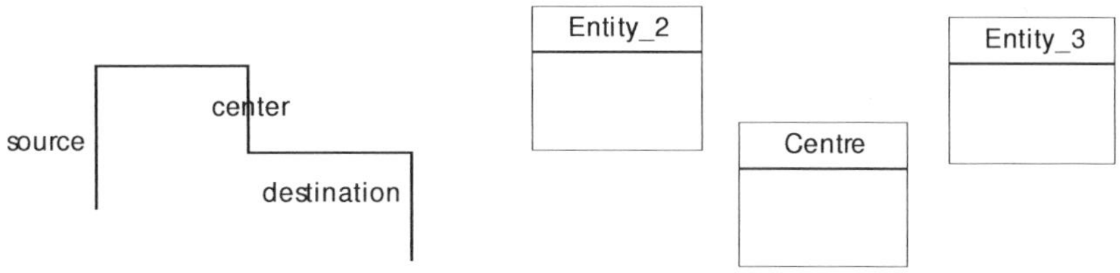 • Flip Vertical - flips the selected symbols through the vertical center of the group. Where appropriate, the orientation of an individual symbol may also be changed. For example, here is a line and three entities before applying 'Flip Vertical': 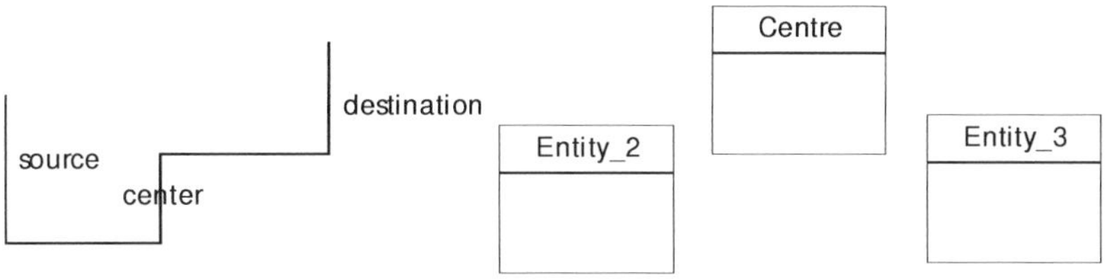 and after: 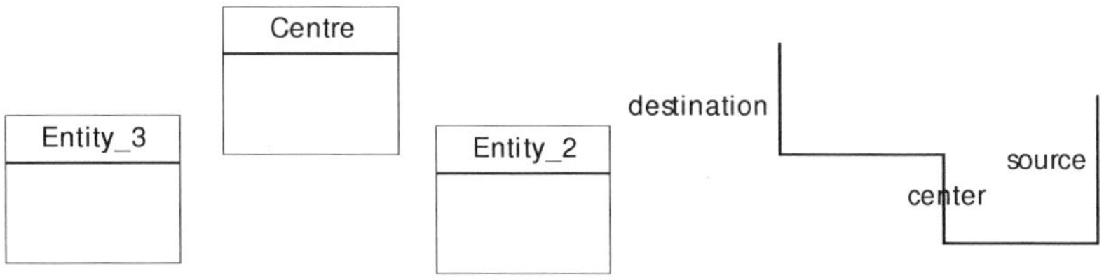

Option	Description
	• Arrange Symbols – distributes the selected symbols evenly, both horizontally and vertically. For example, the following entities and relationships would be re-arranged, from this: 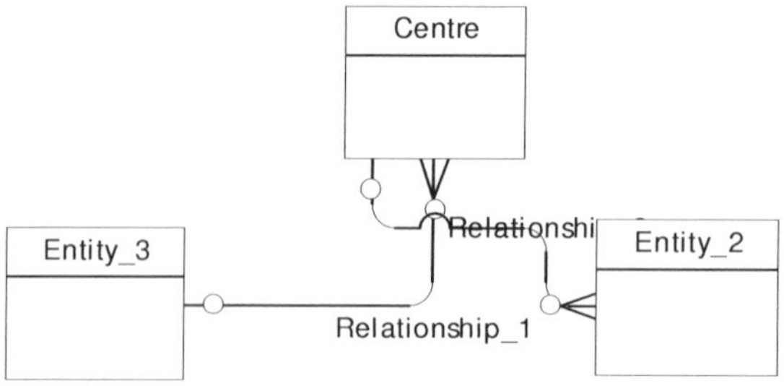 to this: 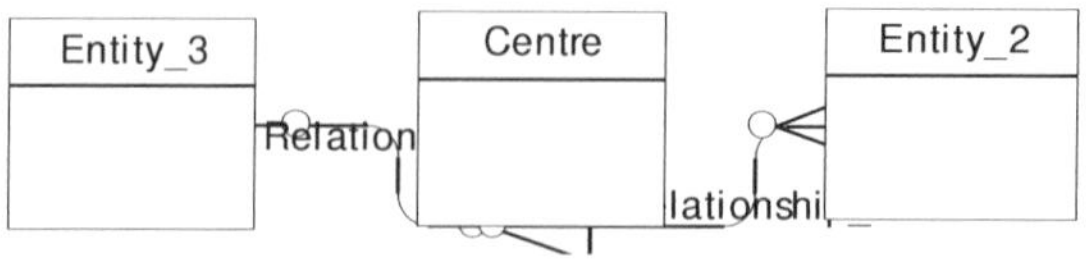 Now apply the Horizontal Disposition to the relationships in this example, to create the following: 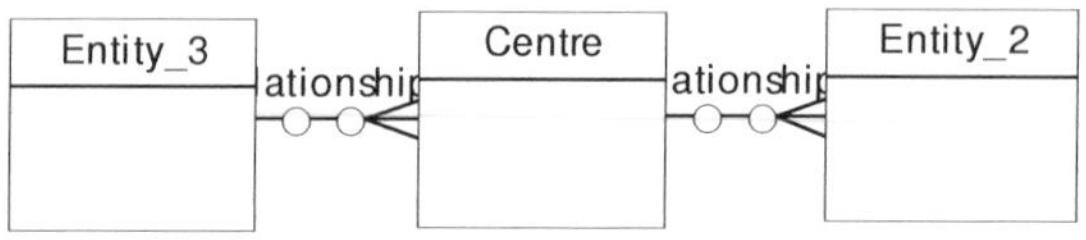 • Arrange Connectors – straightens the selected link symbols and centers their endpoints in the objects that they connect. this is a useful way of re-arranging a relationship • Arrange Attach Points - centers the endpoints of the selected link symbols in the objects that they connect. • Arrange Attached Text – returns text objects associated with the selected link symbols to their default position.
Order	Promotes or demotes the selected symbols in terms of layers within the diagram. This can be useful when you have overlapping symbols and want to have one appear above the other. The following options are available: • Bring to Front • Send to Back • Bring Forward • Send Backward By default, when you insert a free symbol (for example, a note) on a model object symbol (for example, a table), the free symbol is always inserted behind object symbols. Priority is given to the front-most symbols. When symbols overlap, it may not be possible to select the symbol in the background, even if its handles are visible.

If you want to prevent anyone from changing your symbols, you can protect them using 'Protect Symbols' on the Symbols menu. If you do this, remember three things:

- The object is not protected, merely the symbol
- Only direct access to the symbol is prevented - changes made via Display Preferences can still affect symbols
- You can only unprotect a symbol by unprotecting all protected symbols on a diagram – of course you can re-apply protection immediately afterwards.

Bending and Straightening Link Symbols

You can change the corners on link symbols. The results depend on the style of your line, specifically whether or not it has right-angled corners. See "Display Preferences for Relationships" in Chapter 13, to find out more about line corner styles.

You can add one or more handles to a line by holding down <Ctrl> and clicking on the line. In Figure 10.45, we have added two handles.

Figure 10.45 Two new handles

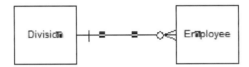

If the line style does not have right-angled corners, we can drag the two new handles to change the shape of the line, as shown in Figure 10.46.

Figure 10.46 A lightning strike

If the line style does have right-angled corners, attempting to drag individual handles may just result in the removal of the handles you added. You need to drag the line segments – the parts in between the handles. See Figure 10.47.

Figure 10.47 Dragging a line segment

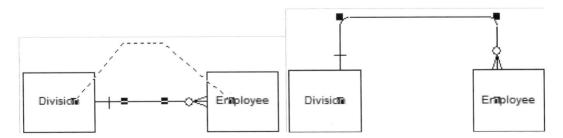

There is an exception to the above rule – you can drag a right-angled corner to a new location and re-route the whole line as shown in Figure 10.48.

Figure 10.48 Dragging a right-angled corner

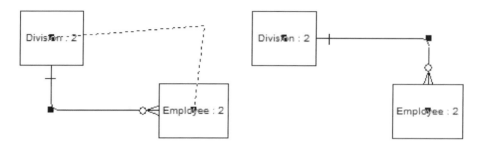

You can also drag a line or portion of a line up and down or left and right, to alter the location it attaches to a symbol. This is useful when you have more than one line attached to one side of a symbol, as shown in Figure 10.49.

Figure 10.49 Moving a line

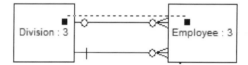

To remove a handle (and corner), press <Ctrl> and click on the handle you want to remove. Pressing <Ctrl+H> or <Ctrl+L> may also have the desired effect. See "Laying Out Diagrams", later in this chapter.

Connecting a Link Symbol to a Different Object

You can drag a link symbol from one object to another. This works for any kind of link, even CDM/LDM relationships and PDM references.

1. Click a link symbol in the diagram.
2. Drag one of its end handles to a different object.

In the left-hand image in Figure 10.50, the line handle that had been inside the entity **Division2** was dragged across to the entity **Employee2**. The left-hand image shows the result – when the mouse button was released, the line end was moved, so the line now connects **Employee2** to itself. In technical terms, the relationship became a recursive (or reflexive) relationship – see Chapter 5 to find out what these are.

Figure 10.50 Moving the end of a line

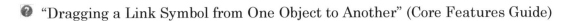

● "Dragging a Link Symbol from One Object to Another" (Core Features Guide)

You can also change the entity or table at either end of a relationship or reference via their property sheet.

Renaming Objects and Symbols

How easy is it to change the name of an object or model? It is very easy! In fact, there are several methods available.

By the way, some of these methods work just as well for sub-objects.

The Two-click Method for Renaming an Object

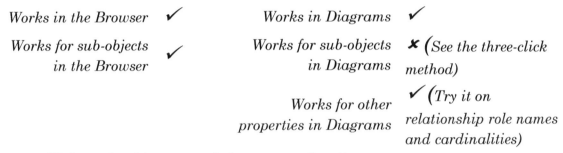

Works in the Browser ✔   *Works in Diagrams* ✔

Works for sub-objects ✔   *Works for sub-objects* ✘ *(See the three-click*
in the Browser   *in Diagrams* *method)*

                                Works for other ✔ *(Try it on*
                       properties in Diagrams *relationship role names*
                                          and cardinalities)

1. Click on the object or symbol name to select it
2. Click again to edit the name.

If your clicks are too close together, you'll open the property sheet instead; that's not a problem, because you can change the name there as well.

The Three-click Method for Renaming an Object

Works for sub-objects in Diagrams ✔

1. Click on the symbol to select it
2. Click on a sub-object name to select it
3. Click again on the sub-object name to edit it

The <F2> Method for Renaming an Object

Works in the Browser ✔   *Works in Diagrams* ✔

Works for sub-objects ✔   *Works for sub-objects* ✘ *See the three-click*
in the Browser   *in Diagrams* *method*

1. Select the name of an object in the Browser or select a symbol on a diagram
2. Press <F2>, and change the name
3. Press <Enter> or click anywhere else to save the new name

The Property Sheet Method for Renaming an Object

Open the property sheet and change the object name in the 'General' tab.

The Two-handed Method for Renaming an Object

Works in the Browser ✗ *Works in Diagrams* ✓

On a diagram, hold down <Ctrl> and right-click the symbol text to select it for editing.

Accessing Objects from a Diagram

Most of the symbols on a diagram represent underlying objects, so you can use symbols to access the object definitions. You can also use them as a pathway to other related diagrams. We will have a brief look at this in Chapter 16.

To find the underlying object in the Browser, either:
- Right-click the symbol and select 'Find in Browser'
  Or
- Select the symbol and press <Ctrl+B>.

There are several ways to access the object's property sheet from a symbol:
- Double-click the symbol
- Right-click the symbol and select 'Properties'
- Select the symbol and press <Alt+Enter>.

Showing and Hiding Symbols

The *Show Symbols* dialog (Figure 10.51) lists all the objects that you can display on the diagram and allows you to choose which ones to show or hide. When you hide a symbol, you do not delete the symbol or the object, the symbol is merely hidden from view. If you re-select the object later, it will re-appear in the same position as it was before you hid it.

Figure 10.51 Show symbols dialog

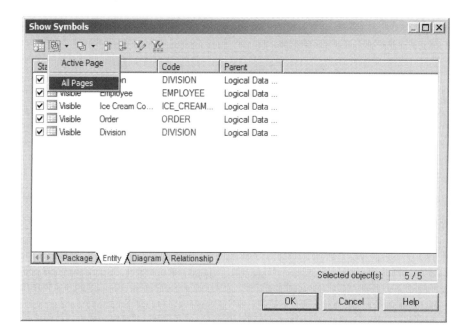

There are three ways to open the Show Symbols dialog:

- `Symbol|Show Symbols`
- Right-click the diagram background and select `Diagram|Show Symbols`
- Right-click the diagram name in the Browser, and select `Show Symbols`.

Each sub-tab in Figure 10.51 shows one type of object. If shortcuts, extended dependencies and/or free symbols are present in the package, they appear on their own sub-tabs. You show and hide symbols by selecting or deselecting them. The *Select All* and *Deselect All* tools allow you to select or deselect all objects on the current tab, or all tabs. The option shown in Figure 10.51 will include all the objects on all the tabs.

If you have other models of the same type open, you can use the *Add Objects* tool to select objects in other models of the same type. Any objects selected are included in your model as shortcuts. For example, if you include the entity **Order** from another model, it will appear in the list of entities for your current model, with a shortcut arrow on the icon.

When you hide or show links or objects with links, the following rules apply:

- Hide an object - Links attached to the hidden object are also hidden
- Show an object - Links attached to the object are shown if the object at their other extremity is already visible
- Show a link - The objects at both ends are also shown.

In a CDM, the following rules apply:

- Hide a parent entity - Inheritances for which the hidden entity is the parent are also hidden.
- Show an association - Entities and association links attached to the association are also shown.
- Show an association link - Entities and associations attached to the association link are also shown.
- Show an inheritance - Parent and child entities and inheritance links attached to the inheritance are also shown.
- Show an inheritance link - Parent and child entities and inheritances attached to the inheritance link are also shown.

To hide one or more symbols without using this dialog, select them and choose `Hide Symbols` from the `Symbol` menu. You can also right-click one of the selected symbols and choose `Edit|Hide Symbols` from the contextual menu.

To show a symbol without using the dialog, simply drag the object into the diagram from the Browser or another diagram. If you drag the symbol from another package or model, a shortcut to the object will be created in the destination model.

> It may be better to hide a symbol than to delete it from a diagram. If you hide a symbol and then decide to show it again, it will re-appear in the same position. If you delete a symbol and then decide to show it again, you will have to decide where to put it. This could save a great deal of time if you need to hide and then re-display many linked symbols.

There is another way to add missing link symbols – the 'Complete Links' command. See "Including Missing Relationships" in Chapter 13.

ⓐ "Showing and Hiding Symbols" (Core Features Guide)

YOUR TURN TO PLAY

1. Open any diagram in the Project Management LDM and open the Show Symbols dialog.
2. Look through the tabs and select some symbols to add to the diagram. Include at least one of the more unusual types of symbols, such as other diagrams, and then click on <OK>. The symbols will now appear on your diagram in the default style.
3. Open the 'Show Symbols' dialog again, de-select at least one symbol, and click <OK>. The symbol will have disappeared from the diagram.
4. Open the 'Show Symbols' dialog for a third time, and check the entries for the symbols you de-selected in step 2 - they are listed as 'hidden'. Select them again and click <OK>. The symbols will reappear on the diagram.

Communicating Your Message

A diagram is a communication tool. For communication to be effective, the message needs to be clear and unambiguous. The content, layout, and style of the diagram are key factors in communicating the message.

There are several ways of improving the readability of your diagram:

- Add a title box, annotations, comments, and other graphical symbols
- Add external files and link them to your model objects
- Exclude objects or properties of objects that are not relevant to the audience
- Exclude sub-objects (such as attributes in an entity symbol) that are not relevant to the audience
- Use color, line, and font styles to convey meaning
- Align your entity symbols to make it easier to visually scan across and down the diagram.

For a more comprehensive discussion of improving readability, see Steve's book *Data Modeling Master Class Training Manual 2nd Edition* (Hoberman, 2011, Module 7).

We'll discuss re-arranging the layout in Chapter 13, where we show you how to create and work with relationships.

Figure 10.52 illustrates some of the graphical embellishments that are available via the Toolbox. None of the embellishments affect the underlying model at all.

Two of the symbols have been changed from their original image via their contextual menu. Just right-click any image and select 'Change Image'. You can replace the current image with clip art, PowerDesigner icons, Windows icons, or anything else you like. If you change the symbol image for a real object such as an entity, you may need to add the object name as a separate text box, as most images cannot contain object properties. You can avoid this issue by using the 'Custom Shape' tab from the format menu to change the symbol shape.

Figure 10.52 Graphical embellishments

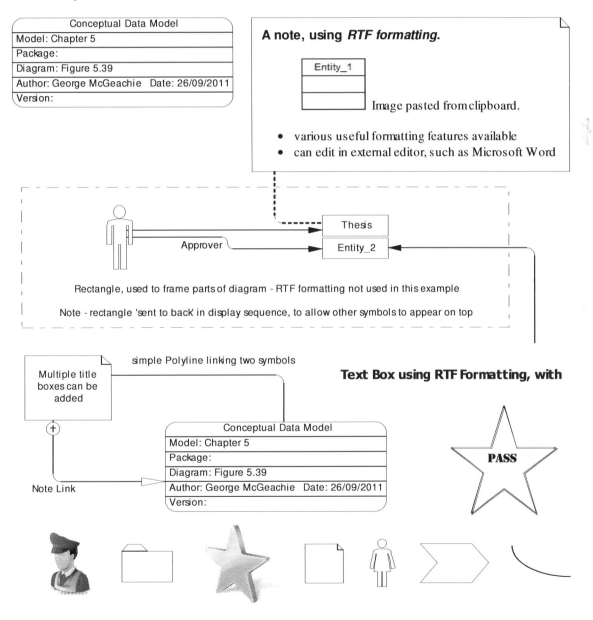

The lines connecting symbols on Figure 10.52 are known as 'Traceability Links'. We're using them to link decorative symbols, so they're only recorded in the diagram. On Figure 10.53, we'll see another type of link which *does* affect the underlying objects.

The way you create decorative symbols is no different from how you created entities. The first step is to click on a tool on the Toolbox; what you do next depends on the type of symbol.

For link symbols, click on the first symbol and drag the mouse to the second symbol. If you release the mouse button in empty space, you will create a bend in the link. Create as many bends as you want to, and then click on the second symbol.

For other symbols, you have two choices:

- Click on the diagram to create the symbols in their default size, in the same way you would create entities

    or

- Click on the diagram and drag the mouse; then let go of the mouse button when your symbol is the required size.

You can change the format of any symbol or link. In Figure 10.52, for example, I changed the symbols at the end nodes on the line that connects the title box to a note.

❷   "Symbols" (Core Features Guide)

You can also import external images, by pasting from the Windows clipboard, or by importing from a file. See the 'Import Image' option on the 'Edit' menu.

In Figure 10.53, we can see examples of presentation techniques that expose the details of the data model, and examples of the formatting capabilities. We are constrained by the monochrome presentation of this book, which prevents us from demonstrating the use of color and shading.

Figure 10.53 Format and content of object symbols

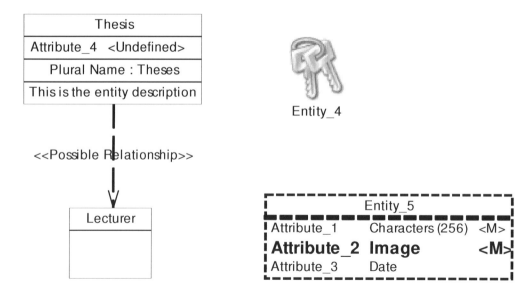

Each of the four entities in Figure 10.53 is displayed differently, due to changes in the selection of content and style.

The *Thesis* entity symbol shows the list of attributes, the plural name, and the description, it also has a shadow. Note that the plural name is not a standard PowerDesigner property – it was introduced via a model extension, which we will discuss again later. The line style and fonts were changed in **Entity_5**, and we're also showing more detail of the attributes. The symbol for **Entity_4** has been completely replaced by an image of door keys.

The dashed line between **Thesis** and **Lecturer** is a traceability link, telling us that **Thesis** is influenced in some way by **Lecturer**. We have chosen to classify the link as a <<Possible Relationship>> by updating the Link Type. You will try this for yourself in Chapter 18.

"Creating Traceability Links" (Core Features Guide)

Changing the Content of Symbols

As we showed in Figure 10.53, you have a lot of control over the object properties displayed in a symbol.

You'll remember that you can access the Display Preferences by right-clicking a blank area of the diagram. You can see the dialog in Figure 10.54.

Figure 10.54 Display Preferences dialog

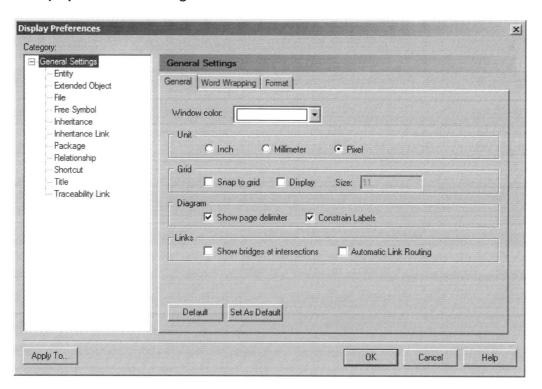

All the standard types of symbols in the model are listed on the left. The term 'Free Symbol' refers to the graphical embellishments we looked at earlier.

The General Settings category allows you to control the general look of the diagram. The 'Word Wrapping' tab allows you to change the way in which long object names are handled. Word wrapping is turned off by default. The 'Format' tab allows you to set the default format (but not font) for all symbols.

Figure 10.54 shows the General Settings applicable to data models. The two settings under the 'Links' category were introduced in PowerDesigner Version 16. Further settings are available for other types of models.

When you select one of the symbol types in the dialog, you will be presented with two tabs, 'Content' and 'Format'. We will look at the 'Format' tab in the next section.

Figure 10.55 shows the default 'Content' tab for entities – it shows the properties that are currently available for display on entity symbols. If you select a different type of symbol on the left, the content tab changes appropriately.

Figure 10.55 Selecting symbol content

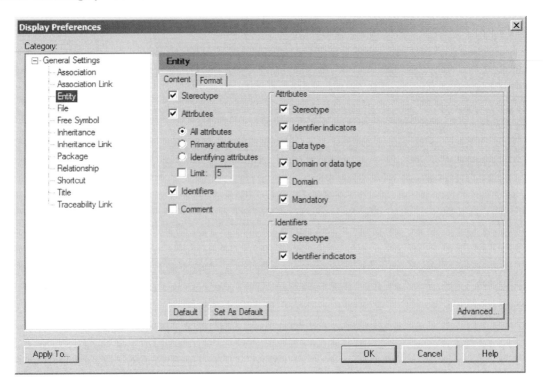

The checkboxes in Figure 10.55 allow you to choose the properties to display on symbols. If you click the <Default> button, the preferences are reset to the current default values for this type of model. Click the <Set As Default> button to set the current Display Preferences as the default for this type of model – PowerDesigner will apply these preferences to all new diagrams of this type. You will also see these buttons in other dialogs, such as 'Model Options', where they have the same affect.

Once you have configured your preferences, you can apply them to the current diagram by pressing <OK>.

Alternatively, click on <Apply To> to select other diagrams to apply the changes to. After selecting your diagrams, you will be asked whether you want to apply your changes to all the symbols in the selected diagrams. If you select 'Yes', all existing and new symbols will reflect your changes to the Format, General, and Content display preferences. If you select 'No', only new symbols will reflect your changes.

When you click on <OK> in the 'Display Preferences' window, you have a choice of how to apply the changes in the current diagram:

All symbols   Apply the changes to all symbols on the diagram

Selected Symbols   Apply the changes to selected symbols on the diagram

New Symbols   Existing symbols are untouched, and new symbols will comply with
                       the new preferences

If you want to apply different Display Preferences to just *some* of your symbols, you must select those symbols and access `Display Preferences` via the `Tools` menu, **not** by right-clicking the diagram.

To change the list of available properties, click on the 'Advanced' button. Figure 10.56 shows the result.

Figure 10.56 Customizing symbol content

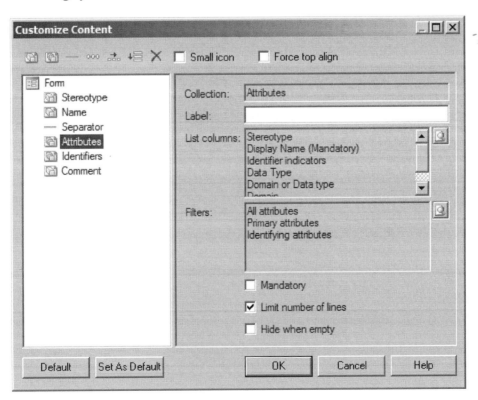

The left-hand side of the 'Customize Content' dialog shows the properties currently selected for display on entity symbols. The right-hand side shows the detail of the property selected on the

left, in this case the *Attributes* property. This is a collection of sub-objects, so we can choose the sub-object properties available for display, as well as define a set of filters to limit the sub-objects displayed.

The <Default> and <Set As Default> buttons have the same effect as those in Figure 10.55.

In this dialog, you need to remember the distinction between Attributes in entities, and attributes as object properties, that we mentioned before. The word 'Attributes' in Figure 10.56 refers to Attributes in entities. In the next few paragraphs, we refer to 'attributes' as properties of PowerDesigner objects. Most of the properties listed on the left-hand side of Figure 10.56 are simple properties of objects, referred to as 'attributes'. If you select such a property on the left-hand side, the right-hand pane is simpler than shown in Figure 10.56. You will be able to change the following:

Label	Used in the list of properties in Display Preferences – this defaults to the property name, so you only need to enter something here if you want to use different words.
Prefix and Suffix	Used to label the entry on the symbol. Remember to add any padding or special characters (such as a colon), because PowerDesigner does not pad the label for you. For example – "Plural Name : ".
Alignment	Choose how you want to align the property value within the symbol
Mandatory	If you select this box, the property will always be displayed on the symbol and cannot be de-selected in the Display Preferences dialog.

Figure 10.57 explains the toolbar icons found at the top of the "Customize Content" form shown in Figure 10.56.

Figure 10.57 Toolbar for customizing content

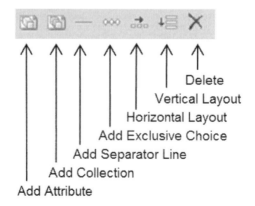

The Horizontal and Vertical Layout options were introduced in PowerDesigner Version 16. They allow you to arrange properties side by side or one under the other. Vertical Layouts are often used in conjunction with a Horizontal Layout, to provide several columns of attributes.

In addition, there are two checkboxes:

Small icon   Places a small object icon in the top-left corner of the symbol in detail mode. The icons can be varied according to the values of the property.

Force top align   Forces top alignment in the symbol for object attributes, such as Name. If this option is not selected, these properties are centered on the vertical axis.

When you click on the 'Add Attribute' button, you are presented with a list of the available property attributes. Figure 10.58 shows the attributes available for entity objects. Most of them are common to all types of object, some are specific to entities.

There are two tabs shown in Figure 10.58, one for standard Attributes, and the other for Extended Attributes, introduced via model extensions.

Figure 10.58 Choose from the available properties (attributes)

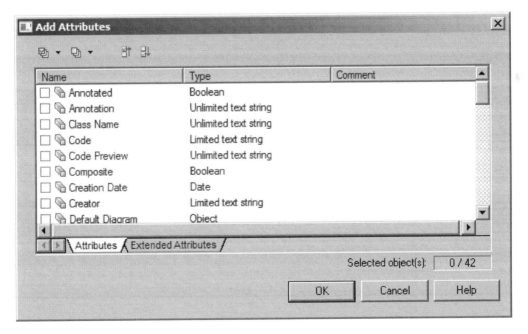

Just select the attributes that you want to have available for display and click on <OK>.

To add one or more Collections, start by clicking the 'Add Collection' button in Figure 10.57, and continue in the same way as you would when adding Attributes.

"Customizing Content Display Preferences" (Core Features Guide)

YOUR TURN TO PLAY

1. Right-click any data model diagram that displays entities, select 'Display Preferences', and click on 'Entity' on the left. Ensure all the checkboxes on the right are cleared and click <OK>. In the 'Changing Formats' window that appears next (Figure 10.59), choose 'All Symbols' and click <OK>. All the entity symbols will change to a simple rectangle, containing only the entity name. The symbols may have shrunk due to the reduction in content.

Figure 10.59 Changing Formats window

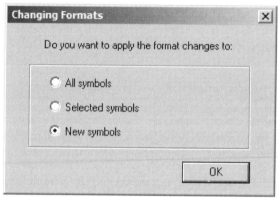

PowerDesigner will ask you if you want to apply the preferences to all the symbols in the selected diagram(s), and gives you the following options:

- Yes – All existing and new symbols will reflect your changes to the Format, General, and Content display preferences.
- No – Only new symbols will reflect your changes. Only the General and Content display preferences are applied to existing symbols. The Format changes are canceled.
- Cancel – Your changes will not affect any symbols in any diagrams except the current one.

2. Now open the 'Display Preferences' again, select 'Entity', and click on <Advanced> to show the list of available properties. Follow these steps to add the *Description* property to the list:
- Select the *Attributes* property and click the 'Add Separator Line' button.
- Click the 'Add Attribute' button.
- Select the *Description* property and click on <OK>.
- The *Description* property is added to the property list in the 'Customize Contents' window, separated from the *Attributes* property; click on <OK> to close this window.
3. Click on <OK> to close the Display Preferences, select 'All Symbols' in the 'Changing Formats' window, and click <OK>.
4. If your entities have Descriptions, they will appear in the symbols – add a Description to an entity and see what happens.
5. Add some Free Symbols from the Toolbox, and add links between symbols. Remember to drag the mouse from one symbol to another when creating links.

Figure 10.60 shows the new list of available properties.

Figure 10.60 Revised list of available properties

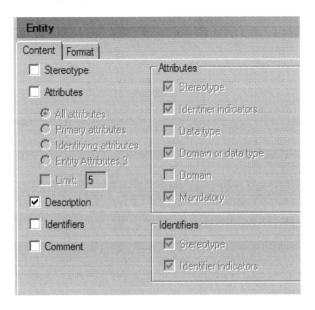

Formatting Symbols

You can change the size, line style, fill, shadow, font, alignment, shape, and content of symbols in the Symbol Format dialog. Some items may not be available if your modeling methodology restricts the modification of symbol format or content.

You will arrive at the Symbol Format dialog when changing the format of:

- One or more individual symbols – select the symbols and press <Ctrl+T>, or select `Format` on the `Symbol` menu, or select `Format` from the contextual menu.
- All symbols - via display preferences (see "Changing the Content of Symbols", earlier in this chapter).

Figure 10.61 shows a typical Symbol Format dialog and Table 10.9 describes each tab. Note that the 'Sub-Objects' and 'Content' tabs are only available for selected objects, not via Display Preferences.

The Content tab allows you to show a different set of properties on selected symbols – for example, you could show more or less detail of the attributes.

The Sub-objects tab can be used to hide selected sub-objects from a symbol, such as attributes on an entity symbol.

There is a useful keyboard shortcut to adjust symbols to fit their content – select all the symbols you wish to adjust and press <Ctrl+J>.

"Symbol Format Properties" (Core Features Guide)

Figure 10.61 Symbol Format dialog

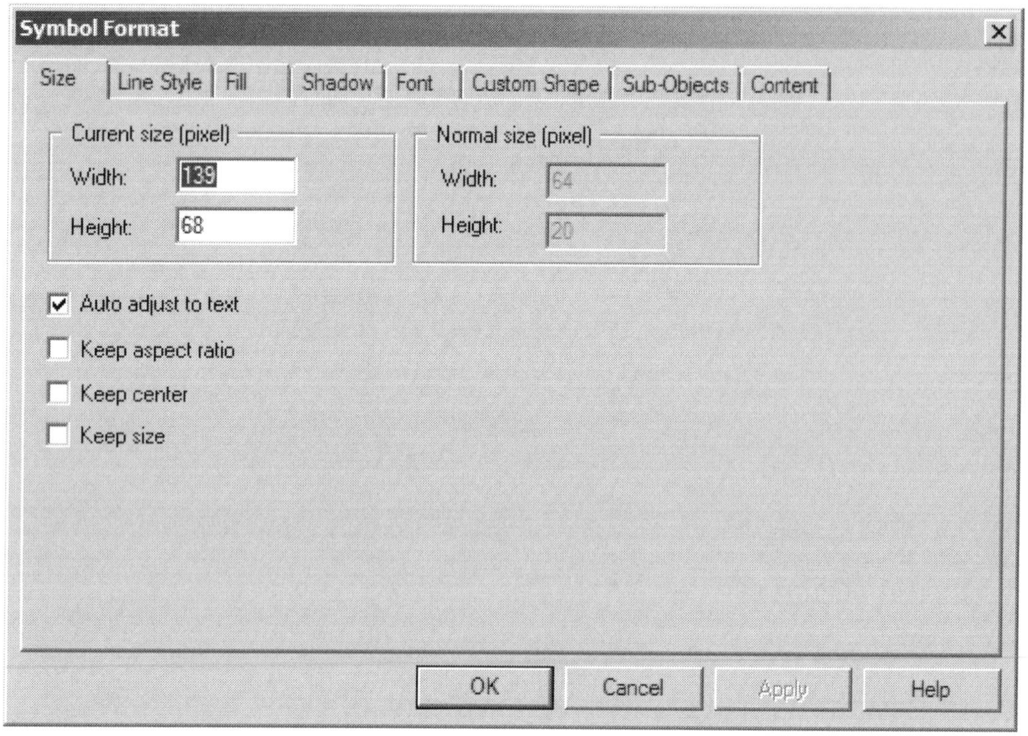

Get and Apply Format

On the contextual menu for symbols, you may have noticed the commands `Get Format` and `Apply Format`. They provide a simple, effective way of transferring the style and content selection from one symbol to another. It even works between different types of objects and between different types of models. For example, you can 'get' the style of a table in a PDM, and 'apply' it to relationships in a CDM.

The first step is to right-click a symbol whose style you want to mimic elsewhere, and select `Get Format`. To apply the style to one symbol, just right-click that symbol, and select `Apply Format`. If the symbols represent the same type of object, all the format and content preferences are copied to the second symbol. Where the symbol types or model types are different, the results vary, but you should probably see some changes.

To apply the format to multiple symbols at the same time, select the symbols, right-click on any one of them, and select `Apply Format`.

	"Selecting, Editing and Resizing Symbols" (Core Features Guide) "Bending and Straightening Link Symbols" (Core Features Guide) "Aligning Selected Symbols" (Core Features Guide) "Arranging Symbols Using the Symbol Menu" (Core Features Guide)

Table 10.9 Symbol Format dialog tabs

Tab	Description
Size Tab	The 'Size' tab controls the size of the symbol and how the size can be manipulated.
Line Style Tab	The 'Line Style' tab controls the color, size, and format of lines (for link and other one-dimensional symbols) and borders (for two-dimensional symbols, such as classes or tables). You can modify the line style of any symbol in the model.
Fill Tab	The 'Fill' tab controls the color, content, and effects for symbol filling.
Shadow Tab	The 'Shadow' tab allows you to add a standard, 3D effect or gradient shadow to objects in a diagram.
Font Tab	The 'Font' tab allows you to define the display preferences for the font, size, style, and color of text associated with symbols in the model. When you modify font preferences, they apply to all existing and new symbols. ⊖ Remember – the object name is NOT the first entry in the list of properties on this tab.
Text Alignment Tab	The 'Text Alignment' tab allows you to define the alignment of text in text boxes and rectangles, ellipses, rounded rectangles, and polygons. Note: You can only control the text alignment for these shapes, and not for model object symbols. When working with RTF, all the options but Vertical are disabled.
Custom Shape Tab	The 'Custom Shape' tab allows you to define a new symbol shape for most non-link symbols.
Sub-objects Tab	The 'Sub-objects' tab is only available when you open the 'Format' tab after having selected a single object that is displaying sub-objects. It gives you very fine control over the sub-objects that you want to display inside your object symbol. For each individual sub-object, you can decide whether to display it or not, and what font to use for its display. Note: For a collection of sub-objects to be available for selection and customization, the collection must be selected for display in the object's content display preferences. Where the number of lines to display for a collection is limited in the display preferences, that limit will take precedence over any choices you make here. Each collection of sub-objects that is enabled in the display preferences has its own sub-tab. For each sub-object, you can: • Select to display or hide it in the parent object symbol by selecting or deselecting its checkbox in the [D]isplay column. • Apply a specific font to its display by clicking the Select font tool or the ellipsis button in the Specific Font column. Note: When not all sub-objects in a collection are selected for display, the parent object symbol will display ellipses to indicate that more items are available.
Content Tab	The 'Content' tab allows you to specify the information that you want to display on the symbol. The properties that are listed on this tab as being available for selection are controlled by the content display preferences.

YOUR TURN TO PLAY

1. Right-click on the name of the Project Management LDM in the Browser, click on New, and then Logical Diagram. The property sheet for the new diagram is displayed. Change the diagram name to 'New Diagram 1' and click on <OK>. The new diagram appears in the list of diagrams in the Browser. That's how easy it is to create a diagram.

2. Here's another way to create a new diagram. Open the 'Main Diagram' and select the 'Employee' entity; then select the menu option Edit|Select Connected Symbols; five more entities are now included in the selection. Hold down the <Shift> key, and click on the **Activity** entity to add that to the selection. You may need to press <F8> to view the whole diagram, so you can see the **Activity** entity. Right-click on any one of the selected symbols, and select Create Diagram from Selection. A new diagram is created with a default name, containing the selected symbols – the symbols have the same appearance and layout as they did in 'Main Diagram'. This is the easiest way to create a diagram with the same display preferences as an existing one.

3. Let's assume that this view of the model doesn't require the **Member** entity, so select it and press <Delete>. PowerDesigner asks you if you want to delete the object itself, or just the symbol. See Figure 10.62.

Figure 10.62 Confirm Deletion

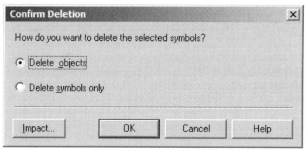

4. Select 'Delete Symbols Only' and click on <OK>. The entity has been removed from the diagram, but you can still see it in the Browser.

When PowerDesigner asks if you also want to remove the object definition, the default answer is 'Yes'. If you accidentally remove definitions, press <Ctrl+Z> to bring them back.

Remember that you can hide symbols instead of deleting them – see "Showing and Hiding Symbols", earlier in this chapter.

5. Now to change the information displayed on Entity symbols. Right-click a blank area of the diagram and select 'Display Preferences'. Click on 'Entity' in the list on the left-hand side, and make sure that all of the checkboxes are blank so the Entity symbols will only contain the Entity name. Now click on the 'Format' tab, and then click on 'Modify'. Figure 10.63 shows the options available. Select the 'Font' tab.

Figure 10.63 Modifying Symbol Format

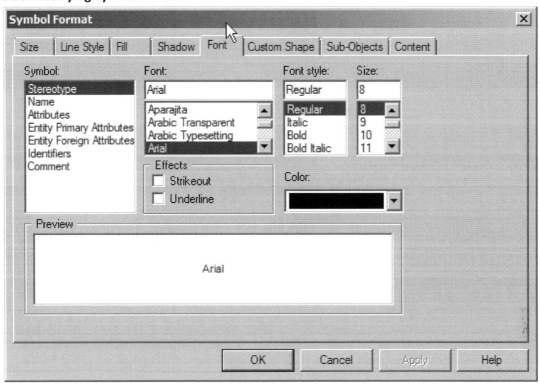

This is the standard Symbol Format window, which you can use to format selected symbols or to set diagram defaults. Have a look at the tabs and try out some of the options, if you like, but make sure that you at least change the name format. Click on the 'Font' tab and PowerDesigner will present a list of Symbol properties on the left, with the font options for each one to the right of that. To change the font for the Symbol name, click on 'Name' on the left and change the font to Arial, Bold, Size 12.

The first entry in the list of Symbol properties is NOT the name. I have lost count of the number of times that I intended to change the format of the Name, but forgot to select it on the left first. Remember you can always undo any change you make accidentally, or cancel the whole operation.

6. Press <OK> and click on 'Apply To' in the 'Display Preferences' dialog. This allows you to apply the formatting changes to other diagrams in your model. Select the diagram called 'Symbol Test' and click on <OK>.
7. In the confirmation window, select 'Yes', and the 'Display Preferences' window is re-displayed. Click on <OK> to apply the changes.
8. PowerDesigner now displays the 'Changing Formats' window (see Figure 10.56). Choose 'All Symbols', so that the style is applied to all the symbols on the diagram, as well as to new symbols.

The entities in your diagram have all been re-sized, and the entity names are now in a larger, bolder font, as shown in Figure 10.64.

Figure 10.64 Project Management LDM in progress

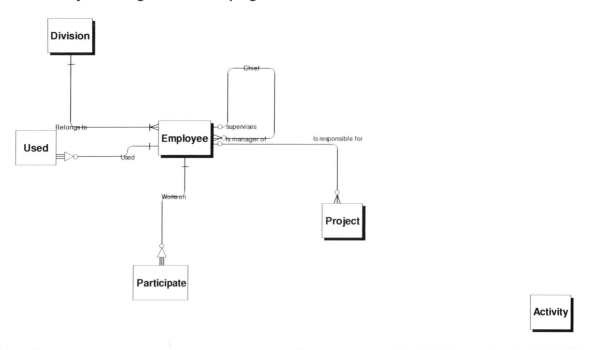

You can change the display preferences for one or more selected symbols. Select the symbols you want to change, click on the `Tools` menu, and then click on `Display Preferences`. Make your changes and choose to apply the changes to 'Selected Symbols'.

"Content Display Preferences" (Core Features Guide)

YOUR TURN TO PLAY

The entities are now more widely spaced than they need to be, so you should re-arrange them, placing **Employee** at the top.

1. Drag the **Employee** entity to the top and middle of the diagram.
2. Use the mouse and the <Shift> key to select all the other entities, and then drag them to below **Employee**.
3. Click on the 'Evenly Space Horizontally' button on the Layout toolbar.
4. Click on the 'Align Top' button on the same toolbar.
5. On the `Symbol` menu, select `Align| Same Width`. Now sort out the relationships.
6. Double-click the relationship tool in the Logical Diagram palette to select all the relationships.
7. On the `Symbol` menu, select `Disposition|Arrange Connectors`.

Most of the lines now look much neater, but there may still be room for improvement. Make sure all of the relationships are still selected, press <Ctrl+H>, and then press <Ctrl+L>. These commands straighten out any lines that can easily be made horizontal or vertical. The result should look something like Figure 10.65.

Figure 10.65 Partially re-organized diagram

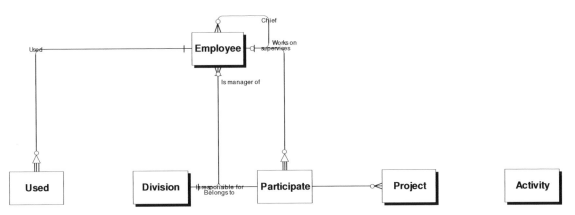

There are just two things to do now: get rid of the entity shadows and move some of the relationship lines. Let's do the easy part first. Select all symbols and press <Ctrl+W>. All of the shadows will disappear – if not, just press <Ctrl+W> again.

Moving the relationships can be a bit trickier. Lines can be moved by dragging the lines, or by dragging the relationship handles, which show up as small squares at the line ends and on any corners. The handles are shown in Figure 10.66; note that the end handles are inside the entity symbols, not on the edges.

Figure 10.66 Relationship handles

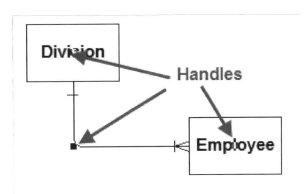

You can slide relationships along entity edges by dragging one of the end handles horizontally or vertically. The line itself is usually a bigger target, so try it now. Click on a line and hold the mouse button down; the line should change into a dashed line which you can easily drag around to reroute the line. In the example shown in Figure 10.66, the line can be dragged to where the word 'Handles' is shown, and it will reroute itself to form a right-angle in a different position. If you have problems dragging the vertical part of the line, try dragging the horizontal part instead.

If you want to resize an entity, select it; you'll see that it also has handles. Drag one of the handles to stretch or shrink the entity in one or both dimensions. If you press <Ctrl+J>, all selected symbols will resize to fit their contents.

Looking at the diagram, it seems that the **Division** entity should be above the **Employee** entity. You could drag it with the mouse, but there's another way, which also ensures that it moves in a straight line. Select the entity; press the <up arrow> key on the keyboard until the entity is as high as you want, and use the left and right arrow keys to move it sideways. The relationship line is continually re-drawn by PowerDesigner. Move the entity around until the relationship line takes a favorable route.

If you now have a gap in the lower entities, select the ones you want to sort out and experiment with the icons on the Layout toolbar (or via the Symbol menu) to line them up and even out the spacing. You can select several entities and use the arrow keys to move them all together, if you like. Finally, you may need to re-adjust the relationship lines. The labels on relationships can also be moved around, as long as you do not try and move them too far from the line. The result may look like Figure 10.67. We have not changed the content or meaning of the model at all, but we have created a new view of part of the model that differs greatly from the original view.

Figure 10.67 The finished diagram

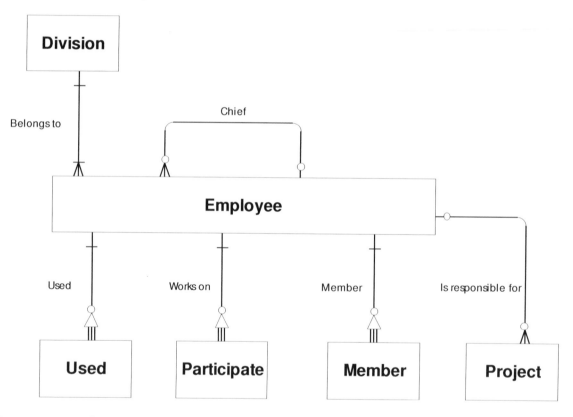

In Figure 10.67, the labels shown for relationships are the relationship names. By default, PowerDesigner places these in the middle of the line. I moved them sideways for clarity. Relationship role names (which have been hidden in Figure 10.67) would be positioned so that they can be read in a clockwise fashion.

To reset relationship labels to their default positions, select them all, and select Disposition|Arrange Attached Text on the Symbol menu.

Perform a quick experiment – in 'Display Preferences', make sure that 'Automatic Link Routing' is disabled. Now move the **Division** entity to the right using the cursor keys: – the entity and relationship will slide sideways, until the entity reaches the **Chief** relationship. From this point, the **Belongs To** relationship will stop moving sideways. Now move **Division** back to where it started. In 'Display Preferences', enable 'Automatic Link Routing', and move **Division** to the right again. PowerDesigner will continually reroute the relationship and move other relationships, if necessary.

Laying Out Diagrams

PowerDesigner can automatically re-arrange whole diagrams or selected symbols in diagrams for you. There are several different layout styles available; just choose one, and PowerDesigner will rearrange the symbols, simplifying the routing of links by minimizing node and link overlaps, and reducing the distances between related nodes.

Select `Symbol`|*Auto-Layout* to open the Auto-Layout window. You can also click on the Auto-Layout tool ▨ on the Layout menu. The Auto-Layout window is shown in Figure 10.68. Only the styles relevant for the current diagram can be selected.

Figure 10.68 The Auto-Layout window

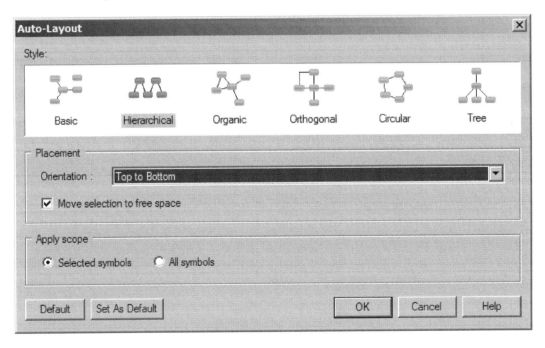

The available layouts are described in Table 10.10. The diagrams in the table show the effect of applying the layout option to the diagram shown in Figure 10.69.

Figure 10.69 The original diagram

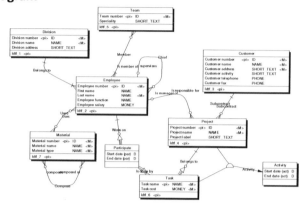

Table 10.10 Auto-layout options

Layout Type	Description
Basic	Provides minimal rerouting for any diagram style. This can be repeated, resulting in different layouts.
Hierarchical	Highlights the main direction or flow within a diagram. You can specify an orientation[5] for the flow. This example was produced using Left to Right orientation: In this example, the parent entity in a relationship (Entity 1) is always on the left. Supertype entities are always on the right. Choosing the 'Right to Left' orientation would reverse the direction of every relationship:

[5] "Top to Bottom", "Bottom to Top", "Left to Right", and "Right to Left"

Layout Type	Description
Organic	Re-arranges entities to reduce crossing relationships. No attempt is made to define a standard direction for relationships.
Orthogonal	For undirected diagrams. You can specify an orientation[6] for the flow within the graph. This example was produced using Left to Right orientation:
	The result does run from left to right, but individual relationships may be oriented in any direction. Choosing the 'Right to Left' orientation would reverse the direction of every relationship.
Circular	Produces interconnected ring and star topologies to emphasize group and tree structures within a network. You can additionally specify a cycle (ring) or radiation (star) shape.
	After applying the 'Cycle' option:
	After applying the 'Radiation' option:

---

[6] "Top to Bottom", "Bottom to Top", "Left to Right", and "Right to Left"

Layout Type	Description
Tree	To create directed or undirected trees. You can additionally specify an orientation for the flow within the graph. This example was produced using Left to Right orientation: 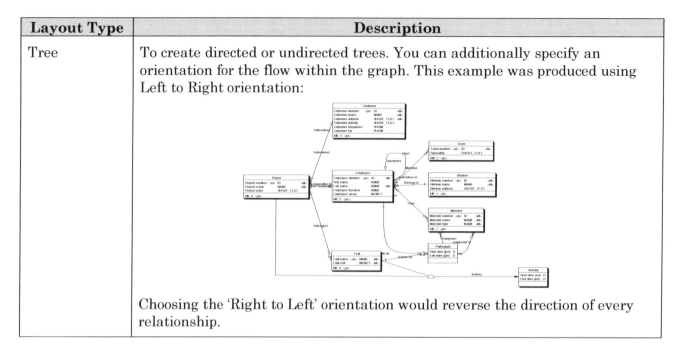 Choosing the 'Right to Left' orientation would reverse the direction of every relationship.

You don't have to apply the layout to the whole diagram. If you have selected two or more symbols, you can specify if you want to apply the auto-layout to all symbols or only to the selected symbols.

When applying Auto-Layout to a selection, you can additionally select the 'Move selection to free space' option to extract the selected symbols from the main body of the diagram and place them in free space.

🚫 If your selection includes supertype and subtype entities, ensure that you also include the inheritance symbol.

Click <OK> to apply the auto-layout and return to the diagram.

Note: You can click the <Default> button to revert to the default auto-layout settings. Click the <Set As Default> button to set the currently selected style as the default.

PowerDesigner may create graphical synonyms (see next page) for certain symbols in (or adjoining) the selection to minimize the length of connecting links.

If you subscribe to the school of thought that describes effective diagram layout using the phrase 'Dead Crows Fly East'[7], try out the orthogonal 'Right to Left' orientation.

Unless your diagram is very simple, it may be best to apply auto-layout selectively. There are other tools on the Layout toolbar and the Symbol menu to help you to align and re-size symbols to improve the readability of your diagrams.

---

[7] Nicely illustrated at http://integrated-modeling-method.com/data-structure-modeling/dead-crows-fly-east/

Graphical Synonyms

A graphical synonym is a duplicate symbol for an object on a diagram. Sometimes, creating multiple symbols for an object in a diagram can improve readability by reducing the length or complexity of links. You can create a graphical synonym by right-clicking a symbol and selecting Edit|Create Graphical Synonym.

To find graphical synonyms of a symbol, right-click the symbol, select Edit|Find Graphical Synonym, and then select a graphical synonym from the list. The graphical synonym will be selected and centered in the diagram window, as shown in Figure 10.70.

Figure 10.70 Selecting a graphical synonym

If Find Graphical Synonym doesn't appear on the menu, that tells you that the symbol does not have graphical synonyms on that diagram.

There are various ways you can access the 'Find in Diagram' window in PowerDesigner, such as right-clicking the object name in the Browser. This window allows you to choose which graphical synonym you wish to have centered in the diagram, as shown in Figure 10.71. To find out more about Graphical Synonyms, see Chapter 13.

Figure 10.71 Find in diagram window

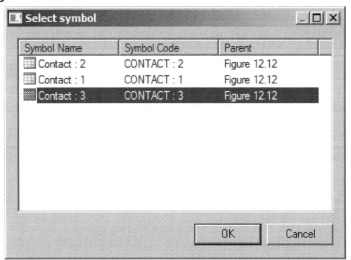

Menus Depend on Models

The menu options available in PowerDesigner depend almost entirely on the currently viewed diagram. If you do not have any diagrams open, most menus will not be available, including the 'Model' menu. There are other ways of accessing the commands on that menu, which we will see shortly.

YOUR TURN TO PLAY

On the `Window` menu, select the option `Close All` to close all the diagrams open in the Canvas. Now open any diagram in the *Project Management LDM* and any diagram in the *Project Management PDM,* and use the `Window` menu to tile them horizontally or vertically. Click on one of the diagram tabs, and then on the `Tools` menu. Now click on the other diagram tab, and again on the `Tools` menu. The list of commands for the PDM is longer than the list for the LDM. There are more generation options, and more automation for common operations. The `Database` menu is only present when the PDM diagram is current. If you open an XML model, the `Database` menu is replaced by a `Language` menu.

When you have many models and/or diagrams open, make sure you are aware of the 'current' model before you access the menus. If necessary, click anywhere on a diagram to make it 'current'. Any selections you make in the Browser will NOT affect the available menus.

Workspaces

In PowerDesigner, you are always working in a Workspace. The Workspace consists of all the Folders, Projects, Models, and External Files you can see in the Browser. You can save the structure of the Workspace in a file, which you can re-open later to recreate your working environment.

A workspace contains all the information you need to perform a modeling task with PowerDesigner. During a work session, every change in the hierarchy of folders and models is saved locally in the workspace. Workspaces tend to be personal, containing folders, files, and projects of interest to a modeler.

So far, we've carried out all our work in a single workspace. You can create multiple workspaces, but you can only work in one workspace at a time. Workspaces are saved in files whose names end in '.sws'. They do not have property sheets. You can create the following new items in a workspace by right-clicking the workspace in the Browser and selecting `New|Item`:
- Projects
- Models and multi-model reports
- Folders.

In addition, you can add existing items (including external files, such as text files or Microsoft Office files) to a workspace by:

1. Right-clicking the workspace in the Browser
2. Selecting Add from the contextual menu
3. Browsing to the item in your Windows folders
4. Clicking <OK>.

You can also drag files into the workspace from Windows Explorer.

When you have external files referenced in a workspace, you can open them with a double-click – they will open in the default software according to your Windows settings.

You can create a hierarchy of folders in a workspace if you choose to. Please remember that these folders are not 'real'; they do not exist in your file system anywhere, they are just containers that help you organize your PowerDesigner objects (including other folders).

When you close PowerDesigner, you'll be asked whether or not you want to save the current workspace. You don't have to do this, of course, but it will make your life easier if you do. You'll also be asked if you want to save any models that have unsaved changes; this includes the option to say 'Yes' or 'No' to saving changes for all unsaved models. Be careful how you use this option if you don't save models regularly; you may lose changes you made a couple of hours ago but forgot to save.

Each model or file entry in a Workspace is a shortcut to the location of a file in the file system. The shortcut is 'absolute' rather than 'relative'; it points to an actual file location, such as 'X:\Server\Folder\Folder\Project\Project Model.ldm'. The supplied Demo workspace is different – the filenames include the named path %_EXAMPLES%

If you attempt to open a model and the shortcut doesn't work, it may have been moved or renamed. PowerDesigner allows you to browse the file system to find the file.

If you only work on one project or on one set of models, you only need one workspace. If you work on multiple projects, it may be useful to have a workspace for each project.

Keep original models and their corresponding generated models in the same workspace, preferably within the same project.

"Workspaces" (Core Features Guide)

Models

Models are the basic work unit in PowerDesigner. You must create a model before you can begin modeling.

Creating a Model

You can create a new, empty model by clicking the *New* tool on the Standard toolbar, or by selecting 'New Model' on the File menu. PowerDesigner will display the New Model window. The New Model window is highly configurable via Model Category Sets, which we will discuss briefly in Chapter 23. Your administrator may hide options that are not relevant to your work, or provide templates or predefined models to guide you through model creation. When you open the window, one or more of the following buttons will be available on the left hand side:

Categories   Provides a set of predefined models and diagrams sorted in a configurable category structure.

Model types   Provides the classic list of PowerDesigner model types and diagrams.

Template files   Provides a set of model templates sorted by model type.

Figure 10.72 demonstrates two of these views. The background shows the 'Model Types' view, with the 'Categories' view in the foreground. In the 'Model Types' view, the left-hand pane lists the types of model your license allows you to create, and the right-hand pane shows the types of default diagrams that can be created in the selected type of model. The Category view groups diagram types rather than model types. Select a Category on the left, and the available types of diagrams are displayed on the right. Use the '*Views*' tool on the upper right hand side of the dialog to switch between large icons and a list in the right-hand pane. Below these two panes, the two views show the same fields, which you should check before creating a model.

Figure 10.72 New model window

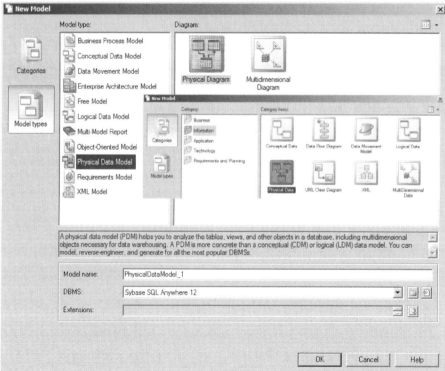

1. Select either 'Categories' or 'Model types'.
2. Select an entry in the left-hand pane.
3. Select an option in the right-hand pane.
4. Enter a model name. The model name will be the default file name when you save the model for the first time – you can, of course, change the model name after creating it, via the Browser.
5. [PDM] Select a target resource file, which customizes PowerDesigner's default modifying environment with target-specific properties, objects, and generation templates. In Figure 10.72, the resource files available provide specific support for different DBMS. If you need to change the DBMS after creating the model, use the option Change Current DBMS on the Database menu.
6. [optional] Click the 'Select Extensions' button (if available) and attach one or more extensions to your model.
7. Click <OK> to create and open the model – the model will probably contain one blank diagram of the type selected in the right-hand pane. If your model is based on a template model, the content will depend on the template.

The code of the model, used for script or code generation, is derived from the model name using the model naming conventions.

There is also a simple way to create a new model in the Browser:

1. Right-click a folder or Project node
2. Select New
3. Choose the type of model you want to create
4. The New Model window opens, but only shows the selected type of model.

In this book, we are only concerned with three types of models: Conceptual Data Model (CDM), Logical Data Model (LDM), and Physical Data Model (PDM). See Chapter 25 to find out about the other types of models.

During model generation, PowerDesigner will create models automatically – see Chapter 18.

◉ "Creating a Model" (Core Features Guide)

Removing an Unsaved Model

If you have not saved a new model, it only exists in the workspace, not in the file system. If you've created a model by mistake, or just decide you don't need to keep it, it is easy to remove: just right-click the model name in the Browser, and select Detach from Workspace. PowerDesigner will ask if you want to save it, so click <No> – the model will disappear from the workspace, and all traces of it will be removed.

You can also delete a model by selecting the model name in the Browser, and pressing <Delete>, or by closing the project and/or workspace without saving changes.

GUIDs

When you save a model for the first time, PowerDesigner automatically assigns a unique identifying number called a GUID (Global Unique ID) to the model, and creates a backup copy of your file with the same identifying number. The GUID is used to identify documents in the Repository and during model generation. Every object within the model also has a GUID.

GUIDs are vital for keeping models in sync with the repository, and for linking models to each other. The use of GUIDs allows PowerDesigner to maintain model and object links, even when you rename or move them. GUIDs are actually surrogate keys, which we will discuss in Chapter 7.

Saving Models

If a Project or model contains unsaved changes, PowerDesigner appends an asterisk to the name in the Browser ⊞ Project Management (CDM) * . You can save one Project or model at a time, or all the models in the workspace.

The following formats are available when you save a model for the first time:

XML [default format]   Larger and somewhat slower to load than binary, but the model file can be edited in a text editor outside of PowerDesigner. Recommended for small to medium-sized models.

Binary   Smaller and faster to load than XML, but cannot be edited outside of PowerDesigner. Recommended for large models.

To save your model, do one of the following.

- *To perform a standard save – just one model*: Select File|Save, click the 'Save' tool ⊞, or right-click the model entry in the Browser and select Save from the contextual menu. If you did not define a file name when you created the new model, the Save As dialog box asks you to provide a name and a path for the file of the new model.
- *To save the model in a different format*: Select File|Save As, or right-click the model node in the Browser and select Save As. Change the file type in 'Save as type'. Unless you supply a different file name, the existing file will be overwritten with the new format.
- *To save changes to the workspace and save all changes in every open Project and model*: Either click on the 'Save All' tool ⊞, press <Ctrl+F3>, or select Save All on the File menu. When you close a workspace, you are prompted to save unsaved changes to projects, models, or the workspace itself.
- *To save the model as a new model with the same GUID*: Select File|Save As, or right-click the model node in the Browser and select Save As. This allows you to create a backup version of a model with the same GUID as the original. The model will have the same name as the original model, but the filename will be different.

- *To save the model as a new model with a new GUID*: Select File|Save As New Model, or right-click the model node in the Browser and select Save As New Model. This allows you to develop two separate models in parallel, starting from the same set of model objects. Note that if you check the new model into a Repository, the Update mode will not be available. External shortcuts located in the new model may also not work properly since the identity of the model has changed.

Table 10.11 describes scenarios where you would use Save As and Save As New Model.

Table 10.11 Saving strategies

Action	New model GUID	When to use
Save As	same as original model GUID	To create a replica of a model, perhaps to share work between modelers, or to experiment with alternative approaches. You can merge the replica back into the original model, either locally using Tools|Merge Model, or by checking it in to the repository (you may need to rename it to match the original model name).
		To save the model in a different format (e.g. save in binary format to improve performance).
Save as New Model	different from original model GUID	To create a new model initially based on the contents of an existing model, where the new model will change radically from the original. If you need to do this frequently, consider saving the original model as a template model, or share it via the Library facility.

A side effect of saving as a new model is that the shortcut in the workspace is changed: it will now reference the new file, not the original one. If you just want to make a backup copy of a file, you should do that in Windows Explorer. If you really do want a copy of the model with a new GUID, you should tread very carefully, or you may find that a Project refers to the wrong file. You may even try to check in the new file instead of the old one (PowerDesigner will not allow you to do this – it knows that it is not the same model, that's what the GUID is for).

To avoid the shortcut changing permanently, close the workspace without saving it. When you re-open it, the shortcut will be OK, though you may have lost other workspace changes.

- "Saving a Model" (Core Features Guide)
- "Models" (Core Features Guide)

Backup Files

Every time you save a model, PowerDesigner creates a backup file, so you can revert to the previously saved version of a file if a catastrophe strikes. The backup file is saved in the same folder as the original file, and the backup file name is derived from the original filename, by replacing the last letter of the file type with 'm'. For example, the file "Chapter 10.cdb" is the backup for "Chapter 10.cdm".

In addition, you can tell PowerDesigner to save backup files periodically, depending on the Autosave setting in General Options.

This setting instructs PowerDesigner to save changes to all open models to a recovery backup file at the specified interval. Enabling this option provides you with a recovery option if PowerDesigner or your computer crash before you have had a chance to save your changes. The save will take place after the interval has passed, but only when PowerDesigner is idle for more than ten seconds. Note that saving large or multiple models may take several seconds, and that PowerDesigner will not be responsive while it is performing the save.

Deleting a Model

In "Removing an Unsaved Model" we saw that you can detach a model from the workspace. You can also delete a model from the PowerDesigner workspace. This is almost the same action as detaching the model from the workspace – the difference is that you have the opportunity to run an impact analysis first.

To delete a model, select the diagram node in the Browser and press the <Del> key. The standard confirmation window is displayed in Figure 10.73.

Figure 10.73 Confirmation window

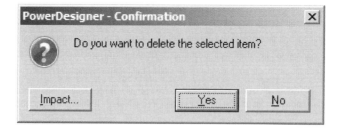

Click on <Yes> to delete the model; click on <No> or press <Esc> to change your mind. Click on <Impact...> to run the impact and lineage analysis for the model, to find out about connections between this model and others. You can find out more about this in Chapter 23 – look for "Impact and Lineage Analysis".

When you click <Yes>, the entry for the model is removed from the workspace, and from any project diagrams (see the next section) it appears on, but the file containing the model is not deleted. Any references to the model in other models are also not deleted.

The model can be added back to the workspace at any time.

Projects

A Project allows you to group together all the models and other types of documents you need for a particular modeling task, and save them as a single entity in your repository.

Unlike Workspaces, Projects have been designed for sharing with co-workers, either via a common folder, or via the repository. A project can contain one or more project diagrams, which show the connections between models and other documents in the Project. Remember PowerDesigner uses a briefcase icon to represent a project in the Browser.

PowerDesigner uses the phrase 'Project Directory' to refer to the Windows folder where the model files are located, and the phrase 'Project Folder' to refer to the Project container in the Browser. To avoid confusion, we use the same convention. Every project has its own Project Directory, usually with the same name as the Project, and project files can be inside or outside the folder – any file that is outside the folder has a shortcut symbol on the Browser icon. PowerDesigner will move any such file into the Project directory if you need to – just right-click the shortcut symbol, and select `Move to Project Directory`.

Creating a Project

You can create a project from scratch or from a template. Just click on the briefcase icon on the standard toolbar, and the 'New Project' window will open as shown in Figure 10.74.

Figure 10.74 Creating a project

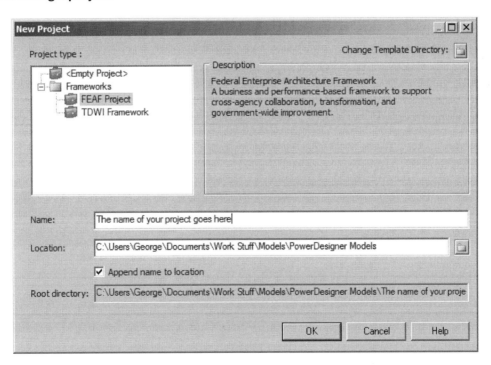

Here you can choose to create an empty project, or a project based on a framework. A framework is a pre-defined project template – see Chapter 23 for an example. Give your project a name, carefully review the location where it will be created, and click <OK>. PowerDesigner will create the project directory; if you have chosen a framework, then all default content will be created within the project. See Chapter 23 for an example.

● If a model is part of a project, do not include it in any other project; the model is aware of the parent project. If you need access to the model from more than one workspace, include the Project (not just the model) in each workspace.

● If a model is part of a project, you must open the project before opening the model. If you open a Project model without the Project being in the workspace, the message in Figure 10.75 appears.

Figure 10.75 Opening outside the project

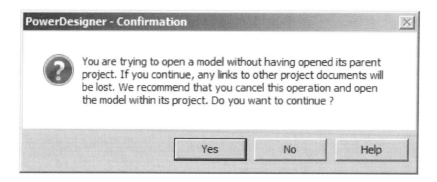

We recommend that you cancel this operation, open the Project, and then open the model from the Browser. Remember, the model file will probably be in the same Windows folder as the project file.

● "Projects and Frameworks" (Core Features Guide)

Adding Models to a Project

There are two ways to create a new model in a project:

- Right-click the Project name in the Browser, select New, and choose the type of model
- Select the Project name in the Browser, and use the tool bar or File menu shortcuts to create a model.

When you create a model this way, the Project Directory is the default location for saving them.

Project Diagrams

When you create a project, PowerDesigner automatically creates a project diagram for you. Project diagrams show models, external files, and the links between them. For example, Figure 10.76 shows a simple project diagram. Each box represents a model, and each link represents a target model connection. The name on each link describes the reason why the link exists. It is possible for models to have several links connecting them.

Over time, the project diagram may get out of date. On the `Tools` menu, select `Rebuild Dependency Links` to bring it up to date.

Figure 10.76 A project diagram

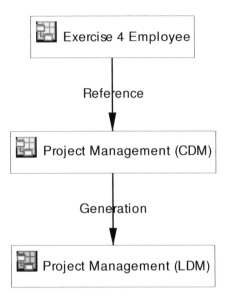

Double-click a box to open a model, or double-click a link to see summary information about it. The detail shown in the 'Dependencies' tab will vary depending on the type of dependency, and whether or not the linked models are open. For example, Figure 10.77 shows the 'Dependencies' tab for the 'Reference' link in Figure 10.76. Here you can see details of the actual objects concerned. Each entry is active – you can double-click it to open the property sheet.

Figure 10.77 Model dependencies

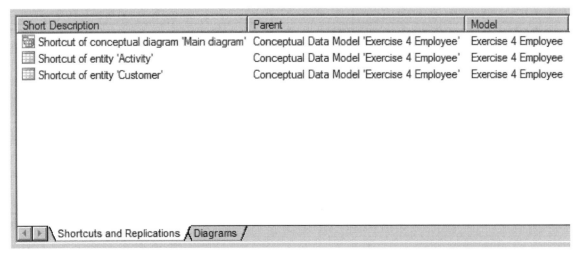

● "Project Diagrams" (Core Features Guide)

Using Frameworks

If your Project includes a Framework Diagram, then you will have access to shortcuts that enable you to do more than just create an empty diagram. See Chapter 23.

Opening a Model, Project, or Workspace

The best way to open a model, project, or workspace is in the Browser, although you can open one from Windows Explorer, as well (see below).

If you have opened the model before, the shortcut to it may exist in one of the workspaces you opened previously. Remember, each model entry in a Workspace or Project is a shortcut to a model file. See Figure 10.78 for examples. The best way to open a model is to double-click the model name. Alternatively, right-click the model name, and select Open or Open as Read-only. When you select a model shortcut in the Browser, PowerDesigner displays the model path at the foot of the PowerDesigner window.	**Figure 10.78 Model shortcuts in the Browser** 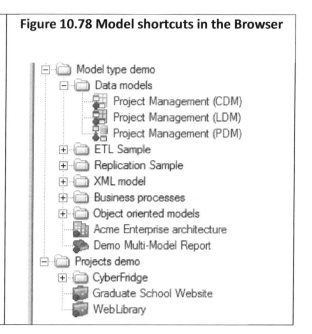

Two options on the File menu provide access to files, projects, and workspaces you opened recently, depicted in Figure 10.79. It is always advisable to open a workspace or project before opening a model.

Figure 10.79 Recent files

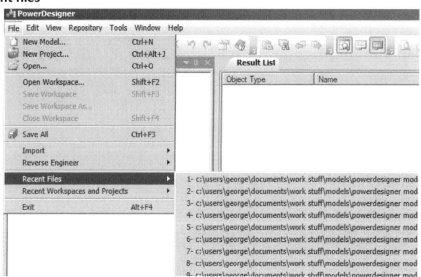

Moving Models Around

Workspaces contain links to projects, models, and file. Projects contain links to models and files. Models contain links to other models. Each link is a shortcut to the location of the model or file. These links will all work forever if none of the files move. In real life, files are moved between folders, and files do get renamed.

If you double-click a model shortcut in your workspace and the file does not exist in the expected location, PowerDesigner will ask you for help. If the file exists in the repository, it will display the options shown in Figure 10.80, giving you the option of retrieving the model or file from the repository. If you choose not to do that, or the model is not in the repository, PowerDesigner will display the options shown in Figure 10.81. Click on <Yes>, and then browse your folders to find the model. If it really is missing, all may not be lost – rename and open the backup file that PowerDesigner created for you.

Figure 10.80 File not found 1st option

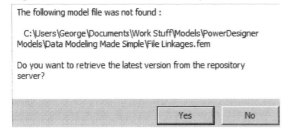

Figure 10.81 File not found 2nd option

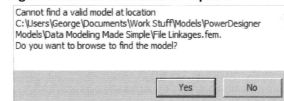

When a model contains links to other models, PowerDesigner refers to those 'other' models as 'Target Models'. When you have a model open, select `Target Models` on the `Tools` menu to see a list of target models. You can edit this yourself, if you know the new location of the file.

When you open a model, PowerDesigner checks this list of target models. If a target model file was renamed or moved, PowerDesigner will attempt to find the model itself, using the model GUID. Sometimes it will ask for confirmation with a message similar to that in Figure 10.82. In this case, the filename for the target model was changed – just click <Yes> to link to the new file name.

Figure 10.82 An unresolved target model

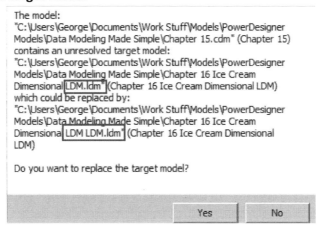

If you delete an entry from the list of target models, every link to that model will be removed – this can include shortcuts, replicas, generation links, and traceability links.

Absolute vs. Relative File Shortcuts

This is a dry topic for a data modeling book, so please bear with us. You may never need to understand this topic, but it may help you to understand what happens when PowerDesigner cannot find a file.

There are two types of file shortcuts maintained by PowerDesigner, absolute and relative.

Absolute The shortcut describes the exact location of the file, such as
`C:\Users\Fred\Documents\Models\My Project\My LDM.ldm`.
If you move or rename My LDM.ldm, PowerDesigner will not be able to find it.

Relative The shortcut describes the location of the file, relative to the location of the current file. The simplest form of relative shortcut just provides a filename – the file is assumed to be in the same folder as the current file.

Figure 10.83 shows the potential links between files in PowerDesigner, and the type of shortcut used for each one.

Figure 10.83 File shortcuts

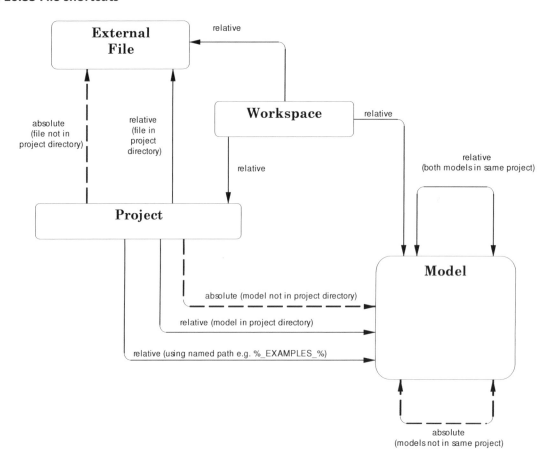

A few simple conclusions can be drawn from Figure 10.83. Follow these and your life will be easier:

- Always use projects to manage related models, and never move individual project files – always move the entire project
- Always keep project files in the project directory
- Keep your models in a dedicated folder structure, with one folder for each project.

Partitioning a Model

Dividing a large model into manageable chunks is a common feature of data modeling tools; they may be called submodels, subject areas, packages, etc. In PowerDesigner, you can divide a model using packages.

Packages

A package is a subset of a model. When working with large models, you can split them into smaller subdivisions to avoid manipulating the entire model at once. Packages can be used to organize your model into different tasks and subject areas, and to assign parts of it to different modelers.

You can create as many packages as you need in a model, just remember that every package name must be unique within the model. You can create packages within packages – there is no limitation to the number of package layers.

Packages can contain the same kinds of items as models:

- Model objects
- Other packages
- Diagrams.

Each package has its own default diagram, which will always be present. This is demonstrated by Figure 10.84, which shows the Browser view of an LDM called 'Chapter 5', created to provide images for this book. The highlighted entry (**Figure 5.20**) is a package: packages are always shown at the top of the content of a model or parent package. The model also contains two diagrams (called **Figure 5.19** and **Figure 5.70**) and several entities. One of the entity entries (**Member**) has a shortcut symbol in the corner of the icon – this tells you that this entity is a shortcut to an object held elsewhere. Figure 10.85 shows what happens when you include this entity in a model diagram - the entity symbol includes a shortcut arrow to indicate that the object is a shortcut, and the name of the package (**Figure 5.20**) to which the entity belongs.

By default, a package uses the parent *namespace* – the names of objects within the package must be unique in the model. The *Use parent namespace* property on the 'General' tab of the property sheet allows you to override this behavior – unchecking this option allows the objects in the package to have the same name as objects elsewhere in the model.

Figure 10.84 A package example   **Figure 10.85 Shortcut to a package entity**

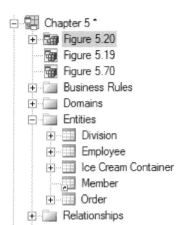

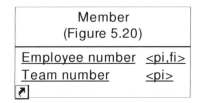

You can right-click the package name in the Browser to view lists of objects in the package and sub-packages, in the same way as you can for the full model.

When to use Packages in Data Models

- To group entities by subject area
- To manage access privileges in the repository
- To hold shortcuts to objects created outside the model – these shortcuts are added to the model when you add traceability links
- To hold objects that you do not want to have generated into new models – this is useful in a PDM, where you want to retain (but not generate) tables that have been denormalized via transformations.

- "Packages" (Core Features Guide)
- "Converting a Diagram to a Package" (Core Features Guide)
- "Moving a Diagram to a Package" (Core Features Guide)
- "Moving Entities Between Packages in a CDM" (Core Features Guide)

Model Extensions

We have mentioned model extensions a few times. PowerDesigner uses extensions to provide new objects, additional properties for objects, new connections between objects, and changes to the standard property sheets. If you add a new property to an entity for example, a new extension is automatically created in the model. Extensions are visible in the Browser. Figure 10.86 shows a model with three extensions. The two with a shortcut symbol in their icon are shortcuts to extension files – these are files containing common extensions. The third extension (Entity properties) exists within the model, not in an external file.

You will create your own local extension in Exercise 18. Also see Chapter 23 for more on extensions.

Figure 10.86 Extensions in the Browser

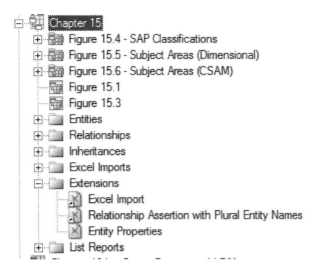

Attaching Extensions to an Existing Model

1. Select `Model|Extensions` to open the List of Extensions.
2. Click the '*Import*' tool to open the *Select Extensions* dialog.
3. Review the different types of extensions available by clicking on the sub-tabs, and then select one or more to attach to your model.
    - Ensure that you open the property sheet for the extension and read the *Comment* property, which will provide guidance on how to get the best out of the extension
    - For example, the *Comment* property for the extension **Relationship Assertion with Plural Entity Names** lists four steps you must follow in order for the extension to be effective within a model:

1. Select `Tools|Model Options|Assertion template`.
2. Select this extension file in the Assertion Extension list.
3. Replace the standard template in the main text box with the following call to the plural template: %pluralAssertion%
4. Click <OK> to save your changes.

Finding Things Again

Have you lost an entity? Do you want a list of entities with no Description?

You need to run 'Find Objects'. There are three ways to do this:

- Search local models that are currently open
- Search the repository – this provides the same features as a local search, but you can search all the models you have access to
- Search via the PowerDesigner web portal – this searches the repository, and provides more comprehensive capabilities, and the ability to save search criteria.

Searching Local Models

Look on the Edit menu, or press <Ctrl+F>. The Find Objects dialog is shown in Figure 10.87.

Figure 10.87 Finding objects

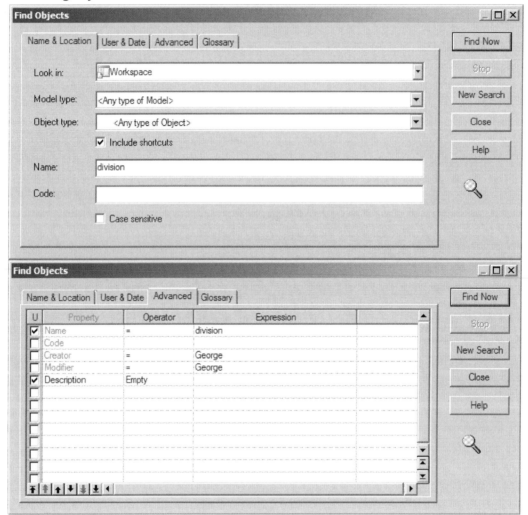

You can search the workspace, a folder, a project, or a model, and you can supply an expression for name searches. The first tab shown in Figure 10.87 shows a search for objects called 'division'. The second tab shows that we can specify additional criteria: in this case, we're looking for objects with an empty description.

The results of a search are displayed in the 'Result lists' window; you can see a sample in Figure 10.88.

Figure 10.88 Search results

Object Type	Name	Code	Location	Match Type
Shortcut of Entity	Thesis	THESIS	Chapter 7::Figure 7.14	
Entity	Thesis	THESIS	Chapter 7::Figure 7.14	
Entity	Thesis	THESIS	Chapter 7	

A summary of the search results is also shown in the 'General' tab on the 'Output' window.

Our search found two entities and a shortcut to an entity. We can access any of these objects: double-clicking will open the property sheet, and right-clicking on the name will display the contextual menu, which will allow us to find the object in the Browser or diagram, carry out an impact analysis, open the object's property sheet, or clear the results list. We can also copy an entity to the clipboard or delete it.

The result list stays in place until we clear it, hide it, run another search, or shut down PowerDesigner.

 Remember that you can use the View toolbar to hide and display the Result list.

Searching the Repository

To search the repository, select `Find Objects` on the `Repository` menu, or press <Ctrl+Alt+F>. The repository search works in the same way as the local search, except that the 'Glossary' options have been replaced with options regarding 'Repository Dates'.

Searching via the Web Portal

The portal provides a quick search facility, which allows you to search for uses of textual terms. The advanced search facility allows you to specify more complicated and multiple search criteria.

After performing a search, you can:

- generate an Excel or PDF version of your results
- search within your results
- modify your search string
- make your search available for reuse.

Unless your search has a very narrow focus, or you only need to search models you have not checked in, you should always search the repository. You will have more success, as it will search every model you have access to.

 "Finding Objects" (Core Features Guide)
"Finding Objects in the Repository" (Core Features Guide)
"PowerDesigner Portal Search" (Core Features Guide)
"Find Parameters" (Core Features Guide)
"Defining a Filter Expression" (Core Features Guide)

YOUR TURN TO PLAY

1. Open the three *Project Management* models, and then press <Ctrl+F> to open the `Find Objects` dialog.

2. Take a look at the tabs, and then come back to the 'Name & Location' tab'.
3. In 'Look In', select the Workspace option.
4. In 'Model type', select 'Any type of model'.
5. Type the following into 'Name' - *employee*.
6. Click on 'Find Now'.
7. Open the 'General' tab on the 'Output window' to see a summary of the search results; right-click the summary, and select 'Clear'.
8. Open the 'Result List' window to see the detailed search results. This looks a lot like a list of objects, although it contains more than one type of object, and the results cannot be filtered. However, you can sort the list by clicking on the column headings.
9. Right-click any object in the list to access a contextual menu. This shows options you've seen before except for the 'Clear' option, which will clear the contents of the Result list.
10. Double-click any column in the list to open the property sheet.
11. Click on the 'Property Sheet Menu' (to the right of the 'Less' or 'More' button), and select 'Parent Properties' to open the property sheet for the table that contains the column. See Figure 10.89.

Figure 10.89 Accessing parent properties

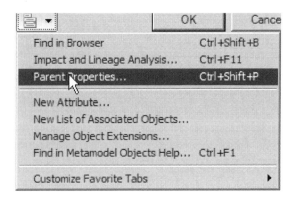

12. Click on the 'Property Sheet Menu' in the property sheet for the table, to open the property sheet for the model.
13. Close the property sheets.

EXERCISE 8: Creating your own Workspace, Project and Models

This is your first exercise using PowerDesigner, so we'll guide you through what you need to do.

Here's a summary of what you're going to do:

1. Open the Demo workspace, and save two of the Demo models as new files
2. Create a new workspace for exercises, called 'Exercises'
3. Create a folder and project in the Exercises workspace, both called 'Exercise 8', then bring the copies of the Demo models into your project and look at the project diagram
4. Move the files into your Project directory, and look again at the project diagram

5. Create a new Free Model with the 'Excel Import' extension attached, and then detach it from the workspace
6. Create a new CDM, copy several entities across from the existing CDM, create shortcuts to several others, and then look again at the project diagram
7. Create a new diagram in the new CDM, and add selected entities
8. Rename or delete several items via the Browser, then add missing relationships
9. Decorate the diagram with notes and other symbols
10. Change the appearance and layout of the project diagram
11. Use Windows Explorer to see the files in the project directory
12. Close and save the workspace.

Start PowerDesigner, and you are ready to begin.

1. Open the Demo workspace, and save two of the Demo models as new files

Use Windows Explorer to create a new folder called 'Exercises', wherever you intend to keep your PowerDesigner models.

Open the Sybase Demo workspace that we've looked at before. If you still have the Welcome screen in front of you, select 'demo.sws' from the list of recent projects and workspaces. If you hover the mouse over the name, the tooltip will tell you which folder it's in. You can also see the same list of recent projects and workspaces via the `File` menu. Select `Recent Workspaces and Projects`, and the Demo workspace will be near or at the top of the list.

Open the model called 'Project Management (CDM)', right-click the model name, and choose `Save As`. Save the model in your new folder, and call it 'Exercise 8.cdm'. Do the same with the model 'Project Management (LDM)', calling it 'Exercise 8.ldm'.

Now close the Demo workspace without saving any models. Don't worry, your new files will be OK, you've already saved them.

2. Create a new workspace for exercises, called 'Exercises'

You now have an empty workspace displayed. Use `File|Open` to open the two new models. If you're following these steps, the 'Exercises' folder is the last place in which PowerDesigner saved anything, so it's the suggested location for opening models.

PowerDesigner has a very small memory for folders; it only remembers the last place you saved 'something'. It is up to you to remember where your models are. Remember that you can see lists of recent files, projects, and workspaces via the `File` menu.

In the `File` menu, select `Save Workspace`, and save it in the 'Exercises' folder. Call it 'Exercises.sws'.

3. **Create a folder and project in the 'Exercises' workspace, both called 'Exercise 8', then bring the copies of the Demo models into your project and look at the project diagram**

In the Browser, right-click the word 'Workspace', select New, and then Folder. Type 'Exercise 8' and press <OK>. In the File menu, select New Project, and then type 'Exercise 8'. Make sure that the *Location* property contains the path to your 'Exercises' folder, and that 'Append name to Location' is selected. Now press <OK>. You should now have two models at the top level of the workspace, along with a folder, which contains a project. The drawing Canvas will be blank, as it shows an empty project diagram.

In the Browser, select both of the models, and drag them onto the project name. They will move into the hierarchy below the project, and icons for them will appear on the project diagram. They will be connected by a line labeled 'Generation', reflecting the fact that the LDM was generated from the CDM. Notice that both model icons have a shortcut arrow on them because the files are stored outside the project directory.

4. **Move the files into your Project directory, and look again at the project diagram**

Select one of the models, right-click the mouse, and then select Move to Project Directory. Do the same with the other model. In the Window menu, select the entry starting with 'PRJ Exercise 8', to bring the project diagram to the front. You'll see that the shortcut arrows have been removed from the icons. At this point, it is a good idea to click the 'Save All' button on the 'Standard' toolbar. This will save all the models, the project, and the workspace.

5. **Create a new Free Model, with the 'Excel Import' extension attached, and then detach it from the workspace**

In the Browser, select the 'Exercise 8' folder, and then click on the 'New Model' button on the 'Standard' toolbar. The window you can now see allows you to create any type of model. Select 'Free Model', and call it anything you like, because we're not going to keep it. Before you click on <OK>, click on the 'Select Extensions' button near the bottom right corner. The 'Select Extensions' window allows you to select extensions to PowerDesigner; select any or all of them that sound interesting, then click on <OK>, and <OK>, again. The Browser folder will contain a new Free Model, and the default diagram will be open on the Canvas.

As the name suggests, Extensions provide the ability to extend or alter PowerDesigner's capabilities. We'll tell you more about this later, but please don't expect a detailed tutorial!

Let's assume that we did this by mistake, and we don't want to keep this model. Because we haven't saved it yet, we can just remove it from the workspace. Right-click the model name in the Browser, and select 'Detach from 'Workspace'. PowerDesigner will ask if you want to save it, so click on 'No'; the model is gone from the workspace. Selecting the model name and pressing <Delete> will also do the trick.

6. **Create a new CDM, copy several entities across from the existing CDM, create shortcuts to several others, and then look again at the project diagram**

Right-click the project, select 'New', and create a Conceptual Data Model called 'Exercise 8 Employee'. Make sure you select both of the available extensions.

In the 'Project Management (CDM)' model, open the 'Main diagram', and select the following entities, along with all the relationships connecting them. The <Shift> key will be useful here:

Entities: **Division, Employee, Team.**

Hold down the <Ctrl> key, drag the selection into the Browser, and drop it onto the name of the CDM you created. The entities will be copied into the new model, and should still exist in 'Project Management (CDM)'. If they have been removed from 'Project Management (CDM)', you forgot to hold down <Ctrl>. Use the Undo tool ↶ to undo the changes, and try again.

In the 'Project Management (CDM)' model, select the following entities in the Browser, then copy them using the main menu, contextual menu, or keyboard shortcuts:

Entities: **Activity, Customer.**

Now right-click the name of the CDM you created, select Edit and Paste As Shortcut.

The new CDM will now contain five entities, two of which are shortcuts to the original CDM. It should look something like Figure 10.90.

Figure 10.90 Five entities, so far

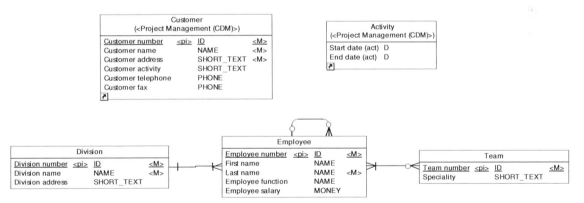

Now click on the 'Save All' button. PowerDesigner will ask if you want to save the unsaved models; click 'Yes', and then click 'Save' to save the new CDM with the default file name (which is the same as the model name).

7. **Create a new diagram in the new CDM, and add selected entities**

Right-click the name of the new CDM, select New, then Conceptual Diagram. Call the diagram 'Exercise 8', and select 'Default Diagram'. Click on <OK>.

Select the **Division,** **Employee,** and **Team** entities in the Browser, and drag them onto the new diagram. The entities will appear on the diagram, but not the relationships, although the relationships do appear in the Browser. We'll get back to them in a minute.

8. Rename or delete several items via the Browser, then add missing relationships

The content and style of the entities will be the PowerDesigner default, unless you have saved any of your previous Display Preferences as the default. Press the <F8> key to center the model in the Canvas, then press <F6> to zoom in (and <F7> to zoom out), as many times as you need for the entity symbols to be a good size to work with.

Select the **Employee** entity in the diagram and click on the name. It should turn into an 'edit box', allowing you to retype the name. Change the name to **Old Entity**; the entity name will change in the Browser as well. Now change the name back to **Employee**, this time using the Browser.

In the Browser, select 'Diagram_1' in the CDM you created. Press <Delete>, and click on <Yes> when you're asked if you're sure.

Now select the **Activity** entity, and then press <Delete>. Don't click on <Yes> or <No> just yet, click on the <Impact...> button. This opens up the 'Impact and Lineage Analysis' window, using the standard 'delete' rule set. If you want to see the properties of the entity to which this is a shortcut, double-click where it says "Shortcut 'Activity' [Delete]", and the property sheet will be opened. Close the impact analysis window, and click 'No' to deleting the entity.

Select the **Activity** and **Customer** entities, and drag them onto the 'Exercise 8' diagram. They are shortcuts to entities in a different model, so the symbols include the shortcut symbol in the corner.

The relationships are still missing from the diagram, and there are two ways to include them. First, the Show Symbols command is on the Symbol menu and on the diagram contextual menu, within Diagram. Run the command, and you will see a screen containing three tabs that allow you to select any of the entities, relationships, or diagrams in the model. That's right, a diagram can contain a shortcut to another diagram, even a diagram in a different model.

It is possible to add entities to the diagram this way by accident, by including a relationship that involves an entity that you do not have on the diagram.

The quickest and best way to include missing relationships is to use the 'Complete Links' command. You can access this via a button on the 'Diagram' toolbar, the Tools menu, or by pressing <Ctrl+F5>. With this method, you cannot choose what will or will not be included on the diagram, but you do not have to work out what is missing. PowerDesigner will add every relationship that should be on the diagram because both of the participating entities appear on the diagram.

Run 'Complete Links' whichever way you prefer, to add the missing relationships. Experiment with the options on the 'Layout' toolbar or the symbol menu to create a tidy diagram. There are only three relationships, so it will not take long.

Click on the 'Save All' button.

9. Decorate the diagram with notes and other symbols

Carry on working in the diagram called 'Exercise 8'.

Select the *Title* tool ⬛ in the Free Symbols palette in the Toolbox, and draw a title box. Press the right mouse button to return to the arrow pointer, then right-click the title box and select Format – change the line style and font to make the Title stand out better.

Now double-click the Title box – the property sheet for the model will open. By default, the 'General' and 'Notes' tabs are available. Click on the <More> button to display all the tabs. The model has a standard set of tabs, just like other objects.

Click on the 'Related Diagrams' tab and click on the *Add Objects* tool ⬛ to display the 'Add Objects' dialog, as shown in Figure 10.91.

Figure 10.91 Add objects dialog

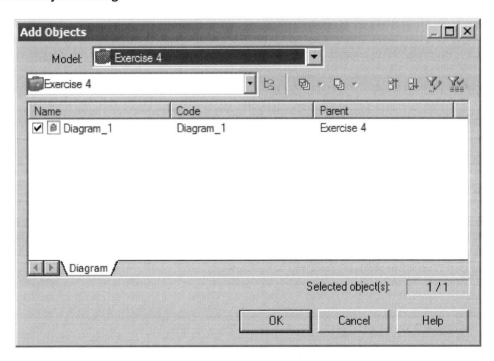

This allows you to select any diagram(s) in any project or model that is currently open. Select the Exercise 8 Project diagram and click <OK>. PowerDesigner will create a dependency between the CDM and the Project Diagram. This is visible on the 'Related Diagrams' tab of the CDM's property sheet, and on the 'Dependencies' tab of the project diagram's property sheet. To see the dependency, right-click the project diagram in the Browser, select Properties from the contextual menu, and then select the 'Dependencies' tab.

Select the 'Rectangle' tool on the 'Free Symbols' palette, and draw a rectangle on the diagram – make sure that two of your entities are completely inside the rectangle. Change the cursor back to the standard arrow pointer. Double-click the rectangle to open the Text window, and select the 'RTF' radio button. Select the *Format* tool, and change the default font style and size; now type a label for the rectangle, and press <OK>. The label will appear inside the rectangle – the exact position will depend on the display preferences.

Try out the ordering of symbols. From the rectangle's contextual menu, select Order|Bring to Front – it will obscure everything that falls within its borders. Now do it again, this time selecting Send to Back. Finally, select Format from the Contextual Menu, change the Line and Fill colors to any colors you like, and the Text Alignment to 'Left' and 'Top', and press <OK>. If you want to, you can change the font.

Now use the 'Note' tool on the 'Predefined Symbols' palette to draw a Note symbol; change the cursor back to the standard arrow pointer, right-click the rectangle symbol, and select Get Format from the contextual menu. Select Apply Format on the contextual menu for the Note symbol. The Note will now have the same format as the rectangle. The result should look something like Figure 10.92.

Figure 10.92 Apply format

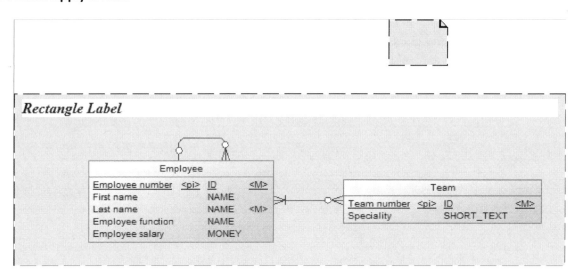

Select the *Link/Traceability Link* tool on the 'Free Symbols' palette, and draw a link from the Note to one of the entities inside the rectangle. Part of the line is behind the rectangle, so use the contextual menu for the link to bring the link to the front. Double-click the link – the text box you see here is similar to the text box for the rectangle, except that it allows you to specify up to three blocks of text, each of which will appear at a different point on the line.

Finally, on the contextual menu for the note, select 'Change Image'. The 'Select Image' dialog (see Figure 10.93) allows you to choose another image for the symbol. Browse the options available, and choose a symbol.

Most of the images available will obscure any text you may have added to the note.

Figure 10.93 Change the image

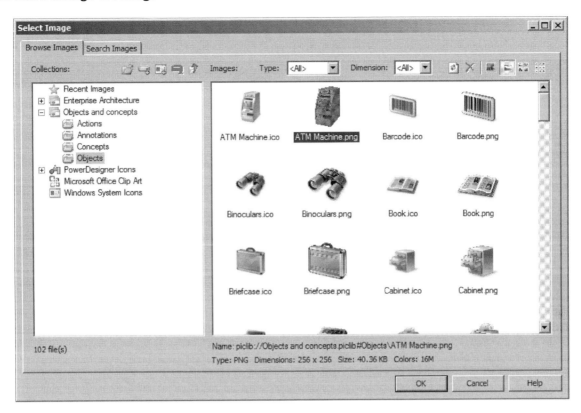

10. Change the appearance and layout of the project diagram

On the `Window` menu, select `Close All` to tidy things up. Open the Project diagram called 'Diagram_1', and run 'Show Symbols' to include your new CDM.

The 'Model' icon has been added to the diagram, along with a link to 'Project Management (CDM)', labeled 'Reference'. If you double-click the line, it will open the property sheet for the link – click on the 'Dependencies' tab to see details of the objects . You may need to click on 'More >>' to make the tab visible.

If the original CDM is open, you will see a list of the entities you copied across as shortcuts. You can double-click the entities, and open their property sheets. If your original CDM is closed, you will only see the name of the project diagram here.

Please close any open property sheets.

Now for some quick cosmetic changes. Select all symbols on the diagram, and then press <Ctrl+Q>. The model icons are replaced with boxes. Now select `Auto-Layout` on the `Symbol` menu, and select the 'Hierarchical' layout, with 'Top to Bottom' orientation. You may also want to click on <Set as Default> to save your choice as the default layout for that type of diagram. When you click on <OK>, the diagram will be re-drawn as a vertical hierarchy.

11. Use Windows Explorer to see the files in the project directory

Use Windows Explorer to open the folder you created in step 1. It should contain a folder called 'Exercise 8', and the workspace file (Exercises.sws). Open the folder 'Exercise 8': this is what PowerDesigner calls the *Project Directory*. It will contain the project file (Exercise 8.prj), and three model files (two CDMs and one LDM). It will also contain backup files that Power Designer has created,

12. Close and save the workspace

Close the workspace, making sure to save all the models.

See the Appendix for the final CDM and project diagrams.

Key Points

- The interface can be as cluttered or uncluttered as you want it to be.

- Contextual menus are available everywhere.

- Menu options depend on the current diagram on the canvas.

- Object property sheets allow you to do much more than just edit a single object.

- Common sorting, selection and filtering functions in any list of objects or sub-objects.

- Save frequently - don't forget that you can still undo.

- An object can have many symbols, sometimes more than one on a diagram.

- Let PowerDesigner route your links for you.

- Add relationships and other objects to diagrams using 'show symbols'.

- Decorate diagrams and customize symbol images and content to aid communication.

- Workspaces and projects are essential tools for managing multiple models.

- Search via the repository for best results.

CHAPTER 11
How do I create entities in PowerDesigner?

Draw, import, refine
Relationships add the lines
Attributes, detail

In this chapter, we will show you how to create a simple data model with six entities, shown in Table 11.1. Make sure you understand the content of Chapter 10 before you start.

Table 11.1 Our six entities

Entity Name	Definition
Ice Cream Cone	An edible container which can hold one or more ice cream scoops.
Ice Cream Container	A holder of ice cream that is either edible, in the case of an ice cream cone, or recyclable, in the case of an ice cream cup.
Ice Cream Cup	A recyclable container that can hold one or more ice cream scoops.
Ice Cream Flavor	The distinctive taste of one ice cream product over another. Flavors are recognized and selected by consumers. Examples include Chocolate, Vanilla, and Strawberry.
Ice Cream Theme	A group of ice cream flavors that share at least one common property. For example, the Brownie Ice Cream and Cake Batter Ice Cream flavors are grouped into the Cake Ice Cream Theme.
Order	Also known as an ice cream sale, an order is when a consumer purchases one or more of our products in a single visit to our ice cream store.

There are three main methods for creating entities: drawing them on a diagram, adding them via the Browser, and adding them via object lists.

Drawing New Entities

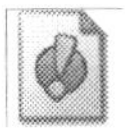

You'll probably create most new entities by drawing them on a diagram. To add any type of symbol on a diagram, you have to click on a tool in the Toolbox. Objects, such as Entities or Tables, can be created independently in any free space in the diagram, while links, such as relationships, are drawn as connections between existing objects.

To create a new Entity in a Conceptual Data Model, click on the ▦ tool in the Conceptual Diagram palette in the Toolbox. You'll notice that the cursor shape has changed from a pointer to the entity icon ▦. If the icon is not available on the Toolbox, then your current diagram is not a Conceptual Diagram. You can bring the Conceptual Diagram to the front by clicking on the diagram's tab.

While the cursor displays the entity icon, you can click anywhere on the Canvas, and a new entity symbol will appear. Each time you click, another entity appears. To start creating a different type of object or symbol, click on another Toolbar tool. To stop drawing entities, simply right-click anywhere, or re-select the Pointer tool from the Standard palette. To revert to a previously selected tool, hold down <Ctrl> and perform a double right-click.

The default names for new entities will be 'Entity_nn'. The value of 'nn' will depend on the names of existing entities. If you prefer to edit the entity name as soon as you draw one, you can do that by selecting 'Edit in place after creation' in the first tab of the General Options. Now, you are offered the chance to edit the name of each entity after you've added it. When you have finished editing, just click again to create the next entity.

YOUR TURN TO PLAY

Open the workspace you created in Exercise 8, and create a new top-level folder called 'Chapter 11'. Now create a new Conceptual Data Model by clicking on the 'New Model' option on the 'File' menu. Call the model 'Chapter 11'. As soon as you've created the model, press <Ctrl+S> to save it in the 'Exercises' folder. You should have 'Diagram_1' open on the Canvas. Rename the diagram to 'Chapter 11 CDM'.

Open the 'General Options' on the Tools menu, select 'Edit in place after creation', then click on <OK>. Now click on the ▦ button in the Toolbox, and then click on the Canvas, edit the entity name, and repeat for the other two entities. Use the first three entity names shown in Table 11.1. When you have finished adding entities, click the right mouse button, then save the diagram again.

The appearance of the entity symbols will depend on the default display preferences in your model. By default, they will probably start out looking like Figure 11.1, assuming you are using the 'Entity/Relationship' notation.

Figure 11.1 Default entity symbol

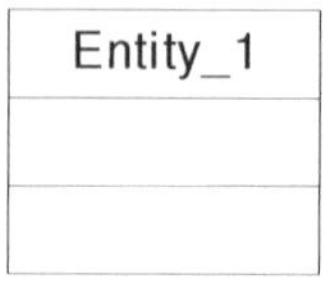

Entity_1

This symbol has three compartments. The entity name is always in the top compartment, never outside the symbol. The other compartments display two of the entity's properties, which are blank because those properties are not defined. The format and content of the symbol are determined by the diagram Display Preferences, described later in this chapter.

Changing Model Notation

If your entity symbols don't look the way you expect, you may need to change the Model notation via the Model Options. For example, rounded corners on all entity symbols are a sign that the notation is 'Barker'. See Chapter 9 for more information.

Creating Entities in the Browser

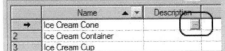 In Exercise 8, you created new entities by copying them in the Browser. Of course, you can also create new entities from scratch in the Browser; in fact you can create any object in the Browser. The following instructions will work for any type of object.

1. Right-click the location in the Browser where you want to create the entity. If you right-click the name of a model or package, select New, and then Entity, to open a new default property sheet. You can also right-click the Entities folder in the Browser, and then select New.

2. Type an object name in the 'General' tab of the property sheet, and then add any other relevant properties in the remaining fields of this or the other tabs. Note that PowerDesigner updates the entity code for you, if *Name to code mirroring* is enabled, which is the default setting in the Model Options.

3. Click OK to confirm the creation of the entity. The entity is now listed under the heading 'Entities', and its symbol has been added to the current diagram.

YOUR TURN TO PLAY

Follow the instructions above to create the remaining entities from Table 11.1. You should now have three entities on your diagram, and six in the Browser.

Editing via the List of Entities

YOUR TURN TO PLAY

1. Right-click the model name in the Browser, select List of and then Entities. The list of entities will open.

2. Click on the 'Customize' tool to customize the columns; refer to Figure 10.30 if you need help to find the tool. In the list of columns, uncheck 'Code' and check 'Description' (**not** 'Description Text'), then click <OK>.

	Name	▲ ▼	Description
→	Ice Cream Cone		
2	Ice Cream Container		
3	Ice Cream Cup		

3. Next click on the 'Description' cell for one of the entities, and then click on the ellipsis button that appears to the right.
4. Now you can type in the entity description from Table 11.1. Use the formatting tools shown in Figure 11.2 to change the font and style, if you want. Click <OK> when you're finished, then click on <Apply> to save the changes.

Figure 11.2 Editing a description

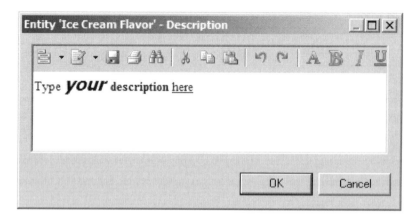

5. To edit the next description, take a different approach. In the list of entities, double-click the row number for another entity to open the property sheet for the Entity. Select the 'Notes' tab, and then type the description. If you have Microsoft Word installed, click on the 'Edit with ...' button on the toolbar above the description, and Microsoft Word will start up. You will probably have to confirm that the document is in RTF format. Try pasting text or images from the clipboard into the description. When you close Word, the description will update in PowerDesigner.
6. When you have finished entering descriptions, click on <OK> to close the object list and save any changes you have not previously applied. Now make sure that all your entities are on the diagram. Use the 'Show Symbols' feature we showed you in Chapter 10.
7. Right-click any data model diagram that displays entities, then select `Display Preferences` from the contextual menu. In the 'Display Preferences' window, select 'Entity' on the left, then select the 'Format' tab. As you can see from Figure 11.3, the 'Format' tab shows the current default and format for entity symbols in the current diagram. Including the name, there are five possible compartments – the number and layout of the compartments depends on the properties selected for display.

This shows you how and where the available properties will be displayed, if you choose to display them. To change the formatting, click on <Modify>, and the Symbol Format dialog will be displayed. Make some changes to the entity format, such as altering the shadow style and the font used for the entity name, then click <OK>. Your changes will be reflected in the sample symbol shown in the 'Format' tab. Now you can commit the changes to your symbols, use the settings to reset the defaults, or choose the diagrams to apply the preferences to, as discussed in the previous section.

Figure 11.3 Default symbol format

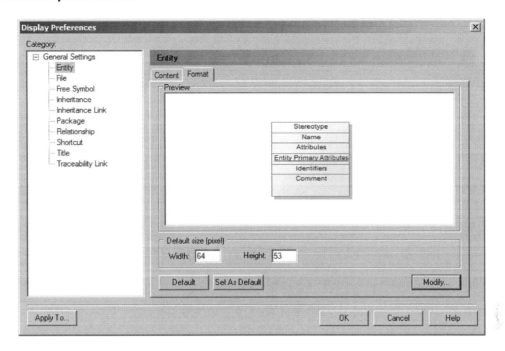

Exporting the Diagram Image

PowerDesigner provides an easy way of saving your diagram as an image file, in either color or monochrome. Just select the symbols you want to export, click on the Edit menu, select Export Image, and then choose the file location, name, and format. For color exports, select Export in Color on the Edit menu first.

Object Property Sheets

We first looked at property sheets in Chapter 10. They are a powerful feature of PowerDesigner, and their contents vary depending on the type of object, so we will continue to introduce them to you gradually.

Before we look at the content of these tabs, let's look at some of the options we have regarding property sheets. You'll remember that we told you about 'Favorite' tabs in Chapter 10, and showed you some of the tabs.

You have control over several aspects of how PowerDesigner handles the display of property sheets via the 'Dialog' section of General Options, available on the Tools menu. The ringed options in Figure 11.4 are particularly useful.

Figure 11.4 General options - dialog

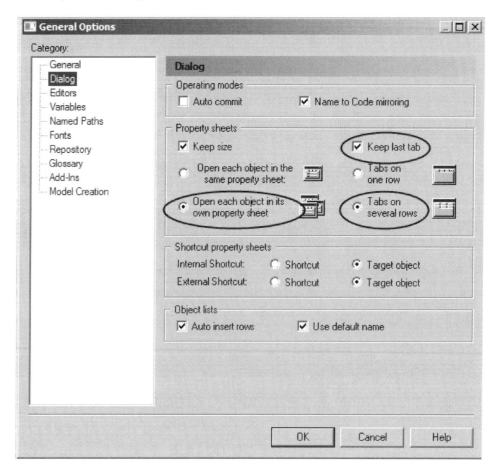

❷   "Dialog Box General Options" (Core Features Guide)

The following two figures show the content of two of the tabs for an entity. All of the standard Entity tabs are visible in both figures.

There is a difference between the 'General' tab in Figure 10.17 and that in Figure 11.5 – there is a new property called *Plural name*, which was added when a model extension was loaded. You can find out more about this model extension in Chapter 13: look for the section on Assertion Statements.

The 'Traceability Links' tab in Figure 11.6 shows a traceability link that was drawn on a diagram. Double-clicking the entry would open the property sheet for the linked object, in this case the 'Lecturer' entity.

Importing Entities from Excel Files

Entities and other objects can be imported and updated from Excel workbooks. See "Excel Import" in Chapter 21 for more information.

Figure 11.5 The entity 'Thesis' – General tab

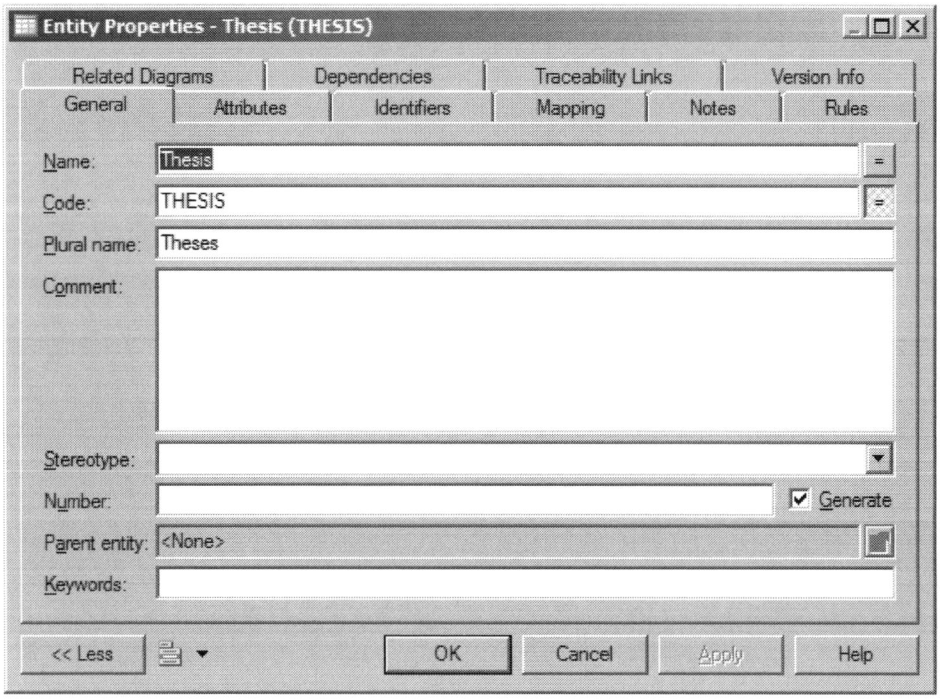

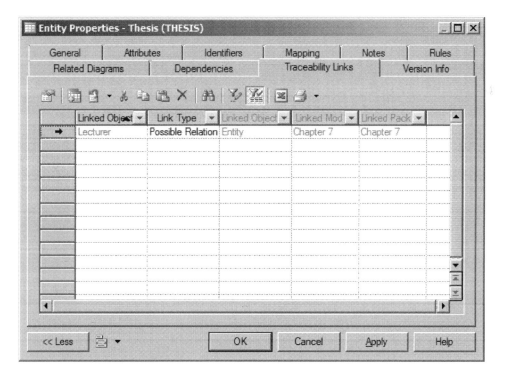

Figure 11.6 The entity 'Thesis' – 'Traceability Links' tab

EXERCISE 9: Creating LDM Entities in PowerDesigner

Within the 'Exercises' workspace you created in Exercise 8, create a folder called 'Exercise 9'. In the folder, create a LDM called 'Exercise 9a'.

Create six entities in the new model, using the information in Table 11.2. Experiment with the content and style of the entity symbols. Entities marked with '*' can be copied from the 'Chapter 11' CDM.

Table 11.2 Our six entities

Entity Name	Definition
Color *	A primary color within the spectrum of visible light.
Ice Cream Cone	An edible container that can hold one or more ice cream scoops.
Ice Cream Container *	A holder of ice cream that is either edible, in the case of an ice cream cone, or recyclable, in the case of an ice cream cup.
Ice Cream Cup *	A recyclable container that can hold one or more ice cream scoops.
Order *	Also known as an ice cream sale, an order is when a consumer purchases one or more of our products in a single visit to our ice cream store.
Order Line	A product purchased during a single visit to our ice cream store.

Customize the view of a list of entities – ensure that you include at least the following properties: Name, Modification Date, Generate, and Description. Use the 'Export to Excel' tool to export the entities to Excel. Keep this file – you will need it in Chapter 21.

Key Points

- Use the *Description* property for descriptions, rather than the *Comment* property.

- Entities can be created by drawing them on a diagram, adding them via the Browser, or adding them via object lists.

- Make use of existing documentation using the Excel Import wizard.

- Object lists provide a complete editing environment.

- It's easy to export the diagram as an image file.

Data Items, Terms
Domains, Attributes, Columns
Elementary!

The level of support provided for data elements by data modeling tools can be summarized in the following categories.

Category	Attribute	Column	Domain	Elementary Data Item
Minimal	-	✓	-	-
Useful	✓	✓	-	-
Essential	✓	✓	✓	-
Comprehensive	✓	✓	✓	✓

Minimal support only allows you to model databases; that's a start, but there's a lot more to data modeling than databases.

Useful support allows you to create logical data models as well as model databases, but doesn't provide Domains to help you manage data element characteristics.

Essential support allows you to use Domains to manage the consistency of data types and values of reference data.

Tools that fall into the *Comprehensive* category provide a key additional feature, the ability to record facts or definitions of data independently of entities. This is a key benefit for business and data analysts, and for the organization as a whole – finally, we can describe our data in business terms without modeling first!

The level of support that PowerDesigner provides for data elements is beyond the *Comprehensive* level: the Glossary features introduced in PowerDesigner 16 allow us to record the vocabulary of the business as Terms, and to use those Terms as the basis of a naming standard for data elements and other objects.

We discuss the different types of data models in Section IV, so we don't provide too much detail here. It's sufficient for now to say that data elements play a vital role in all three types of data models that PowerDesigner provides, the Conceptual, the Logical, and the Physical Data Models.

Data Items, Attributes, and Columns are all data elements, just as we outlined in Chapter 4. There are key differences between them due to the context in which they're used, which we'll discover later; it's what they have in common that we're interested in here.

In PowerDesigner, the 'Elementary Data Item' is known as a Data Item; a Data Item is a 'conceptual' data element, independent of any model objects such as entities. They are integral to the Conceptual Data Model, where every attribute automatically references an underlying Data Item.

An Attribute defines a data element within the context of an Entity in a Conceptual or Logical Data Model, whereas a Column defines a data element within the context of a Table in a Physical Data Model.

All the PowerDesigner data models allow you to define Domains to manage the characteristics of your data elements.

In this chapter, we will outline a simple strategy for how and when to use each of the types of Data Elements in PowerDesigner, as well as introduce you to the PowerDesigner Glossary.

Table 12.1 illustrates the types of Data Elements in PowerDesigner. The arrows show the 'generation' links that are created as you transform one type of model into another type of model. We'll discuss this topic more in Chapter 18. For now, we'll just say that the Conceptual, Logical, and Physical Data Models can form a chain of linked models. We create that chain by generating one model from another, thereby also creating a chain of related data elements. You can create each of the models manually, and manually map them to each other if you choose to, but letting PowerDesigner do that work for you will deliver better results.

Table 12.1 Data elements and generation links

Type of Object	Type of Data Model		
	Conceptual	Logical	Physical
Data Item	✓		
Domain	✓ ⇒	✓ ⇒	✓
Attribute	✓ ⇒	✓ ⬎	
Column			✓

Domains are transferred from the Conceptual model to the Logical model, and then to the Physical model. Attributes are transferred from the Conceptual model to the Logical model, and then converted into Columns in the Physical model. As we'll see in Chapter 18, it's also possible to generate a Physical Data Model directly from a Conceptual Data Model, and vice versa.

Table 12.1 shows the standard "top-down" generation links. In reality, the possibilities are more complex; PowerDesigner also allows you to work "bottom-up", generating a Logical Data Model from a Physical Data model, and a Conceptual Data Model from a Logical Data Model. You can also generate a new model of the same type as the original.

Properties are transferred between data elements when we generate the chain of data elements we referred to earlier. "Transferring Properties", later in this chapter, will provide you with more details.

There are differences in the support for Attributes in Conceptual and Logical Data Models, so to avoid confusion, we will use the following phrases when referring to Attributes:

Conceptual Attribute   an attribute in a Conceptual Data Model

Logical Attribute   an attribute in a Logical Data Model

Attribute   an attribute in either type of model

Standard Properties for Data Elements

In addition to the "common" properties described in Chapter 10, there are standard properties shared by all the types of data elements in PowerDesigner, shown in Table 12.2.

Table 12.2 Standard data element properties

Data type, length, and precision	Data type specifies the nature of the data, such as character, numeric, or date. The length is the number of characters or digits the data element will allow. The precision applies to numeric data, and specifies the number of possible digits after the decimal point. The precision is NOT part of the length; if you need to represent the number 1234.56, the Length must be set to '4', and the Precision must be set to '2'.

If your DBMS supports them, you can define your own Abstract Data Types in Physical Data Models.

"Abstract Data Types (PDM)" (Data Modeling) |
| *Check parameters* | PowerDesigner allows you to define constraints to control the range and format of data. You can specify constraints on the 'Standard Checks' and 'Additional Checks' tabs. See "Managing Allowable Values" and "Exporting and Importing Lists of Values".

You can create data formats to reuse in constraints for multiple objects by clicking the New button to the right of the Format field on the 'Standard Checks' tab. Data formats are informational only. |
| *Mandatory property* | Specifies whether or not a value must be assigned when we create an instance of the object containing this data. |

- "Attribute Properties" (Data Modeling)
- "Column Properties" (Data Modeling)
- "Data Item Properties" (Data Modeling)

- "Domain Properties" (Data Modeling)
- "Creating Data Formats for Reuse" (Data Modeling)

In the next section, we'll show you where to find all of these properties in a Domain; the instructions also apply to other types of data elements. These properties can be transmitted from data element to data element; see "Transferring Properties", later in this chapter, for more information.

Domains in PowerDesigner

In PowerDesigner, Domains help you to standardize data characteristics within your Data Items, Attributes, and Columns. We will let you explore Domains for yourself by creating several Domains in a Conceptual Data Model. Before you do that, though, take a look at Figure 12.1, which shows all the tabs on the property sheet for a domain.

Figure 12.1 Domain properties – all tabs

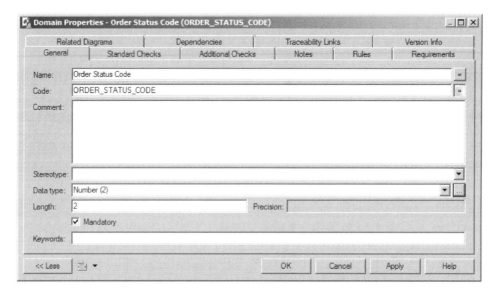

YOUR TURN TO PLAY

1. Open the workspace you created in Exercise 8, and create a new top-level folder called 'Chapter 12'. Now create a new Conceptual Data Model by clicking on the 'New Model' option on the 'File' menu. Call the model 'Chapter 12'. You should have 'Diagram_1' open on the Canvas. Rename it to 'Chapter 12 CDM'.
2. Now save the model in the 'Exercises' folder.
3. We will not be using the diagram in this exercise, but do not close the diagram, or we will not have the correct menu options displayed.
4. Click on the 'Model' menu, and then select 'Domains'. An empty list of domains is displayed; you need to create three domains, so click on the *add a row* tool three times. The result is shown in Figure 12.2.

Figure 12.2 List of domains

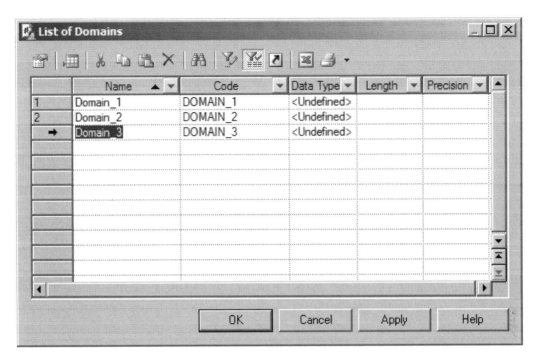

5. Overtype the three domain names with the following, in any sequence, and click on <Apply>:
- Date
- Person Name
- Order Status Code.

Remember – you can easily move between the items in the list using the cursor (arrow) keys.

The 'Domains' folder, containing three new entries, now appears in the Browser.

6. We'll continue to work in the list of domains for a while. Click on the 'Data Type' entry for the 'Date' domain, and select 'Date' from the drop down list of values. Click on the 'Data Type' entry for 'Order Status Code'; Figure 12.3 shows the result.

Figure 12.3 Our three domains

	Name ▲ ▾	Code ▾	Data Type ▾	Length ▾	Precision ▾
1	Date	DATE	Date		
➡	Order Status Code	ORDER_STATUS_C	<Undef ▾ …		
3	Person Name	PERSON_NAME	<Undefined>		

7. Now click on the tool with three dots on it, in the 'Data Type' column; this opens a simple dialog (see Figure 12.4) which allows you to choose one of the standard data types, then specify the length and precision, where appropriate.

Figure 12.4 Standard data types

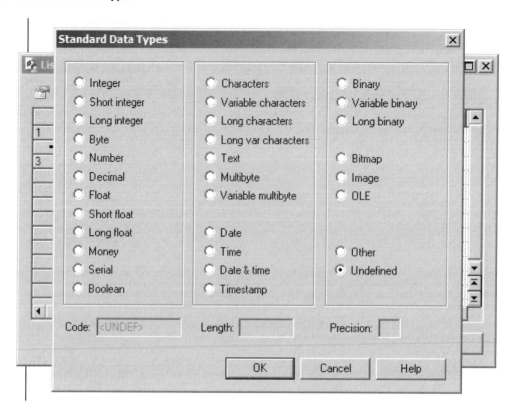

8. Set the Data Type for **Order Status Code** to 'Number', and the Length to '2', then click <OK>. At this point, the domain details have been updated in the list of domains, but the changes have not been applied to the model, so click on <Apply>.

If you press the <Esc> key, all unapplied changes will be ignored.

9. Now, double-click the row number or arrow to the left of 'Person Name'. The property sheet for the domain will open. You should see the contents of the 'General' tab displayed. If a different tab appears, that is because you selected 'Keep Last Tab' in the General Options (see Figure 11.4).

10. In the 'General' tab, select the data type 'Characters (%)', and set the length to 120. Select the 'Mandatory' check box, which will force all data elements attached to this domain to be mandatory. Click <OK> to close the property sheet, and then click <OK> to close the Domain List.

11. It would be wise to save the model at this point.

12. Now it's time to add definitions to our domains. Open each domain, in turn, via the Browser or the list of Domains, whichever you prefer. For each Domain, enter the descriptions from Table 12.3 into the *Description* property in the 'Notes' tab.

Table 12.3 Domain descriptions

Domain	Description
Date	The standard Date Domain for XYZ Inc. This must be utilized for all Dates for which a more specialized Domain does not exist.
Order Status Code	A code that identifies a valid overall status of an Order. It is updated as a result of actions carried out relating to the whole Order, or against individual Order Lines within the Order.
Person Name	The standard format for a defined part of a Person's name, such as 'Person First Name' or 'Person Family Name'.

13. We have some values we need to add to 'Order Status Code', so open the domain again, and then select the 'Standard Checks' tab. Type the values shown in Table 12.4 into the *List of Values* property.

Table 12.4 Values for Order Status Code

Value	Label
01	Open
02	Shipped
03	Closed
04	Returned

14. Check the 'Complete' check box to indicate that there are no missing values.

15. ☐ If your list of values is in a table in a spreadsheet or document, you may copy and paste them into the 'List of Values' only if there is at least one value already in the List. Here's how to do it:

- Ensure your values are in two columns – Value and Label. The first row is assumed to contain labels
- Select any existing value in the list of values in the Domain by clicking on the row number; if you paste into an empty list, only the first value is pasted

- Paste, using <Ctrl+V> or the 'Paste' button on the list of values toolbar.
- Your values are appended to the existing values.

PowerDesigner prevents you from entering duplicate values in the list by suffixing the duplicate value with a number.

 PowerDesigner does NOT check whether your values match the Domain data type.

16. Now let's create another Domain that is similar to an existing domain. In the Browser, select the Domain 'Order Status Code', and then press <Ctrl+C> to copy the Domain into the Clipboard. Select the 'Domains' folder in the Browser, and press <Ctrl+V>; the Domain will be pasted from the Clipboard into a new Domain called 'Order Status Code2'.

Copy and Paste works in the Browser – you can even copy and paste between several models, provided they are the same type of model. To copy objects between models of different types, you need to use the generation capabilities – see Chapter 18.

17. Now we need to edit the new Domain. Click on the Domain **Order Status Code2** in the Browser, then either press <F2> or click on the name again, to enable name editing. Change the name to 'Order Line Status Code', and press <Enter>.
18. Double-click 'Order Line Status Code' in the Browser to open the property sheet. The properties we need to change are the description and the values. In the 'Standard Checks' tab, add one further value:

05 Cancelled

19. In the 'Notes' tab, provide the following Description, then click on <OK>:

'A code that identifies a valid status for an Order Line.'

Figure 12.5 shows the list of Domains with the four domains.

Figure 12.5 Our four domains

	Name	Data Type	Length	Precision	Description
1	Date	Date			The standard
2	Order Line Status Code	Characters (2)	2		A code that
3	Order Status Code	Number (1)	1		A code that
→	Person Name	Characters (120)	120		The full name

Enforcing Non-divergence from a Domain in a Data Model

Domains help you to standardize data characteristics within your Data Items, Attributes, and Columns. In the following paragraphs, we refer to these collectively as 'Data Elements'.

The Model Options allow you to decide which properties are to be enforced. On the Tools menu, select Model Options. Figure 12.6 shows the default options relating to Domains.

Figure 12.6 Data model options for domains

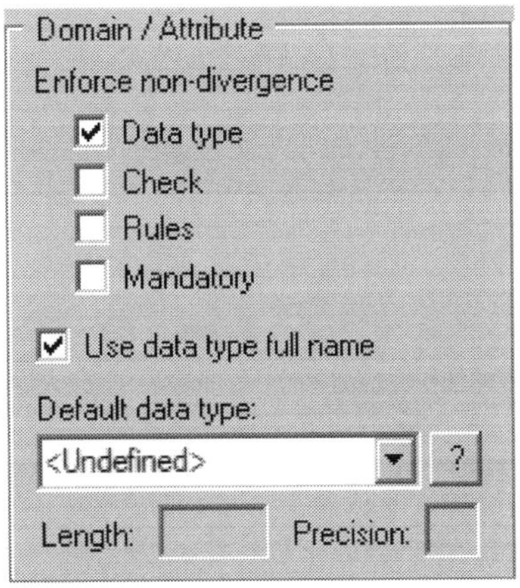

Select the check boxes of the data element properties that are not permitted to diverge from the domain definition. You can specify any or all of:

Data type	data type, length, and precision
Check	check parameters such as minimum and maximum values
Rules	business rules
Mandatory	mandatory property of the attribute or column
[PDM only] Profile	test data profile

Which properties you enforce will depend on how you're using Domains. If you use them to manage lists of values, then you'll need to select 'Check' to prevent the creation of multiple lists of values for the same data.

If you subsequently modify any of a domain's properties specified here as non-divergent, the corresponding properties of the Data Elements attached to that domain will be updated automatically.

⊖ Properties specified as non-divergent appear dimmed and are non-editable in Lists and Data Element property sheets. If you want to modify a non-divergent property, you must detach the Data Element from its domain, or change the divergence properties for the domain.

When you set the 'Enforce non-divergence' options, you are asked if you want to apply domain properties to Data Elements currently attached to the domain. If you click <OK>, the Data Element properties are modified to be consistent with the properties of the domain to which they belong. See the 'Dependencies' tab on the Domain property sheet to see the linked Data Elements.

Whenever you amend a Domain, PowerDesigner checks to see whether any Data Elements use the Domain. If so, an update confirmation box (see Figure 12.7) is displayed, asking if you want to cascade the domain changes. Remember, changes to Domains could be cascaded to a whole chain of data elements in many models, so it is wise to check the impact analysis before making changes.

Figure 12.7 Cascading domain changes

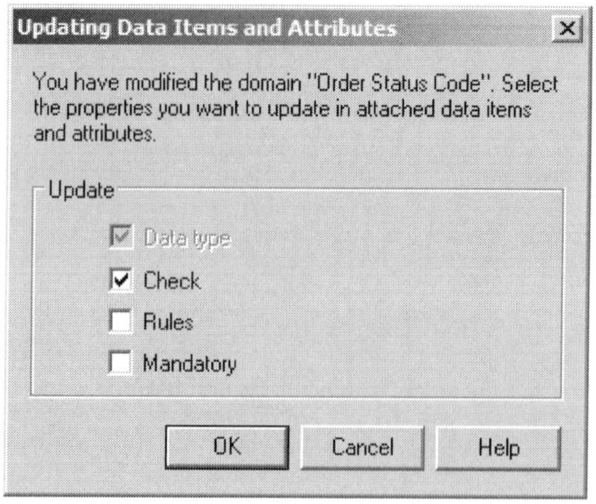

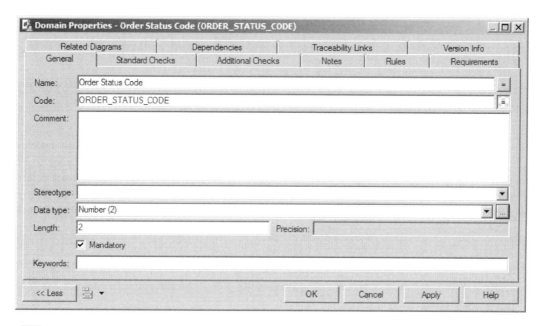

The 'Check', 'Rules', and 'Mandatory' boxes should be selected only if those properties have been amended. In Figure 12.7, the 'Data Type' check box cannot be amended, because we have (via the model options) decided to enforce the data type for all Domains.

When you check a model, any differences between Domains and the objects attached to them are reported. See "Compare and Merge" in Chapter 23.

The Result of our Edits

Figures 12.8 to 12.10 show the key tabs for one of our domains, "Order Status Code".

Figure 12.8 Order Status Code – 'General' tab

Note the ☐ tool to the right of Data Type; this opens the 'Standard Data Types' selection window you saw in Figure 12.4.

Figure 12.9 Order Status Code – 'Standard Checks' tab

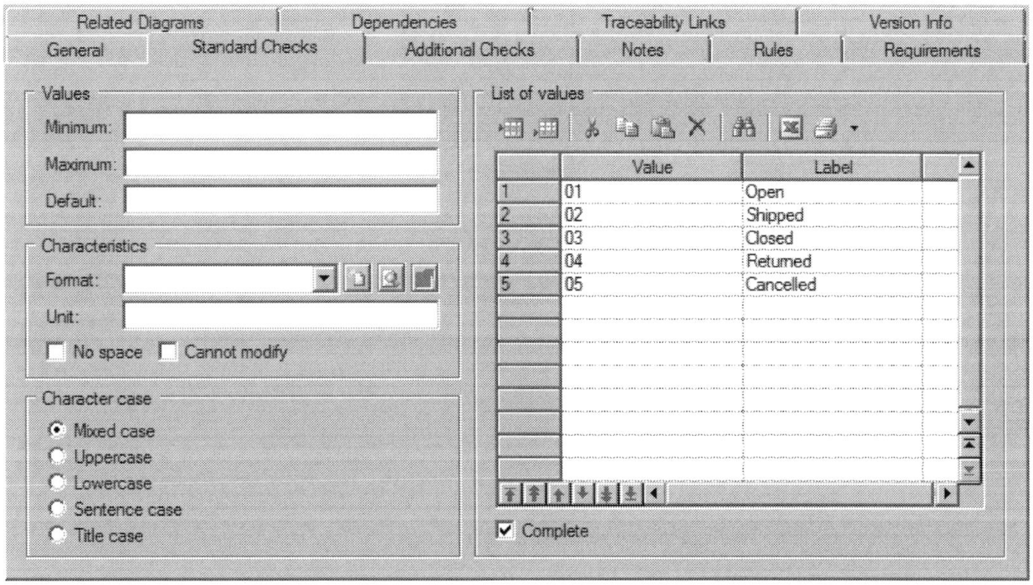

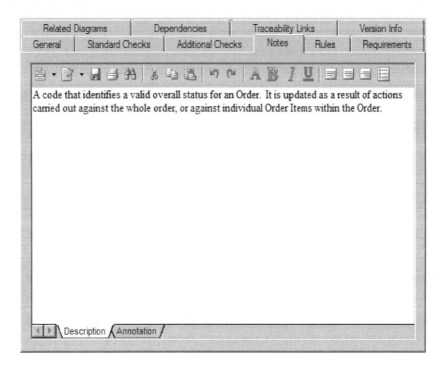

Figure 12.10 Order Status Code – 'Notes' tab

In the next two sections, we will use these Domains in Data Items and Attributes, and come back to the other Domain tabs.

"Domains (CDM/LDM/PDM)" (Data Modeling)

Data Items in PowerDesigner

A Data Item is a 'conceptual' data element that exists independently of any model objects, such as Entities or Tables. Data Items are integral to the Conceptual Data Model, where every attribute automatically references an underlying Data Item. They are not present in the Logical Data Model or Physical Data Model. We do not usually start a paragraph with a gotcha, but we have to here, because there is a fundamental point about Data Items that will affect how you decide to use them.

In a Conceptual Data Model, an Attribute is a Data Item that has been included in an Entity. If you amend an Attribute, you amend the Data Item, and *every* other Attribute in the model that is based on that Data Item.

There are two approaches you can take to create a pairing of Data Item and Attribute; the approach you take depends on your policy regarding the use of Data Items. See "Should we reuse Data Items within a model?" later in this chapter.

Approach 1   Include an existing Data Item in an Entity to create an Attribute – this may result in a Data Item being referenced by more than one Attribute

Approach 2   Create a new Attribute in an Entity, without selecting a Data Item

Both approaches are supported by the 'Attributes' tab in the Entity property sheet, and we'll try them both in the next section - see "Creating a Conceptual Attribute".

Figure 12.11 Data Item Property sheet

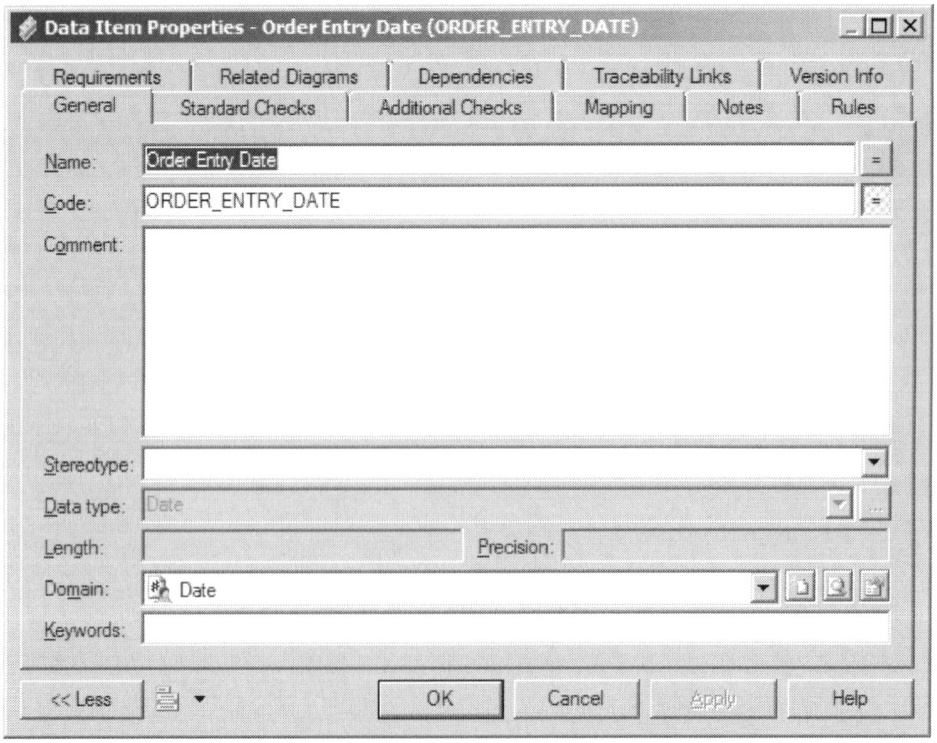

Figure 12.11 shows the 'General' tab on the property sheet for a Data Item; you'll see that it's virtually identical to the property sheet for a Domain, shown in Figure 12.1. The difference here is that you cannot edit the Data Type. The Data Item references the 'Date' Domain, so it inherits the Data Type from that Domain, and the Model Options prevent us from overriding the inherited Data Type.

Controlling Uniqueness and Reuse of Data Items

By default, PowerDesigner allows you to use a Data Item to create more than one attribute. For example, you can define a **Zip Code** Data Item once, and reuse it in whichever entities contain addresses. If you then update the Data Item, your changes will simultaneously cascade to all the attributes that use it. Remember, all these attributes are identical.

You can change this behavior via the 'Model Settings' section of 'Model Options'. Table 12.5 lists the options available, and their effect.

Table 12.5 Model options – reuse of data items

Option	When selected	When cleared
Unique code	Each data item must have a unique code. If you try to select this option and some existing data items are already sharing a code, the following error will be displayed: "Unique Code option could not be selected because two data items have the same code: *data_item_code*" To be able to select the option, you must first assign unique codes to all data items.	Multiple data items can have the same code, and you differentiate them by the entities that use them. The entities are listed in the Used By column of the list of data items. Note: To make an item visible in a list, click the *Customize Columns and Filter* tool in the list toolbar, select the appropriate check box from the list of filter options displayed, and click <OK>.
Allow reuse	One data item can be an attribute for multiple entities.	Each data item can be an attribute for only one entity.

Should we reuse Data Items within a model?

Should we allow Data Items to be used by more than one entity in a single data model? Remember the 100% match between a Data Item and an Attribute. If we use a Data item in three entities, the three Attributes are identical; every property (including the name) is identical.

In Chapter 16, we discussed how to normalize a data model; in essence, we make sure that each item of data only appears once in a data model, in the 'correct' entity. This implies that multiple uses of a Data Item is wrong, and indicates that the modeler's work is not complete. However, this is not necessarily true. As in so many aspects of data modeling, 'it depends'.

Mostly, it depends on the type of model you're creating. It is very likely that a Conceptual Data Model would not be fully normalized, so some duplication of attributes may be acceptable. The decision we really have to make is whether to allow <u>identical</u> attributes in different entities. It can be tempting to speed up the modeling process by reducing the time we spend describing our Attributes, and reusing Data Items certainly allows us to do that; however, it could easily result in generic descriptions that lead to confusion and misunderstandings. We must avoid that at all costs; see Chapter 6 for a discussion of the importance of names and definitions.

In Table 12.6, both attributes use the same Data Item. Because the Data Item has to describe two similar but different concepts, it has a generic description. The descriptions do not tell us enough about the attributes; they are not complete.

Table 12.6 Forcing attributes to be identical

Entity	Attribute Name (Data Item Name)	Description
Customer Application	Birth Date	The date a Person was born.
Employee	Birth Date	The date a Person was born.

For Table 12.7, we changed our naming standard for attributes, and renamed the two attributes from Table 12.6. We now have two Data Items with descriptions that are specific to the use of the data.

Table 12.7 Resolving the differences

Entity	Attribute Name (Data Item Name)	Description
Customer Application	Customer Application Birth Date	The date of birth of the Customer, according to information entered by the customer on their application.
Employee	Employee Birth Date	The date of birth of the Employee, verified by sight of their birth certificate or passport when they commenced employment.

A side effect of this approach is the longer name on each Data Item – they include the name of the entity. This makes the Data Items more useful as the core of a Data Dictionary. It is also a potential concern for models further down the line, as we'll discuss in 'Managing Object Names and Codes' in Chapter 20.

When to Use Domains instead of Data Items

Let's think again about managing the definition of a *Zip Code*. If you need all *Zip Code* attributes to have the same generic description, then you could define a Data Item called **Zip Code**. A better approach would be to provide a generic description of **Zip Code** as a Term in the Glossary, and define a Domain called **Zip Code**, to ensure that all Zip Codes use the same format and validation. If you use this approach, you will make effective use of domains, and the traceability that PowerDesigner provides along the chain of data elements:

Term (in the Glossary) →Domain →Data Item →CDM Attribute →LDM Attribute →PDM Column.

This topic is discussed in more depth in Chapter 20 – see "Managing Names and Codes" and "The Lineage of Data Elements". See also "Replica Data Items in one Model" later in this chapter.

Incorporating Data Items in Governance

Data Items can assist you with governing a single data model, or governing all your data models. They allow you to take advantage of previous analysis work by creating a 'catalog' of approved data definitions, waiting to be incorporated into your model(s); 'Data Dictionary' is a common name for such a catalog. You could extend the properties of Data Items to record Data Ownership, Approval Date and Status, and other organization-specific information.

Data Items allow you to manage your elementary data definitions. If you use PowerDesigner for Business Process Modeling, Data Items provide the link from your data models to the elementary Data objects referenced by your business processes.

We recommend that you incorporate PowerDesigner Data Items into your data governance process. The strategy must be applied consistently, a corporate strategy that applies to all models; individual models shouldn't follow different rules, or it will be impossible to integrate them in the future if that becomes necessary.

A catalog of Data Items is simple to import from Excel using the Excel Import Wizard. Alternatively, you can generate them from any type of PowerDesigner object by defining your own Object Generation. For example, you may want to create a Data Dictionary from a set of 'Data' in a Business Process Model.

We recommend that you clear 'Allow reuse' in the CDM model options, and select 'Unique Code'.

To share a set of Data Items with other modelers, check the CDM into the Library folder in the Repository; this will automatically be pushed out to all repository users. Modelers reuse the Data Items by creating Replicas of the Data Items, in their own models. See "Replica Data Items", later in this chapter. This shared CDM is also ideal for sharing standard domains.

"Generating Model Objects" (Core Features Guide)

Model Checks

You can run the Model Check to validate your Data Items. These checks include identifying Data Items:

- That are not used
- That are used multiple times
- Whose name is not unique
- Whose code is not unique
- That does not match the referenced Domain.

You can also use a Dependency Matrix to list Data Items that are or are not being used, as we'll see shortly.

⊚ "Example: Building a Data Dictionary in a CDM" (Data Modeling)

⊚ "Data Item Checks" (Data Modeling)

Attributes and Columns in PowerDesigner

Attributes are present in both Conceptual and Logical Data Models; Physical Data Models have Columns. In this chapter, we focus on Attributes, but you can carry out the same tasks with Columns; you will have a chance to create your own Columns in Chapter 17.

Attributes are sub-objects; they can only exist within an entity. Like Data Items, they do not have symbols; unlike Data Items, you can display their properties on an Entity symbol, and edit them via the Entity symbol.

Figure 12.12 shows the 'General' tab on the property sheet for an attribute in a Conceptual Data Model; this attribute uses the data item shown in Figure 12.11. Compared to Figure 12.11, there are additional properties referencing the data item, and the entity that contains this attribute. Remember the 100% match between the data item and attribute; any changes you make here will also affect the data item.

If you want to, you can click any of the 'Properties' buttons 🖼 on the right hand side, to access the property sheet for the Entity, Data Item, or Domain. You can also create a new Domain with the 'Create' button 🗔, or open a selection window to choose a Domain with the 'Select Object' button 🔲.

There is a property we haven't seen before, called 'Displayed'. If this is not checked, the attribute will not be shown on any entity symbols.

To prevent an attribute from being displayed on a particular symbol, see "Communicating Your Message" in Chapter 10.

Figure 12.12 Conceptual attribute

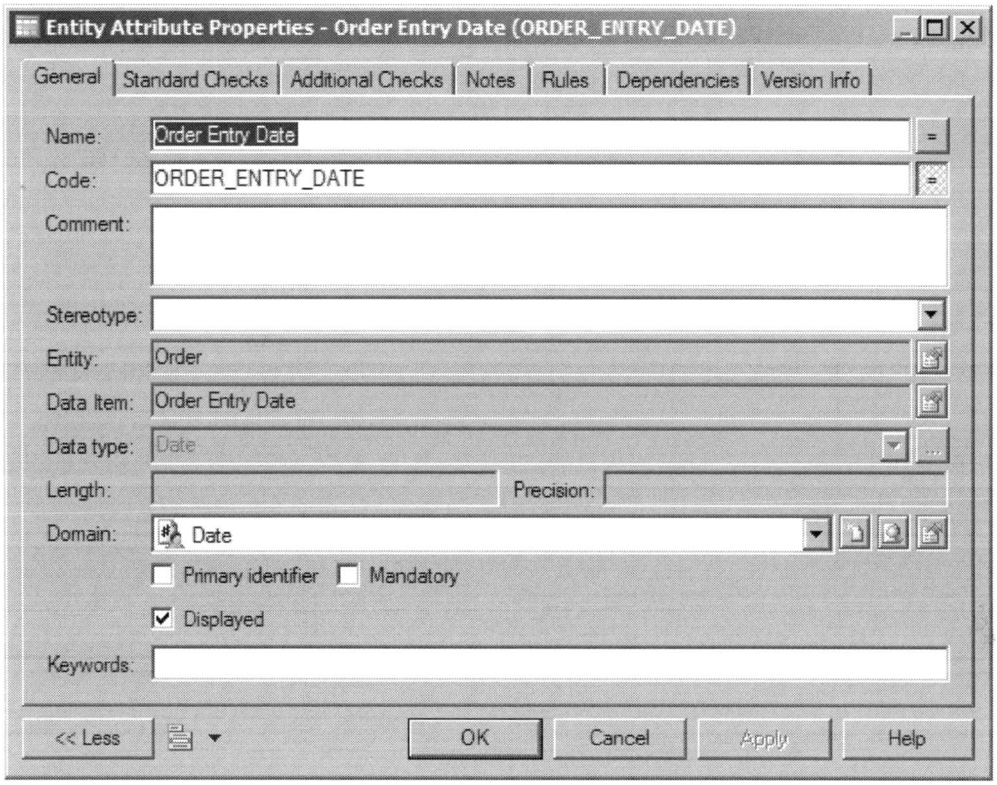

Entity Attribute Properties - Order Entry Date (ORDER_ENTRY_DATE)

| General | Standard Checks | Additional Checks | Notes | Rules | Dependencies | Version Info |

Name: Order Entry Date

Code: ORDER_ENTRY_DATE

Comment:

Stereotype:

Entity: Order

Data Item: Order Entry Date

Data type: Date

Length: Precision:

Domain: Date

☐ Primary identifier   ☐ Mandatory

☑ Displayed

Keywords:

<< Less   OK   Cancel   Apply   Help

Creating a Conceptual Attribute

If you've decided that the concept of a Data Dictionary is a useful one, then we suggest you create Data Items before you create your Attributes. You can create a Data Item via the Browser or a List of Objects. You cannot create a Data Item on a diagram, as they do not have symbols.

- Select `Model|Data Items` to access the List of Data Items, and click the *Add a Row* tool

or

- In the Browser, right-click the model or package, and select `New|Data Item`

or

- If you already have Data Items in the model, right-click the *Data Items* folder, then select `New`

You could just create attributes, and let the data items be created automatically, but, as we said earlier, this could result in duplicate data items. To avoid this, consider pre-loading candidate data items using the Excel Import feature. You'll probably create most of your attributes in the 'Attributes' tab in the entity property sheet. You can create attributes using the same methods used to create entities via the Object List you saw in Figure 11.2. As attributes are sub-objects, there are extra tools on the Toolbar, shown in Figure 12.13, and described in Table 12.8.

Figure 12.13 The sub-objects Toolbar on a list

Table 12.8 describes the purpose of the four important extra tools in a Conceptual Data Model.

Table 12.8 Adding attributes to a conceptual entity

Icon	Tool Name	Action
	Reuse Data Item	Opens a Selection window (see Figure 12.14) listing all the data items available in the model. Select one or more data items in the list and then click OK. This is the only way to guarantee that you will not create duplicate data items. This option is only available if 'Allow Reuse' has been enabled in the Model Options.
	Insert a Row *(the arrow is in the middle of the icon)*	Inserts a new attribute at the current position in the list of Attributes, and creates a new data item. If you have enabled the 'Allow Reuse' model option, the new data item can be reused as an attribute for other objects. If you have enabled the Allow Reuse and Unique Code model options, and you type the name of an existing data item, it will be reused.
	Add a Row *(the arrow is at the foot of the icon)*	Appends a new attribute and creates a new data item. If you have enabled the Allow Reuse model option, the new data item can be reused as an attribute for other objects. If you have enabled the Allow Reuse and Unique Code model options, and you type the name of an existing data item, it will be reused.
	Add Data Item	Opens a Selection window (see Figure 12.14) listing all the data items available in the model. Select one or more data items in the list and then click OK. If the data item has not yet been used, it will be linked to the object. If the data item has already been used, it will be copied (with a modified name, if you have enabled the Unique code model option) and the copy will be attached to the object.

Now it's time for some more practice.

YOUR TURN TO PLAY

1. Open the 'Chapter 12' Conceptual Data Model you created earlier. This contains four Domains.
2. Click on the 'Model' menu, then select 'Data Items' to open the list of data items. Now add the data items shown in Table 12.9; refer back to Chapter 11, if you need to. If you prefer, add them via the Browser.

Table 12.9 Add these data items

Data Item Name	Domain	Description
Order Status Code	Order Status Code	A code that identifies a valid overall status for an Order. It is updated as a result of actions carried out against the whole order, or against individual Order Lines within the Order.
Order Entry Date	Date	The date on which the Order was entered into the Order Processing system.

3. The description of 'Order Status Code' is the same as the Description for the domain of the same name, so you can use the Windows clipboard to copy it across.
4. Now open the diagram in your Conceptual Data Model, right-click the canvas, and then select 'Model options'. Select 'Allow reuse', and click <OK>. It would be a good idea to save the model now.
5. Create an entity called 'Order'. Open the Entity's property sheet and click on the 'Attributes' tab. Click on the *Reuse Data Item* tool 🖼 on the Toolbar, and a list of existing data items is presented, like the one in Figure 12.14. If the button is not on the Toolbar, then you've forgotten to change the Model Options to allow reuse of data items.

In this example, I selected 'Order Entry Date' to be included in my entity. When I click on <OK>, a new attribute is created. If you click on the 'Add Data Item' button instead, the process is similar, but a new Data Item is created.

 The Selection window in Figure 12.14 is a standard PowerDesigner feature. You will see similar windows wherever you need to choose objects to process, such as when editing reports, generating models, or comparing or merging models.

Figure 12.14 Selecting data items

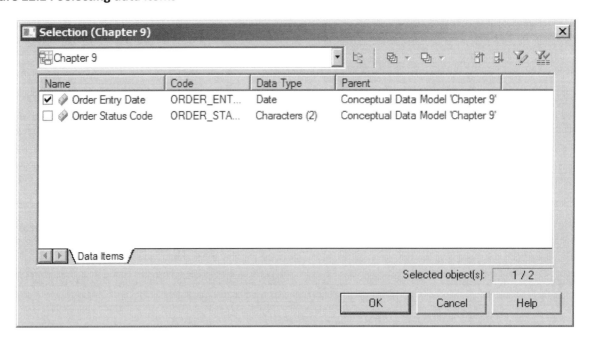

Using the tools on the toolbar, you can select or de-select all the entries on a tab, re-sequence them, and filter the list. You can also re-sequence the entries by clicking on the column headings. If more than one type of object is available for selection (such as when generating a model), more than one tab will be displayed. You can swap between tabs to select and de-select objects, or click on one of the down-arrows (circled in Figure 12.15) to select or de-select all objects in all tabs.

Figure 12.15 Selection window toolbar

❷ "Creating a Data Item" (Data Modeling)

❷ "Adding an Item from a Selection List" (Core Features Guide)

Creating a Logical Attribute

The property sheet for an attribute in a Logical Data Model appears in Figure 12.16. You can see that it is almost identical to the property sheet for a conceptual attribute in Figure 12.12.

There are two extra properties in Figure 12.16 that do not apply to conceptual attributes:

Inherited From	The name of the supertype entity this attribute was inherited from
Foreign Identifier	Indicates whether this attribute is a foreign identifier

Figure 12.16 Logical attribute

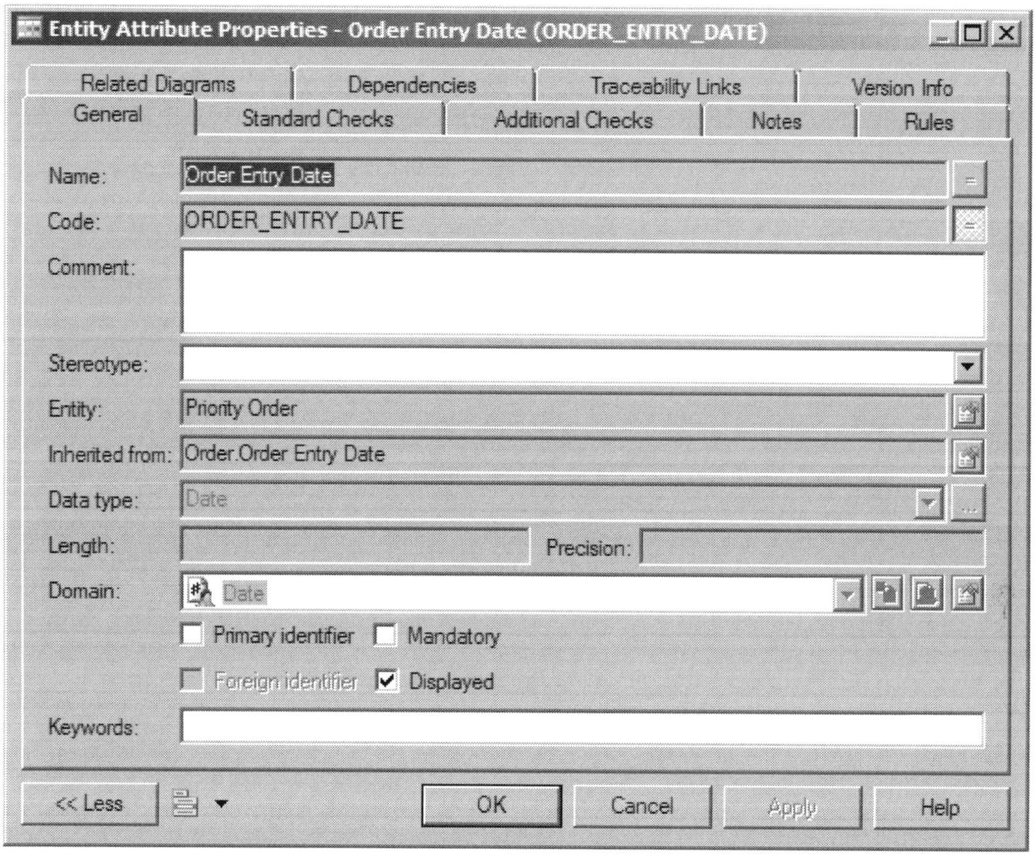

When adding logical attributes to an entity, the Toolbar looks the same as it does in Figure 12.13, but the effect of the buttons is different; there are no data items in a Logical Data Model. See Table 12.10 for an explanation.

Table 12.10 Adding attributes to a logical entity

Icon	Button Name	Action
	Insert a Row	Inserts a new attribute at the current point in the list.
	Add a Row	Appends a new attribute to the list.
	Add Attributes	Opens a Selection window listing all the attributes available in the model. Select one or more attributes in the list, and then click <OK> to copy them into the entity. The new attributes are copies of the original ones, and there are no restrictions on what you can do with them. The original attribute and the new attribute are not linked in any way.
	Replicate Attributes	Opens a selection window listing all of the attributes available in the model. Select one or more attributes in the list, and then click <OK> to create replicas of them in the entity. See "Replica Attributes" below.

⊚ "Creating an Attribute" (Data Modeling)

Replica Attributes

A Replica Attribute is a synchronized copy of the original attribute. By default, most of the properties are synchronized with the original attribute, and can only be edited in the original attribute. In a replica attribute, most properties are grayed out, and cannot be edited.

To change this behavior, you need to change the properties of the replication. Click on the 'Version' tab of the replica attribute to access a link to the original attribute:

- Click the *Delete* tool to break the replication link and convert the attribute into an independent object.
- Click the *Properties* tool to access the replication properties, which allow you to choose which properties to synchronize. Any properties that you don't synchronize can be edited in the replica object.

You can also access replication properties via the list of replications on the Model menu.

If you view the *Dependencies* property of the original attribute, any replica attributes will be shown as links on the sub-tab called 'Replications'. If the sub-tab doesn't appear, that means that the attribute does not have any replicas.

Replica Entities

You can replicate most types of objects between models of the same type, such as two Conceptual Data Models. Open the model(s) containing the original object(s), then open the model in which you want to create the replicas. Now click on the Edit menu, and select Replicate Objects; you can select any object in any of the open models of the same type.

As you will see shortly, using the right mouse button to drag an object also allows you to create a replica of the object.

You cannot edit the synchronized properties in the replica entity, but you can create new attributes, and add or remove relationships.

Replica Data Items

Via 'Replicate Objects', you can also replicate data items. For example, you could maintain a master Data Dictionary in a Conceptual Data Model with restricted update access. Your analysts can create their own Subject Area Models (as separate PowerDesigner Conceptual Data Models), and replicate the data items that they need. They will be able to change the name of the replica Data Item if they need to.

If the replica data items refer to domains, the domains referred to are also replicated. The replica data items and domains are read-only; apart from adding keywords, you can only amend them in the original model. You have control over the use of your definitions, and you also have traceability; you can traverse the link between the original and replica objects in both directions.

Replica Data Items in one Model

If you need to create two or more very similar Data Items in one model, you could define the 'standard' definition first, then create Replicas within the same model. For example, you could create a Data Item called **Birth Date**, and then create replicas called **Customer Application Birth Date** and **Employee Birth Date**.

Listing Replicas

To see a list of all the replicas in your model, select `Model|Replications`.

Each object and sub-object has a *Replica* property set to 'True' if it is a replica. This property can be included in lists of objects and list reports.

❓ "Creating Replicas" (Core Features Guide)

Display Preferences for Attributes and Columns

The Display Preferences give you control over which properties of attributes appear on entity symbols, and which properties of columns appear on table symbols. While these properties are essentially the same in meaning, they are presented differently. Figures 12.17 and 12.18 demonstrate this for you. The arrows link the selection of a property to its default location on a symbol.

Figure 12.17 Attribute properties in entity symbols

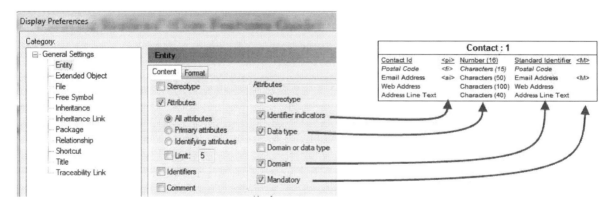

Figure 12.18 Column properties in table symbols

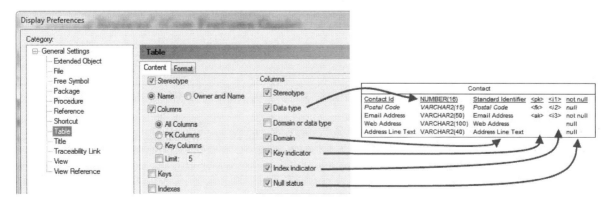

The display of attribute properties differs for Barker notation. The settings for 'Identifier Indicators' and 'Mandatory' are ignored, because the Barker notation introduces an additional set of symbols, which are ringed in Figure 12.19.

Figure 12.19 Attribute properties in entity symbols (Barker)

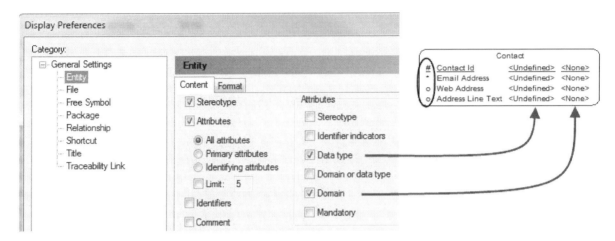

The symbols tell you the following:

\#   This attribute is part of the primary identifier of the entity

*   This attribute is mandatory

o   This attribute is optional.

YOUR TURN TO PLAY

You're going to create a Logical Data Model by generating it from the 'Chapter 12' Conceptual Data Model, and then create more attributes. Then you'll try out different ways of editing those Attributes.

1. Close any models you have open, and open the 'Chapter 12' Conceptual Data Model you created in the previous 'Your Turn' exercise.
2. Click on the 'Tools' menu, and select 'Generate Logical Data Model'; you'll be presented with the LDM Generation Options shown in Figure 12.20 - we'll look at this in more detail in a later chapter. By default, a new Logical Data Model will be created with the same name as the Conceptual Data Model.
3. Click on <OK>, and PowerDesigner will create a new LDM that matches the CDM. It will contain one diagram, four domains, and one entity. The Data Item **Order Status Code** will be transferred to the LDM, as it is not referenced by any attributes, although unused domains **are** transferred.
4. If you look at the diagram tabs, you'll see two new ones – 'Diagram_1' and 'Result List'. The 'Diagram_1' tab is the diagram in the new LDM, the other tab shows the results of the model check that ran before the LDM was generated.
5. Rename the new diagram to '**LDM**', and one of the tab names will change from 'Diagram_1' to 'LDM', as shown in Figure 12.21.
6. Save the new LDM in the same location as before. You should also save the original CDM, which has been updated with links to the objects in the new model.

Figure 12.20 LDM Generation Options

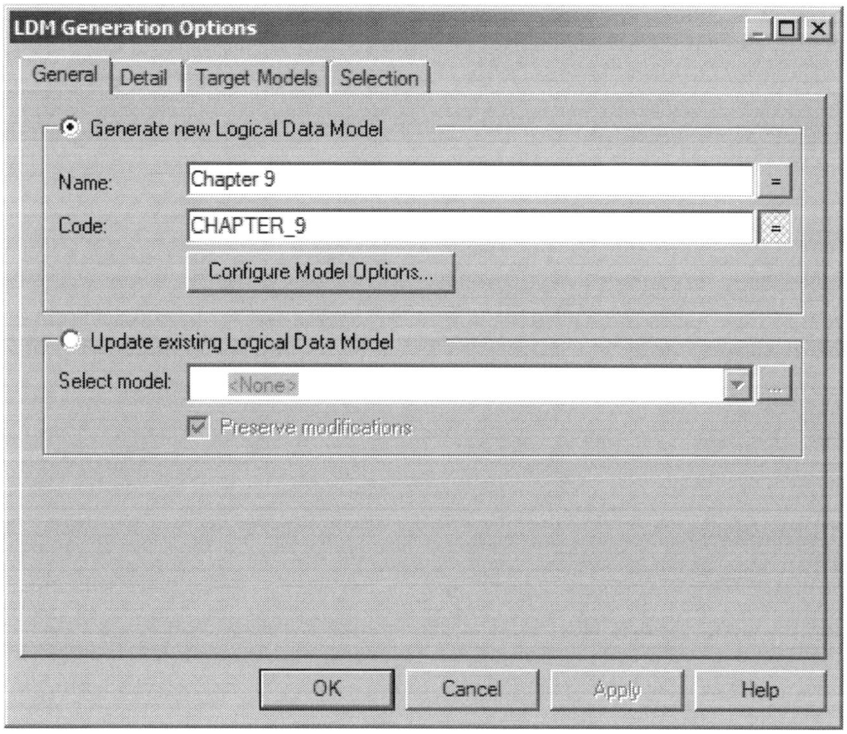

Figure 12.21 - Diagram tabs

Viewing Generation Links

You can see the links between the models via the Generation Links Viewer. On the `Tools` menu, click on `Generation Links`; you can then click on either `Origin Model` or `Derived Models`, depending on which of the two models is the current one. Either way, you'll see a window similar to that in Figure 12.22. You'll need to expand the entries for each model – I've done that for you.

In this viewer, you can see a list of every object in both models. In this case, the only object that wasn't generated to the LDM was the List Report. There are a few other types of objects that also wouldn't be generated, such as Extensions and Reports. These objects can't be directly translated from one model type to another. If you had generated another CDM from your CDM, the List Report would have been copied.

If you double-click any of the object names, you can open a read-only property sheet for that object. In small models such as these, it's easy to see the generation links. In larger models, or models that have generation links to multiple models, you may need to take advantage of the toolbar in the Target pane to filter the items displayed.

❷ "The Generation Links Viewer" (Core Features Guide)

Figure 12.22 Generation Links Viewer

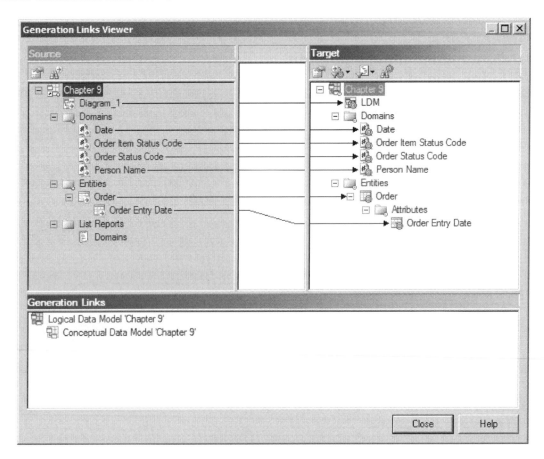

YOUR TURN TO PLAY

1. Close the viewer, and open the 'Version' tab on the property sheet for any object in the LDM; here you can see details of the object from which it was generated, and a tool that allows you to open the property sheet for the original object. Now open the 'Dependencies' tab for any entity in the CDM (see Figure 12.23); you'll see a sub-tab called 'Generated As', which provides information about the entity you generated – double-click the entry to open the property sheet for the generated entity. You'll also see a sub-tab called 'Diagrams', which lists the diagrams that display the entity. Again, double-clicking an entry in this list will open the diagram.

2. On the 'Generated As' sub-tab, click on 'Impact and Lineage Analysis'. Figure 12.24 shows part of the result. This is a fairly simple analysis; later in the book we'll show a more complicated example.

3. Ensure that 'LDM' is the current diagram – click on the diagram's tab if you need to be certain.

4. Create two more entities, called **Order Line** and **Customer**.

Figure 12.23 Generation Dependencies

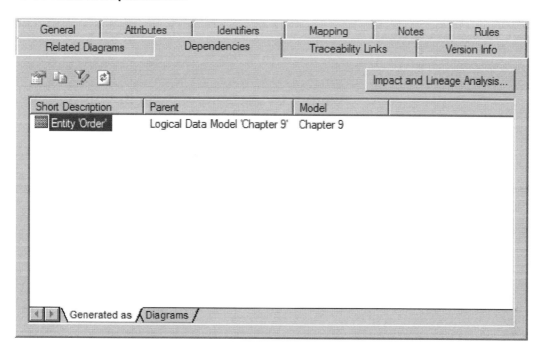

Figure 12.24 Impact and Lineage Analysis

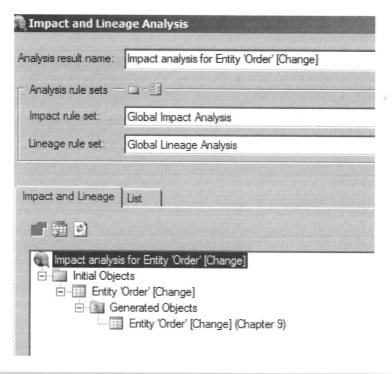

5. Let's continue working with the same LDM diagram. In the Browser, expand the entry for the 'Order' entity until you can see the name of the attribute. Now use the left mouse button to drag the attribute to the **Order Line** entity, and hold down the <CTRL> key while you release the mouse button. You have copied the attribute to a new entity. If you repeat the exercise, you can create another copy of the attribute, with the name suffixed by '2'.

6. Now you're going to create another copy of the attribute via the diagram. First, center the whole diagram by pressing <F8>. Now zoom until you can see all entities clearly; you can press <F6> to zoom in, and <F7> to zoom out. Alternatively, press <Ctrl>, and scroll with the mouse wheel. You can also use the combination of <Shift> and the mouse wheel to scroll sideways. Click on the **Order** Entity, then click on the **Order Entry Date** attribute. Your entity should look like Figure 12.25, with the selected attribute highlighted.

Figure 12.25 Selecting an attribute

7. Now drag the attribute name onto the **Customer** entity, and drop it into the 'attribute' part of the symbol. You have moved the attribute to a new entity.
8. Now drag the attribute back to 'Order', this time holding down <Ctrl>, and copy the attribute. Both entities now have an attribute called 'Order Entry Date'. Repeat this three more times, so you have four attributes in 'Order'. Notice that you can choose where to drop the attribute in the list – use the line that appears on the target entity to help you locate the new place for the attribute.
9. Drag two or three of the attributes in 'Order' to a new position in the same symbol. You can select multiple attributes by pressing <Ctrl> or <Shift> when you click on a series of names; this is standard Windows behavior.
10. After selecting an attribute on an entity symbol, you can open the attribute's property sheet – just double-click the attribute name after selecting it on the symbol.
11. To edit the name of an attribute in the symbol, select the attribute, pause briefly, then click on the name again. You can also select the attribute and press <F2>. Move up and down the list using <Tab> or the cursor (arrow) keys.
12. Remember that you can 'undo' any of these actions.
13. Attributes can also be deleted via the entity symbol. Make sure you still have the CDM open before you do this – in the LDM diagram, select the original **Order Entry Date** attribute in the entity **Order**, and press <Delete>. PowerDesigner will ask if you really want to do this – click on the <Impact> button. The Impact and Lineage Analysis window shows the impact of deleting the attribute, but it does not yet show the lineage. In the drop-down 'Lineage Rule Set', select 'Global Lineage Analysis'. The analysis results are re-calculated, as shown in Figure 12.26. Here you can see the links back to the CDM attribute (ringed), the data item (highlighted), and the original domain (ringed).

Figure 12.26 Impact of deletion

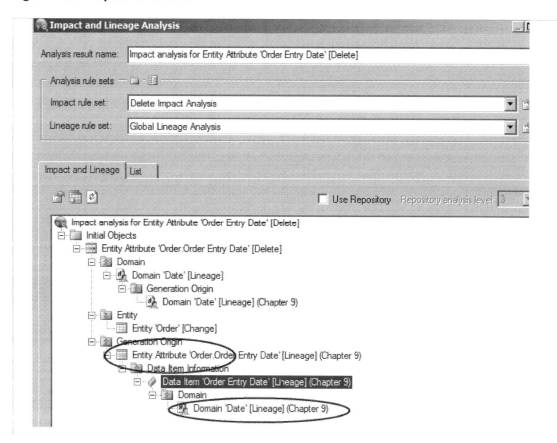

Each entry in the analysis is labeled with an action description:

[Delete]   The attribute that you're proposing to delete, and anything else that would also be deleted

[Lineage]   objects that precede the attribute you're proposing to delete, such as the domain it references, the Conceptual attribute it was generated from, and the data item that the Conceptual attribute uses

[Change]   objects that will be changed if you delete the attribute, in this case the entity

Double-clicking any of the entries in the analysis results, will open the property sheet for that object.

YOUR TURN TO PLAY

1. Click on 'Close' to close the window, and then click on 'No', so you don't delete the attribute. There's one last thing to try out with attributes on symbols; dragging with the *right* mouse button. Select any attribute on a symbol, and hold down the *right* mouse button while dragging the attribute to another entity. When you release the button, the menu shown in Figure 12.27 appears.

2. You have a choice of three actions – to copy, move, or replicate the attribute. Just click on the required action. This also works in the Browser.

Figure 12.27 After dragging with right mouse button

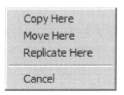

You can drag and drop attributes to copy or move them, or to create a shortcut or a replica:

* between entities in the Browser
* between entity symbols on a diagram
* from the Browser to an entity symbol
* from an entity symbol to the Browser
* from a result list (e.g. from Find Objects) to the Browser

See "Creating Objects in a List of Objects"

Click the 'Add a Row' tool ⊞ to add a new entity at the end of the list. You can also create a new entity by using the arrow keys. When you open a list, the name of the first entity is automatically highlighted for editing. Press the down arrow on your keyboard, and you select the second entry. Keep moving the arrow downwards and eventually you'll move to empty rows, which automatically become entities.

This works in any column in the list: move down the list of modified dates, and you'll eventually reach empty rows and start creating entities. If you have too many rows, select the rows you want to get rid of, and press <Delete>.

The new entities will not actually exist until you apply the changes via the <Apply> or <OK> buttons, or by double-clicking one of the new entities to access the property sheet. When you do this, you are asking PowerDesigner to edit an object that does not yet exist, so it will ask you to commit all the changes you have just made, first. That means ALL the changes, not just the entity you double-clicked. See Figure 10.33.

Figure 10.33 Commitment required

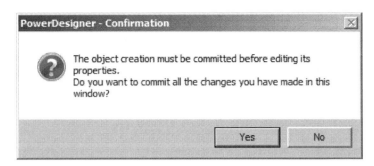

Click <Yes> to carry on, or <No> to go back to the list of objects without applying any changes.

"Object Lists" (Core Features Guide)

"Customizing Object List Columns and Filtering Lists" (Core Features Guide)

"Defining a Filter Expression" (Core Features Guide)

"Customizing Columns in Lists Containing Multiple Types of Objects" (Core Features Guide)

See "Moving, Copying and Deleting Objects" in Chapter 10.

Domain Dependencies

YOUR TURN TO PLAY

1. You now have several copies of **Order Entry Date**, all of which reference the **Date** domain. In the Browser, open the property sheet for the domain **Date**, and you'll see that there are several entries. It should look like Figure 12.29.

2. In Figure 12.29, I customized the properties displayed (see Chapter 10), and also sorted the rows by clicking on the column headings; just click on *Name* or *Parent* to sort by the values in that column.

As well as dragging attributes between entities, you can also drag them around the 'Attributes' tab of the entity's property sheet.

Open the property sheet for the **Order** entity, and select the 'Attributes' tab. Each entry in the list of attributes has a number; you can select the attribute by clicking on that number. Using the <Ctrl> or <Shift> keys, you can select more than one attribute.

Figure 12.29 Domain Dependencies

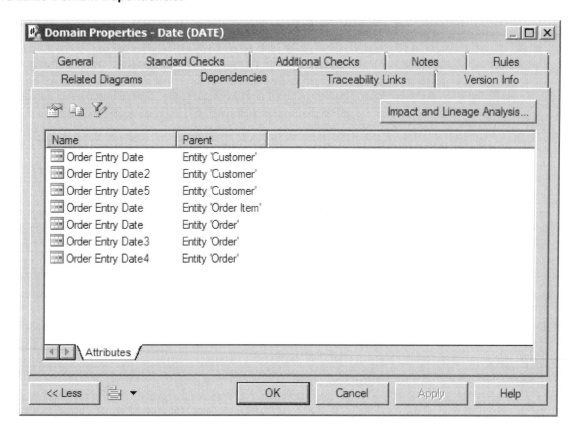

You can move the selected attribute(s) to another point in the list in two ways:

* drag them with the mouse

* use the buttons on the re-sequencing toolbar at the foot of the list of attributes, shown in Figure 12.30. The outer buttons move the selection to the top or bottom of the list; the other buttons move them up or down one row at a time.

Figure 12.30 The re-sequencing toolbar

You can drag attributes from the Browser into the list of attributes. You can only copy attributes this way, not move them; nor can you drag them in the opposite direction.

The PowerDesigner Glossary

In environments with a repository, administrators can deploy a glossary of Terms; a Term is a word or phrase that forms part of a controlled vocabulary.

In the 'Naming Conventions' section of the Model Options (see Figure 12.31), you can enable the use of the Glossary for auto-completion of names in a model. This will also enable you to check the names of objects for compliance with the terms in the glossary.

Figure 12.31 Enabling the Glossary in a model

If you enable the Glossary in a model, terms are suggested from the Glossary as you type in the name of an object. If you type a recognized synonym for a term, then PowerDesigner suggests that you use the term, instead. The glossary auto-complete feature is limited – it does not work within object and sub-object lists (List of..., 'Attribute' tab in Entity properties, etc.).

We don't assume you have access to a glossary, so we won't ask you to do anything yourself. Figure 12.32 shows a fragment of a Glossary.

Figure 12.32 Business terms and synonyms

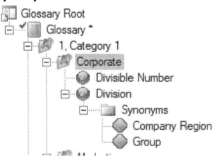

Note the term 'Division' and its synonym, 'Company Region'; also note the term 'Divisible Number'. In Figure 12.33, I'm part-way through typing in the name of a new data item. After I typed the third letter, PowerDesigner suggested two possible terms that I might wish to use. When I hover the mouse over a term, it displays the term's 'comment' property to help me make my choice.

⊖ The comment is extracted from the repository entry, not from the local Glossary.

All I have to do to comply with the Glossary is to select one of the suggested terms; I can then carry on typing the name, and save it when finished. When I save the new object, it is automatically linked to the term in the Glossary. This linkage can be seen via the *Dependencies* property of the entity or term, and also via their Impact and Lineage Analysis.

Figure 12.33 PowerDesigner suggested two possible terms

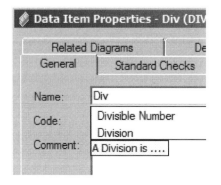

Figure 12.34 shows what happens if I type 'Gro' in the name. The word 'Group' is a synonym of 'Division', so PowerDesigner suggests that I use 'Division' instead.

Figure 12.34 Suggesting the preferred term

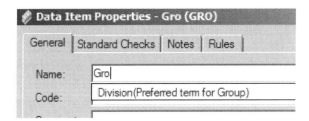

As well as using the terms in the Glossary to help me decide on object names, I can also use them to validate the names in my model when I run the Model Check. Figure 12.35 shows some of the options available.

Figure 12.35 Checking the model against the Glossary

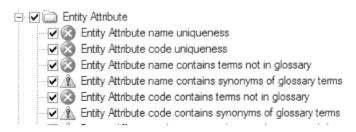

See Chapter 20 to find out more about the Glossary.

Transferring Properties

As you've progressed through the previous exercises, you have seen that objects can depend on each other in various ways. Sometimes, the properties of an object are derived from the properties of another object; the property values have been transferred. This happens either by synchronization or by generation.

Synchronization

The property values in a dependent object are the same as those of the equivalent property in another object, which we'll call the original object. If we change the property value in the original object, the values in the dependent objects also change. Here are some examples that you've seen so far:

- Data items and attributes inherit property values from domains
- Conceptual attributes inherit all their properties from data items
- Replica objects inherit all their properties from the original objects, unless changes are made to the replication properties
- The inheritance of attributes by a subtype entity.

Generation

When we generate a new model from an existing model, new objects are generated from existing objects. In some cases, such as domains, the new object is identical to the original object. In other cases, the new object is derived from the original object: for example, a table is derived from an entity.

You can amend the original object and the derived object independently of each other. By default, the links between the original objects and the derived objects are stored when you generate the new model; this allows you to bring them back into line later on. To do that, you run the model generation again, this time updating the model rather than creating a new one.

You will find out more about model generation in Chapter 18.

Managing Allowable Values

PowerDesigner allows you to record lists of values on any data element, so where you record them depends on your strategy for the use of data elements. All data elements have the same 'Standard Checks' tab, where you can maintain a list of values – look at Figure 12.36 for a reminder.

Figure 12.36 'Standard Checks' tab

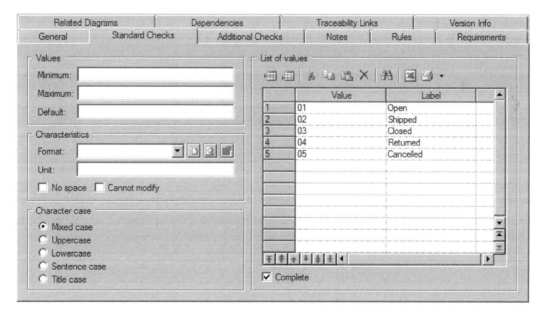

The best type of object to record values is the domain. If you choose to, via the Model Options, you can ensure that all data items, attributes and columns that use the domain automatically inherit changes to the domain values. If a new domain is generated from the original domain by generating a new model, you can ensure that the values are consistent by re-generating the target model(s). If you are unsure of which models you need to re-generate, check the impact analysis for the domain.

The next best place to record values is a data item: this will ensure that the values are the same in conceptual attributes. Re-generating models will ensure that dependent attributes and columns in other models are up to date. Again, check the impact analysis for the data item.

If you prefer not to use domains or data items, identify a single Logical or Physical Data Model as the repository of your lists of values. Whatever approach you take, remember that you can partition any type of data model into packages, and each package can hold a distinct set of data items, entities, or tables, which would allow you to maintain a single model with multiple lists of values for the same thing. Just make sure each package has its own namespace. However, domains are model-level objects – you can only have one domain with a given name in a model.

See "Exporting and Importing Lists of Values", in Chapter 21.

Dependency Matrices

The Dependency Matrix is a really useful PowerDesigner feature. You can create dependency matrices to review and create links between any two types of objects.

You can create an individual matrix from the Browser, or define a matrix in a model extension for reuse by others. You can also copy them between two models of the same type, but only by merging the models. You cannot use the Windows Clipboard, because PowerDesigner views them as a type of diagram.

For data elements, there are a few essential dependencies that we may be interested in:

- Data items used by entities (via attribute)
- Domains used by data items, attributes, or columns
- Domains (or other objects) and the domains they were generated from.

They are also useful for other objects we have seen so far:

- Entities and the diagrams they appear on
- Terms and the data items they're used by.

Creating a dependency matrix is a simple operation - right-click a model or package node in the Browser and select New|Dependency Matrix to open the matrix property sheet on the 'Definition' tab. To define a matrix, you must:

- Select an object type from the current model to populate your matrix rows and another to populate the matrix columns. Now specify how the rows and columns of your matrix will be associated, by selecting a dependency from the list. You can think of a 'dependency' as being a property of the objects in the rows.
- Only direct dependencies are available from the list. You can specify a more complex dependency by clicking the 'Advanced' button to open the Dependency Path Definition dialog. We will see an example of this shortly.
- For certain dependencies, the object type on which the dependency is based will be displayed, and you can select an object attribute to display in the matrix cells. You can

also select the 'No value' symbol, which is displayed if that attribute is not set in any particular instance.

- Click the 'General' tab and enter a name for the matrix (for example 'Domains vs. Data Items').
- Click OK to complete the definition and open your matrix.

Figure 12.37 shows an example with entity attributes in the rows, and domains in the columns.

Figure 12.37 Domains vs. logical attributes – 'Definition' tab

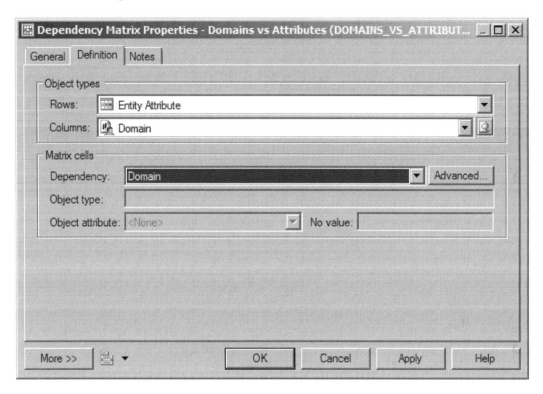

The selected dependency here is the *Domain* property shown on the property sheet for each logical attribute. If you want to have domains in the rows, the dependency would be 'Attributes' – this is the name of the sub-tab on the Domain dependencies tab. Figure 12.38 shows the resulting matrix.

From the matrix, you can access the property sheet of any object listed – just double-click the object name. You can also update the dependency; simply select a cell and press the spacebar or <v>. If the attribute is already linked to a domain, then you will have to select the cell containing '✓', and delete the contents. After this, you can link the attribute to another domain.

You cannot update this way in every matrix. Whether or not you can update entries will depend on the types of objects, the connection between them, and the type of property displayed. For example, you cannot update links to terms from the Glossary with a matrix, although you can display them.

Figure 12.38 Domains vs. logical attributes - matrix

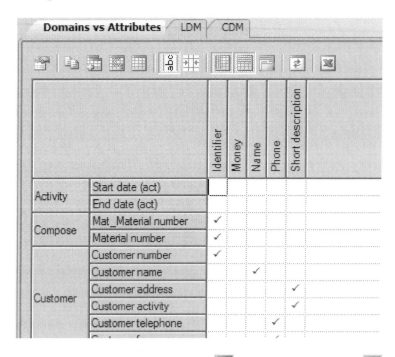

The Toolbar allows you to select only empty rows or populated rows , and also to open a selection window where you can choose the attributes and domains to be included. The selection window is shown in Figure 12.39.

Figure 12.39 Selecting matrix objects

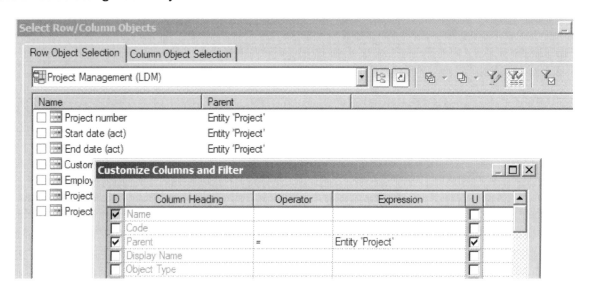

In this example, the selection list is limited to attributes of the entity 'Project'.

Whenever you open a matrix, the content is refreshed using the rules in the selection window. In the above example, the content would include any new domains or attributes in the 'Project' entity. You can also refresh the content of a matrix while it is open, by clicking on the *Refresh* tool ⟳, or pressing <F5>. Some new content will appear automatically when you create it, but it is best to be certain that everything you need is included.

The content of the matrix can be exported to an Excel file by clicking on the *Export to Excel* tool ⊠, or by right-clicking the matrix name in the Browser and selecting `Export|Excel`.

❷ "Working with Dependency Matrices" (Custom Features Guide)

⊖ If your model contains shortcuts to objects in other models, they will appear in the matrix; you will not be able to distinguish them from objects that are not shortcuts. You can de-select them in the selection window shown in Figure 12.38, by simply clicking on the *Include External Shortcuts* tool ⟳.

Advanced Dependencies

You can examine dependencies between two types of objects that are not directly associated with each other by using the Dependency Path Definition dialog, which is accessible by clicking the 'Advanced' button shown in Figure 12.36. This allows you to specify a path passing through as many intermediate linking objects as necessary. For example, assume we need to create a matrix showing the link between data items and entities. The objects are not linked directly, they are linked via an intermediate attribute, and so we have to define the path between the objects. Figure 12.40 shows the necessary selections.

Matrices that display advanced dependencies cannot be used to update the model, because the property(s) displayed in the matrix has been derived.

❷ "Specifying Advanced Dependencies" (Custom Features Guide)

Figure 12.40 The path from data item to entity

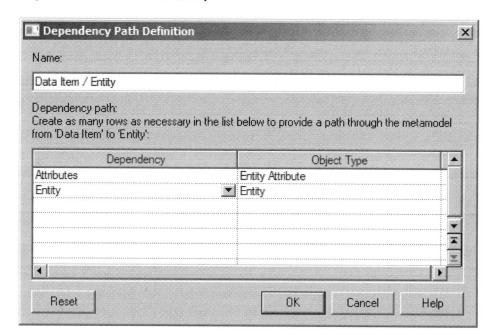

EXERCISE 10: Creating a new Conceptual Data Model in PowerDesigner

Create a new Project in your workspace, called 'Exercise 10'; make sure the project directory has the same parent directory as the previous projects you created. Find the Excel file that you used to create entities in Exercise 9, and use the Excel Import wizard to create a new Conceptual Data Model from the spreadsheet; call this model 'Exercise 10'. Rename the diagram to 'Exercise 10 CDM'. You should now have six entities in the Browser – Color, Ice Cream Cone, Ice Cream Container, Ice Cream Cup, Order, and Order Line. Create the domains shown in Table 12.11. Create some via the Browser, and some via a List of Domains.

Table 12.11 Domains

Domain	Data Type	Length	Precision	List of Values
Color Code	Characters	1		b=blue
Short Name	Characters	20		
Sugar or Wafer Indicator	Characters	1		S = Sugar W = Wafer
Height	Number	3		
Ice Cream Container UPC	Number	16		
Standard Identifier	Number	10		
Standard Date	Date			
Standard Large Value	Number	4	2	

Create the data items shown in Table 12.12. Again, try different ways of creating them.

Table 12.12 Data items

Data Item	Domain	Description
Color Code	Color Code	The short name of one of the standard ice cream colors.
Color Name	Short Name	The full name of one of the standard ice cream colors.
Ice Cream Cone Sugar or Wafer Indicator	Sugar or Wafer Indicator	Determines whether the ice cream cone is made of a sugar-based or wafer-based material.
Ice Cream Container Height	Height	The height, in millimeters, of the container. Used by inventory to determine how many containers can fit on a storage shelf.
Ice Cream Container Name	Short Name	The name our store employees use for communicating with consumers on what they would like to order.
Ice Cream Container UPC	Ice Cream Container UPC	A numeric code used to identify a specific product across the ice cream industry.

Reuse all the data items you've just created to create the attributes shown in Table 12.13.

Table 12.13 Attributes for Color, Ice Cream Cone, and Ice Cream Container

Entity	Data Item
Color	Color Code
Color	Color Name
Ice Cream Cone	Ice Cream Cone Sugar or Wafer Indicator
Ice Cream Container	Ice Cream Container Height
Ice Cream Container	Ice Cream Container Name
Ice Cream Container	Ice Cream Container UPC

Create the attributes on the Order entity as shown in Table 12.14 – the data items do not exist yet.

Table 12.14 Attributes for Order

Attribute	Domain	Description
Order Number	Standard Identifier	The unique number assigned to each order placed by a consumer. It is a numeric sequence number that never repeats.
Order Placed Date	Standard Date	The date the order was placed.
Order Total Value	Standard Large Value	The total value of the order in the default national currency, including any applicable sales tax.

Key Points

- For every Conceptual attribute, there is always a data item.

- Use domains to manage the characteristics of your data elements.

- Combine data items and the Glossary for data governance.

- Data element properties are transferred between objects and between models.

- A replica is a synchronized copy of the original object; you control the synchronization.

- The generation links viewer eases visualizing the impact of change at the model level.

- Impact and lineage analysis visualizes the impact of change at the object level.

- 'Drag and drop' saves time - remember to drag with the right mouse button.

- Use dependency matrices to review and create links between any two types of object.

Relationships now
PowerDesigner has them
Connecting the dots

In Chapter 5, we identified three levels of relationship, all of which PowerDesigner supports:

Subject Area   Relationships in Conceptual or Logical Data Models

Logical   Relationships in Logical Data Models

Physical   References in Physical Data Models

The fundamentals of relationships are the same for all three levels; all relationships and references are 'link objects'. Once you have created a link object, it can be modified in the same way as any other object. See Chapter 10 if you need a refresher.

In this chapter, we focus on Relationships in the Conceptual and Logical Data Models. We will see how different References are in the Physical Data Model in Chapter 17.

Rules that you cannot describe using relationships can be defined in PowerDesigner as Business Rules, and linked to any object in any model. If your organization has documented requirements in Microsoft Word documents, you can import those documents into PowerDesigner Requirements models, and link the requirements to any object in any model. See Chapter 23.

Creating Relationships in PowerDesigner

You can create a relationship from the palette, the Browser, or the Model menu.

Creating a Relationship from the Palette

In PowerDesigner, each type of diagram has a specific drawing palette. As you see in Figure 13.1, the palettes for the different types of data models have a lot in common. Nearly all of the tools that you would use to create a relationship or reference show two connected symbols; the only exceptions are the 'Create Association' and 'Create Association Link' tools on the Conceptual Diagram palette, which are gray, as the selected model notation does not support Merise objects.

Table 13.1 shows the three basic drawing actions and the tools associated with them in each palette.

Figure 13.1 The Diagram palettes

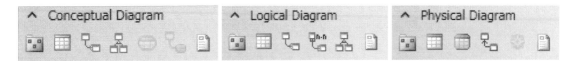

Table 13.1 Relationship drawing actions

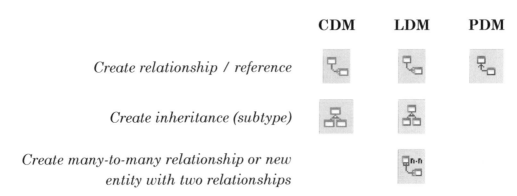

	CDM	LDM	PDM
Create relationship / reference	⬚	⬚	⬚
Create inheritance (subtype)	⬚	⬚	
Create many-to-many relationship or new entity with two relationships		⬚	

To create a relationship in a Conceptual or Logical Diagram, select the appropriate Relationship tool in the diagram Palette. Decide which direction the relationship needs to go. In Figure 13.2, the modeler wants to draw a new relationship between **Entity_7** and **Entity_6**. There are several ways of visualizing this situation, just use whichever you're comfortable with:

- **Entity_7** is the *parent* entity, and **Entity_6** is the *child* entity
- **Entity_7** is at the *one* end of the relationship, and **Entity_6** is at the *many* end
- **Entity_7** is the parent entity, and **Entity_6** is the child entity
- The relationship goes *from* **Entity_7** *to* **Entity_6**

Click inside the first entity to link and, while continuing to hold down the mouse button, drag the cursor to the second entity. Release the mouse button inside the second entity, and PowerDesigner will draw the line for you. Drawing an inheritance requires a different technique – see "Subtypes in PowerDesigner" later in this chapter.

Figure 13.2 Drawing a relationship

The left-hand image in Figure 13.2 shows a relationship being drawn from **Entity_7** to **Entity_6**. When the mouse button is released over **Entity_6**, the relationship shown in the right-hand image is automatically created.

New relationships are zero-to-many, and completely optional. To revise the optionality and cardinality, open the relationship's property sheet – see later in this chapter.

If you make a mistake, and draw the relationship in the wrong direction, all is not lost. Double-click the relationship, and then reverse the entities listed in 'Entity 1' and 'Entity 2' on the 'General' tab of the relationship's property sheet. See Figure 13.5 for an example.

If you are using 'free angle corners' or you haven't enabled 'Automatic Link Routing' in your Display Preferences (see later in this chapter), you can choose the route for the link yourself. Click inside the first entity to link and, while continuing to hold down the mouse button, drag the cursor to the first point at which you want the link to change direction, and release the mouse button. Now click the mouse button wherever you want to create another corner; click on the second entity to complete drawing the line.

If you have enabled 'Automatic Link Routing', PowerDesigner will ignore your suggested route.

Every new relationship is given a default name and cardinalities; it is a fully-optional one-to-many relationship.

When you draw a relationship with the mouse, the positions where you click in the entity symbols become the default positions for the 'handles' that form the ends of the relationship. When you lasso symbols to select them, the relationship is only included in the selection if both handles are inside the selection box.

In Chapter 10, we told you about the `Disposition` options – remember that `Arrange Attach Points` causes the relationship handles to move to the entity centers, which may result in changes to the routing of the relationship line.

YOUR TURN TO PLAY

1. Open the "Exercises" workspace, and create a new top-level folder called 'Chapter 13'. Now create a new CDM called 'Chapter 13', and save it in your Exercises folder.

2. Access the Display Preferences for the diagram in the new model, and make the following settings:

Show bridges at intersections	Enabled
Automatic Link Routing	Not Enabled
Relationship Content	only include 'Name'
Relationship Format	set corners to the first option (free angles):

Corners: [‾‾‾‾⌐_‾‾‾ ▼]

3. Draw four entities on the diagram, with the names and approximate positions illustrated in Figure 13.3. The style and content of the entity symbols doesn't matter.

Figure 13.3 New diagram - draw these entities

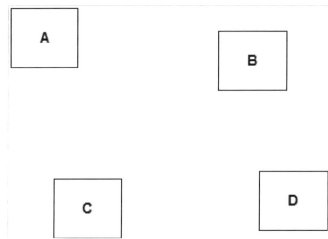

4. Draw a relationship from the middle of entity **A** to the middle of entity **B** – don't attempt to add any corners.
5. Draw a relationship from entity **B** to entity **C** – add several corners along the way by clicking on the Canvas (you have to release the mouse button to create the first corner).

Creating a Relationship from a List

Select `Model|Relationships` to access the list of Relationships, and click the *Add a Row* tool. If you don't want to use the default name (see below), type in the name of the relationship. Select the entities via the drop-down lists called 'Entity 1' and 'Entity 2': if you don't select two entities, you will not be able to create the relationship. When you click on <Apply> or 'Create', the relationship will automatically appear on the diagram.

Remember that you can customize the list of Relationships, so you can display and edit any relationship properties.

YOUR TURN TO PLAY

1. Open the list of relationships via the 'Model' menu – your two relationships will be shown in the list. Use the *Customize Columns and Filter* tool to customize the columns displayed in the list to match Figure 13.4.

Figure 13.4 Relationship properties

	Name ▲ ▾	Entity 1 ▾	(1)->(2) ▾	M ▾	(2)->(1) ▾	M ▾	Entity 2 ▾
1	Relationship_1	A	0,n	☐	0,1	☐	B
2	Relationship_2	B	0,1	☐	0,1	☐	C
→	Relationship_3	A	1,n	☑	0,n	☐	C

List of Relationships

Table 13.2 lists the properties that you need to include. In some cases, the column heading in the list of relationships is different from the property name, so we've highlighted these differences for you.

Table 13.2 Relationship properties to include

Column Heading	Property Name in List
Name	Name
Entity 1	Entity 1
(1)->(2)	Entity 1 -> Entity 2 Role Cardinality
M	Entity 1 -> Entity 2 Role Mandatory*
(2)->(1)	Entity 2 -> Entity 1 Role Cardinality
M	Entity 1 -> Entity 2 Role Mandatory
Entity 2	Entity 2.

* this column needs to be moved up the list of properties – select the entry and click the 'up' arrow to do this.

2. In the list of relationships, add a new entry to the end of the list, and set Entity 1 to 'A', and Entity 2 to 'C'. Amend the properties of the relationships to match Figure 13.4.

Creating a Relationship in the Browser

This is easy – just right-click the model or package in the Browser, and select `New|Relationship`. An empty property sheet is opened for the Relationship, showing the 'General' tab. You have to choose your two entities before you can create the relationship or switch to a different tab. Remember to click <OK> or <Apply> to save the new relationship.

Relationship Properties

The object properties for relationships look very similar to those of other objects. Figure 13.5 shows the General' properties tab for a relationship. This is where you provide the name of the relationship, and select the two entities joined by the relationship.

Note the tools to the right of the entity names – working from right to left, these allow you to display the properties of the selected entity, select an entity from a list, and create a new entity. This last option is useful if you need to link the relationship to an entity that doesn't yet exist – you can create the entity object, amend the relationship, and add the new entity to the current diagram in one single action.

At the top of every tab in the property sheet is a depiction of the relationship using the default style for the diagram; the depiction changes in step with changes you make to the relationship properties. The labels 'Entity 1' and 'Entity 2' above the entity symbols are actually tools – just click on the label to access the property sheet for the entity.

Figure 13.5 Relationship 'General' tab

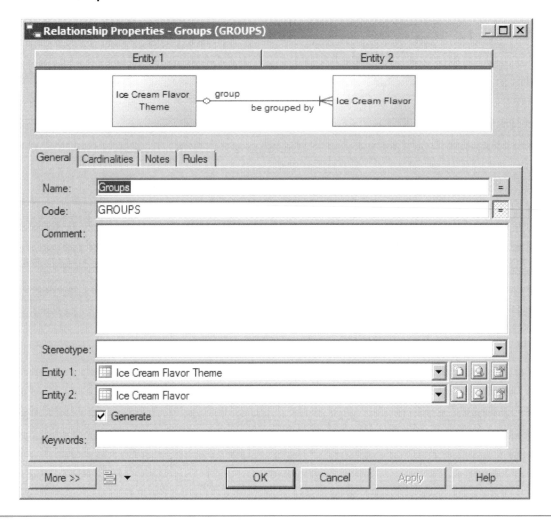

PowerDesigner automatically creates relationship names, but you really should change them as soon as you can. The default names, such as **Relationship_6**, are not very helpful when you are looking at a list of relationships in the Browser, or trying to find a relationship to include on your diagram. Use full names such as "Ice Cream Flavor Dispensed as Scoops". On the 'Cardinalities' tab, you can also provide a role name for each 'direction' of the relationship, and you can elect to show all, none, or any of these names for display on a diagram.

Relationship names have to be unique where a pair of entities is connected by two or more relationships. For example, you cannot have two 'manages' relationships between the **Employee** and **Department** entities.

Relationship names do not have to be unique within a model, but the equivalent 'codes' may have to be unique, depending on the model options. By default, the code is automatically generated from the name, so it makes life much easier if you make the names unique. See "Names and Codes in PowerDesigner Objects" in Chapter 10.

"Defining a Code Option for Relationships" (Data Modeling)

The Cardinalities Tab

You have already seen the content of most of the tabs for a relationship, because they are the same as the tabs for other objects. The tab you really need to see now is the 'Cardinalities' tab, shown in Figure 13.6. This is the key tab for a relationship, where you specify *how* the two entities are related.

Figure 13.6 Relationship 'Cardinalities' tab

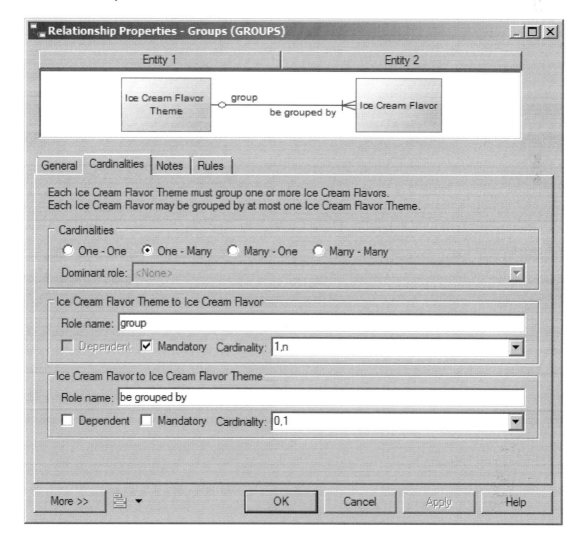

There is a lot of information on the 'Cardinalities' tab. The overall cardinalities are set by your choice of one of the four radio buttons at the top. The two drop-down cardinality properties allow you to fine-tune the cardinalities. For example, you could overtype '1,n' in Figure 13.6 with '0,4', which would make the relationship completely optional, and also set the maximum number of Flavors in a Theme to four. Using the Display Preferences, you can display the cardinalities on a diagram. See later in this chapter.

If your relationship cardinalities are 'One – One', you can choose the 'Dominant' role in the relationship – the primary identifier attributes of the 'dominant' entity are migrated along the relationship to the other entity. See "Identifier Migration Along Relationships", in Chapter 14.

If the child entity is partially identified by the relationship, then you must select the _Dependent_ property.

❷ "Relationship Property Sheet Cardinalities Tab" (Data Modeling)

The Importance of Role Names

In Figure 13.6, the relationship has two role names, one for each direction of the relationship. A role name describes _how_ **Ice Cream Flavor Theme** is related to **Ice Cream Flavor**, or vice versa. PowerDesigner uses the role names to generate "assertion statements" for the relationships – see "Assertion Statements" below, for more information.

PowerDesigner will also use the relationship role name to construct the name of attributes migrated via relationships of inheritance links. See "Attribute Migration Settings", in Chapter 14. When creating a role name, you should use the infinitive phrase that describes the relationship of one entity to the other. For example, each Order may _contain_ one or more lines.

YOUR TURN TO PLAY

1. In the Browser, create a relationship from entity **B** to entity **D**. Set the cardinalities to the entries shown in Figure 13.7.
2. Check the location of the new relationship on the diagram. This is where you realize that, even though you were very careful, you made a mistake. You really meant to add a relationship from **C** to **D**, not from **B** to **D**. Re-open the property sheet for **Relationship_4**, and use the drop-down list to change Entity 1 from **B** to **C**. The diagram will now look something like Figure 13.8.

Figure 13.7 New relationship via Browser

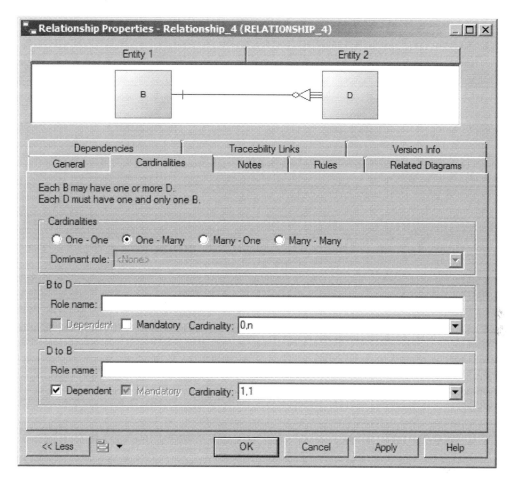

Figure 13.8 2nd new diagram

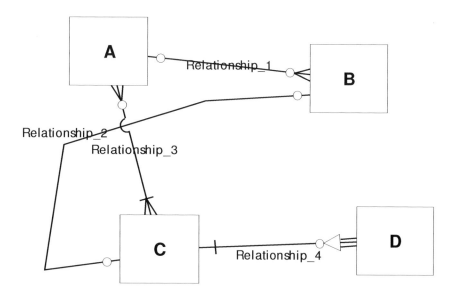

Assertion Statements

It often makes sense to show relationship role names on a diagram, as well as, or instead of the relationship names. Figure 13.9 shows a simple example.

Figure 13.9 Relationship role names

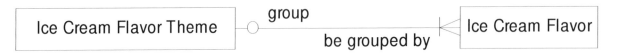

On the 'Cardinalities' tab for a relationship, the entity role names and relationship cardinalities are combined into 'assertion' statements. These statements describe the relationship in plain English, and can be extracted in Reports and List Reports (select the *Assertion* property). As you change the cardinalities and role names in Figure 13.9, the depiction of the relationship changes, as do the 'Assertion Statements'.

In Figure 13.9, the relationship has two role names, and PowerDesigner has placed them on the diagram in a way that makes assertion statements easier to read. You just read them in a clockwise fashion. Therefore, we have:

Ice Cream Flavor Theme – *group* – **Ice Cream Flavor**

and

Ice Cream Flavor – *be grouped by* – **Ice Cream Flavor Theme**

PowerDesigner combines these words with the relationship cardinality and optionality to create the assertion statements:

Each **Ice Cream Flavor Theme** must *group* one or more **Ice Cream Flavors**

Each **Ice Cream Flavor** may *be grouped by* at most one **Ice Cream Flavor Theme**.

There is a standard model extension[8] that converts entity names to the plural equivalent, which can be imported into any CDM or LDM. In the example above, this extension has been imported, and PowerDesigner has generated the plural name for the 'Ice Cream Flavor' entity. PowerDesigner creates the plural name by suffixing the entity name with 's'; this doesn't work for some entities, so you also have the option of adding your own plural name via a new property in the entity's 'General' tab. You can try this out in Exercise 11. See Chapter 23 to find out how to ensure this extension is available for all new data models.

---

[8] Called "Relationship Assertion with Plural Entity Names"

YOUR TURN TO PLAY

The relationships don't have meaningful names yet, so change the names to those shown in Table 13.3, and add the role names shown in the table. The quickest place to change the names is in the list of relationships. If you customize the list of relationships again, you can also display the role names.

Table 13.3 New relationship names and role names

Entity 1	Entity 2	Original Name	New Name	Entity 1 > Entity 2 role name	Entity 1 > Entity 2 role name
A	B	Relationship_1	owns	own	be owned by
B	C	Relationship_2	contains	contain	be within
A	C	Relationship_3	apply for	apply for	be applied for by
C	D	Relationship_4	request	request	be requested by

The second role names have been padded out with 'be' and 'by' to improve the assertion statements. For example:

Each *C* may **request** one or more *D*.

Each *D* must **be requested by** one and only one *C*.

The list of relationships is sorted by the relationship name; when you open the list after changing the relationship names, they will, of course, be in a different sequence.

An Entity's Relationships

On the property sheet for an entity, there is no 'Relationships' tab; relationships are just one example of the dependencies an entity may have, so they have a sub-tab on the 'Dependencies' tab. If you prefer to have a separate tab for relationships, you can create one via a model extension. The 'Dependencies' tab is shown in Figure 13.10; remember that you can open the property sheet for a relationship by double-clicking the relationship name in the list.

Figure 13.10 Entity 'Dependencies' tab

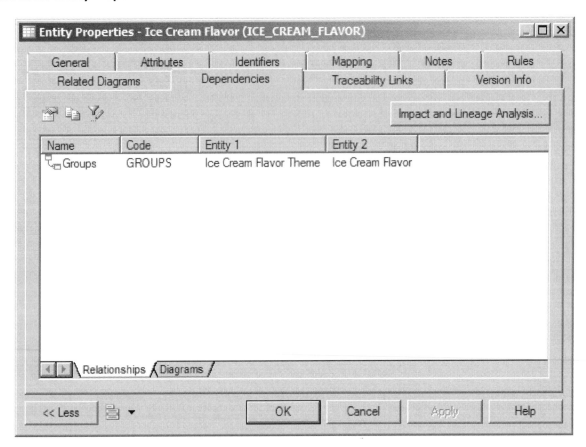

Display Preferences for Relationships

The Display Preferences give you control over the appearance of relationships on a diagram. Look at Figure 13.11 for an example of a relationship that is displaying the role names and cardinalities. Note also the curved right-angled corner on the relationship line.

Figure 13.11 Relationship with role names and cardinalities

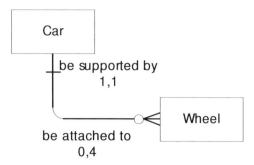

Did you notice that the relationship role names in Figure 13.11 do not use the same verb? In most relationships, you would use the same verb for both role names, but that is not compulsory. Use the verbs that provide the most meaning for each direction of the relationship.

Figure 13.12 shows the Display Preferences for the relationships in Figure 13.11. This works in the same way as the display preferences for entities, except for the split between the source, center, and destination part of the line. As with entities, you can choose which diagrams to apply a style to, and set a default style.

Figure 13.12 Relationship display preferences

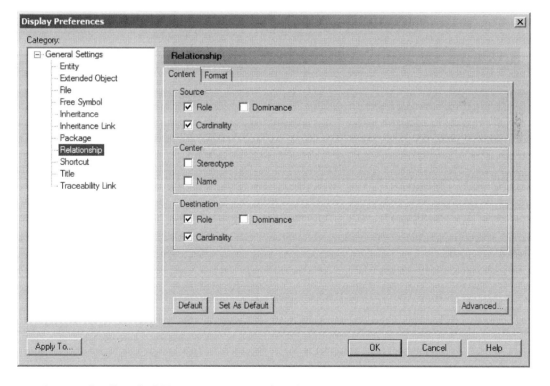

Figure 13.3 shows the Symbol Format options for the Relationships, which you can access from Figure 13.2 by selecting the 'Format' tab, then clicking on <Modify>. The format options are similar to those for entities, though there are fewer tabs, and additional options for the line style.

Figure 13.13 Relationship symbol format options

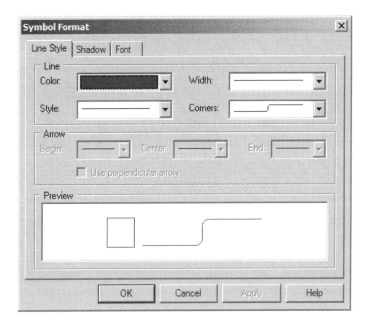

Figure 13.14 shows some of the style options available. You can override the notation style for lines, and choose to use dashed lines instead, and you can choose between four corner styles. For an individual relationship, you can choose between a large number of arrowheads for each end, but we wouldn't recommend that, except when presenting a simplified data model[9] using a specially-constructed diagram. In general, you should use the line style that comes with the notation you're using.

Figure 13.14 Relationship style options

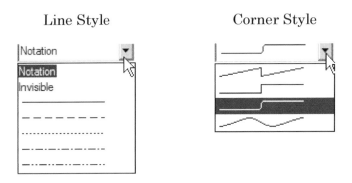

Figure 13.15 illustrates the different corner styles that are available to you, in the order presented above.

---

[9] For example, the 'Fact Model' described in (Ross & Lam, 2011, pp. 103-130)

Figure 13.15 Corner Styles illustrated

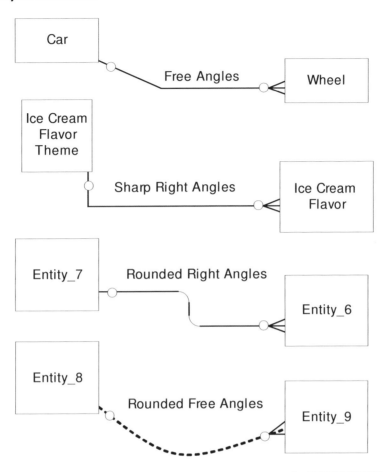

YOUR TURN TO PLAY

During analysis, we discover that there is a maximum 6 instances of *D* in the *request* relationship. Open the properties for the relationship.

1. Change the cardinalities of 'C to D' from '0,n' to '0,6' – simply replace the 'n' with '6'.

2. Now change the Display Preferences to show more information – display both role names and both cardinalities. Remember to apply it to 'all symbols'. The resulting diagram should look like Figure 13.16.

Okay, the diagram is messy, but you can see that PowerDesigner places the role names and cardinalities at the appropriate end of the relationship, and in such a position that they can be read in a clockwise fashion.

Figure 13.16 More relationship properties displayed

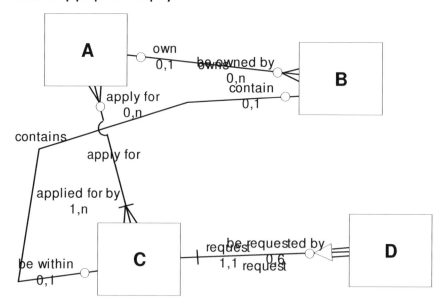

Routing Relationships

PowerDesigner allows you to take complete control of the routing of your relationships, and also offers to manage the routing for you. To allow PowerDesigner to route your lines, ensure that your default corner style has right-angled corners, and select 'Automatic Link Routing' in the Display Preferences. It is also useful to select 'Show bridges at intersections', as well.

See "Routing Link Objects" in Chapter 10, to remind yourself of the capabilities.

YOUR TURN TO PLAY

It's time to reformat and straighten our relationship lines, *without* dragging anything around.
1. Select all symbols on the diagram (I use <Ctrl+A>), and right-click on one of the relationship lines. If the contextual menu that appears does not have the `Reroute link` option at the top, then you missed the target, and right-clicked on something else, instead. Once you have the correct menu displayed, select `Reroute link`.

Nothing happened, did it?

PowerDesigner will only automatically route relationships for you if the corner style has right-angled corners, and yours are all 'freestyle'. Via Display Preferences, change the corner style to 'rounded right angles' , and apply this to all symbols.

When you change the corner style this way, PowerDesigner automatically reroutes the links for you, but they can still be improved. The easiest fixes to apply are the horizontal and vertical alignments – select all symbols, then press <Ctrl+H>, followed by <Ctrl+L> - the sequence doesn't matter, as relationships would only be affected by one or the other, not both. You should see some improvements, but that long, winding relationship from **B** to **C** will not have changed, so we have to give that one special treatment.

2. Right-click the relationship from **B** to **C**, and select `Arrange Connectors` from the `Disposition` options. The line will now be shortened, but will probably (it does on my diagram) overlap the relationship from **C** to **D**. Undo the last change, to revert back to the long, winding line.

3. It's time to let PowerDesigner take control of routing – in Display Preferences, enable 'Automatic Link Routing'. Now select the **B** to **C** relationship, and run 'Arrange Connectors' again. The line will be rerouted differently from before, and other lines have probably been moved slightly to make room for it. Any additional minor adjustments will have to be made manually.

4. Your relationships will probably look clearer if your entities are better aligned – try to re-create the layout shown in Figure 13.17. First, use the mouse to drag the entities into approximately the right positions. Second, select vertical or horizontal groups of entities, and use the tools on the layout toolbar or the symbol menu to align them.

You can achieve a neater result when centering symbols if you select relationships, as well as entities. For example, use the mouse to roughly line up entities A, C, and D vertically, and then use a selection box to select all three entities and their connecting relationships. Right-click any selected symbol to open a contextual menu, and select `Center on Horizontal Axis` from the Align menu (or press <Ctrl+H>). Ensure that all the symbols remain selected, re-open the contextual menu, and select `Evenly Space Vertically` from the `Align` menu (or press <Ctrl+L>).

As well as using the mouse, you can use the keyboard arrow keys to move selected symbols. As you move entities, the relationships are continually re-drawn. For final adjustments, drag segments of relationships sideways, or drag relationships sideways by their end handles. You can also drag the relationship names and role names around if they get in each other's way. You may need to drag the *owns* relationship to a different location (I had to) – use the corner handle to do this.

In Figure 13.7, the Display Preferences were changed, to hide the relationship names.

Select different combinations of entities, and play with the facilities on the layout toolbar. Once you get used to them, they'll enable you to make clear, easy-to-follow diagrams quickly. Try the `Flip Horizontal` and `Flip Vertical` options on the `Disposition` menu, too.

Figure 13.17 A finished diagram

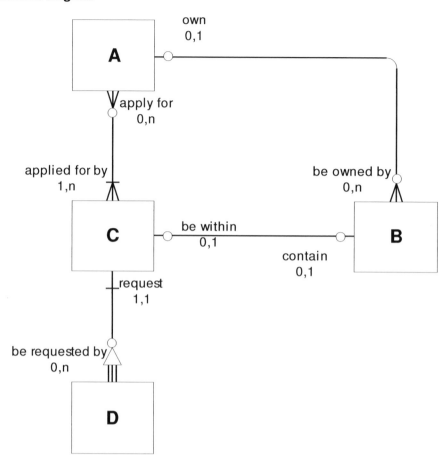

Graphical Synonyms

We introduced the concept of graphical synonyms in Chapter 10. Remember, a graphical synonym is an additional symbol for an object on a diagram. Sometimes, creating multiple symbols for an object in a diagram can improve readability by reducing the length or complexity of links. You create a graphical synonym by right-clicking a symbol and selecting `Edit|Create Graphical Synonym`.

You can create as many graphical synonyms as you want within the same diagram. You can even create graphical synonyms of graphical synonyms, and of object shortcuts. Each graphical synonym displays the name of the object followed by a colon and the number of the synonym. In Figure 13.18, **Contact : 1** and **Contact : 2** both represent the **Contact** entity.

If you create a Graphical Synonym from a relationship, graphical synonyms of the related entities are also created. Note that though you cannot visually distinguish a graphical synonym of a relationship from a normal relationship (unless you display the name attribute), when you select a link symbol, it is identified as a graphical synonym in its tooltip.

You can create Graphical Synonyms for any data model symbols except for inheritances and inheritance links in the CDM and LDM.

Figure 13.18 Graphical synonyms

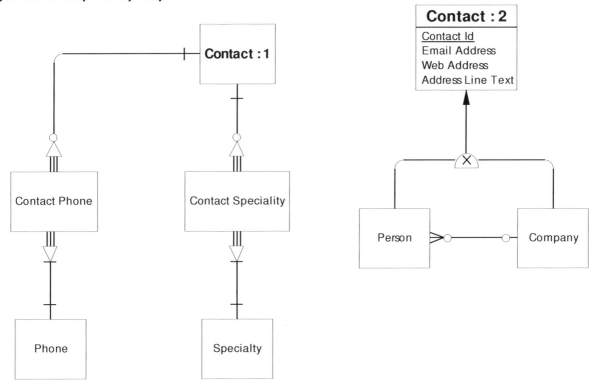

You can move relationships between graphical synonyms if you want to – to create Figure 13.18, I dragged the end handle of the inheritance link (the arrow head) from **Contact : 1** to **Contact : 2**. If you wish, you could edit the Display Preferences for one of the graphical synonyms to show different content – I did this in Figure 13.18.

If you delete a graphical synonym, all of its linked symbols are connected to one of the other graphical synonyms, or the original symbol, if the last graphical synonym has been removed.

It is possible to create Graphical Synonyms accidentally, by dragging a relationship onto a diagram; if one or both of the related entities is already present on the diagram, graphical synonyms are created. To avoid this happening, hold down the <Shift> key when you drag the relationship onto the diagram.

YOUR TURN TO PLAY

1. Select all of the symbols in your diagram, and right-click on one of the symbols. Select Create Diagram from Selection to create an identical diagram.
2. In the new diagram, select entity **C,** and then select Create Graphical Synonym on the Edit menu. Drag the new symbol to the left of entity **C : 1.** Now select the **request** relationship, and drag the top handle to the center of entity **C : 2.** That part of the diagram should now look like Figure 13.19.

Figure 13.19 Two copies of the entity

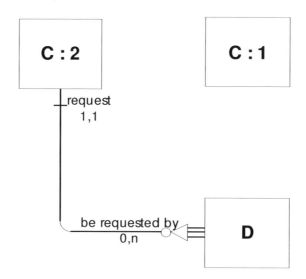

3. Open the property sheet for the **request** relationship to confirm that it's still connected to entity **C**. Now delete either of the symbols for entity **C**; all the relationships are now connected to the remaining symbol.

Many-to-many relationships

To create a many-to-many relationship in a CDM, create a relationship as you would normally, then select the 'many-to-many' option on the 'Cardinalities' tab.

By default, the LDM does not support many-to-many relationships. You can enable them if you want to via the model options (they are disabled by default).

PowerDesigner refers to 'many-to-many' relationships as 'n-n' relationships, so the option is called 'Allow n-n relationships'.

There is a special tool in the LDM palette for creating many-to-many relationships. When you connect two entities using this tool, PowerDesigner will do one of two things, depending on whether or not 'n-n relationships' have been enabled via the Model Options:

Disabled (default) PowerDesigner will create a new entity instead of a relationship, with one-to-many dependent relationships to the two entities you wanted to relate to each other. See the first example in Figure 13.20.

Enabled PowerDesigner will draw a many-to-many relationship. See the second example in Figure 13.20.

Figure 13.20 Many-to-many relationships in the LDM

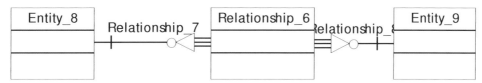

Table 13.4 Many-to-many relationships and model generation

Target Model Type	Action
CDM	Identical many-to-many relationships generated.
LDM	Before you generate the target model, you can change the model options to enable many-to-many relationships. However, many-to-many relationships always resolve into an associative entity and two relationships, similar to the first example in Figure 13.20.
PDM	Many-to-many relationships are converted into an associative table and two references, similar to the first example in Figure 13.20.

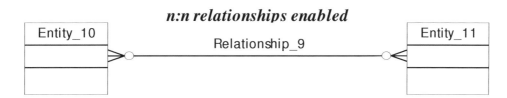

When you generate a new model, how many-to-many relationships are treated depends on the options available in the new (target) model. See Table 13.4 for details.

YOUR TURN TO PLAY

1. Create a new LDM called 'Chapter 13' in your 'Chapter 13' folder. Draw four entities in this pattern:

A	B
C	D

2. Check the model options, making sure that 'Allow n-n relationships' is **not** selected. Now select the 'n-n Relationship' tool , and draw a relationship from entity **A** to entity **B**. PowerDesigner will automatically create an 'associative' entity and two relationships, as shown in Figure 13.21.

Figure 13.21 The new associative entity

3. Change the model options to allow n-n relationships, and draw a many-to-many relationship from entity **C** to entity **D**. This time, the result is a single many-to-many relationship.
4. Draw a one-to-many relationship from entity **C** to entity **D**. Your diagram should now look like Figure 13.22.

Figure 13.22 Our three relationships

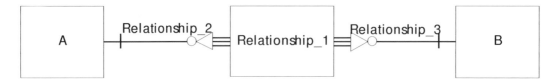

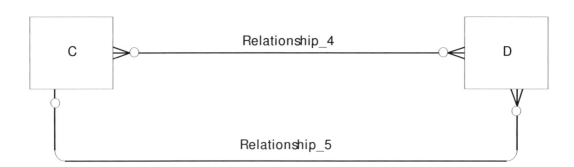

5. Open the contextual menu for **Relationship_5,** and select Change to Entity. The relationship will be converted into an entity and two relationships. Note that the original cardinalities have been preserved – an instance of entity **D** can still only be related to one instance of entity **C.**
6. Now change the model options again, to disable n-n relationships. Did you see what happened to the many-to-many relationship, **Relationship_4**? It was converted into an entity and two relationships.
7. Save the model.

If you right-click any relationship, and select Change to Entity, PowerDesigner will convert the relationship into an entity and two relationships.

Resolving Many-to-many Relationships

Converting a many-to-many relationship into a new entity and two relationships is often referred to as 'resolving' the many-to-many relationship. The new entity is referred to as an 'associative' entity. The simplest way to resolve a many-to-many relationship in PowerDesigner is to right-click it in the Browser or on a diagram, and select `Change to Entity` on the contextual menu. The name of the new entity will be the same as the name of the original relationship.

❓ "Changing a Relationship into an Associative Entity" (Data Modeling)

Recursive (Reflexive) Relationships

Recursive relationships are simple to draw from the palette; in fact you may create them by accident. When drawing the relationship, click once on the entity symbol, drag the mouse a short distance inside the symbol, and then release the mouse button.

➖ Remember that PowerDesigner uses the term 'reflexive', rather than 'recursive'. In PowerDesigner, you can make one or both ends of a reflexive relationship mandatory, and even make the relationship dependent, causing potential problems when you generate further models. Fortunately, the model checker does report these for you.

YOUR TURN TO PLAY

Carry on working in your LDM. Draw a relationship from entity *A* to itself. Simple, isn't it?

❓ "Creating a Reflexive Relationship" (Data Modeling)

Subtypes in PowerDesigner

In PowerDesigner, subtype structures are called 'Inheritances', and the links between entities and the subtype symbol are called 'Inheritance Links'. The modeling notations support them in different ways (see Chapter 9). Each Inheritance is an object in its own right, so it has a default name; in Figure 13.23, I chose to change the name to **Ice Cream Container**, reflecting the name of the supertype entity.

Figure 13.23 Inheritance with two child entities

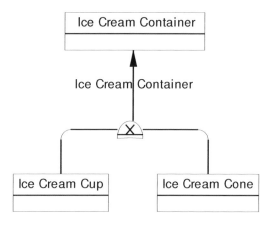

It's a good idea to give inheritances meaningful names, so you can tell them apart in the Browser.

The Inheritance is represented by the half-moon symbol; the arrow points to the parent (supertype) entity, and the straight lines link the child (subtype) entities. The 'X' in the Inheritance symbol tells us that the subtypes are mutually exclusive – an Ice Cream Container cannot be both an Ice Cream Cup and an Ice Cream Cone at the same time. The double line at the bottom of the half-moon tells us that the list is complete – there are no more children (subtypes). A single line would indicate that there may be other subtypes that are not shown on the diagram.

Creating an inheritance via the palette is subtly different from creating a standard relationship. To create a new inheritance, instead of dragging from parent to child, you must drag the link from the child to the parent entity – the subtype node is created for you, as shown in Figure 13.24. For further inheritance links, drag from the child entity to the half-moon symbol, or add the child entity via the 'Children' tab in the Inheritance property sheet.

Figure 13.24 Creating an inheritance from the palette

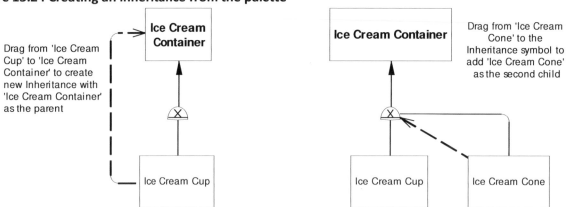

PowerDesigner will let you create more than one inheritance for a given parent entity; this is unusual, but not illegal in conceptual data modeling. For example, your analysis may reveal that some cones and cups are perishable, and others are not. Perishable containers have specific attributes (such as the shelf life) and relationships. There are several different ways to represent this in a data model. Which method you choose will depend on the purpose of your data model. If you want to make the distinction crystal-clear in a Subject Area Model, you could add new subtypes of **Ice Cream Container**, called **Perishable Container** and **Non-perishable Container**. The left-hand image in Figure 13.25 shows the new subtypes within the same hierarchy as the original subtypes. The problem with this model is the subtypes themselves – a given instance of **Ice Cream Container** cannot be allocated to just one of the subtypes. An **Ice Cream Cone** must also be perishable or non-perishable. This issue is referred to as overlapping subtypes, and it will cause problems in implementation.

Figure 13.25 Two hierarchies or one?

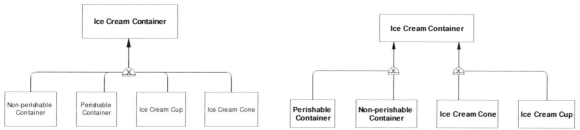

The right-hand image in Figure 13.25 shows the new subtypes in a separate inheritance structure. A given instance of **Ice Cream Container** can now be represented by two subtypes – in effect, there are two separate categorization schemes for Ice Cream Containers.

Inheritance Properties

To view or edit an inheritance's properties, double-click its diagram symbol, or entry in the Browser or a list. Figure 13.26 illustrates the 'General' tab of the property sheet.

Figure 13.26 Inheritance properties – 'General' tab

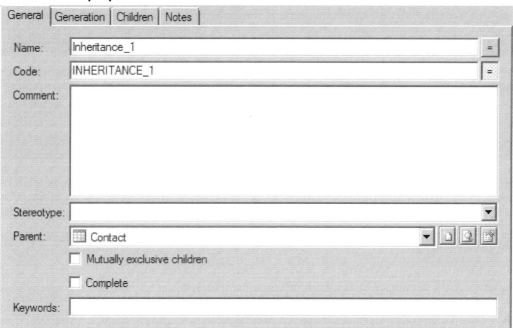

This is where you give the inheritance a name, select the parent entity, and provide two pieces of information about the set of child entities – exclusivity and completeness:

Mutually Exclusive Children   When selected, the subtypes are mutually exclusive, meaning an entity instance must be one or the other of the subtypes, but cannot be more than one of them at the same time. In Figure 13.24, an **Ice Cream Container** could not be both an **Ice Cream Cone** and an **Ice Cream Cup**. When 'Mutually Exclusive Children' is selected, the Inheritance symbol displays an X, as in Figure 13.23.

Complete	When selected, the list of children is complete – every instance of the parent entity must also be an instance of one of the children. If the example in Figure 13.24 is marked as 'Complete', then every **Ice Cream Container** must be either an **Ice Cream Cone** or an **Ice Cream Cup**. When 'Complete' is selected, the Inheritance symbol displays a double line on the base, as in Figure 13.23.

The 'Generation' tab, shown in Figure 13.27, allows you to specify how the inheritance structure will be generated to a PDM. It also allows you to decide which sets of attributes will be inherited by child entities in the LDM. Refer to Table 13.5 for a description of the results of each choice on this tab.

Figure 13.27 Inheritance properties – 'Generation' tab

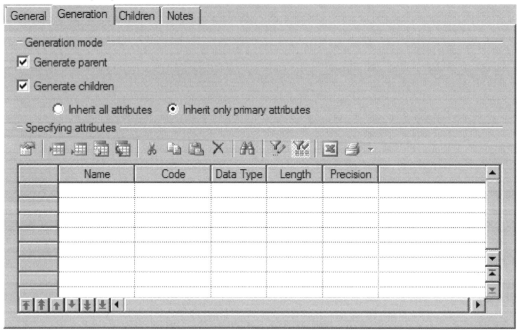

Table 13.5 Generation policy

Choice	Result
Generate parent	When a PDM is generated, this causes the PDM to contain a table corresponding to the parent entity. If one or more child tables are not generated, the parent will take on their columns and references.
Generate children	In the LDM, this property determines the way in which attributes from the parent entity are inherited by child entities. This is not relevant in the CDM, because attribute inheritance is not supported in the CDM. When a PDM is generated, this causes the PDM to contain a table corresponding to each child entity. The primary key of each child table is the concatenation of the child entity identifier and the parent entity identifier. You must additionally choose between: *Inherit all attributes* – Each table inherits all the attributes of the parent entity *Inherit only primary attributes* - Each table inherits only the identifier of the parent entity.

You can control the generation of individual child tables using the Generate option in the property sheet of each child entity.

If you choose to generate the parent table and not the children, the *Specifying Attributes* property allows you to define one or more new attributes to differentiate between occurrences of the children. In the example shown in Figure 13.28, we may wish to add an attribute called 'Contact Type', with values of 'Person' and 'Company'.

The 'Specifying Attributes' are shown in the property sheet for the parent and child entities, but they can only be edited via the Inheritance. These attributes will be removed from the Inheritance if you select 'Generate Children'.

The 'Children' tab, shown in Figure 13.28, allows you to view the list of child entities; you can also add or remove child entities here.

Figure 13.28 Inheritance properties – 'Children' tab

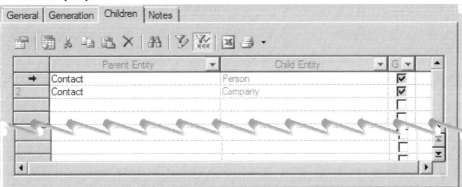

YOUR TURN TO PLAY

1. Create a new diagram in your LDM, and follow the steps shown in Figure 13.24 to create a hierarchy of three entities. Add the following attributes to the **Contact** entity: **Contact Identifier**, **Name**, **Telephone Number**. Ensure that **Contact Identifier** is flagged as part of the primary key.
2. Notice that all three attributes are inherited in the child entities. Open the property sheet for one of the child entities; note that the attributes are not editable here. Open the property sheet for one of the child attributes, and see that it says it's inherited from **Contact.*attribute name***. Click on the properties tool to the right of that entry to open the property sheet for the parent attribute.
3. Open the 'Generation' tab on the property sheet for the inheritance (the half moon symbol); select 'Inherit only primary attributes', and press <OK>. Two attributes disappear from each of the child entities. Remember though, that they are implicitly still present. An **Ice Cream Cup** is an instance of **Ice Cream Container**, and inherits all the attributes and relationships of the parent entity – PowerDesigner gives you the option of hiding or showing all of the inherited attributes.

If you want to show more than just the primary key attributes in child entities, but hide some of the other inherited attributes, you can. Remember the *Displayed* property on every attribute? It is available for inherited attributes as well – uncheck the *Displayed* property for an attribute and it will never appear on a diagram. The attribute will still exist, and will be generated into new models, unless you uncheck the *Generate* property. Remember that you can also hide attributes in a given entity via the 'Sub-Objects' tab on the Symbol Format dialogue, accessible via the contextual menu for the entity symbol.

YOUR TURN TO PLAY

Open the property sheet for the inheritance you created earlier. In the 'Generate' tab, uncheck 'Generate Children'; the 'Specifying Attributes' properties are now available. Here you can create one or more *specifying* attributes in the parent entity, which differentiate between occurrences of each child. Create an attribute here called **Contact Type**, and click <OK>. The **Contact Type** attribute appears in the entity, but can only be edited via the inheritance.

If you enable the 'Generate Children' option, the specifying attribute(s) are deleted from the parent. If you want to keep them, copy them to another entity first.

Subtypes in Barker Notation

The Barker notation does not use inheritances to represent subtypes. Instead, subtypes are represented by placing the child entities inside the parent entity symbol, as shown in Figure 13.29.

Figure 13.29 Barker subtypes

To make an entity a subtype of another entity, just drag it onto the supertype entity symbol, and drop it when a small '+' symbol appears. You can also drag and drop in the Browser. To create a brand-new subtype entity, there are three options:

- Open a diagram, select the *Entity* tool as if you were drawing entities, then click within the supertype symbol.
- Via the 'Subtypes' tab in the property sheet for the supertype entity
- In the Browser, right-click the supertype entity, then select New|Entity from the contextual menu.

You can't 'hide' subtypes via Show symbols, but you can delete the entity symbols.

If you know the entity has subtypes but they are not shown on the diagram, check the display preferences for entities; ensure that 'Composite Editable view' is selected. If you need to adjust the size of the supertype symbol, select it and press <Ctrl+J>.

To include a subtype entity onto a diagram, drag it onto the diagram from the Browser. If you drop it onto a supertype symbol, it will be nested within the supertype symbol. If you drop it onto an empty area of the diagram, a supertype symbol will be added (as a graphical synonym if necessary).

Including Missing Relationships

As you work on a data model, you may create more than one diagram, create objects in the Browser, or remove symbols from diagrams. All of these activities may result in symbols being missing from a given diagram. We have already discussed the two ways of including missing symbols:

Show Symbols	See "Showing and Hiding Symbols", in Chapter 10
Complete Links	See "Showing and Hiding Symbols", in Chapter 10

The `Complete Links` command is available on the `Tools` menu, and via the *Complete Links* tool 🔧 on the standard Toolbar. When you run the command, any link that could be on the diagram is automatically included – this includes relationships, inheritance links and traceability links. If you have any symbols selected when you run the command, you will have the option to complete links for the whole model or just the selected symbols.

In Figure 13.30 for example, **Entity_9** appears to be unconnected to any other entity on the diagram.

Figure 13.30 An unconnected entity

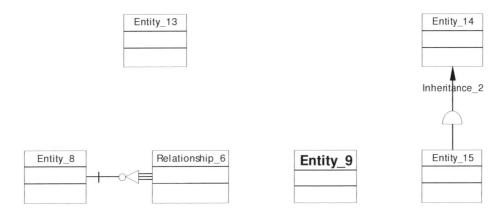

Figure 13.31 shows the diagram after selecting **Entity_9** and running `Complete Links`. The diagram now has an additional relationship, an inheritance link, and a traceability link, all connected to **Entity_9**. Remember, these connections already existed, all we've done is include them on the diagram.

Figure 13.31 Connections added

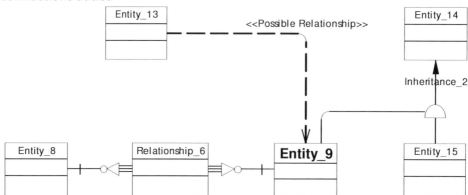

YOUR TURN TO PLAY

Create a new diagram in your LDM. In the Browser, select the inheritance you created earlier, and drag it onto the diagram. PowerDesigner adds the inheritance and the parent entity to the diagram, but not the child entities. Now select Show Symbols via the Symbol menu, or right-click the diagram background and select Diagram|Show Symbols. In the 'Inheritance Link' tab, shown in Figure 13.32, you will see the child entities listed. If you have more than one inheritance in your model, check the *Name* property shown in the list – it's a composite value, derived from the names of the parent entity, the inheritance, and the child entity.

Figure 13.32 Selecting your inheritance links

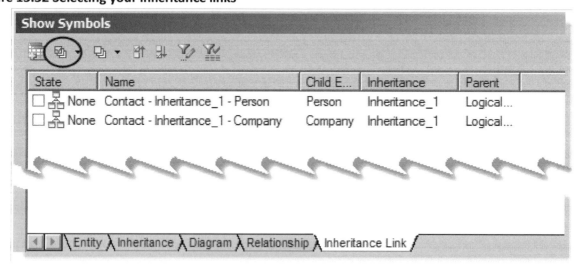

Use the 'Select All' tool (circled above) to select all the inheritance links, and click on <OK>. The child entities are added to the diagram, complete with links to the inheritance.

The quickest way to add a missing inheritance structure is to add all the inheritance links via Show Symbols – this will add the parent and child entities, the inheritance, and all the links.

YOUR TURN TO PLAY

Now drag all the remaining entities onto the diagram; note that none of the relationships have been included. Now click on the 'Complete Links' tool – all the missing relationships have been added. Select all the newly-added entities and relationships and experiment with auto-layout – use the auto-layout tool ⊠ on the layout Toolbar.

● "Inheritances (CDM/LDM)" (Data Modeling)

EXERCISE 11: Creating Relationships in PowerDesigner

Create a new Project in your workspace, called 'Exercise 11'; make sure the project directory has the same parent directory as the previous projects you created. Create a LDM in the Project, also called 'Exercise 11'. Add the extension 'Relationship Assertion with Plural Entity Names' to the model (see instructions in Chapter 10).

Create the model shown in Figure 13.33. Concentrate on the diagram contents, don't worry about definitions or attribute properties. You will use this model again in Exercise 18.

Figure 13.33 The target model

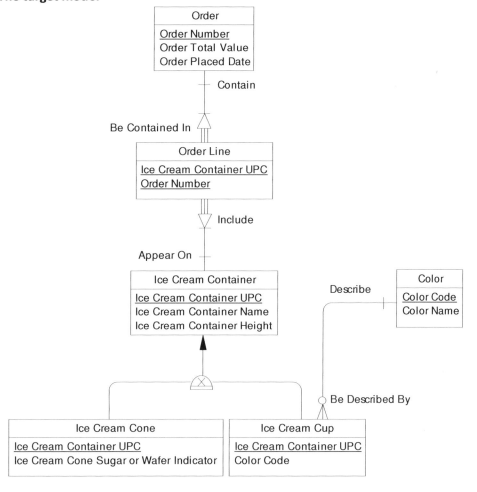

EXERCISE 12: Naming an Associative Entity

Figure 13.34 illustrates a common scenario in a Conceptual Data Model, of a many-to-many relationship between two entities. In this example, a person can be assigned to many or no projects, and a project must have at least one person working on it.

Figure 13.34 A many-to-many relationship

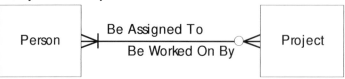

In a Logical Data Model, we decide to resolve this relationship, and convert it into an entity, and the result is shown in Figure 13.35. What names do you suggest we use for the two relationships and the associative entity?

Figure 13.35 The entity and relationships to rename

Key Points

- PowerDesigner supports every type of relationship.

- Agree on standards for relationship and inheritance names and for using role names.

- Draw relationships from the 'one' entity to the 'many entity'.

- Draw a new inheritance from the child to the parent, and draw inheritance links from the child entity to the sub-type symbol.

- Let PowerDesigner manage relationship routing for you.

- The property sheet includes a depiction of the relationship - use this to confirm your changes before you click <ok>.

- The 'Cardinalities' tab is where you specify how two entities are related.

- The entity 'Dependencies' tab lists relationships.

- Use 'Show Symbols' to add existing relationships to a diagram.

- You can convert a relationship into an entity.

- Use graphical synonyms to improve readability of a diagram.

- By default, all parent attributes are inherited by child entities.

- Rules that you cannot describe using relationships can be defined as Business Rules.

In Business Models
We are Identifiers
Physical keys too

In Chapter 7, we introduced Candidate Keys, Primary Keys and Foreign Keys. These are all standard data modeling artifacts that are supported by PowerDesigner. See Table 14.1.

Table 14.1 PowerDesigner support for keys

Concept	Model(s)	Object Type	Notes
Candidate Key	CDM and LDM	Identifier	You can create as many identifiers as you need for an entity.
Alternate Key	CDM and LDM	Identifier <ai>	An identifier that does not have the *Primary Identifier* property selected. You can create as many alternate identifiers as you need for an entity.
	PDM	Key <ak>	A key that does not have the *Primary Key* property selected. You can create as many alternate keys as you need for a table.
Primary Key	CDM and LDM	Identifier <pi>	You can only have one 'Primary' identifier for an entity. It is indicated via the *Primary Identifier* property on the 'General' tab on the property sheet (see Figure 14.1).
	PDM	Key <pk>	You can only have one 'Primary' key for a table. It is indicated via the *Primary Identifier* property on the 'General' tab on the property sheet.
Foreign Key	CDM	None	The CDM does not support the concept of inheritance of attributes – there are no foreign keys.
	LDM	None <fi>	Entities contain attributes migrated from other entities via inheritance links or relationships. There is no separate 'foreign key' object.
	PDM	Key <fk>	Tables contain columns migrated from other tables via references. There is no separate 'foreign key' object.

"Identifiers (CDM/LDM)" (Data Modeling)

"Keys (PDM)" (Data Modeling)

287

Creating Candidate Identifiers

There are several ways of creating identifiers in a PowerDesigner CDM or LDM. The process is essentially the same when creating keys in the PDM. In Exercise 13, you'll have the chance to try out the options marked with ⬚.

In the Entity Property Sheet

- ⬚ Open the 'Attributes' tab, select one or more attributes, and then click the Create *Identifier* tool ⬚. The selected attributes are associated with the identifier and listed on the 'Attributes' tab of its property sheet. Identifiers created in this way are not *Primary* by default, so this is a good way to create candidate identifiers.

- ⬚ Open the 'Attributes' tab, and check the 'P' column for each attribute that you want to include in the primary identifier. When you apply the changes, the identifier is created or updated.

- ⬚ Open the 'Identifiers' tab, and click the *Add a Row* tool ⬚. A new, empty, identifier will be created. You need to open the identifier's property sheet to edit the details.

In the Browser

- Right-click the entity name; in the contextual menu select *New*, and then *Identifier*. The property sheet of the new identifier will open – see below for details.

- If an entity already has one or more identifiers, right-click the *Identifiers* folder below the entity name, and select *New*. A property sheet will open – see below for details.

In an Entity Symbol

This will only work if you have selected *Identifiers* in the display preferences.

⬚ Select an entity symbol, select any identifier, right-click any identifier name, and then select edit|insert; a new, empty, identifier will be created. You need to open the property sheet to edit the details.

In a Relationship Property Sheet

⬚ In the 'Cardinalities' tab, you can declare the relationship to be dependent. When you declare a relationship to be dependent, the migrated attributes will be included in the primary identifier of the child entity. The identifier will be created, if necessary.

Via an Excel Import

You can use the Excel Import feature to create identifiers and link them to attributes, using a similar approach to that described in "Using Excel Import to Create Surrogate Keys", in Chapter 21.

Entity Identifier Properties

An entity identifier or a table key is a sub-object – it can only exist within an entity or table. You will generally access identifiers and keys via the 'Identifiers' tab on an entity property sheet, or the 'Keys' tab on a table property sheet. Just like other sub-objects you have seen, identifiers and keys have their own property sheets. Figure 14.1 shows a typical identifier, the primary identifier of the entity **Class**.

Figure 14.1 Entity identifier properties

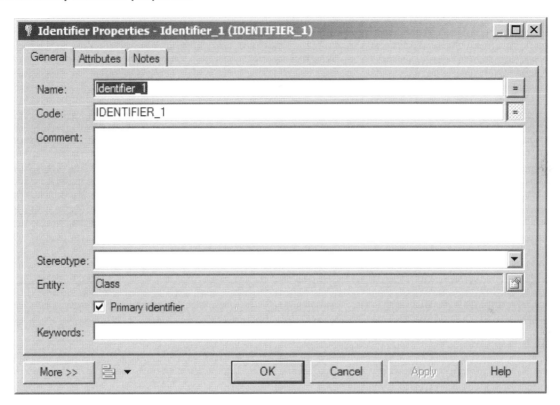

Figure 14.2 shows the 'Attributes' tab of the same identifier. The identifier contains a single attribute, **Class Full Name**. As before, you can double-click the attribute name on the 'Attributes' tab to open the attribute's property sheet.

If you want to link an identifier to the business need for it, you can link identifiers and keys to any Business Rules or Requirements that are relevant.

Object Lists

Like every other sub-object or object in PowerDesigner, you can access a grid-based object list via the `Model` menu. Identifiers and keys are sub-objects, so you can edit and delete them via an object list, but you cannot create them this way.

Figure 14.2 The 'Attributes' tab

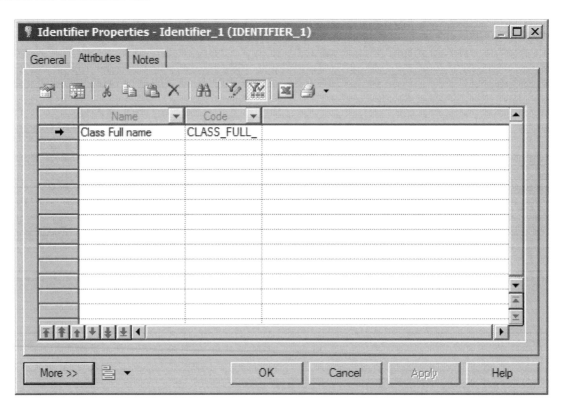

Identifiers on Entity and Table Symbols

Identifiers and keys can be displayed within entity or table symbols on diagrams – just select *Identifiers* or *Keys* within Display Preferences. Figure 14.3 shows an entity and a table – the LDM entity **Attendance** has an identifier called **Identifier_1**, which contains just one attribute, **Class Full Name;** the entry *<pi,fi1>* after the attribute name tells us that the attribute is part of the primary identifier, and is also a foreign identifier, inherited via a relationship.

The PDM table **Attendance** has one primary key called **Key_1**, which contains just one column, **Class Full Name**; the entry *<pk,fk1>* after the column name tells us that the column is part of the primary key, and is also a foreign key, inherited via a dependent relationship. The entries in the bottom section of the table symbol are indexes, one for each foreign key; they are automatically created when the PDM was generated from the LDM.

Changing Identifier Content

To revise the list of attributes in an identifier, open the 'Attributes' tab on the identifier's property sheet. For the primary identifier, you can change the *Primary Identifier* property on the identifier's attributes, via a list of attributes (from the Model menu), the list of attributes for an entity, or an attribute's property sheet.

Figure 14.3 Entity and table symbols

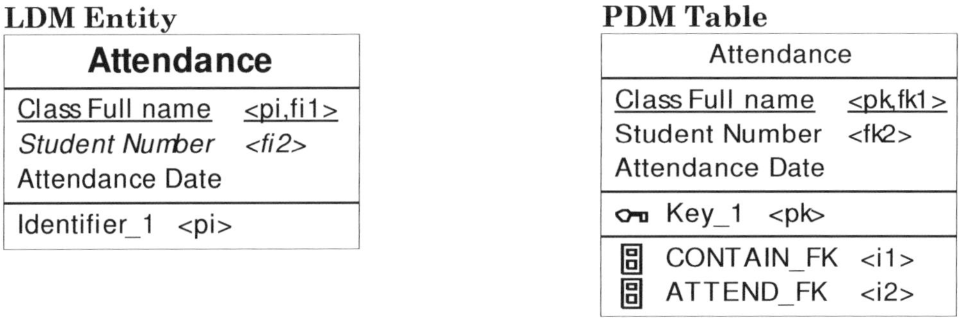

LDM Entity

Attendance	
Class Full name	<pi,fi1>
Student Number	<fi2>
Attendance Date	
Identifier_1 <pi>	

PDM Table

Attendance	
Class Full name	<pk,fk1>
Student Number	<fk2>
Attendance Date	
⚷ Key_1 <pk>	
⊞ CONTAIN_FK	<i1>
⊞ ATTEND_FK	<i2>

Identifier Migration Along Relationships

Foreign attributes are migrated instantaneously in a LDM, or during model generation when you generate a PDM from a CDM or LDM. Table 14.2 shows the rules used by PowerDesigner when migrating attributes in a LDM.

Table 14.2 Attribute migration in different types of LDM relationships

LDM Relationship type	Migration
Dependent one-to-many	Foreign identifiers become attributes of the primary identifier of the child entity.
Many-to-many	No attributes are migrated.
Dominant one-to-one	Primary identifier attributes migrate from the dominant entity.
Mandatory one-to-many	If the child to parent role is mandatory, migrated attributes are mandatory.

PowerDesigner allows you to choose which attributes to migrate, and which identifier to migrate them from (if you have more than one, of course).

❷ "Identifier Migration Along Relationships" (Data Modeling)

❷ "Automatic Reuse and Migration of Columns" (Data Modeling)

Attribute Migration Settings

The way in which data elements migrate along relationships and references varies between the types of data model, as described in Table 14.3.

Table 14.3 Attribute migration approaches

Model Type	Migration
CDM	No attributes are migrated, ever.
LDM	Attributes are automatically migrated from primary identifiers into child entities. Attributes are also automatically migrated via inheritance links, and you have control over which attributes are migrated - see "Inheritance Properties" in Chapter 13.
PDM	Columns are automatically migrated from primary keys into child tables.

In a LDM, the Model Options shown in Figure 14.4 give you a degree of control over the migration process.

Figure 14.4 LDM Migration Settings

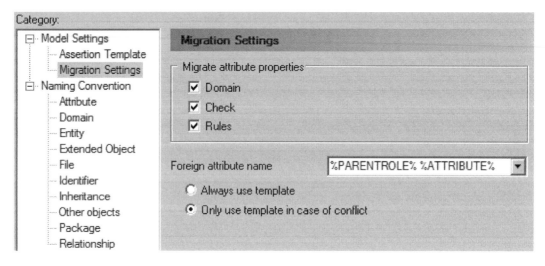

There are two parts to these settings. In *Migrate attribute properties,* you can choose whether or not the migrated attributes inherit the original attribute's Domain, Checks, and associated Rules. By default, all the options are enabled, and you are advised to leave them as they are.

The second part controls the names of attributes migrated via a relationship. The drop down list contains templates that you can use to construct the name of the migrated attribute. For example, the template shown in Figure 14.4 will prefix the original attribute name with the role name from the 'parent' end of the relationship.

Figure 14.5 demonstrates the effect of the template on the 'contain' relationship from our model – the foreign key attribute is called ***contain* Class Full Name**.

Figure 14.5 Appending a role to an attribute name

The parent role name (**contain**) has been appended to the name of the original attribute to create the name of the migrated attribute, **contain Class Full Name**. If you intend to use this template in your models, you will probably want to ensure that your role names use initial capital letters, such as **Contain** instead of **contain**.

Several default templates are available, or you can create your own template from a combination of the options shown in Table 14.4. The template is not applied to attributes migrated through an inheritance link.

If you manually rename a migrated attribute, future changes to the template will not affect the attribute name.

Table 14.4 Options for constructing migrated attribute names

%PARENT%	Name/Code of the parent entity
%ATTRIBUTE%	Name/Code of the parent attribute
%IDENTIFIER%	Name/Code of the identifier constraint attached to the relationship
%RELATIONSHIP%	Name/Code of the relationship
%PARENTROLE%	Role of the entity that generated the parent entity. If no role is defined on the relationship, %PARENTROLE% takes the content of %PARENT% to avoid generating an attribute with no name

By default, PowerDesigner will apply templates only when necessary to avoid creating duplicate attribute names in an entity. Alternatively, you can apply the template to all migrated attribute names.

The example in Figure 14.6 shows the results of applying the same template to every migrated attribute in a different model. Without applying a template, all the attributes in **Entity_6** would be called **Attribute A**, which we cannot allow. The relationship from **Entity_7** does not have a role name, so the name of the migrated attribute is prefixed with the entity name, which will be replaced by the relationship parent role name when you define it.

Entity_8 and **Entity_9** illustrate a problem with this approach – the attributes have been migrated along two or three relationships, so their names have two or three prefixes. The work-around here is to rename migrated attributes where the generated name is not suitable. Future changes to the relationship name or role name will still affect the name of the migrated attributes, so this type of amendment should be carried out at a late stage in modeling if you want to avoid rework.

Figure 14.6 Applying a naming template

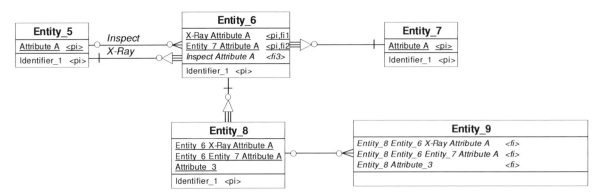

Figure 14.7 shows the same model, with the naming template used when required. The **X-Ray** relationship was created first, so the name of the attribute migrated via that relationship does not have a prefix.

Figure 14.7 Prefix attribute names only when required

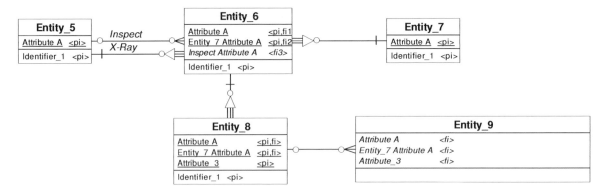

This is a contrived situation, partly showing the pitfalls of giving every attribute the same name; it's likely that the impact on a real-life model will not be quite so onerous. Figure 14.8 shows a more realistic scenario. The **Parent** relationship was the first to be created, which explains why it is the attribute inherited from the **Child** relationship that has the qualified name.

Figure 14.8 A more realistic scenario

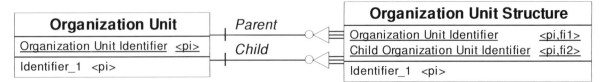

The default template in PowerDesigner is "%.3:PARENT%_%ATTRIBUTE%". This prefixes the attribute name with first three characters of the entity name followed by an underscore, which will result in attribute names such as "Cla_Class Full Name".

Changing the Migration Settings for a model will affect the model immediately, and could potentially rename all of the migrated attributes.

"Migration Settings (LDM)" (Data Modeling)

Migrating a Different Identifier

PowerDesigner allows you to select any of the keys of a parent entity to form the foreign key in a child entity. For example, you could choose to propagate the attributes from an alternate key, rather than the primary key. A *join* is a link between an attribute in a parent entity and an attribute in a child entity (attribute pair), defined within a relationship. Using the 'Joins' tab in the relationship property sheet (see Figure 14.9), you can choose which key to use in the join, and which attributes in the child entity form the foreign key.

Figure 14.9 Choosing a different identifier to join with

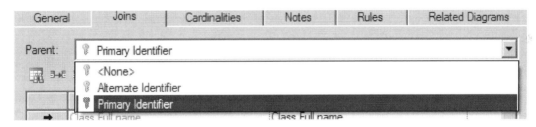

This flexibility can cause you potential problems when, for example, you create surrogate identifiers in an existing model, and convert the original primary identifiers into alternate identifiers.

This feature is also available for references in the PDM.

If you convert an existing primary identifier into an alternate identifier, the alternate identifier will continue to be used in the join, and the attributes in the alternate identifier will continue to be propagated as foreign identifiers. If you then create a new surrogate identifier attribute, and make that your primary identifier, PowerDesigner will not change the relationship joins for you.

To prevent this from happening, always create the new primary identifier attribute first, and mark it as Primary. Only then should you create your new alternate identifier. It is OK if you do all this in the same editing session, it's the sequence of events that counts.

If you decide to apply surrogate identifiers to an existing LDM, prepare your model first. Follow these steps to make life simpler:

1. Open the list of identifiers via the *Model* menu
3. If necessary, customize the list to display the Entity property
4. Rename the existing primary identifiers that will become alternate identifiers

   - replace the name of the identifiers with the name *Alternate* (or another name if you prefer), highlight the new name, and copy it into the Windows clipboard

   - use the arrow keys to move up or down the list of identifier names, pasting the new name into each using <Ctrl+V>

   - de-select the *P* column for each identifier you need to change

5. Click <OK> to commit the changes

After preparing the existing identifiers, create the surrogate identifiers, but don't adjust the relationships just yet. After creating all your surrogate identifiers, it's time to adjust your relationships. To do this, open the list of relationships via the `Model` menu, and customize it to include the *Parent Identifier* property, as shown in Figure 14.10. Using the drop-down lists, you can select the identifier for each relationship – click <OK>, and the changes are applied. If it helps, sort the list by the value of 'Parent Identifier' – just click on the column heading.

Figure 14.10 Choosing a different identifier

Name ▲ ▼	Entity 1 ▼	Entity 1 -> E ▼	Depend ▼	(1)->(2) ▼	Parent Identifier ▼	Entity 2 ▼
Attend	Student	attend	<None>	0,n	Primary Identifier	Attendance
Contain	Class	contain	<None>	0,n	Alternate Identifi ▼	Attendance
Relationship_3	Student Enrollment Ty	Classify	<None>	0,n	<None>	Student
Relationship_5	Entity_5	X-Ray	<None>	0,n	Alternate Identifier	Entity_6
Relationship_6	Entity_7		<None>	0,n	Primary Identifier	Entity_6
Relationship 7	Entity 5	Inspect	<None>	0,n	Primary Identifier	Entity 6

Instead of a list of relationships, you could also use a List Report of Relationship Joins, making sure that you include the property *Parent Identifier* under the *Parent* group (see Figure 14.11).

Figure 14.11 Selecting the *Parent Identifier* property in a list report

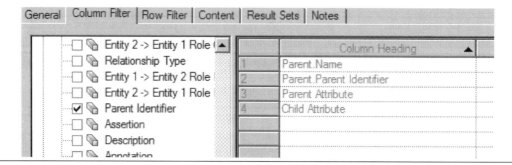

Naming Your Identifiers

Within a CDM or LDM, the names of identifiers only really matter for two reasons:

1. You have more than one identifier for an entity, and you need to tell them apart
2. You intend to generate a PDM.

When you generate a PDM from a CDM or LDM, PowerDesigner will convert your entity identifiers into table keys. The default identifier names (such as **Identifier_1**) are converted into default key names (such as **Key_1**), which are used to form the names of the constraints on the database. Save yourself work in the PDM; name your entity identifiers in such a way that they generate acceptable database constraint names.

Attributes and Columns in Identifiers and Keys

As ever, the place to look for ways in which an attribute or column has been used (apart from being a sub-object within an entity or table) is the 'Dependencies' tab on the property sheet. Figure 14.12 shows the 'Dependencies' tab for an attribute called **Attribute A**, which has been migrated into two other entities, as **Attribute A** and **Inspect Attribute A**.

Figure 14.12 The attribute 'Dependencies' tab

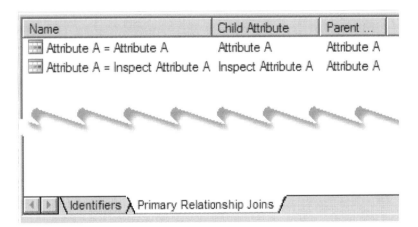

The sub-tabs provide the information shown in Table 14.5 by default – the contents can be customized in the usual way.

Table 14.5 Sub-tabs for dependencies

Sub-tab	Content
Identifiers	Links to the identifier(s) that contain Attribute A
Primary Relationship Joins	Links to the relationship joins that result in Attribute A being migrated to other entities – the name of the join includes the names of the parent and child attributes. In Figure 14.12, we can see that one of the child attributes is called *Inspect Attribute A*.

A key point to remember about the 'Dependencies' tab is that it will never contain *empty* sub-tabs. For example, the presence of the two tabs shown in Figure 14.12 tells us that the attribute is referenced by at least one identifier, and by at least one relationship join.

EXERCISE 13: Constructing Identifiers

Figure 14.13 shows a simple model, similar to the model in Chapter 7. The bottom portion of each entity symbol is where the identifiers would be shown; they are all empty, because no identifiers have been defined yet.

Figure 14.13 Data model before candidate keys have been identified

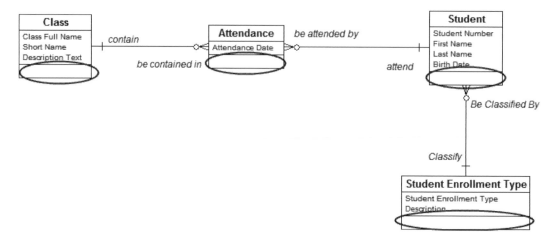

Our analysis identified the candidate identifiers shown in Table 14.6.

Table 14.6 Candidate Identifiers

Entity	Identifier Number	Candidate Identifiers
Attendance	1	*Composite identifier:* - identifier inherited from *Student* - identifier inherited from *Class* - Attendance Date
Class	1	Class Full Name
Class	2	Class Short Name
Student	1	Student Number
Student Enrollment Type	1	Student Enrollment Type

In the following pages, you will create the candidate identifiers in a LDM, using the techniques marked ⌗ at the beginning of the chapter.

YOUR TURN TO PLAY

In the 'Exercises' workspace, create a new folder and LDM in the folder – call both 'Exercise 13'. Create the entities and relationships shown in Figure 14.13. Ensure that you have selected *Identifiers* in the entity display preferences.

Create Identifiers via the Entity Property Sheet

1. Open the 'Attributes' tab on the property sheet for the entity **Student**, and then:
2. Select the attribute **Student Number**
3. Click on the *Create* Identifier tool ⚲ - a new identifier will be created, and the property sheet will be opened
4. Click <OK> to close the identifier's property sheet, then click <OK> to close the entity's property sheet
5. On your diagram, the Identifier name will appear in the **Student** symbol, and the attribute name will be suffixed with <ai>. The attribute will not be migrated to the entity **Attendance**, because the identifier has not been flagged as the *Primary* identifier.
6. On the diagram, open the contextual menu for **Student Enrollment Type** and select *Identifiers*. The entity's property sheet will open at the 'Identifiers' tab. Click either the *Add a Row* ⊞ or *Insert a Row* ⊞ tool. A new identifier will appear in the list – click on the *Properties* ⊞ tool to open the property sheet for the identifier. Click on <Yes> when you're asked to commit changes as shown in Figure 14.14 – you can't edit the identifier until it has been created.

Figure 14.14 Commitment Required

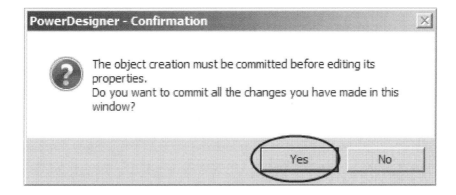

7. Via the 'Attributes' tab, add **Student Enrollment Type** to the identifier. Click <OK> to save the changes to the Identifier. The symbol for **Student Enrollment Type** will change to reflect the new identifier; again, this is not a primary identifier, but we'll soon change that. The property sheet for the entity will still be open – in the 'Identifiers' tab, the P column has not been selected (see Figure 14.15), telling us that this is not the primary identifier.

Figure 14.15 The empty 'P'

8. To convert the identifier into a primary identifier, select P in the 'Identifiers' tab, then click on <OK> or <Apply>. In the diagram, notice the changes that have been made to Student Enrollment Type and Student. The attribute Student Enrollment Type has been migrated to Student.

The Quickest Way to Create a Primary Identifier

There is a quicker way to create a primary identifier, via the 'Attributes' tab on the Entity Property Sheet. In the 'Attributes' tab, the P column indicates whether or not an attribute is part of the primary identifier. In Figure 14.16, we can see that **Student Enrollment Type** is part of the primary identifier.

Figure 14.16 The P column for attributes

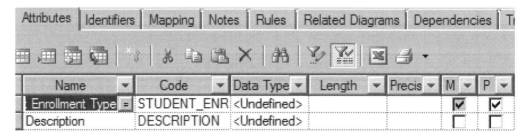

If you were to de-select column P, the attribute would be removed from the primary identifier, and the primary identifier would still exist. Re-select P and the attribute will again be included in the primary identifier. We can take advantage of this behavior to create the primary identifier with just a single mouse-click.

YOUR TURN TO PLAY

Open the property sheet for the entity **Class**; in the 'Attributes' tab, select column P for the attribute **Class Full Name**. Notice that the M (mandatory) column is automatically selected as well — attributes in the primary identifier are mandatory. Switch to the 'Identifiers' tab, and you'll see that a primary identifier has been created, as shown in Figure 14.17.

Figure 14.17 Making Class Full Name part of the primary identifier

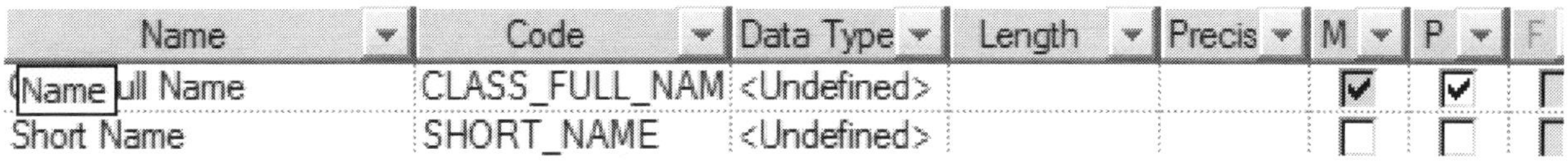

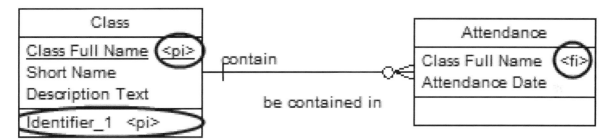

Name	▾	Code	▾	Data Type	▾	Length	▾	Precis	▾	M	▾	P	▾	F
[Name] ull Name		CLASS_FULL_NAM		<Undefined>						☑		☑		☐
Short Name		SHORT_NAME		<Undefined>						☐		☐		☐

Look at the diagram fragment in Figure 14.18, and you'll see the changes that have been made - each change has been circled on the diagram. The **Class** entity now has a primary identifier, the attribute **Class Full Name** is now flagged as <pi>, and the format of the name has changed accordingly. The attribute **Class Full Name** has been migrated to the entity **Attendance**.

Figure 14.18 The revised diagram

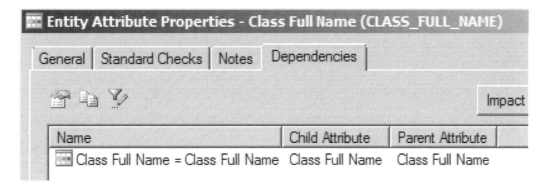

🌑 Do not use this method to convert an existing candidate identifier into a primary identifier. If the entity does not have a primary identifier already, selecting the *P* column for any attribute will *always* create a new identifier.

The new **Class Full Name** attribute is, of course, dependent upon the original attribute in **Class**. This dependency is visible in the property sheet for both of the **Class Full Name** attributes; just open the property sheet for either attribute, and look at the 'Dependencies' tab. The original attribute will have a sub-tab called *Primary Relationship Joins*, and the migrated attribute will have a sub-tab called *Foreign Relationship Joins*. Both sub-tabs contain a link to the relationship that joins them. Figure 14.19 shows the sub-tab on the migrated attribute.

Figure 14.19 The attribute depends on a relationship

Your Turn To Play

Double-click the name of the dependency (Class Full Name = Class Full Name) to open the 'Joins' tab on the relationship, shown in Figure 14.20.

Figure 14.20 The 'Joins' tab for a relationship

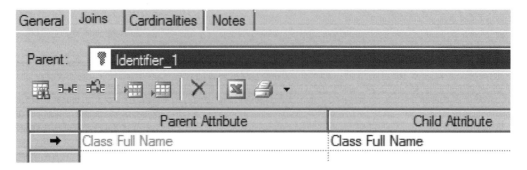

Here you can see the name of the primary identifier in **Class**, and the names of the original and migrated attributes. You have the option here to change the attribute migration policy for the relationship, perhaps to link the relationship to a different attribute in the **Attendance** entity. Any such changes have to be carefully considered, and are outside of the scope of this book.

"Relationship Property Sheet Joins Tab (LDM)" (Data Modeling)

Convert a Candidate Identifier into a Primary Identifier

Your Turn To Play

Open the list of identifiers for the model, via the `Model` menu. This list also has a *P* (primary) column – the identifier for **Student** is the only one not checked. See Figure 14.21. To convert it, just check the *P* column and click <OK>.

Figure 14.21 Three primary identifiers

Name	Code	Entity	P
Identifier_1	IDENTIFIER_1	Student Enrollment Type	☑
Identifier_1	IDENTIFIER_1	Student	☑
Identifier_1	IDENTIFIER_1	Class	☑

Look at the diagram in Figure 14.22 – can you see the changes that have been made to **Student** and **Attendance**? The changes are listed in Table 14.7.

Figure 14.22 Demonstrating attribute migration

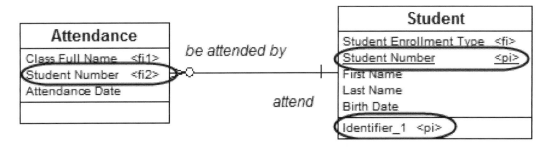

Table 14.7 Entity Changes

Student	* the identifier is tagged with <pi> instead of <ai> * Student Number is tagged with <pi> instead of <ai>, and the font style may have changed (depending on your display preferences)
Attendance	* Student Number has been migrated to the entity Attendance, where it is flagged as <fi>

Make a Relationship Dependent

YOUR TURN TO PLAY

Open the 'Cardinalities' tab on the property sheet for the relationship shown in Figure 14.22; select 'Dependent' for the 'Attendance to Student' direction, and click on <OK>. The result is shown in Figure 14.23, and the changes are listed in Table 14.8.

Figure 14.23 Dependency changes

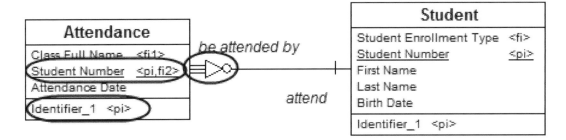

Table 14.8 Dependency changes

Attendance entity	* new primary identifier created * Student Number now included in primary identifier, flagged as <pi> and <fi>, and the font style will probably have changed (depending on your display preferences)
Relationship	* displays the 'dependent' notation

Change the Name of a Migrated Attribute

YOUR TURN TO PLAY

Open the property sheet for the entity **Attendance**, and change the name of **Student Number** to **Attending Student Number**. The two attributes are still linked, but they no longer have identical names.

Make a Migrated Attribute 'primary'

YOUR TURN TO PLAY

In the entity Attendance, open the property sheet for the attribute **Class Full Name**, select *Primary Identifier* on the 'General' tab, and click <OK>.

Look at Figure 14.24 – can you see the change to Attendance? Class Full Name is now tagged as <pi>. The relationship from Class has also changed – it is now a dependent relationship, so the symbol has changed.

Extending a Composite Identifier

Figure 14.24 Composite Identifier

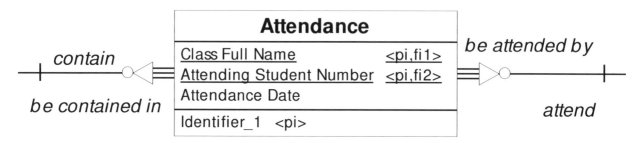

So far we have created most of the candidate identifiers listed in Table 14.6, and all of our entities now have primary identifiers. Only one entity (**Attendance**) is incomplete - it is an associative entity with a composite identifier, made up of two migrated attributes that PowerDesigner created automatically for us, when we created the primary identifiers for the two parent entities. Look back at Table 14.6, and you will see that the candidate key for **Attendance** is not complete; we still need to include the attribute **Attendance Date**.

Editing the Identifier via the Entity Symbol

YOUR TURN TO PLAY

In the diagram, select the **Attendance** entity, and then select **Identifier_1.** Now double-click **Identifier_1** to open the identifier's property sheet. In the 'Attributes' tab, use the *Add Attribute* tool 🖼 to add **Attendance Date.**

Creating a Candidate Identifier via the Entity Symbol

YOUR TURN TO PLAY

The entity **Class** needs an additional identifier that references the **Short Name** attribute; we can also create this via the entity symbol. On the diagram, select **Class**, then select **Identifier_1**. Now right-click **Identifier_1**, select Edit, and then select Insert. A new identifier will appear on the symbol. Edit the identifier name, and press <Enter> when you're ready. Use any of the approaches you've used before to add the attribute **Short Name** to the new identifier. You can also create an identifier in the symbol by pressing <Ctrl+I> after selecting **Identifier_1**.

📄 This approach will work for any sub-object; just select an existing sub-object of the required type, first.

The Finished Diagram

Now that we have created all the identifiers, your diagram will look something like Figure 14.25.

Figure 14.25 The finished diagram

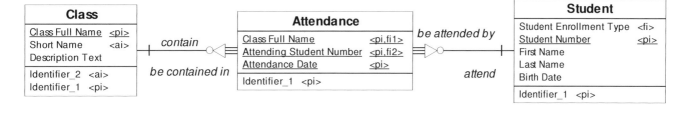

Key Points

- PowerDesigner uses the word 'identifier' in the CDM and LDM, and 'key' in the PDM.

- The easiest way to create a primary identifier/key is to check the 'P' column in a list of attributes or columns.

- PowerDesigner allows you to choose which identifier/key a relationship/reference uses to migrate attributes or columns.

- In the LDM, choose your template for constructing the name of migrated attributes; make sure you have a policy for this.

Section IV introduces the data model pyramid, then explores the three different levels of models: subject area, logical, and physical. A subject area model (SAM) represents a business need. It is a very broad view, containing only the basic and critical concepts for a given scope. The logical data model (LDM) represents a detailed business solution, capturing the business requirements without complicating the model with implementation concerns such as software and hardware. The physical data model (PDM) represents a detailed technical solution. It loses some of the precision of the LDM, but this loss usually comes with gains in performance and usability within a given hardware and software set.

In addition to these three levels of detail, there are also two different modeling mindsets: relational and dimensional. Relational modeling is the process of capturing how the business works, while dimensional modeling is the process of capturing what the business is monitoring or measuring. Relational modeling captures how the business works, and captures business rules, such as "A Customer must have at least one Account", or a "Product must have a **Product Short Name**". Dimensional modeling captures what the business uses to measure how well it is performing. For example, examining sales at a day level and then, after getting the answer, looking at sales at a month or year level, or a product or brand level, or a city or country level. Dimensional modeling is all about playing with numbers by summarizing or aggregating data such as Sales Value Amount.

The table on the facing page summarizes these three model levels and two mindsets, leading to six different types of models.

		Mindset	
		Relational	**Dimensional**
Types of models	**SAM**	Key concepts and their business rules, such as a "Customer can place many Orders."	Key concepts focused around one or more measures, such as "I want to see Gross Sales Value Amount by Customer."
	LDM	All data elements required for a given application or business process, neatly organized into entities according to strict business rules and independent of technology, such as "**Customer Last Name** and **Customer Shoe Size** depend completely on **Customer Identifier**."	All data elements required for a given reporting application, focused on measures and independent of technology, such as "I want to see Gross Sales Value Amount by Customer and view the Customer's first and last name."
	PDM	The LDM modified for a specific technology, such as database or access software. For example, "To improve retrieval speed, we need a non-unique index on **Customer Last Name**."	The LDM modified for a specific technology, such as database or access software. For example, "Because there is a need to view **Gross Sales Value Amount** at a Day level, and then by Month and Year, we should consider combining all calendar data elements into a single table."

The purpose and characteristics of each of these six models are explained in detail in this section, along with specific instructions for creating them in PowerDesigner.

Chapter 15 goes into detail on the subject area model, discussing the variations along with how to build and manage this type of model in PowerDesigner.

Chapter 16 focuses on the relational and dimensional logical data model.

Chapter 17 focuses on the physical data model, going through the different techniques for building an effective design, such as denormalization and partitioning. Slowly Changing Dimensions (SCDs) are also discussed in this chapter.

Chapter 18 focuses on managing model dependencies, and describes the PowerDesigner model generation process.

The Data Model Pyramid

Many practitioners of data modeling use a pyramid to illustrate the different types of models and the relationships between them. This particular shape is well suited to the task for two reasons:

- It supports the principle of 'layers of models'
- As we move down the layers, everything grows – the number of models, their complexity, and the number of objects included

The pyramid consists of four layers, providing increasing detail as you move towards the base. PowerDesigner connects models in adjacent layers using 'Link and Sync' connections; they can also be connected manually via mappings made using the Mapping Editor.

Figure IV.1 The data model pyramid

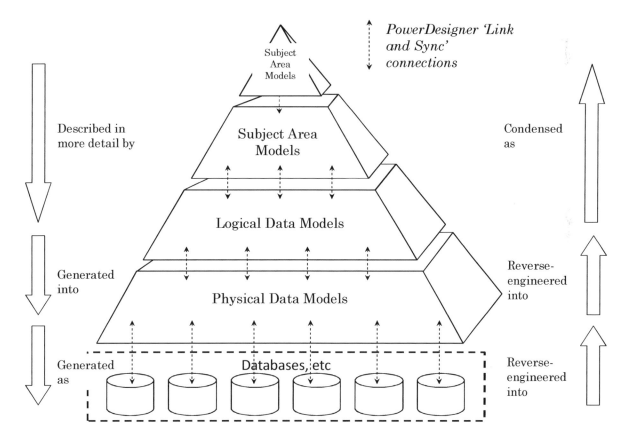

For Subject Area Models, see Chapter 15. For Logical Data Models, see Chapter 16. For Physical Data Models, see Chapter 17.

Which PowerDesigner model types should I use?

In Chapter 9, we discussed the three types of data models provided by PowerDesigner, the Conceptual Data Model, the Logical Data Model, and the Physical Data Model.

Nobody can force you to use these models in the way Sybase intended, but there is an obvious synergy between our three levels of data models and the PowerDesigner models, shown below. To avoid confusion, we refer to the PowerDesigner models by their 3-letter model types, CDM, LDM, and PDM.

	Relational	PowerDesigner Model Type	Dimensional	PowerDesigner Model Type
SAM	*'One-pager' on how something works*	CDM	*'One-pager' on what is monitored*	CDM
LDM	*Detailed business solution on how something works*	LDM or CDM *	*Detailed business solution on what is monitored*	LDM
PDM	*Detailed technical solution on how something works*	PDM	*Detailed technical solution on what is monitored*	PDM *(consider using Multidimensional diagrams)*

* PowerDesigner cannot currently generate XML Models from LDMs, but you can generate XML Models from CDMs, so you might want to consider using the CDM to create a Logical Data Model to manage XML Schemas. You can also consider using a PDM or an Object-oriented class model for this task.

Need the Big Picture?
No common definitions?
Hero, build a SAM!

The highlighted row in Table 15.1 shows the focus of this chapter – the subject area model (SAM).

Table 15.1 The Subject Area Model is the focus of this chapter

	Relational	**Dimensional**
Subject Area Model (SAM)	**'One-pager' on how something works**	**'One-pager' on what is monitored**
Logical Data Model	Detailed business solution on how something works	Detailed business solution on what is monitored
Physical Data Model	Detailed technical solution on how something works	Detailed technical solution on what is monitored

A subject area model shows the key concepts in a particular area and how these concepts interact with each other. This chapter defines a subject area, followed by an explanation of the importance of the subject area model and subject area definitions. Then the three types of subject area models are discussed, including the application subject area model, where both relational and dimensional variations exist. Then we provide a summary of the ten-step approach to building a subject area model. We conclude this chapter with a description of the support provided by PowerDesigner for Subject Area Models, and a couple of exercises to reinforce what we've told you.

Subject Area Explained

A subject area is a key concept that is both *basic* and *critical* to your audience. "Basic" means this term is probably mentioned many times a day in conversations with the people who represent the audience for the model. "Critical" means the business would be very different or non-existent without this concept.

The majority of subject areas are easy to identify and include concepts that are common across industries, such as Consumer, Customer, Employee, and Product. An airline may call a Customer a Passenger, and a hospital may call a Customer a Patient, but they are all people who receive goods or services. Each subject area will be shown in much more detail at the logical and physical phases of design. For example, the Consumer subject area might encompass the logical entities Consumer, Consumer Association, Consumer Demographics, Consumer Type, and so on.

Many subject areas, however, can be more challenging to identify, as they may be subject areas to your audience, but not to others in the same department, company, or industry. For example, Account would most likely be a subject area for a bank and for a manufacturing company. However, the audience for the bank subject area model might also require Checking Account and Savings Account to be on their model, whereas the audience for the manufacturing subject area model might, instead, require General Ledger Account and Accounts Receivable Account to be on the model.

In our example with the business card, a basic and critical concept can be Address, but Mailing Address can also be basic and critical. Should the subject area model for contact management contain Mailing Address as well? To answer this question, we need to know whether Mailing Address is basic and critical to your audience. The key point about subject area modeling is to model at a level where the audience for the model would agree that each subject area is a key concept.

Subject Area Model Explained

A subject area model is a set of symbols and text representing the key concepts and rules binding these key concepts for a specific business or application scope, for a particular audience, that fits neatly on one page. It could be an 8 ½ x 11, 8 ½ x 14, (A4 or A3 in Europe), or similar sized paper, but it cannot be a plotter-sized piece of paper. Limiting the subject area model to one page is important because it forces the modeler and participants to select only key concepts. We can fit 10, 20 or 50 concepts on one page, but not 500 concepts. A good rule of thumb, therefore, is to ask yourself if the audience for this model would include this concept as one of the top 10 or 20 or 50 concepts in their business. This will rule out concepts that are at too low a level of detail; they will appear in the more detailed logical data model. If you're having trouble limiting the number of concepts, think about whether or not there are other concepts into which the ones you're discussing could be grouped. These higher concepts are the ones you should be including in the subject area model.

The subject area model includes subject areas, their definitions, and the relationships that show how these subject areas interact with each other. Unlike the logical and physical data models, as we will see, subject area models may contain many-to-many relationships. A sample subject area model appears in Figure 15.1.

Figure 15.1 Healthcare Facility Appointment Subject Area Model

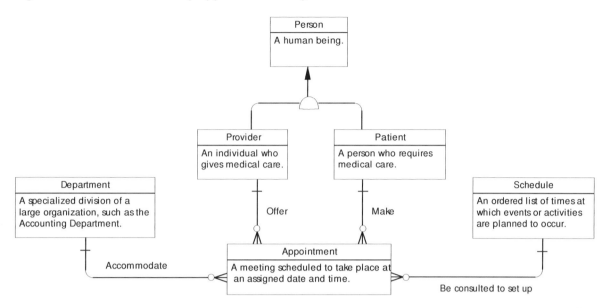

In this diagram, the display preferences in PowerDesigner have been changed to display the Subject Area descriptions.

Business Rules (listed in the order we would typically walk someone through the model):

- Each Person may be a Provider, a Patient, or both a Provider and a Patient. Note that when the subtyping symbol does *not* have an 'X' in its center (as shown in Figure 15.1), it indicates that a member of the supertype can play more than one subtype role. This is called an inclusive (overlapping) subtype. For example, a particular person can be both a provider and a patient.
- Each Provider is a Person.
- Each Patient is a Person.
- Each Provider may offer one or many Appointments.
- Each Patient may make one or many Appointments.
- Each Schedule may be consulted to set up one or many Appointments.
- Each Department may accommodate one or many Appointments.
- Each Appointment must involve one Provider, one Patient, one Department, and one Schedule.

Notice on the model in Figure 15.1, that concepts such as Patient and Provider are likely to be considered subject areas throughout the healthcare industry. There are also slightly more detailed subject areas on this model, such as Schedule and Appointment, which are considered basic and critical, and are therefore subject areas for the particular audience for this subject area model. Yet these more detailed subject areas may not be considered subject areas within a different department, such as accounting and marketing, in this same healthcare company.

During the subject area modeling phase, definitions of the concepts should be given a lot of attention. All too often, we wait until it is too late in the development process to get definitions.

Waiting too long usually leads to not writing definitions at all, or doing a rush job by writing quick definition phrases that have little or no usefulness. If the definitions behind the terms on a data model are nonexistent or poor, multiple interpretations of the subject area become a strong possibility. The names of subject areas in SAMs are likely to be operands in logical expressions that define business rules. Imagine a business rule on our model that states that an Employee must have at least one benefits package. If the definition of Employee is lacking, we may wonder, for example, whether this business rule includes job applicants and retired employees.

Remember the three main functions of definitions in Chapter 6? Subject area models are especially relevant for one of these – "**Helps initiate, document, and resolve different perspectives of the same concept**". If we can agree on the definitions of our business concepts, we are one step closer to creating a holistic view of the business.

By agreeing on definitions at the concept level, the more detailed logical and physical analysis will go more smoothly and take less time. For example, definitions can address the question, "Does Customer include potential customers or only existing customers?" See the cartoon in Figure 15.2 for an example of what not to do.

Figure 15.2 Clarify key concept definitions early!

We need to do a better job of capturing definitions. In fact, during a recent presentation to over 100 business analysts, I asked the innocent question, "How many of you have an agreed-upon single definition of Customer in your organization?" I was expecting at least a handful of the 100 participants to raise their hands, but no one in the room raised their hand!

When the subject area model is complete, which includes subject area definitions, it is a powerful tool that can provide a number of important business benefits:

- **Provides broad understanding**. We can capture extremely complex and encompassing business processes, application requirements, and even entire industries on a single piece of paper. This enables people with different backgrounds and roles to understand and communicate with each other on the same concepts, agreeing on or debating issues.
- **Defines scope and direction**. By visually showing subject areas and their business rules, we can more easily identify a subset of the model to analyze. For example, we can model the entire Logistics department, and then scope out of this a particular logistics application that we would like to build. The broad perspective of a subject area model can help us determine how planned and existing applications will coexist. It can provide direction and guidance on what new functionality the business will need next.
- **Offers proactive analysis**. By developing a subject area-level understanding of the application, there is a strong chance we will be able to identify important issues or concerns, saving substantial time and money later on. Examples include subject area definition differences and different interpretations of project scope.
- **Builds rapport between IT and the business**. A majority of organizations have some issues of internal communication between the business and IT departments. Building a subject area model together is a great way to remove or reduce these communication barriers. On one occasion, a key business user and I sketched out a Contact Data Mart subject area model, which built not just business understanding, but also a strong relationship with this key user.

Types of Subject Area Models

There are three types of subject area models. I've coined acronyms for them that are easy to remember: the Business Subject Area Model (BSAM), the Application Subject Area Model (ASAM), and the Comparison Subject Area Model (CSAM). The BSAM is a subject area model of a defined portion of the business, the ASAM is a subject area model of a defined portion of a particular application, and the CSAM is a subject area model that shows how something new fits within an existing environment.

Business Subject Area Model (BSAM)

The BSAM is a subject area model of a defined portion of the business (not an application). The scope can be limited to a department or function such as manufacturing or sales. It can be as broad as the entire company or industry. Company data models are often called enterprise data models. In addition to all the concepts within an organization, they can also contain external concepts such as government agencies, competitors, and suppliers. Besides serving as a foundation for an enterprise architecture, a BSAM is also a very good place to start capturing the subject areas and business rules for a new application. All future subject area and logical data models can be based on this initial model.

Figure 15.3 contains an example of a BSAM. The purpose of this model was to understand the concepts and high-level business rules within the consumer interaction area, in preparation for building a consumer interaction reporting application. A good first step is to understand how the consumer interaction business works. We could ask questions to learn more about what the business needs, such as:

- What is a Consumer? That is, can a Consumer be someone who has not yet purchased the Product?
- Can one Interaction be placed by more than one Consumer?
- Does an Interaction have to be for a specific Product, or can an interaction be for something more general than a Product, such as a Brand?
- What types of Complaints do you receive?

In Figure 15.3, the name of each relationship is displayed, and the role names (if any) have been hidden. Remember that we can select which relationship names to show on a diagram via the Display Preferences.

Figure 15.3 Consumer Interaction BSAM

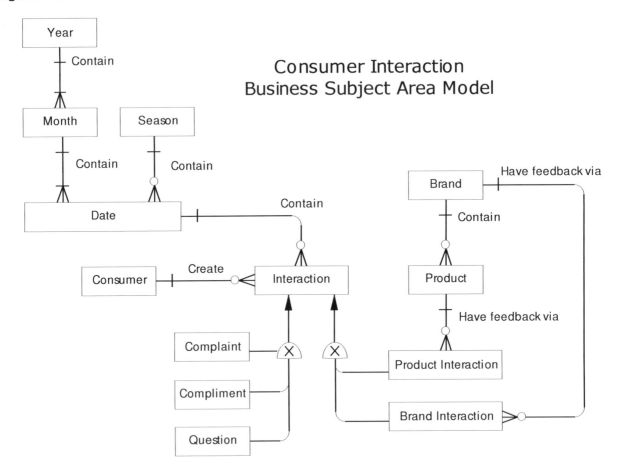

Subject area definitions:

Brand A grouping of products that is recognized by consumers. A brand means something to a consumer in terms of the experience they will have if they purchase a product within this brand.

Brand Interaction A contact initiated by one consumer about a specific brand.

Complaint Negative feedback that we receive on one of our products or brands.

Compliment Positive feedback that we receive on one of our products or brands.

Consumer Someone who buys or receives products or services from us with the intent of the products or services being used and not resold; in other words, the final recipient of the product or service. For example, we are a consumer any time we purchase a product from one of our customers.

Date A period of time containing 24 hours.

Interaction A contact between an employee and a consumer for a specific product or brand. An interaction can take place through a variety of mediums, such as through phone, email, and mail. Interactions fit into one of three categories: complaints, compliments, or questions. Here are examples of some of the interactions:

  - "I love your product." (compliment)
  - "I hate your product." (complaint)
  - "I found a strange object in your product." (complaint)
  - "Where can I buy your product?" (question)
  - "I found your product difficult to assemble." (complaint)

Month One of the twelve major subdivisions of the year.

Product The goods or services that are offered for sale.

Product Interaction A contact initiated by one consumer about a specific product.

Question An inquiry that we receive on one of our products or brands.

Season A season is one of the major divisions of the year, generally based on yearly periodic changes in weather.

Year A period of time containing 365 days (or 366 days in a leap year).

Business Rules (listed in the order we would typically walk someone through the model):

- Each Year must contain exactly 12 Months.
- Each Month must belong to one Year.
- Each Month must contain one or more (up to 31) Dates.
- Each Date must belong to one Month.
- Each Season may contain one or more Dates.
- Each Date must belong to one Season.
- Each Brand may contain one or more Products.
- Each Product must belong to one Brand.
- Each Consumer may create one or more Interactions.
- Each Interaction must be created by one Consumer.
- Each Date may contain one or more Interactions.
- Each Interaction must occur on one Date.
- Each Interaction may be a Complaint, Compliment, or Question.
- Each Complaint is an Interaction.
- Each Compliment is an Interaction.
- Each Question is an Interaction.
- Each Interaction may be a Product Interaction or a Brand Interaction.
- Each Product Interaction is an Interaction.
- Each Brand Interaction is an Interaction.
- Each Product may have feedback via one or more Product Interactions.
- Each Product Interaction must provide feedback on one Product.
- Each Brand may have feedback via one or more Brand Interactions.
- Each Brand Interaction must provide feedback on one Brand.

This model revealed a reporting challenge. One of the reporting requirements was to determine how many interactions are reported at a brand level. The model shows that interactions can be entered at a product level, which then roll up to a brand. Or interactions can come in directly at the brand level. The challenge is to answer this question: "How many interactions are there at a brand level?" According to our data model, if we just summarize those product interactions up to a brand level (i.e., follow the relationship from Interaction to Product Interaction to Product to Brand), we are missing those interactions that occur only at the brand level. Therefore, we need to summarize product interactions up to a brand and then add those interactions at just a brand level to get the total number of interactions at a brand level to answer this question.

The BSAM is the most frequently built type of subject area model. Many times when we say we are creating a subject area model, we mean the BSAM. Before embarking on any large development effort, we first need to understand the business. If an organization needs a new claims-processing system, it needs to have a common understanding of claims and related subject areas. The BSAM can be created simply to develop an understanding of a business area, or as the beginning of a large development effort, such as introducing packaged software into your organization.

Application Subject Area Model (ASAM)

The ASAM is a subject area model of a defined portion of a particular application. BSAMs are frequently the first step in large development efforts (first understand the business before you understand the application), so they are usually the starting point for the ASAM. The ASAM is often a subset of the BSAM. For example, after creating the BSAM of the Human Resources department, we can now carve out of it an ASAM for an application that will track employee training.

 In PowerDesigner, we would generate the ASAM CDM from the BSAM CDM.

We mentioned earlier that there are two modeling mindsets: relational and dimensional. Relational and dimensional data models lead to relational- and dimensional-based applications, so we have two types of ASAMs: relational and dimensional. Relational ASAMs focus on how the business works through the eyes of the application, while dimensional ASAMs focus on how the business is monitored through the eyes of the application.

I once built a relational ASAM to capture the classifications concept in the Enterprise Resource Planning (ERP) software package, SAP/R3. In an effort to understand how SAP treats classifications (terminology, rules, and definitions), I created this model from studying screens, help files, and a large number of the underlying 350 database tables within Classifications. Figure 15.4 contains a subset of this model.

In Figure 15.3, we showed just the name of the relationship. In Figure 15.4, we decided to display all of the relationship role names, using an italic font. The assertion statements that PowerDesigner generates from the role names match the business rules listed below. The entity symbols display a property we added ourselves, called *Notes and Examples*, to hold text that is useful for helping us understand each entity, but is not necessary for describing them.

Business Rules (listed in the order we would typically walk someone through the model):

- Each Class may contain one or many Classes.
- Each Class may be contained in one Class.
- Each Class must be described by many Characteristics.
- Each Characteristic must describe many Classes.
- Each Characteristic may contain one or many Characteristic Values.
- Each Characteristic Value must belong to one Characteristic.
- Each Class must organize many Objects.
- Each Object must be organized by many Classes.
- Each Object must be assigned many Characteristic Values.
- Each Characteristic Value must be assigned to many Objects.

Figure 15.4 Subset of SAP/R3 Classifications

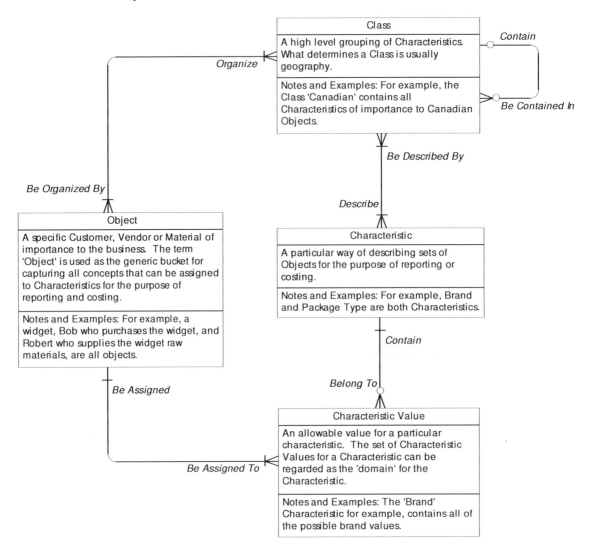

This SAP/R3 ASAM was used for educational purposes, as well as to gauge the effort to customize the application. Notice that on this particular model, showing the definitions directly on the model helps the reader to understand the concepts, as terms such as Object and Class can be ambiguous. This model was first used in a joint IT and business department meeting where the goal was to clearly explain SAP/R3 Classifications in 30 minutes or less. This was not an easy task, as SAP/R3 is a very complicated system, and showing the audience the underlying 350 database tables within the Classifications area would most likely have led to the audience running screaming from the room. Therefore, this model was produced to get the main concepts across to the audience. Somewhere hidden in those 350 database tables are these four key concepts and accompanying business rules. The model was extremely well-received, and I know from the comments and questions from the audience that both the business and IT folks understood it.

We can also build a dimensional ASAM, such as the example in Figure 15.5, which builds on our ice cream example.

Figure 15.5 Dimensional ASAM example

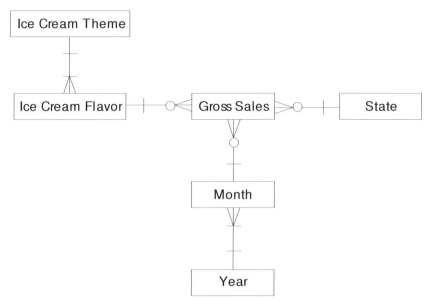

Subject area definitions:

Gross Sales	The total dollar amount charged for all goods or products sold or distributed. Also included in gross sales is sales tax. Returns from melted ice cream are not deducted.
Ice Cream Flavor	The distinctive taste of one ice cream product over another. Flavors are recognized and selected by consumers. Examples include Chocolate, Vanilla, and Strawberry.
Ice Cream Theme	A group of ice cream flavors that share at least one common property. For example, the Brownie Ice Cream and Cake Batter Ice Cream flavors are grouped into the Cake Ice Cream Theme.
Month	One of the twelve major subdivisions of the year.
State	A subset of the United States; one of the fifty states.
Year	A period of time containing 365 days (or 366 days in a leap year).

Navigation paths (listed in the order a user would typically navigate through the model):

"I need to see Gross Sales for each Theme and Year. If there are any surprises, I will need to drill down into the details. That is, drill down from Theme to Flavor, from Year to Month, and add State to my queries."

Notice that with a dimensional model, the focus is more on navigation than on business rules, as in a relational model.

Comparison Subject Area Model (CSAM)

The CSAM is a subject area model that shows how something new fits within an existing environment. It is used primarily for impact analysis and issue resolution. CSAMs build on two or more ASAMs, in which one or more ASAMs represent an existing application environment and (optionally) one or more ASAMs represent proposed changes to an environment.

The CSAM identifies gaps, touch points, and overlaps. It compares something new with something in place to see whether there are gaps or redundancies. Here are some examples where a CSAM would be useful:

- **Proposed data mart within current data warehouse architecture.** The CSAM will show how the new data mart requirements fit into what currently exists within the data warehouse.
- **Proposed additional functionality to an existing operational or data mart application.** The CSAM will highlight the new functionality and show how it fits in with current functionality.
- **Replacing an application.** The CSAM can show the overlap at a subject area level when you are replacing an existing application with a new application.

The CSAM also helps estimate the development effort. Because we are showing the overlap and gaps that a new application will cause within our environment, we can more easily develop a high-level estimate for the development effort. For example, superimposing a new reporting application over an existing data warehouse environment can help us find areas of the reporting application where the programming effort will be greater than in those areas already existing in the warehouse.

The CSAM requires the most effort to build, but of the three types of subject area models, it can provide the most benefits. It requires the most effort because there is more than one viewpoint to represent on a model. More than one perspective often leads to more than one interpretation of a subject area, or the rules between subject areas. It takes time to identify these differences and resolve, or at least document them. The CSAM provides the most benefits because we are showing impact or issues at a high-level of granularity. What's more, it is likely that this high-level, cross-application view has not been captured and explained with such clarity previously. Figure 15.6 includes an example of a CSAM.

In the CSAM in Figure 15.6, we are capturing how a proposed new data mart would impact an existing data warehouse. Building on our ice cream example, the current data warehouse for this ice cream store contains those subject areas that are not shaded in gray. That is, the data warehouse currently contains Ice Cream Cone, Ice Cream Container, Ice Cream Cup, Ice Cream Flavor, and Ice Cream Scoop. The dimensional ASAM example from Figure 15.5 is a proposed data mart. All of the concepts on this proposed data mart are in the ice cream store data warehouse with the exception of those two terms shaded in gray: Ice Cream Theme and Order. (Note that the concepts of Month, Year, State, and Gross Sales from Figure 15.5 are derived from detailed orders. Therefore, Order in Figure 15.6, includes these four concepts.) This CSAM is an excellent tool to explain to the data warehouse and data mart stakeholders what the impact (and therefore, the cost and benefit) of creating this new data mart within the existing data warehouse would be.

Figure 15.6 CSAM example – Ice Cream

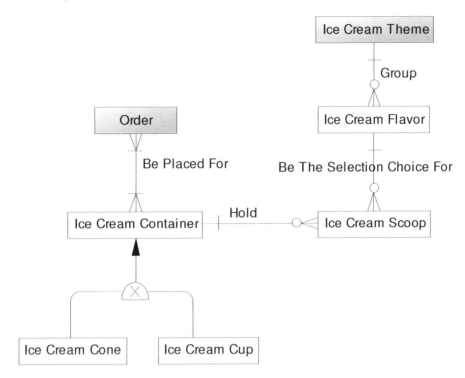

Subject area definitions:

Ice Cream Cone	An edible container which can hold one or more ice cream scoops.
Ice Cream Container	A holder of ice cream that is either edible, in the case of an ice cream cone, or recyclable, in the case of an ice cream cup.
Ice Cream Cup	A recyclable container which can hold one or more ice cream scoops.
Ice Cream Flavor	The distinctive taste of one ice cream product over another. Flavors are recognized and selected by consumers. Examples include Chocolate, Vanilla, and Strawberry.
Ice Cream Scoop	A single ball-shaped unit of ice cream formed in a company-standard size ice cream scoop and packaged in one ice cream container.
Ice Cream Theme	A collection of ice cream flavors that have been grouped together because they share at least one common property. For example, the Brownie Ice Cream and Cake Batter Ice Cream flavors are grouped into the Cake Ice Cream Theme.
Order	Also known as an ice cream sale, an order is when a consumer purchases one or more of our products in a single visit to our ice cream store.

Business Rules (listed in the order we would typically walk someone through the model):

- Each Ice Cream Container may hold one or many Ice Cream Scoops.
- Each Ice Cream Scoop must be held in one Ice Cream Container.
- Each Ice Cream Container is either an Ice Cream Cone or an Ice Cream Cup.
- Each Ice Cream Cone is an Ice Cream Container.
- Each Ice Cream Cup is an Ice Cream Container.
- Each Ice Cream Flavor may be the selection choice for one or many Ice Cream Scoops.
- Each Ice Cream Scoop must contain one Ice Cream Flavor.
- Each Ice Cream Theme may group one or many Ice Cream Flavors.
- Each Ice Cream Flavor must be grouped by one Ice Cream Theme.
- Each Order must be placed for one or many Ice Cream Containers.
- Each Ice Cream Container must appear on one or many Orders.

How to Build a Subject Area Model

Following is a brief summary of the ten steps to complete a SAM (for more on this approach, please refer to Chapter 4 in *Data Modeling for the Business: A Handbook for Aligning the Business with IT using High-Level Data Models*, ISBN 9780977140077, where the SAM is referred to as a High-Level Data Model, or HDM):

1. **Identify model purpose.** Before starting any data modeling effort, first identify why the model needs to be built. The underlying reason for building a data model is communication. We build data models so we can ensure that we and others have a precise understanding of terminology and business rules. In this step, we identify our communication needs. What are we communicating? Who are we communicating it to? Always "begin with the end in mind", as Stephen Covey would say. The most popular reason for building a SAM is to gain understanding of an existing area of the business. We can model a department such as Sales or Accounting, a line of business such as Home Mortgages, or even the entire organization. The SAM is also a very good place to start capturing the concepts and business rules for a new application, so that terminology, rules, and definitions can be agreed upon prior to detailed project analysis.

2. **Identify model stakeholders.** Document the names and departments of those who will be involved in building the SAM, as well as those who will use it after its completion. Roles include architects, analysts, modelers, business users, and managers. Both business and IT roles are required for success. I remember one project I worked on where only IT people showed up to build the SAM. As enthusiastic as we all were to build the model and get support for the project, it was a losing effort because without the business, the model lost credibility and the project, therefore, lost financial support.

3. **Inventory available resources.** Leverage the results from Step 2, as well as identify any documentation that could provide useful content to the SAM. The two

types of resources are people and documentation. People include both business and IT resources. Business people may be management and/or knowledge users. IT resources can span the entire IT spectrum, from analysts through developers, from program sponsors to team leaders. From the people side, this step can be as simple as assigning actual people to the builder roles in Step 2. For example, if we are building a SAM of the manufacturing section of our business, Bob, the business analyst who spent 20 years of his career working in the plant, would be an excellent resource to assign as a builder. Documentation includes systems documentation and requirements documents. Systems documentation can take the form of documentation for a packaged piece of software, or documentation written to support a legacy application. Requirements documents span business, functional, and technical requirements, and can be an essential input to building the SAM.

4. **Determine type of model.** Decide whether the BSAM, ASAM, or CSAM is the most appropriate. Base your selection on the purpose of the model and the available resources.

5. **Select approach**. There are three approaches for building a subject area model: top-down, bottom-up, and hybrid. Even though these approaches sound completely different from each other, they really have quite a lot in common. In fact, the major difference between the approaches lies in the initial information-gathering step. The top-down approach begins with a purely business needs perspective. We learn how the business works and what the business needs from the business people themselves, either through direct meetings with them, or indirectly through requirements documents and reports. The business people are allowed to dream - they should reach for the sky. All requirements are considered possible and doable. The bottom-up approach, on the other hand, temporarily ignores what the business needs and instead focuses on the existing systems environment. We build an initial subject area model by studying the systems that the business is using today. It may include operational systems that run the day-to-day business, or reporting systems that allow the business to view how well the organization is doing. Once the existing systems are understood at a high level, new concepts may be introduced or existing concepts can be modified to meet the business needs. The hybrid approach completes the initial information gathering step by usually starting with some top-down analysis, and then some bottom-up analysis, and then some top-down analysis, etc., until the information gathering is complete. First, there is some initial top-down work to understand project scope and high level business needs. Then we work bottom-up to understand the existing systems. The whole process is a constant loop of reconciling what the business needs with what information is available.

6. **Complete audience-view SAM.** Produce a SAM using the terminology and rules that are clear to those who will be using the model. This is the first high-level model we build. Our purpose is to capture the viewpoint of the model's audience without complicating information capture by including how their perspective fits with that of other departments, or with the organization as a whole. Our next step will reconcile the deliverable from this step with enterprise terminology. Here our purpose is just

to capture *their* view of the world. The initial model can be created by standing at a white board or flipchart with the users. Sometimes 30 minutes at a white board with a business user can reveal more about what they want than spending hours reading requirements documents.

7. **Incorporate enterprise terminology.** Now that the model is well-understood by the audience, ensure the terminology and rules are consistent with the organization view. To build the enterprise perspective, modify the audience model to be consistent with enterprise terminology and rules. Ideally, this enterprise perspective is captured within an enterprise data model. You might have to schedule meetings between the people whose view is captured in the audience-specific model and those who share the enterprise perspective, to resolve any terminology or definition issues.

8. **Signoff.** Obtain approval from the stakeholders that the model is correct and complete. After the initial information gathering, make sure the model is reviewed for data modeling best practices, as well as for meeting the requirements. The signoff process on a SAM does not require the same formality as signoff on the physical design, but it should still be taken seriously. Usually, email verification that the model looks good will suffice. Validating whether the model has met data modeling best practices is often done by applying the Data Model Scorecard®, which will be discussed in Chapter 22.

9. **Market.** Similar to introducing a new product, advertise the data model so that all those who can benefit from it know about it. If the model has a relatively small scope, it is possible that the users who helped you build and validate the model are also the only ones who need to know about it, so marketing requires little effort. However, most SAMs span broad areas, so it is essential to let the appropriate business and IT resources know it is available to them. Techniques include 'Lunch-and-Learns', advertisements on corporate intranets, and presenting the model at periodic management meetings.

10. **Maintain.** SAMs require little maintenance, but they are not maintenance-free. Make sure the model is kept up-to-date. The SAM will not change often, but it *will* change, and we need to have formal processes for updating this model to keep it up to date. What works well is to have two additional steps in your software methodology:

    1. Borrowing from a SAM, and
    2. Contributing back to the SAM.

    After the SAM is complete, and before starting a logical data model, for example, the SAM should be used as a starting point for further modeling. The second step in the methodology requires taking all of the lessons learned during the project and making sure all new concepts are incorporated back into the SAM. In PowerDesigner, create and maintain linkages from your SAM to other CDMs, LDMs, and perhaps PDMs.

Subject Area Models in PowerDesigner

If you have worked through the earlier chapters, you've already tried all the PowerDesigner techniques you need to create a SAM:

> *Chapter 10*   **General 'how-to' knowledge**
> *Chapter 11*   **Creating Entities**
> *Chapter 13*   **Creating Relationships**

We do not suggest that you include attributes in a SAM, hence the above list doesn't include data elements or keys. Always use a PowerDesigner CDM to create a SAM.

CDM Settings

Before you add content to your model, we suggest that you set the options listed in Table 15.2. Remember to click on <Set As Default> within the model options and display preferences.

Table 15.2 CDM settings

Category	Settings
Model Options – Model Settings	Entity/Relationship notation.
	Allow duplicate codes for relationships.
	Enable links to requirements (if you intend to create a Requirements model).
Model Options – Naming Convention	Enable Glossary for auto completion and compliance checking (if you use a Glossary).
Display Preferences – General Settings	Enable the following:
	Show Bridges at Intersections
	Auto Link Routing
	Snap to Grid
	Enable Word Wrapping
	If you have a preference for the color of lines and symbol fill, or for the use of symbol shadows, set them here.
Display Preferences – Entity	Hide all properties, except perhaps the description (you'll need to add this property).
Display Preferences – Relationship	Hide all properties, except the name or the source role name, depending on your approach to naming relationships (see below).
	Set the line style to 'rounded right-angles'.
Display Preferences – Inheritance	Hide all properties.
Display Preferences – Inheritance Link	Set the line style to 'rounded right-angles'.
Display Preferences – Traceability Link	Set the line style to 'rounded right-angles'.

Approaches for Creating a SAM

You can use a variety of techniques to create a SAM in PowerDesigner, depending on whether or not you have existing data models that can 'seed' the new model.

To create SAM (CDM) entities based on CDM entities in PowerDesigner models, copy them from the existing model, and paste them into the new model. It may be appropriate to paste them as replicas. To create SAM entities based on existing LDM entities, open the LDM, and choose `Generate Conceptual Data Model` from the `Tools` menu. Ensure that you update the new SAM (it will need to be open), rather than creating a new model, and that you *do not* keep the generation dependencies. An entity in the SAM is very likely to be related to many LDM entities, so we suggest you maintain the links from the SAM to LDMs another way, which we will describe shortly.

To create attributes based on data items in a 'Data Dictionary' model held in a different CDM, copy the data items from the Data Dictionary model, and paste them as shortcuts or replicas in your SAM.

Use the Excel Import facility to create or update entities in your SAM. This is a great way of making effective use of existing documentation.

Presenting the SAM

In order to achieve the potential benefits of a SAM, it must communicate concepts clearly. Of all data models, this is probably the one where style and format matter the most. Look back at the figures in this chapter, and you will see that we have taken more than one approach regarding the content of symbols – revise the symbol content to suit the audience. As this is a monochrome book, we have not been able to use color in our symbols apart from some shading, but you can use color very effectively in a SAM, and even continue the color scheme to other related models.

Be prepared to create more than one diagram in your SAM, if you need to communicate your message to different audiences. For layout and formatting tips, refer to Chapter 9 in *Data Modeling for the Business: A Handbook for Aligning the Business with IT using High-Level Data Models*, ISBN 9780977140077, where the SAM is referred to as a High-Level Data Model, or HDM.

Linking the SAM to Other Data Models

Every organization's modeling requirements are different, so every organization's model linking requirements are different. See Chapter 18 for a discussion of this topic.

Linking a SAM to other related models is great for impact analysis, and for categorizing the content of related models. The relatively abstract nature of the entities in a SAM means that they are unlikely to match directly to entities or tables in other data models, except those in other SAMs. We suggest that you do not use generation links to link the SAM to other models, even if you generated parts of the SAM from other models. You could use the mapping editor to create these links, but we believe that these links need to be more explicit and obvious than those created by the mapping editor. Instead, we suggest that you use traceability links.

Create a new type of *Traceability Link*, named according to the reason why you are linking models together. Create *Traceability Links* between the objects you need to connect together, perhaps using a Dependency Matrix. See Exercise 19 for an example of this approach. You could share standard Dependency Matrices via template models or a model extension.

Searching the Links

When the linked models are in the repository, the links will show up in repository searches and impact analysis (assuming you select *Use Repository*). You may want to create your own analysis rules to make this easier for users.

You can also create links between the subject areas in a SAM and diagrams in other models by using the *Related Diagrams* feature.

Relationship Names in the SAM

The diagrams in the SAM are simple, and there is no need for complex naming standards for relationships. We suggest you take one of three approaches, listed in Table 15.3.

Table 15.3 Relationship names in the SAM

Approach	When to use
Let the relationship names default, or provide simple unique names; don't display them on diagrams; *do not* create relationship role names	Use in a high-level BSAM, where most or all relationships are many-to-many, and are therefore difficult to name precisely.
Create relationship names that include entity names; *do not* create relationship role names	Use when you do not want to show relationship names on diagrams, but you need to have a meaningful list of relationships in the Browser, the portal, or in reports
Create relationship names that include entity names; also create relationship source role names	Use when you need to have a meaningful list of relationships in the Browser, the portal, or in reports, and you also want to show a shorter name on diagrams. Also use when you want to generate Assertion Statements.

Useful SAM Model Checks

PowerDesigner allows you to verify the validity of your models via the Model Check facility (press <F4> to run the model check). The following checks are particularly useful for a SAM. Check the PowerDesigner documentation to find out more about them.

All Objects
- Name or Code contains terms not in glossary [if glossary enabled]
- Name or Code contains synonyms of glossary terms [if glossary enabled]. PowerDesigner can automatically correct these for you by replacing synonyms with their associated glossary terms.

Entity
- Existence of attributes
- Existence of relationship or association link(s)
- Redundant inheritance
- Multiple inheritance
- Parent of several inheritances

Relationship
- Reflexive dependency
- Reflexive mandatory
- Bijective (completely mandatory one-to-one) relationship between two entities

Inheritance
- Existence of inheritance link

❓ "Checking a Data Model" (Data Modeling)

Additional Information in the SAM

If you have documentation of requirements or business rules, consider importing them into PowerDesigner, and linking them to your SAM entities and relationships.

Promoting and Sharing the SAM

Make the SAM available to as wide an audience as you can. If you do not have a repository, generate an HTML report and add it to your intranet; generate an RTF report, including diagram images, and distribute in whatever format suits you best; use the Excel export and import features to enable non-users to contribute.

If you have a repository, ensure that the SAM and all linked models are checked in, and made available to the portal, and use the 'Composer' license to allow selected experts to amend the SAM via the portal.

EXERCISE 14: Building a Subject Area Model in PowerDesigner

In PowerDesigner, create the BSAM shown in Figure 15.3.

EXERCISE 15: Building a Subject Area Model

Identify an area within your organization that is in desperate need of a SAM and build it for them using the ten-step approach from this chapter. Make sure you document it in PowerDesigner as a CDM.

If you prefer, build one or more of the Subject Area Models described in this chapter.

Key Points

- A subject area is a concept that is both basic and critical to your audience.

- A subject area model is a set of symbols and text that represents key concepts and the rules binding these key concepts for a specific business or application scope and for a particular audience.

- The BSAM is a subject area model of a defined portion of the business.

- The ASAM is a subject area model of a defined portion of a particular application, and may be relational or dimensional.

- The CSAM is a subject area model that shows how something new fits within an existing framework.

- Follow the ten-step approach to building a SAM.

- The CDM is the most appropriate type of model for a SAM in PowerDesigner.

- Pay attention to how you present the SAM to your audience(s).

- Use the PowerDesigner repository and portal to share and link your SAM.

- There is no need for complex relationship naming standards.

What does business need?
Forget the technology
Enter logical

The highlighted row in Table 16.1 shows the focus of this chapter, which is the logical data model.

Table 16.1 The Logical Data Model is the focus of this chapter

	Relational	Dimensional
Subject Area Model (SAM)	'One-pager' on how something works	'One-pager' on what is monitored
Logical Data Model	**Detailed business solution on how something works**	**Detailed business solution on what is monitored**
Physical Data Model	Detailed technical solution on how something works	Detailed technical solution on what is monitored

A logical data model (LDM) takes the business need defined on a subject area model down to the next level of a business solution. That is, once you understand at a broad level the scope of an effort and what business people require to solve their problem, the next step is to come up with a solution for them in the form of a LDM. The logical data model is explained, along with a comparison of relational and dimensional mindsets. Then, for relational models, the techniques of normalization and abstraction are discussed. Then we answer Frequently Asked Questions (FAQ) on dimensional modeling, which leads to explaining terms such as conformed dimensions and factless facts. We conclude by explaining how Logical Data Models are supported by Power Designer, and use four exercises to reinforce the lessons for you.

Logical Data Model Explained

A logical data model (LDM) is a business solution to a business problem. It is how the modeler captures the business requirements without complicating the model with implementation concerns such as software and hardware.

On the subject area model, we might learn, for example, what the terms, business rules, and scope would be for a new order entry system. After understanding the requirements for the order entry system, we create a LDM containing all of the data elements and business rules needed to deliver the business solution system. For example, the subject area model will show that a Customer places many Orders. The LDM will capture all of the details behind Customer and Order, such as the customer's name, their address, the order number, and what is being ordered. While building the LDM, questions or issues may arise having to do with specific hardware or software such as:

- How can we retrieve this information in less than 5 seconds?
- How can we make this information secure?
- There is a lot of information here. What is the best way to manage storage space?

These questions focus on hardware and software. Although they need to be documented, they are not addressed in a data modeling tool until we are ready to start the physical data model. The reason these questions depend on technology is because if hardware and software were infinitely efficient and secure, these questions would never be raised.

Comparison of Relational with Dimensional Logical Models

There are both relational and dimensional logical data models. Relational modeling is the process of capturing how the business works, while dimensional modeling is the process of capturing the information the business needs to monitor how well it is doing. Relational modeling captures how the business works and contains business rules, such as "A Customer must have at least one Account", or "A Product must have a **Product Short Name**." Dimensional modeling focuses on capturing and aggregating the metrics from daily operations that enable the business to evaluate how well it is doing by manipulating the numbers. For example, examining the measure **Gross Sales Value Amount** at a day level and then, after getting the answer, looking at **Gross Sales Value Amount** at a month or year level, or at a product or brand level, or a city or country level. The dimensional model is all about playing with numbers. Recall the Ice Cream CSAM from Figure 15.6, a subset of which appears in Figure 16.1.

Figure 16.1 Ice cream CSAM subset

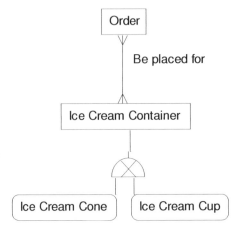

Figure 16.2 contains the relational logical data model for this CSAM.

Figure 16.2 Ice cream relational logical data model

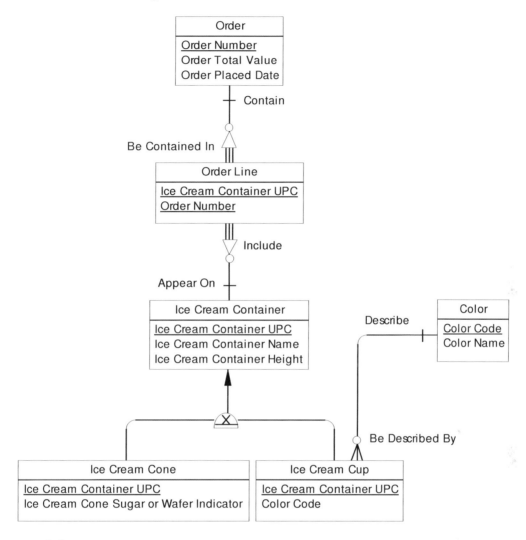

Data element definitions:

Color Code

The short name of one of the primary colors, such as 'b' for 'blue'.

Color Name

The full name of one of the primary colors, such as 'blue', 'red', or 'yellow'.

Ice Cream Cone Sugar Or Wafer Indicator

Determines whether the ice cream cone is made of a sugar-based or wafer-based material. Contains either the value 'S' for 'Sugar' or 'W' for 'Wafer'.

Ice Cream Container Height

The height, in inches, of the container. Used by inventory to determine how many containers can fit on a storage shelf.

Ice Cream Container Name	The name our store employees use for communicating with consumers on what they would like to order. Examples range from the smallest, called "Kid's Cup", to the largest size, called "Kitchen Sink".
Ice Cream Container UPC	UPC (Universal Product Code) is a numeric code used to identify a specific product across the ice cream industry.
Order Total Value	The total dollar amount of the order, including sales tax.
Order Placed Date	The date the order was placed.
Order Number	The unique number assigned to each order placed by a consumer. It is a numeric sequence number that never repeats.

Business Rules (listed in the order we would typically walk someone through the model):

- Each Order may contain one or many Order Lines.
- Each Order Line must be contained in one Order.
- Each Ice Cream Container may appear on one or many Order Lines.
- Each Order Line must include one Ice Cream Container.
- Each Ice Cream Container must be either an Ice Cream Cone or an Ice Cream Cup.
- Each Ice Cream Cone is an Ice Cream Container.
- Each Ice Cream Cup is an Ice Cream Container.
- Each Color may describe one or many Ice Cream Cups.
- Each Ice Cream Cup must be described by one Color.

A **relational logical data model** captures the business solution for how part of the business works. On this ice cream relational logical data model, we are representing the properties and rules for part of an ice cream ordering system, including Order, Order Line, and Ice Cream Container. Our solution, for example, allows us to capture whether an ice cream cone is a sugar or wafer cone, but does not allow us to capture the color of the ice cream cone. We can only capture the color for cups, not cones.

Two additional notes on the model in Figure 16.2:

- The primary key for a subtype must have the same primary key as its supertype. Given "Each Ice Cream Cone is an Ice Cream Container" and "Each Ice Cream Cup is an Ice Cream Container", it makes sense for an Ice Cream Cone to have the same primary key as an Ice Cream Container, and an Ice Cream Cup to have the same primary key as an Ice Cream Container.
- There are more details on the logical data model. Whereas the subject area model contained a many-to-many relationship between Order and Ice Cream Container, the logical model contains more details, including the new entity Order Line, which resolves

the many-to-many relationship between Order and Ice Cream Container. Also, the Color logical entity was not considered basic and critical and therefore did not need to be shown on the subject area model. In fact, it is not uncommon to have ten or more logical entities capture the details behind one subject area.

A **dimensional logical data model** captures all of the information needed to answer business questions where the answers to the questions are measures, and these measures need to be reported at different levels of granularity. Granularity means the level of detail of the measures, such as by a particular level of calendar including day, month, or year, or by a particular level of geography, including city, region, or country. Here are some examples of business questions that focus on measures:

- What is my **Gross Sales Value Amount** by Region, Product, and Month? Now what about by Region and Year? How about by Product Brand and Quarter?
- How many Students majored in Computer Science this Semester? How about for the whole Year?
- What is our **Member Growth Rate** by Region over the last five Years? How about by Country over the last ten Years?

Figure 16.3 contains the dimensional logical data model that is based on the ice cream example from Figure 16.1.

Figure 16.3 Ice cream dimensional logical data model

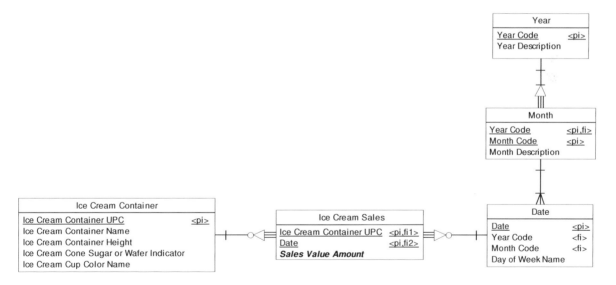

Sales Value Amount is captured at the Date and Ice Cream Container level and then the user (or reporting tool) can navigate and look at **Sales Value Amount** at different levels of detail. "What was the value of our Sales of Sugar Ice Cream Cones in August 2011? Oh, that number is so low. What was the value of our Sales of Sugar Ice Cream Cones each date in August 2011? Or how about the value of Sales for all of 2011 for all Ice Cream Containers?" These are examples of some of the questions that can be answered. Note that all of these questions focus on measures - in this case, **Sales Value Amount**.

Although the symbols are very similar across both the relational model in Figure 16.2 and the dimensional model in Figure 16.3, the modeling mindset required is very different. With the relational model, we ask "How does this business work?" With the dimensional model, we ask "What does the business want to monitor?" On a relational model, we have the building blocks of entity, data element, and relationship. On a dimensional model, we have similar symbols, but they represent different concepts:

- **Measure**. A data element that may be manipulated in or is the result of a calculation (e.g., sum, count, average, minimum, maximum). **Sales Value Amount** is an example of a measure in our ice cream example.
- **Meter**. A meter is an entity containing a related set of measures. It is not a person, place, event, or thing, as we find on the relational model. Instead, it is a bucket of common measures. As a group, common measures address a business concern, such as Profitability, Employee Satisfaction, or Sales. The meter is so important to the dimensional model that the name of the meter is often the name of the application.
- **Grain**. The grain is the meter's lowest level of detail. It should be low enough that the answers to all of the business questions within the scope of the dimensional model are derivable. It is generally a good practice to define the measures and grain as early as possible in the requirements process. The grain in our ice cream example is Ice Cream Container and Date.
- **Dimension**. A dimension is reference information whose purpose is to add meaning to the measures. All the different ways of filtering, sorting, and summing measures make use of dimensions. Dimensions are often, but not exclusively, hierarchies. A hierarchy is when a higher level breaks down into many lower levels, but a lower level rolls up into only one higher level. Our calendar structure in Figure 16.3 is an example of a hierarchy, because every Date rolls up into a single Month, and every Month rolls up into a single Year. Also, every Year contains many Months and every Month contains many Dates. Ice Cream Container is an example of a dimension that is not a hierarchy.
- **Dimensional level**. A dimensional level is one level within the hierarchy of a dimension, such as Month within the Calendar dimension. Dimensional levels are used to facilitate calculating measures at the level(s) the business needs to see. They are not built based on how the business works.
- **Dimensional attribute**. The properties within a dimension, such as Ice Cream Container Height, in the Ice Cream Container dimension.

We've emphasized several times that relational modeling captures how something works and dimensional captures what is being monitored. Let's look at this distinction in another way - there are three main differences between relational and dimensional models: focus, lines, and scope:

- **Focus**. A dimensional model is a data model whose only purpose is to allow efficient and user-friendly filtering, sorting, and summing of measures. A relational model, on the other hand, focuses on supporting a business process. Dimensional models are appropriate when there is a need to massage numbers, such as by summing or averaging. The reason the dimensional model should be limited to numbers is because its design allows for easy navigation up and down hierarchy levels. When traversing hierarchy levels, measures may need to be recalculated for the hierarchy level. For example, a **Gross Sales Value Amount** of $5 on a particular date might be $100 for the month in which that date belongs.

- **Lines**. The relationship lines on a dimensional model represent navigation paths instead of business rules, as in a relational model. Let creativity drive your dimensional structures. The relationships in a dimensional hierarchy do not have to mimic their relational counterparts. You should build dimensions to meet the way the business users think.

- **Scope**. The scope of a dimensional model is a collection of related measures that together address a business concern, whereas in a relational model, the scope may be a broad business process, such as order processing or account management. For example, the metrics **Number of Product Complaints** and **Number of Product Inquiries** can be used to gauge product satisfaction.

Normalization Explained

When I turned 12, I received a trunk full of baseball cards as a birthday present from my parents. I was delighted, not just because there may have been a Hank Aaron or Pete Rose buried somewhere in that trunk, but because I loved to organize the cards. I categorized each card according to year and team. Organizing the cards in this way gave me a deep understanding of the players and their teams. To this day, I can answer many baseball card trivia questions.

Normalization, in general, is the process of applying a set of rules with the goal of organizing *something*. I was normalizing the baseball cards according to year and team. We can also apply a set of rules and normalize the data elements within our organizations. The rules are based on how the business works, which is why normalization is the primary technique used in building the relational logical data model.

Just as those baseball cards lay unsorted in that trunk, our companies have huge numbers of data elements spread throughout departments and applications. The rules applied to normalizing the baseball cards entailed first sorting by year, and then by team within a year. The rules for normalizing our data elements can be boiled down to a single sentence:

> Make sure every data element is <u>single-valued</u> and <u>provides a fact</u> <u>completely</u> and <u>only</u> about its primary key.

The underlined terms require more of an explanation.

'Single-valued' means a data element must contain only one piece of information. If **Consumer Name** contains **Consumer First Name** and **Consumer Last Name,** for example, we must split **Consumer Name** into two data elements - **Consumer First Name** and **Consumer Last Name**.

'Provides a fact' means that a given primary key value will always return no more than one of every data element that is identified by this key. If a **Customer Identifier** value of '123' for example, returns three customer last names ('Smith', 'Jones', and 'Roberts'), it violates this part of the normalization definition.

'Completely' means that the minimal set of data elements that uniquely identify an instance of the entity is present in the primary key. If, for example, there are two data elements in an entity's primary key, but only one is needed for uniqueness, the data element that is not needed for uniqueness should be removed from the primary key.

'Only' means that each data element must provide a fact about the primary key and nothing else. That is, there can be no hidden dependencies. For example, assume an Order is identified by an **Order Number**. Within Order, there are many data elements, including **Order Scheduled Delivery Date**, **Order Actual Delivery Date**, and **Order On Time Indicator**. **Order On Time Indicator** contains either a 'Yes' or a 'No', providing a fact about whether the **Order Actual Delivery Date** is less than or equal to the **Order Scheduled Delivery Date**. **Order On Time Indicator,** therefore, provides a fact about **Order Actual Delivery Date** and **Order Scheduled Delivery Date**, not directly about **Order Number**, so it should be removed from the normalized model. **Order On Time Indicator** is an example of a derived data element, meaning it is calculated. Derived data elements are removed from a normalized model.

You can record **Order On Time Indicator** in PowerDesigner as a Data Item in a Data Dictionary model, a Term in the Glossary, or as a Business Rule. All of these can be linked to the attributes from which the indicator setting is derived.

So, a general definition for normalization is that it is a series of rules for organizing something. The series of rules can be summarized as: *Every data element is single-valued and provides a fact completely and only about its primary key.* An informal definition I frequently use for normalizing is: *A formal process of asking business questions.* We cannot determine if every data element is single-valued and provides a fact completely and only about its primary key unless we understand the data. To understand the data, we usually need to ask lots of questions. Even for an apparently simple data element such as **Phone Number,** for example, we can ask many questions:

- Whose phone number is this?
- Do you always have to have a phone number?
- Can you have more than one phone number?
- Do you ever recognize the area code as separate from the rest of the phone number?
- Do you ever need to see phone numbers outside a given country?
- What type of phone number is this? That is, is it a fax number, mobile number, etc.?
- Does the time of day matter? For example, do we need to distinguish between the phone number to use during working hours, and outside working hours? Of course, that would lead to a discussion on what we mean by 'working hours'.

The answers to questions like these do not have to result in new attributes or changes to attributes. They could lead to the addition of Data Items, Business Rules, or Terms in the Glossary, which you then link to the relevant attributes or entities.

To ensure that every data element is single-valued and provides a fact completely and only about its primary key, we apply a series of rules or small steps, where each step (or level of normalization) checks something that moves us towards our goal. Most data professionals would agree that the full set of normalization levels is the following:

- first normal form (1NF)
- second normal form (2NF)
- third normal form (3NF)
- Boyce/Codd normal form (BCNF)
- fourth normal form (4NF)
- fifth normal form (5NF).

Each level of normalization includes the lower levels of rules that precede it. If a model is in 5NF, it is also in 4NF, BCNF, and so on. Even though there are higher levels of normalization than 3NF, many interpret the term "normalized" to mean 3NF. This is because the higher levels of normalization (that is, BCNF, 4NF, and 5NF) cover specific situations that occur much less frequently than the first three levels. Therefore, to keep things simple, this chapter focuses only on first through third normal forms.

Normalization provides a number of important benefits: (NOTE: In this section, the term data model may also represent the physical database that will be implemented from the data model)

- Stronger understanding of the business.
- Greater application stability.
- Less data redundancy.
- Better data quality.
- Faster building of new models.

Initial Chaos

We have all put together puzzles at one time or another. After you open the box and dump out the pieces, the sight can be overwhelming: hundreds, maybe thousands, of tiny pieces in a large pile. The pile is in a state of chaos. As we pick each piece up and examine it, we understand its properties in the form of its shape. We lack knowledge at this point about how these puzzle pieces connect with each other. We begin the process of fitting the pieces together and, after much effort, we complete our masterpiece. Each puzzle piece is in its proper place.

The term *chaos* can be applied to any unorganized pile, including data elements. We may have a strong understanding of each of the data elements, such as their name and definition, but we lack knowledge about how the data elements fit together. We understand each piece of the puzzle, but we do not yet understand the connections between the pieces. In our business card example, we do not know the relationship between **Mailing Address** and **Phone Number** before normalizing. Just as we need to determine the appropriate place for each piece within our puzzle, we need to determine the appropriate place for each data element within our model.

Recall our four business cards from Figure 1.2, repeated here as Figure 16.4.

Figure 16.4 Four business cards from my nightstand

In this business card example, chaos starts off as one pile of data elements. In other words, all the data elements can be initially assigned to one entity, the business card itself. See Figure 16.5.

Figure 16.5 Initial set of data elements in chaotic state

Business Card
Person Name
Person Title
Company Name
Web Address
Email Address
Mailing Address
Phone Number
Logo Image
Speciality Description

As was noted earlier, it is sometimes easier to think of an entity as a set of spreadsheet columns. Each data element in the entity is a separate column, and the rows in the spreadsheet represent the entity instances. Table 16.2 is a spreadsheet showing the data elements from Figure 16.5 as columns and the four business cards from Figure 16.4 as rows.

Table 16.2 Four sample business cards in spreadsheet format

Card	Person Name	Person Title	Company Name	Web Address	Email Address	Mailing Address	Phone Number	Logo Image	Specialty Description
1	Steve Hoberman	President	Steve Hoberman & Associates, LLC	www. steve hoberman. com	me@steve-hoberman. com	10 Main St New York, NY 10021	212-555-1212	Entity Model. jpg	
2	Steve Jenn		findsonline .com	finds-online. com	Steve@finds online.com Jenn@finds online.com		(973)555 -1212		Internet auction experts
3	Bill Smith		The Amazing Rolando		BillSmith@ TheAmaz-ingRolando. com		732-555-1212		Magic for all occasions Walk around magic Children's parties
4	Jon Smith		Raritan River Club		Reservation s@Raritan-RiverClub.c om	58 Church Avenue New Bruns-wick, NJ 08901	(908)333 -1212 (908)555 -1212 554-1212		Fine fresh seafood

We hit a very interesting data modeling challenge in this step. It is a challenge that many of us face on the job when we first start a modeling project. The challenge is whether to model the medium or the content of the medium. In other words, do we model the form, report, or in this case business card? Or do we model the contents of the form, report, or business card?

In one of my data modeling classes, the students need to model a survey form. Some model the form itself, with a prominent entity in the center called Survey and supporting entities surrounding it. Others model the content of the survey, modeling the questions and creating data elements for the responses.

We need to ask a basic question to know whether we need to model the medium or the contents of the medium: *Why are we building this data model?* If we are building it for a business card company to automate the process of printing business cards, then the business card entity is appropriate. If we are building it for an organization or person to manage their contact information, then the business card is no longer the important concept. Rather, the contents of the business card are important and the business card serves as a grouping mechanism or source for our information.

To make the business card exercise even more fun, let's assume we are modeling this for a contact management organization, and the model you build will be the foundation for a new contact management application. In other words, we will model the content instead of the medium. Therefore, let's update the model as shown in Figure 16.6.

Figure 16.6 Contact management data elements in chaotic state

Contact
Person Name
Person Title
Company Name
Web Address
Email Address
Mailing Address
Phone Number
Logo Image
Speciality Description

Normalizing is a process of asking questions. After asking the key question on model purpose, we now have another important question: What is a **Contact**? This is where we realize how important definitions are to the analysis and modeling process. Contact can mean different things to different people or departments, much the same way as Customer can mean different things to different people or departments. Is **Contact** the person in an organization whose phone number and email address we would like to capture? Is it the organization's phone number and email address itself? Or is **Contact** the person's phone number or email address, and the person or organization becomes the contactee?

After hours of talking to people in different departments in the organization building this contact management application, we have come up with this definition of **Contact**:

A person, a company, or a person at a company who our organization cares about knowing how to reach.

Now that we know what a **Contact** is, how would a businessperson request a specific **Contact**? We need to ask how a **Contact** is identified. We need something that, at least initially, makes a contact unique. If we are replacing an existing contact management system, we can investigate what makes a contact unique in that system and use the same primary key here. If this is a new contact management system, we need to interview business people and consult requirements documents to determine what data element or data elements can uniquely identify a contact.

Let's assume that this is for a new system and the manager of the department building the system would like the system to create a new unique identifier for each **Contact**. The manager would like this **Contact Id** combined with the Contact's email address to guarantee uniqueness. See Figure 16.7 for the Contact model with this new primary key added.

In normalizing, you have to ask a business expert many questions or examine a lot of actual data to answer the questions themselves. Table 16.3 shows the same data from Table 16.2 with the rows divided to show the impact of defining a contact by **Contact Id** and **Email Address**. Note that a business card can have more than one contact. Note also that **Contact Id** is just a meaningless number, and therefore the values do not have to be a sequential counter.

Figure 16.7 Contact entity with primary key

```
┌─────────────────────────────┐
│           Contact           │
├─────────────────────────────┤
│ Contact ID                  │
│ Email Address               │
│ Person Name                 │
│ Person Title                │
│ Company Name                │
│ Web Address                 │
│ Mailing Address             │
│ Phone Number                │
│ Logo Image                  │
│ Speciality Description      │
└─────────────────────────────┘
```

Table 16.3 Four sample business cards in spreadsheet format segmented by Contact

Card	Con-tact Id	Email Address	Person Name	Person Title	Company Name	Web Address	Mailing Address	Phone Num-ber	Logo Image	Specialty Descrip-tion
1	123	me@ steveho-berman.com	Steve Hober-man	Presi-dent	Steve Hoberman & Associates, LLC	www. steve hober-man. com	10 Main St New York, NY 10021	212-555-1212	Entity Model. jpg	
2	54	Steve@ finds-online.com	Steve		finds online. com	finds-online. com		(973) 555-1212		Internet auction experts
	58	Jenn@ finds-online.com	Jenn		finds online.com	finds-online. com		(973) 555-1212		Internet auction experts
3	42	Bill Smith@ The-Amazing Rolando. com	Bill Smith		The Amazing Rolando			732-555-1212		Magic for all occasions Walk around magic Children's parties
4	14	Reser-vations@ Raritan River-Club.com	Jon Smith		Raritan River Club		58 Church Avenue New Bruns-wick, NJ 08901	(908) 333-1212 (908) 555-1212 554-1212		Fine fresh seafood

Now we are going to remove redundancies and assign each data element to its proper entity, following the first three levels of normalization. Recall our initial definition of normalization: *Every data element is single-valued and must provide a fact completely and only about its primary key.* To formalize this slightly, and to more accurately fit the description for the first three levels of normalization, we can rephrase this definition of normalization into: *Every data element must provide a fact about the key, the whole key, and nothing but the key.* First Normal Form (1NF) is the "Every data element must provide a fact about the key" part. Second Normal Form (2NF) is "the whole key" part, and Third Normal Form (3NF) is the "nothing but the key" part.

First Normal Form (1NF)

1NF ensures that "Every data element must provide a fact about the key". 'Key' refers to the primary key of the entity. 'Provide a fact about' is the most important phrase, which we defined earlier and will elaborate on here. It means that for a given primary-key value, we can identify, at most, one of every data element that depends on that primary key. For example, assume **Department Number** is the primary key to the Department entity. Table 16.4 shows some sample values.

Table 16.4 Sample values for Department

Department Number	Department Name
A	Accounting
A	Marketing
B	Information Technology
C	Manufacturing

In this example, **Department Number** A identifies two values for **Department Name**: Accounting and Marketing. Therefore, **Department Name** does not provide a fact about **Department Number**, and this example violates 1NF.

Ensuring each data element provides a fact about its primary key includes correcting the more blatant issue shown in Table 16.4, as well as addressing repeating groups and multi-valued data elements. Specifically, the modeler needs to:

- Move repeating data elements to a new entity
- Separate multi-valued data elements.

Resolve Repeating Data Elements

When there are two or more of the same data element in the same entity, they are called repeating data elements. The reason repeating data elements violate 1NF is that for a given primary key value, we are getting more than one value back for the same data element. Repeating data elements often take a sequence number as part of their name. For example, recall Figure 15.5, a subset of which is reproduced here in Figure 16.8.

Figure 16.8 Ice Cream Theme can group many Ice Cream Flavors

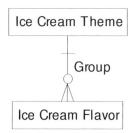

Recall these definitions:

Ice Cream Flavor – The distinctive taste of one ice cream product over another. Flavors are recognized by consumers. Examples include Chocolate, Vanilla, and Strawberry.

Ice Cream Theme – A collection of ice cream flavors that have been grouped together because they share at least one common property. For example, the Brownie Ice Cream and Cake Batter Ice Cream flavors are grouped into the Cake Ice Cream Theme.

Imagine the initial logical model for this ice cream example is the model shown in Figure 16.9. Table 16.5 contains the sample data for this model.

Figure 16.9 Un-normalized ice cream example

Ice Cream Theme

Ice Cream Theme Code
Ice Cream Theme Name
Ice Cream Flavor One Code
Ice Cream Flavor One Name
Ice Cream Flavor Two Code
Ice Cream Flavor Two Name
Ice Cream Flavor Three Code
Ice Cream Flavor Three Name

Table 16.5 Sample values for Ice Cream Theme

Ice Cream Theme Code	Ice Cream Theme Name	Ice Cream Flavor One Code	Ice Cream Flavor One Name	Ice Cream Flavor Two Code	Ice Cream Flavor Two Name	Ice Cream Flavor Three Code	Ice Cream Flavor Three Name
C	Cake - Cake Ice Cream Theme	Br	Brownie	Ca	Cake Batter		
T	Trad – Traditional Ice Cream Theme	Ch	Chocolate	Va	Vanilla	St	Strawberry
W	Winter – Winter Ice Cream Theme	Sn	Snowball Slide				

Note that to resolve this repeating group, we need to ask important business questions such as:

- Is there any significance to the 'One', 'Two', or 'Three' in the name of Ice Cream Flavor? That is, could **Ice Cream Flavor One Name** be the most popular flavor, **Ice Cream Flavor Two Name** the second most popular, and **Ice Cream Flavor Three Name** the third most popular?
- Can you ever have more than three flavors?
- Can you ever have no flavors?

Repeating data elements hide business rules and limit the 'many' in a one-to-many or many-to-many relationship. If a data element is repeated three times in an entity, we can have at most three occurrences of this data element for a given entity instance. We cannot have four, and we waste space if we have only one or two.

Assume there is no significance to the 'One', 'Two', or 'Three' in the flavor name. Figure 16.10 contains the ice cream data model with repeating data elements resolved.

Figure 16.10 Ice Cream example with repeating data elements resolved

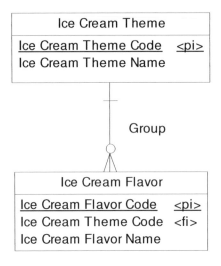

Now we can have any number of Ice Cream Flavors for a given Ice Cream Theme, such as zero, three, or one hundred.

In our contact example, by examining the sample data in Table 16.3 and asking lots of questions of business experts, we learn that a Contact can have more than one phone number and specialty description. We see that Jon Smith has three phone numbers: *(908)333-1212, (908)555-1212,* and *554-1212.* We see that The Amazing Rolando has three specialty descriptions: *Magic for all occasions, Walk around magic,* and *Children's parties.*

We can find ourselves asking many questions just to determine if there are any repeating data elements we need to address. We can have a question template, such as:

"Can a" [[insert entity name here]] "have more than one" [[insert data element name here]] "?"

So these are all valid questions:

- Can a Contact have more than one **Email Address**?
- Can a Contact have more than one **Person Name**?
- Can a Contact have more than one **Person Title**?
- Can a Contact have more than one **Company Name**?
- Can a Contact have more than one **Web Address**?
- Can a Contact have more than one **Mailing Address**?
- Can a Contact have more than one **Phone Number**?
- Can a Contact have more than one **Logo Image**?
- Can a Contact have more than one **Specialty Description**?

Note that you might find yourself rephrasing some of these techie-sounding questions to make them more understandable to a business person. "Can a Contact have more than one **Email Address**?" might be better phrased as "Do you ever have the need to reach a Contact by more than one **Email Address**?"

Assuming that the four business cards we are examining contain a good representative set of data (and that's a big assumption), and that the business people provide answers to our questions that are consistent with this data, a more accurate version of our Contact model would reflect that a Contact can have at most three phone numbers and at most three specialties, as shown in Figure 16.11.

Figure 16.11 More accurate view of Contact

Contact	
Contact Id	<pi>
Email Address	<pi>
Person Name	
Person Title	
Company Name	
Web Address	
Mailing Address	
Phone 1 Number	
Phone 2 Number	
Phone 3 Number	
Logo Image	
Speciality 1 Description	
Speciality 2 Description	
Speciality 3 Description	

If a Contact can have three phone numbers, there is a good chance that one day there will be a Contact that has four phone numbers, or maybe ten. So in general terms, a Contact can have one or many phone numbers, and also one or many specialties. So we need to create separate entities for phone number and specialty, as shown in Figure 16.12.

Figure 16.12 Repeating groups moved to new entities

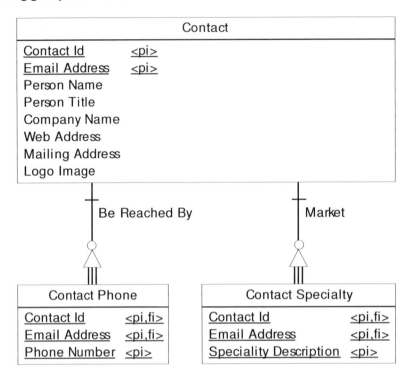

To resolve a repeating data element, you can see that we need to create a one-to-many relationship, or a many-to-many relationship with a new entity that contains the repeating data element.

We are not yet done with completely resolving repeating groups, though. What other questions do we need to ask?

We already asked whether a contact can have more than one of each of its data elements. We also need to ask the other side of the equation, which is – can the values in these repeating data elements belong to more than one contact?

We need to make sure that one-to-many relationships from Contact to Contact Phone, and from Contact to Contact Specialty, are correct, and that they are not many-to-many relationships. So these two business questions need to be answered, as well:

- Can the same **Phone Number** belong to more than one Contact?
- Can the same **Specialty Description** belong to more than one Contact?

By looking at the sample data in Table 16.3 and confirming with business people, we learn that the same phone number and specialty can belong to more than one contact, as Jenn and Steve from findsonline.com both share the phone number *(973)555-1212* and specialty *Internet auction experts*. Therefore, a more accurate model with repeating groups resolved is shown in Figure 16.13.

Figure 16.13 Repeating groups resolved

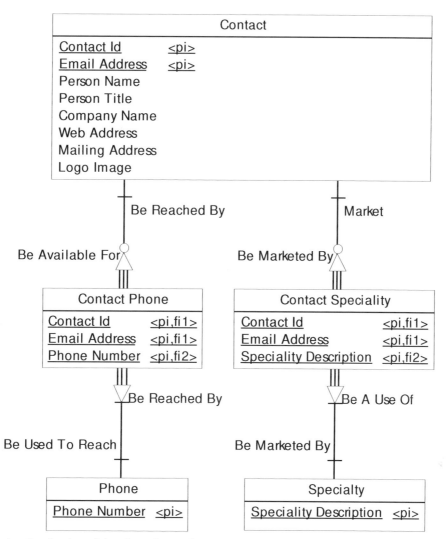

Each of the original relationships has have been converted into two relationships, but the roles they play remain the same, so the verbs ('Reach' and 'Market') are also used in the new relationship names.

Note that what currently makes the phone number and specialty description unique at this point, is the **Phone Number** and **Specialty Description** themselves, respectively. These are not ideal primary keys. but they serve to illustrate normalization in this example.

Resolve Multi-valued Data Elements

Multi-valued means that within the same data element we are storing at least two distinct values. There are at least two different business concepts hiding in one data element. For example, Name may contain both a first name and last name. **First Name** and **Last Name** can be considered distinct data elements, and therefore, "John Smith" stored in Name, is multi-valued, because it contains both "John" and "Smith."

Using our ice cream example from Figure 16.9, with sample values in Table 16.5, recall the values for **Ice Cream Theme Name**:

- Cake - Cake Ice Cream Theme
- Trad – Traditional Ice Cream Theme
- Winter – Winter Ice Cream Theme.

By examining this sample data and then validating it through a business expert, we see that **Ice Cream Theme Name** contains more than just the name of the theme. It also contains a theme description. Therefore, to resolve repeating data elements, we need to break description out from name, as shown in Figure 16.14. This now puts our data model in 1NF.

Figure 16.14 Ice cream example in 1NF

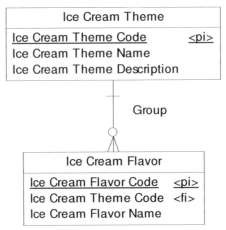

Returning to our contact example, by examining the data in Table 16.3 and the data model in Figure 16.13, and by asking even more questions, we can identify those data elements that need to be broken up into more refined data elements.

We may find ourselves asking many questions just to determine if there are any multi-valued data elements we need to identify. We can have another question template, such as:

"Does a" [[insert data element name here]] "contain more than one piece of business information?"

So these are all valid questions:
- Does a **Contact Id** contain more than one piece of business information?
- Does an **Email Address** contain more than one piece of business information?
- Does a **Person Name** contain more than one piece of business information?
- Does a **Person Title** contain more than one piece of business information?
- Does a **Company Name** contain more than one piece of business information?
- Does a **Mailing Address** contain more than one piece of business information?
- Does a **Logo Image** contain more than one piece of business information?
- Does a **Web Address** contain more than one piece of business information?
- Does a **Phone Number** contain more than one piece of business information?
- Does a **Specialty Description** contain more than one piece of business information?

Often a modeler will encounter multi-valued data elements that do not need to be separated into distinct data elements. This is common when the distinct data element parts are not of interest to the business or industry and the data element is considered to be in its atomic form, even though it contains more than one piece of information. For example, **Phone Number** contains an area code and may contain a country code. We might, therefore, decide to show country code and area code as separate data elements on the model. However, do your business people ever need to see the area code or do they view phone number in the most granular form? The answer to this question determines whether the modeler breaks apart the **Phone Number** data element.

The cost of breaking apart a multi-valued data element unnecessarily is the potential for confusion when explaining the data model, extra development effort to break apart the actual data, and then extra development effort to put the pieces back together for the business user. There is also a chance that in putting the pieces back together, some data may be lost or changed, and the newly combined values no longer match the original data, thereby causing a data quality issue. Looking at the values from Table 16.3, we see that **Phone Number** contains different formats, and one phone number is even missing an area code. Phone Number, therefore, would be an example of a data element that would require extra development effort to break apart.

Assume that in our contact example, **Person Name** and **Mailing Address** are the only two data elements that require being shown in a more granular form. The model in Figure 16.16 resolves these two multi-valued data elements and is therefore in 1NF.

Second Normal Form (2NF)

Recall the summary of all three normalization levels: *Every data element must provide a fact about the key, the whole key, and nothing but the key.* First Normal Form (1NF) is the "Every data element must provide a fact about the key" part. Second Normal Form (2NF) is "the whole key" part. This means each entity must have the minimal set of data elements that uniquely identifies each entity instance.

For example, in Figure 16.15, we have Employee Assignment.

Figure 16.15 Example of model not in 2NF

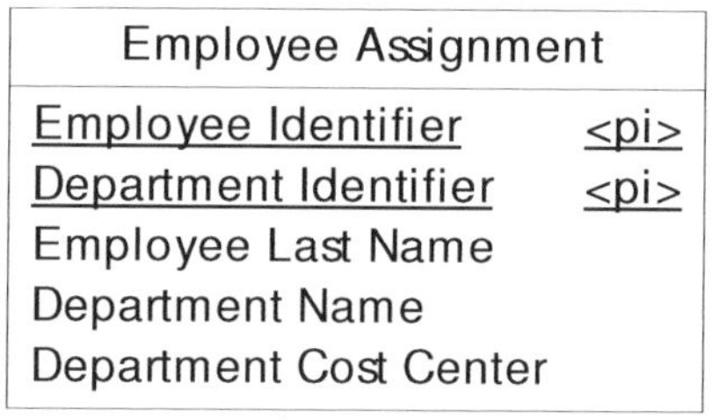

Employee Assignment	
Employee Identifier	<pi>
Department Identifier	<pi>
Employee Last Name	
Department Name	
Department Cost Center	

Figure 16.16 Contact data model with multi-valued data elements resolved, and therefore in 1NF

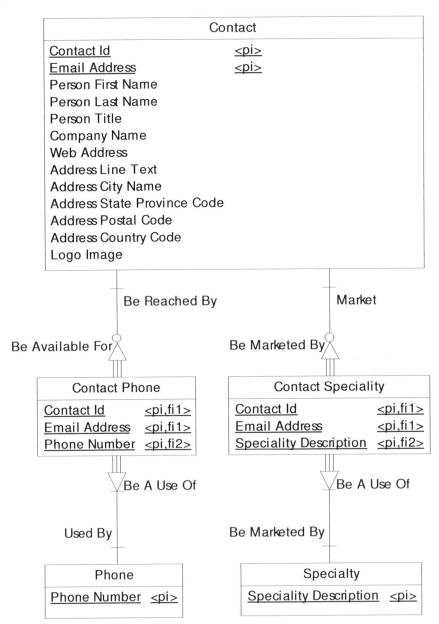

The primary key of Employee Assignment is **Employee Identifier** and **Department Identifier**. Do we have the minimal primary key for each of the non-key data elements? We would need to confirm with business experts whether the **Employee Identifier** is unique within a department or unique across the whole company. Most likely it is unique across the whole company, so we therefore do not have the minimal primary key for each of the non-key data elements. **Employee Last Name** probably needs only **Employee Identifier** to retrieve one value. Similarly, both **Department Name** and **Department Cost Center** most likely need only **Department Identifier** to retrieve one of their values. Therefore, we need to modify this model to get it into 2NF, as shown in Figure 16.17.

Figure 16.17 One option for putting the model in 2NF

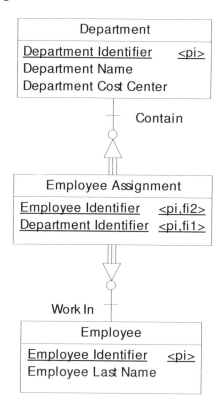

Now **Department Name** and **Department Cost Center** are facts about only **Department Identifier**, and **Employee Last Name** is a fact about only **Employee Identifier**. The associative entity **Employee Assignment** links employees with their departments.

Normalization is a process of asking business questions. In this example, we could not complete 2NF without asking the business "Can an Employee work for more than one Department at the same time?" If the answer is "Yes" or "Sometimes", then the model in Figure 16.17 is accurate. If the answer is "No", then the model in Figure 16.18 prevails.

Figure 16.18 Another option for putting the model in 2NF

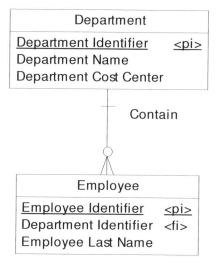

This model assumes answers to two other business questions:

- Can a Department exist without an Employee?
- Can an Employee exist without a Department?

The answers from the business would be "Yes, a Department can exist without an Employee", and "No, an Employee cannot exist without a Department".

As with 1NF, we will find ourselves asking many questions to determine if we have the minimal primary key. We can have another question template, such as:

"Are all of the data elements in the primary key needed to retrieve a single instance of" [[insert data element name here]]?" In the Contact example shown in Figure 16.15, the 'minimal set of primary key instances' are **Contact Id** and **Email Address.**

So these are all valid questions for our contact example:

- Are both Contact Id and Email Address needed to retrieve a single instance of **Person First Name**?
- Are both Contact Id and Email Address needed to retrieve a single instance of **Person Last Name**?
- Are both Contact Id and Email Address needed to retrieve a single instance of **Person Title**?
- Are both Contact Id and Email Address needed to retrieve a single instance of **Company Name**?
- Are both Contact Id and Email Address needed to retrieve a single instance of **Web Address**?
- Are both Contact Id and Email Address needed to retrieve a single instance of **Address Line Text**?
- Are both Contact Id and Email Address needed to retrieve a single instance of **Address City Name**?
- Are both Contact Id and Email Address needed to retrieve a single instance of **Address State Province Code**?
- Are both Contact Id and Email Address needed to retrieve a single instance of **Address Postal Code**?
- Are both Contact Id and Email Address needed to retrieve a single instance of **Address Country Code**?
- Are both Contact Id and Email Address needed to retrieve a single instance of **Logo Image**?

We realize that the answer to all of these questions is "No". We do not need both the **Contact Id** and **Email Address** in the primary key of Contact. Either one of these is enough to uniquely identify a contact and return a single instance of any of the data elements in Contact. Therefore, we only need one of these in the primary key. We have full control over the values of **Contact Id**, so let's use it as the primary key, and make **Email Address** an alternate key. You must also consider the uniqueness of the **Email Address** – can an **Email Address** be shared by several contacts? If the answer is "Yes", then **Email Address** cannot be a primary key, merely a non-unique candidate key.

The updated model is shown in Figure 16.19.

Figure 16.19 Contact model in 2NF

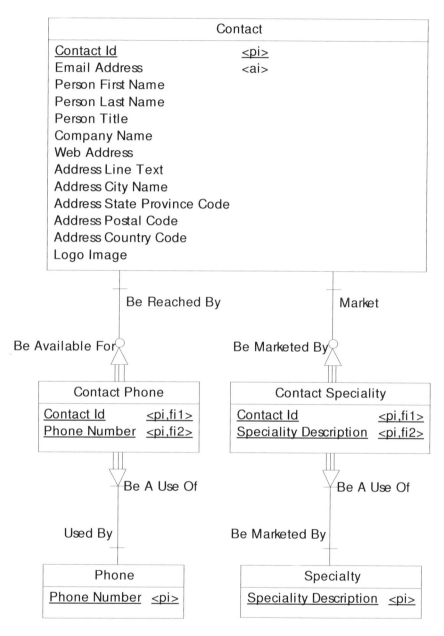

Asking the previous list of questions at this point might lead us to a more descriptive and refined model. For example, we realize there are people and company information in the Contact entity. We can therefore make our model more descriptive and capture more business rules if we introduce subtyping into this structure.

Subtyping captures many more rules, but before we can show them, we need to confirm them with the business by asking more questions. For example, here are the questions we would need to ask to arrive at the model in Figure 16.20:

- Which data elements in Contact are shared by both a Person and Company?
- Which data elements are just for a Person?
- Which data elements are just for a Company?
- Which relationships to Contact are shared by both a Person and a Company?

Note that we learn that the Logo Image is really just for a Company, and not for a Person.

Figure 16.20 Contact model in 2NF updated with subtyping

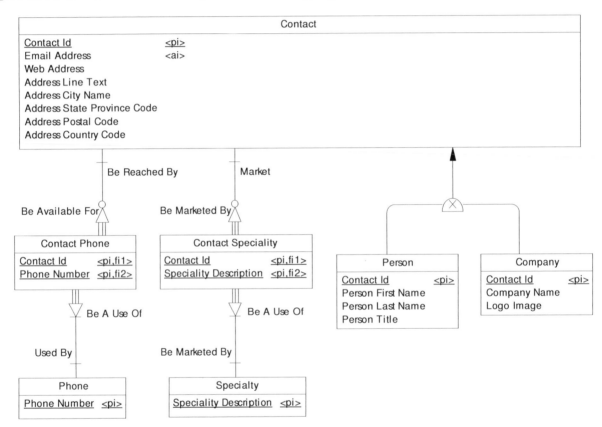

In a subtyping structure, the primary key from the supertype is also the primary key for each subtype. By default, the primary key attributes for the subtype have the same names as the primary key attributes for the supertype, as shown in Figure 16.20. The modeler often renames the subtype primary keys to make them more meaningful. Renaming any foreign key, including a subtype's primary key, is called role naming. For example, we can role name **Contact Id** in Person to **Person Id,** and **Contact Id** in Company to **Company Id. Person Id** and **Company Id** still contain the same value as **Contact Id**, but renaming the subtype's primary key facilitates better communication.

PowerDesigner allows you to rename ordinary foreign key attributes, but it does not allow you to rename inherited supertype attributes. In Figure 16.20, therefore, the subtype entities are both identified by the 'Contact Id' attribute, though we may prefer to rename them to **Person Id** and **Company Id**.

Figure 16.21 shows a simple PowerDesigner model with renamed foreign key attributes, and illustrates the benefits and a potential pitfall of this approach.

Figure 16.21 Telephone Call Model with Attribute Role Names

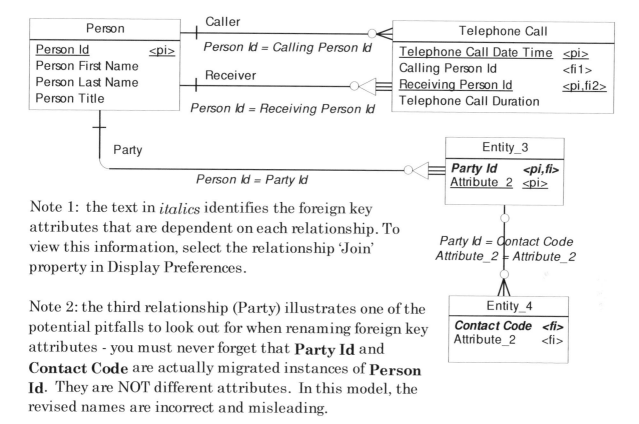

Note 1: the text in *italics* identifies the foreign key attributes that are dependent on each relationship. To view this information, select the relationship 'Join' property in Display Preferences.

Note 2: the third relationship (Party) illustrates one of the potential pitfalls to look out for when renaming foreign key attributes - you must never forget that **Party Id** and **Contact Code** are actually migrated instances of **Person Id**. They are NOT different attributes. In this model, the revised names are incorrect and misleading.

An important relationship that was assumed in Figure 16.1 is missing in Figure 16.20; people work for Companies. By having the data elements together in the same entity in Figure 16.19, we assumed this was the case. Can a Person work for more than one Company? Can a Company contain more than one Person? These questions need to be answered by the business.

Let's assume the answers to these questions are that a Person can only work for one Company, but doesn't have to work for a Company at all, and that a Company can employ many People, but doesn't have to employ any People. The updated model is shown in Figure 16.22. Note that the foreign key attribute in the Person entity has been renamed to 'Employing Company Id', to reflect the relationship role.

Figure 16.22 Contact model in 2NF updated with Person Company relationship

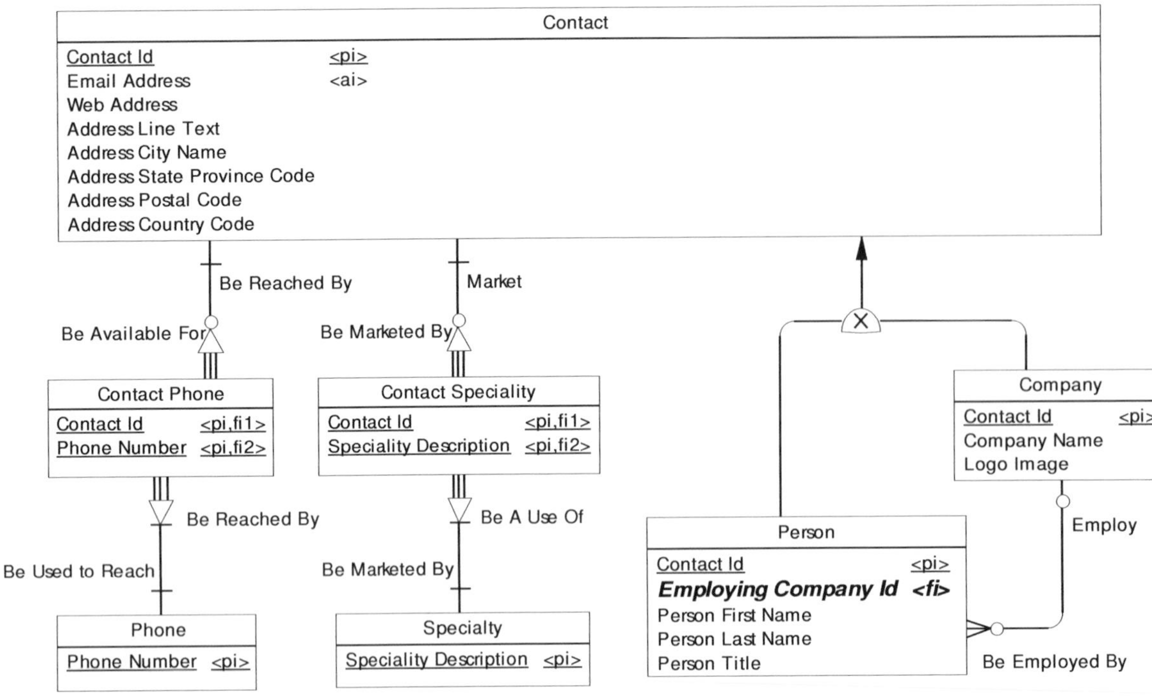

Third Normal Form (3NF)

Again, recall our summary of all three normalization levels: *Every data element must provide a fact about the key, the whole key, and nothing but the key.* First Normal Form (1NF) is the "Every data element must provide a fact about the key" part. Second Normal Form (2NF) is "the whole key" part, and Third Normal Form (3NF) is the "nothing but the key" part.

3NF requires the removal of hidden dependencies. Each data element must be directly dependent on the primary key, and not directly dependent on any other data elements within the same entity.

The data model is a communication tool. The relational logical data model communicates which data elements are facts about the primary key and only the primary key. Hidden dependencies complicate the model and make it difficult to determine how to retrieve values for each data element.

To resolve a hidden dependency, you will either need to remove the data element that is a fact about non-primary key data element(s) from the model, or you will need to create a new entity with a different primary key for the data element that is dependent on the non-primary key data element(s).

As with 1NF and 2NF, we will find ourselves asking many questions to uncover hidden dependencies. We can have another question template, such as:

"Is" [[insert data element name here]] "a fact about any other data element in this same entity?"

So these are all valid questions for the Contact entity within our contact example:

- Is **Web Address** a fact about any other data element within this same entity?
- Is **Address Line Text** a fact about any other data element within this same entity?
- Is **Address City Name** a fact about any other data element within this same entity?
- Is **Address State Province Code** a fact about any other data element within this same entity?
- Is **Address Postal Code** a fact about any other data element within this same entity?
- Is **Address Country Code** a fact about any other data element within this same entity?

We learn from asking these questions that there are some hidden dependencies within the address data elements. If we know the postal code, we can determine the city, state province, and country. Therefore, by moving city, state province, and country to a different entity, as shown in Figure 16.23 our model is now in 3NF.

Figure 16.23 Contact model in 3NF

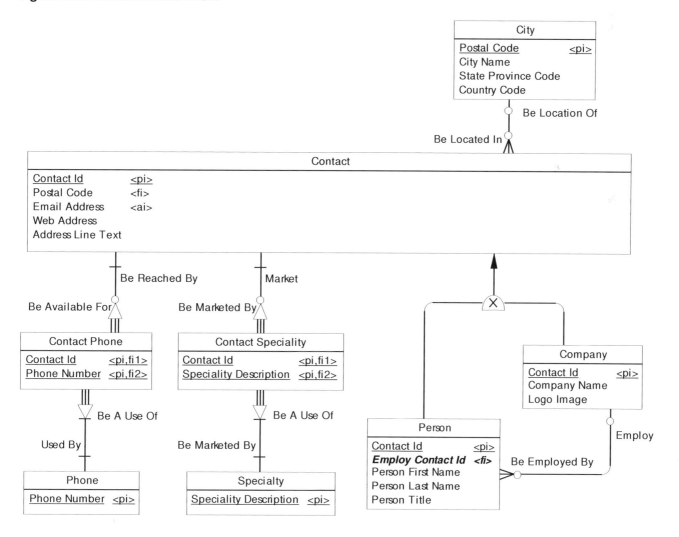

You may be wondering why we did not also move country and state province to their own entities. After all, if we know the city, we should know the state province, and if we know the state province, we should know the country. The reason we did not break these apart is because we do not have enough information to guarantee we can find the single country for a given state province or the state province for a given city. Take *Halifax* for example – there are towns and cities called Halifax in England and Canada, and in North Carolina and Virginia, in the United States.

Note that we needed to ask even more questions to determine the right cardinality on the relationship line between City and Contact:

- Does a Contact have to have a City?
- Does a City have to contain at least one Contact?

We learned from the business that no, a contact does not have to have a city. We also learned that there could be cities in which no contacts reside. Therefore, the answer to the second question is "No".

You will find that the more you normalize, the more you go from applying rules sequentially to applying them in parallel. For example, instead of first applying 1NF to your model everywhere, and then when you are done applying 2NF, and so on, you will find yourself looking to apply all levels at once. This can be done by looking at each entity and making sure the primary key is correct and that it contains a minimal set of data elements, and that all data elements are facts about only the primary key.

Abstraction Explained

Normalization is a mandatory technique on the relational logical data model. Abstraction is an optional technique. As mentioned earlier, abstraction brings flexibility to your data models by redefining and combining some of the data elements, entities, and relationships within the model into more generic terms.

Returning to our contact example, we may decide to abstract Email Address and the phone number structure into a more generic Communication Medium structure. Communication Medium could include any method of communicating with a contact, including email and phone numbers, as well as all future types of communication mediums such as text messaging, or anything else that comes along. This more abstract Contact data model, based on the model from Figure 16.23, is shown in Figure 16.24. The new entity symbols have a bolder line style than the others.

Table 16.6 contains some of the values in the Communication Medium structure.

Figure 16.24 Contact data model with Communication Medium

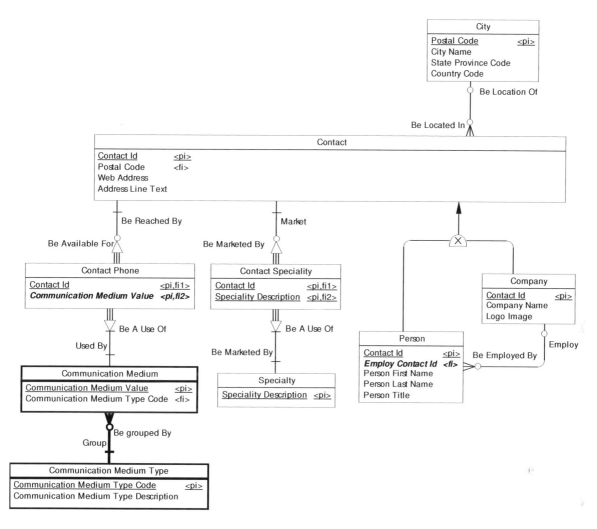

Table 16.6 Business card values in Communication Medium structure

Contact

Contact Id	Web Address	Address Line Text	Postal Code
123	www.stevehoberman.com	10 Main St	10021
54	findsonline.com		
58	findsonline.com		
42			
14		58 Church Avenue	08901

Communication Medium Type

Communication Medium Type Code	Communication Medium Type Description
01	Telephone
02	Fax Number
03	Email Address
04	Text Messaging

Table 16.6 Business card values in Communication Medium structure (continued)

Communication Medium

Communication Medium Value	Communication Medium Type Code
212-555-1212	01
(973)555-1212	01
732-555-1212	01
908-333-1212	01
908-555-1212	02
554-1212	01
me@stevehoberman.com	03
Steve@findsonline.com	03
Jenn@findsonline.com	03
BillSmith@TheAmazingRolando.com	03
Reservations@RaritanRiverClub.com	03

Contact Communication Medium

Contact Id	Communication Medium Value
123	212-555-1212
54	973-555-1212
58	973-555-1212
42	732-555-1212
14	908-333-1212
14	908-555-1212
14	554-1212
123	me@stevehoberman.com
54	Steve@findsonline.com
58	Jenn@findsonline.com
42	BillSmith@TheAmazingRolando.com
14	Reservations@RaritanRiverClub.com

Notice the extra flexibility we gain with abstraction. A new email address for findsonline.com, for example, leads to a new entity instance in Communication Medium and Contact Communication Medium, instead of a new data element on a model, with subsequent database and application changes. Abstraction allows for greater flexibility, but does come with a price. Actually, three high prices:

- **Loss of communication**. The concepts we abstract are no longer represented explicitly on the model. That is, when we abstract, we often convert column names to entity instances. For example, **Email Address** is no longer a data element on the data model in Figure 16.24, but is, instead, an entity instance of Communication Medium, with a **Communication Medium Type Code** value of '03' for 'Email Address'. One of the main reasons we model is for communication, and abstracting can definitely hinder communication.

- **Loss of business rules**. When we abstract, we can also lose business rules. To be more specific, the rules we enforced on the data model before abstraction now need to be enforced through other means, such as through programming code. If we wanted to enforce that a Contact must have one and only one **Email Address,** for example, we can no longer enforce this rule through the abstracted data model in Figure 16.24. In PowerDesigner, we can document the rule as a Business Rule, and the Business Rule can be linked to the abstract entity and/or attributes, whichever makes the most sense.
- **Additional development complexity**. Abstracting requires sophisticated development techniques to turn columns into rows, when loading an abstract structure, or to turn rows back into columns, when populating a structure from an abstract source. Imagine the work to populate the data elements in Communication Medium from a source data element called **Email** that only contains the email address. It would be much easier for a developer to load a data element called **Email** into a data element called **Email Address**. The code would be simple and it would be very fast to load.

So, although abstraction provides flexibility to an application, it does come with a cost. It makes the most sense to use abstraction when the modeler or analyst anticipates additional types of something coming in the near future. For example, additional types of communication mediums, such as text messaging, would be a good justification for using the Communication Medium structure in Figure 16.24. Make sure you only abstract where it makes sense.

Abstract data models must be subject to the same rigorous change control as any other data model. For example, code values such as **Communication Medium Type Code** must be managed in the Logical Data Model, not just in the Physical Data Model. They are not 'just data' that can be added or removed without affecting the underlying model.

Consider using an ASAM to show the non-abstract view of the model. Use this model to agree on exactly what the data requirements are for a proposed change, and then consider the changes to the abstract Logical Data Model.

For a comprehensive review of four possible levels of abstraction for data models, see (Len Silverston, 2009). Chapter 1 introduces the four levels of abstraction, and further chapters describe how they can be applied in different scenarios.

Dimensional Modeling FAQ

In a previous section of this chapter, we discussed the dimensional logical data model. There are quite a few terms and guidelines in dimensional modeling that differ from relational modeling. This section covers these terms and guidelines in the form of Frequently Asked Questions (FAQ).

Recall the dimensional model from Figure 16.3, repeated below as Figure 16.25, as we go through each of these questions.

Figure 16.25 Dimensional logical data model of ice cream

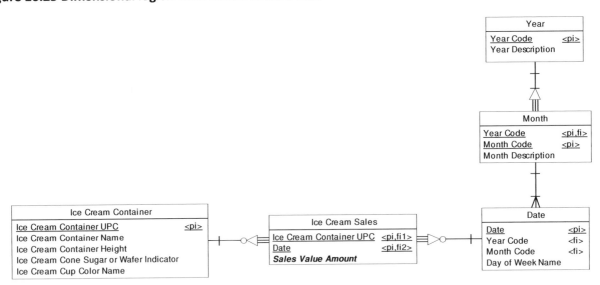

Should you always model the lowest level of detail available in the business? The lowest level of detail for the meter is known as the grain. The grain in Figure 16.25, for example, is Ice Cream Container and Date. Do you design exactly for the questions the business needs answered, or do you add a more detailed grain in anticipation of more detailed questions with the same measures? My belief is that it is OK to provide the richer grain as long as it does not impact performance (e.g. Will it take a lot longer to return results at a date level instead of at a month level?), scope-creep (e.g. Will the project take another month to finish because of the extra grain?), data quality (e.g. Will the business be responsible for checking the quality of additional data?), or user-friendliness (Is the dimensional model no longer easy to understand?).

Can you relate dimensions to each other? Not on a dimensional logical data model. All relationships from dimensions must go through the meter. That is, you can never have relationships between different dimensions. In the dimensional model from Figure 16.25, you cannot show, for example, the rule capturing which Ice Cream Containers are available in a given Year. That is, we cannot create a relationship between Ice Cream Container and Year.

Can you have optional cardinality on the relationship lines connecting dimension levels? No, don't leave navigation paths empty. It is a good practice to avoid null (i.e. empty) foreign keys on a dimensional model, because nulls can be interpreted differently by different databases and reporting tools (and users!). So to avoid unnecessary confusion and data discrepancies, make sure every hierarchy level is populated. If a specific Product does not roll up to a specific Product Line, for example, using a default value instead of leaving the foreign key in Product empty will minimize reporting errors and misunderstandings.

Can you combine relational and dimensional modeling techniques on the same logical model? No, not on the same logical model. A logical model must be relational OR dimensional; it cannot have properties of both. When you get to the physical model, one solution would be to combine them within the same schema. There are pros and cons, though (like everything in the physical). The pros include meeting multiple needs within the same structure, while cons include creating reporting complexity, such as loops. (A loop is when there is more than one navigation path to arrive at the meter.)

What is a conformed dimension? A conformed dimension is one that is shared across the business intelligence environment. Customer, Account, Employee, Product, Time, and Geography are examples of conformed dimensions. The term was made popular by Ralph Kimball and requires the modeler to design the conformed dimension with a much broader perspective than just the requirements for a single data mart. Conformed dimensions allow the navigator to ask questions that cross multiple marts. For example, a user could navigate from a Promotions data mart directly to a Sales data mart to track the impact of certain promotions. Most dimensions need to be conforming. In fact, it is rare to come across dimensions that will only ever be relevant for a single data mart.

What is a factless fact? The meter on a dimensional logical data model, is called a *fact table* on a dimensional physical data model. A fact table that does not contain any facts (i.e. measures) is called a factless fact (good name, huh?). Factless facts count events by summing relationship occurrences between the dimensions. For example, a fact table called Attendance contains no measures. It links to the Student, Course, and Semester dimensions with the goal of counting relationship occurrences of how many students take a particular course in a particular semester.

Logical Data Models in PowerDesigner

If you have worked through the earlier chapters, you have already tried all the PowerDesigner techniques you need to create a Logical Data Model:

> *Chapter 10*   **General 'how-to' knowledge**
>
> *Chapter 11*   **Creating Entities**
>
> *Chapter 12*   **Creating Data Elements**
>
> *Chapter 13*   **Creating Relationships**
>
> *Chapter 14*   **Creating Keys**
>
> *Chapter 15*   **Creating Subject Area Models**

Always use a PowerDesigner LDM to create a Logical Data Model.

LDM Settings

Before you add content to your model, we suggest that you set the options listed in Table 16.7. Remember to click on <Set As Default> within the model options and display preferences.

Table 16.7 LDM settings

Category	Settings
Model Options – Model Settings	Choose the notation required by your modeling standards.
	Enable links to requirements (if you intend to create a Requirements model).
Model Options – Migration Settings	Migrate Attribute Properties
	– select all options
	Foreign Attribute Name
	– set to "%PARENT% %ATTRIBUTE" (that's just one space in the middle)
Model Options – Naming Convention	Enable Glossary for auto completion and compliance checking (if you use a Glossary).
Display Preferences – General Settings	Enable the following:
	Show Bridges at Intersections
	Auto Link Routing
	Snap to Grid
	Enable Word Wrapping
	If you have a preference for the color of lines and symbol fill, or for the use of symbol shadows, set them here.
Display Preferences – Entity	Hide all properties, except the list of attributes. Show the *Stereotype* property if you use it.
	Add the *Description* property to the list of available properties.
Display Preferences – Relationship	Hide all properties, except the name or the role names, depending on your approach to naming relationships (see below).
	Set the line style to 'rounded right-angles'.
Display Preferences – Inheritance	Hide all properties.
Display Preferences – Inheritance Link	Set the line style to 'rounded right-angles'.
Display Preferences – Traceability Link	Set the line style to 'rounded right-angles'.

Approaches for Creating a LDM

You can use a variety of techniques to create a LDM in PowerDesigner. Which approach is appropriate for you will depend on the models and information you have available.

- Create from scratch
- Generate a LDM from a SAM (CDM) or another LDM – see Exercise 19

- Generate a LDM from a PDM
- Copy or replicate entities, etc. from other LDMs, including reference models held in the Library
- Use the Excel Import facility to create or update entities in your LDM. This is a great way of making effective use of existing documentation.

If you want to create a LDM to describe existing XML-based data structures, you will need a slightly more complex approach, using an intermediate model. In the steps listed below, we suggest you use a CDM as the intermediate model, but you could also use a PDM or Object-oriented class model if that's useful to you:

1. Import the XML Schema into a new XML Model (XSM)
2. Generate a CDM from the XSM
3. Generate a LDM from the CDM.

To create new LDM entities based on LDM entities in PowerDesigner models, copy them from the existing model, and paste them into the new model. To create LDM entities based on existing CDM entities, open the CDM, and choose `Generate Logical Data Model` from the `Tools` menu.

Presenting the LDM

In order to achieve the potential benefits of a LDM, it must communicate concepts clearly. Look at the figures in this chapter and in Chapter 15, and you will see that we have taken more than one approach regarding the content of symbols – the content will need to suit the audience. As this is a monochrome book, we have not been able to use color as part of the message, but you can use color very effectively in a LDM, and even continue the color scheme to other related models.

Be prepared to create more than one diagram in your LDM, if you need to communicate your message to different audiences. For layout and formatting tips, refer to Chapter 4 in *Data Modeling for the Business: A Handbook for Aligning the Business with IT using High-Level Data Models*, ISBN 9780977140077.

Linking the LDM to Other Data Models

Linking a LDM to other related models is essential for impact analysis. The most important models to link to are:

1. Subject Area Models
   - See Chapter 15 for a discussion of how to create and maintain these links
2. Reference models that shortcut or replica entities originate in
   - Links are automatically maintained by PowerDesigner when you create shortcuts or replicas

3. The Glossary
   o PowerDesigner automatically builds links from glossary terms to the objects that reference those terms in their names
4. Models that the LDM was generated from
   o PowerDesigner automatically creates and updates Generation Dependencies, unless you tell it not to when generating or updating a model
5. Models that have been generated from the LDM
   o PowerDesigner automatically creates and updates Generation Dependencies, unless you tell it not to when generating or updating a model

⊖ Generation Dependencies are broken if you move attributes between entities

6. Models representing equivalent data structures that are not connected via a common Subject Area Model
   o Use a specific type of traceability link – see Exercise 19 for instructions
7. Dimensional LDMs containing data derived or calculated from data in a Relational LDM
   o In the Dimensional LDM, create *Traceability Links* from derived or calculated attributes to the attributes in the Relational LDM – this is described in Exercise 19

Remember, links between models can be seen in the list of `Target Models` on the `Model` menu.

When the linked models are in the repository, the links will show up in repository searches and impact analysis (assuming you select *Use Repository*). You may want to create your own analysis rules to tailor the analysis results to suit your users.

Dependency Matrices provide a useful way of visualizing and managing links.

You can also create links between objects in a LDM and diagrams in other models, using the *Related Diagrams* feature.

Every organization's modeling requirements are different, so every organization's model linking requirements are different. See Chapter 18 for a discussion of this topic.

Dimensional LDM Notation

There is no specific notation for Dimensional models in the LDM, but there is an easy way to annotate your diagrams to identify the dimensional model concepts we discussed earlier in this chapter. We can use the standard *Stereotype* property, as shown in Figure 16.26.

Figure 16.26 Stereotypes in a dimensional LDM

The <<Stereotype>> property tells you the purpose of each entity and attribute in this dimensional model. You can type anything you like in the Stereotype property, though we created two lists of valid stereotypes via a Model Extension, to provide drop-down lists in the entity and attribute property sheets.

Via *Display Preferences*, we have changed the property display sequence, so that the stereotype appears below the entity name, and in bold type. We also decided to display the stereotype property for attributes.

The font for the *Measure* in this model (Sales Value Amount) has been manually altered to make it stand out.

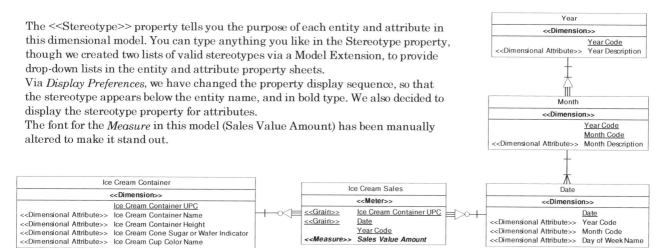

If you want to use different symbols, depending on the entity stereotype, you can, though it is not a two-minute job, unlike the minor customization needed to add the two lists of stereotypes mentioned in Figure 16.26. See Exercise 19 to find out how to add the stereotypes. Adding icons to indicate the Dimensional Type is fairly simple, as long as you have suitable icons. You can see an example of this later, in Figure 17.12.

Relationship Names in the LDM

In a LDM, you need to be stricter with relationship names than in a SAM. We suggest you create meaningful names for your relationships, and create role names. If you have included %PARENTROLE% in the foreign attribute name template in your migration settings, make sure your role names have initial capital letters, so they meet the naming standards for attributes. See "Relationship Properties", in Chapter 13.

Normalization in the LDM

There is no automated process for normalizing a data model in PowerDesigner. The tool cannot possibly understand your business or your model well enough to tell you how to alter the model. The following techniques will help you to amend your model.

- Convert any relationship into an entity
  - o Right-click the relationship symbol, and select *Change to Entity*
  - o Use this technique when your analysis reveals that there is data involved in a relationship, and a new entity is required
- Replicate Attributes
  - o Useful if you need to have identical attributes in sibling subtype entities
- Let PowerDesigner rename Foreign Key Attributes for you, using the relationship role name as a prefix
- Copying and moving attributes
  - o Use drag and drop between symbols, in the Browser, or between symbols and the Browser

- Copy and paste an entity to create an almost identical copy
  - o See Chapter 10 to remind yourself of the limitations of copying this way
- To copy part of a diagram, complete with display preferences, select at least two symbols, and select `Create Diagram from Selection` from the contextual menu
- Use the Hierarchical layout to make entity hierarchies really obvious
- Save versions of your model in the repository
- Before you introduce abstraction in your LDM, make sure you take a copy or version of the LDM so you have something to go back to; or maintain the non-abstract view of the model in a SAM.

Useful LDM Model Checks

PowerDesigner allows you to verify the validity of your models via the Model Check facility (press <F4> to run the model check). All of the checks listed for the CDM in Chapter 15 are useful for a LDM. For the LDM, the following additional checks are worth noting.

Domain

- Detect inconsistencies between check parameters
- Precision > maximum length
- Undefined data type
- Invalid data type

Entity

- Existence of attributes
- Existence of relationship or association link(s)
- Redundant inheritance
- Multiple inheritance
- Parent of several inheritances

Attribute

- Detect differences between attribute and associated domain
- Detect inconsistencies between check parameters
- Precision > maximum length
- Undefined data type
- Invalid data type

Relationship

- 'Many-many' relationships

Inheritance

- Incomplete inheritance with ungenerated ancestor, which means that the 'generate' property for a super-type entity is not selected, and the sub-types are not a complete set. Generating the sub-type entities into a PDM will possibly result in missing data.

❷ "Checking a Data Model" (Data Modeling)

Additional Information in the LDM

If you have documentation of requirements or business rules, consider importing them into PowerDesigner, and linking them to your LDM entities and relationships.

Promoting and Sharing the LDM

Make the LDM available to as wide an audience as you can. If you do not have a repository, generate an HTML report and add it to your intranet; generate an RTF report, including diagram images, and distribute in whatever format suits you best; use the Excel export and import features to enable non-users to contribute.

If you have a repository, ensure that the LDM and all linked models are checked in, and made available to the portal, and use the 'Composer' license to allow selected experts to amend the LDM via the portal.

EXERCISE 16: Creating a Logical Data Model in PowerDesigner

Create a new LDM called "Exercise 16", containing the entities, attributes, and relationship from Figure 16.27.

Figure 16.27 LDM subset

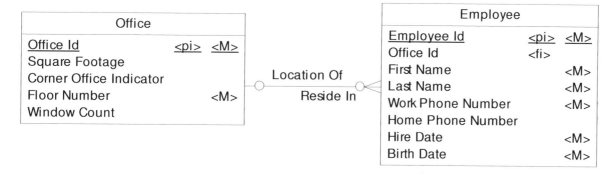

The relationship states:

- Each Office may be the location of one or many Employees.
- Each Employee may reside in one Office.

Note the naming standard we are using for attributes – we don't include the entity name in attribute names. The data element **Employee First Name** is represented by the attribute **First Name** in the entity **Employee.**

EXERCISE 17: Modifying a Logical Data Model in PowerDesigner

Take the LDM you created in the previous exercise.

You need to add the data element **Office First Occupied Date** to this model.

Here is the definition of **Office First Occupied Date:**

Office First Occupied Date is the official date, as recorded in the Human Resources database, when a person first took up residence in an office. It must be a business day (that is, not a weekend day or holiday).

The business expert in this area provided you with the following three rules that need to be captured on this model:

1. **Office First Occupied Date** is a mandatory field for each employee who has an office.
2. Only managers have an office and all managers have an office.
3. A manager has one and only one office.

Modify this model to accommodate this new data element and the three business rules. Add the rules as Business Rules in PowerDesigner, and link them to the entities and attributes that document them.

Extract the Entity and Attribute Names and Descriptions for review by your experts.

See the Appendix for my answers.

EXERCISE 18: Modifying and Normalizing a Logical Data Model in PowerDesigner

---

In this exercise, you will work with the Contact Logical Data Model and work through the normalization steps we described.

Whether or not you create domains in this LDM is your choice. We do not specify data types in this exercise, and only one attribute requires a list of values, so they are not strictly necessary.

Create a new LDM called "Exercise 18", containing the entity shown in Figure 16.28.

Figure 16.28 The initial model

Business Card
Person Name
Person Title
Company Name
Web Address
Email Address
Mailing Address
Phone Number
Logo Image
Speciality Description

First Normal Form

Rename **Business Card** as **Contact**, and create two new entities, called **Contact Phone** and **Contact Specialty**.

Add two new attributes to **Contact**, and add them both to the primary identifier:

- **Contact Id**
- **Email Address**.

Create two dependent relationships:

> Each **Contact** may *Be Reached By* one or more **Contact Phone**

> Each **Contact** must *Market* one and only one **Contact Specialty**

Move the following attributes from **Contact** (by dragging them on the diagram):

> **Phone Number**   to entity **Contact Phone**

> **Specialty Description**   to entity **Contact Specialty**

Add each of these attributes to the entity primary key.

The result should look like the model shown in Figure 16.29.

Figure 16.29 Repeating groups moved to new entities

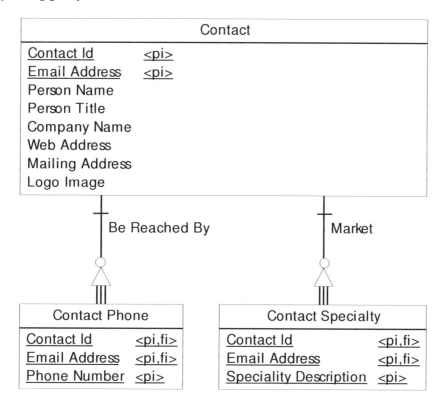

Now convert both relationships into entities, and make the changes necessary to make the model look like Figure 16.30. This includes replacing the attribute **Mailing Address** with five new attributes.

Figure 16.30 Contact data model with multi-valued data elements resolved, and therefore in 1NF

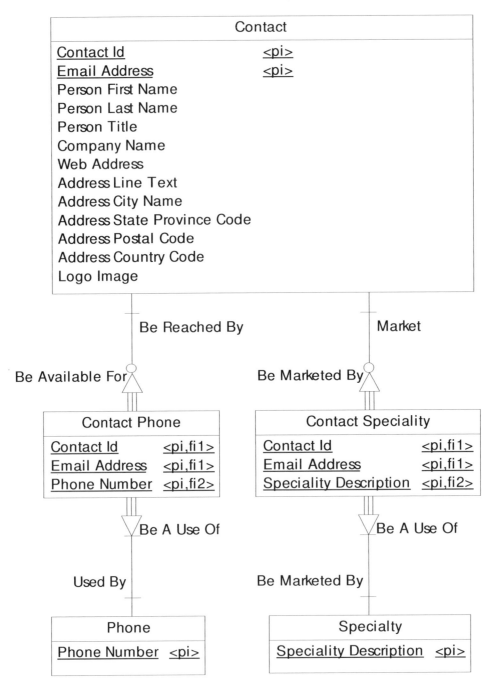

Second Normal Form

Remove the attribute **Email Address** from the primary key of **Contact**. Create a new alternate identifier in **Contact**, and include the attribute **Email Address.**

The result should look like the model shown in Figure 16.31.

Figure 16.31 Contact model in 2NF

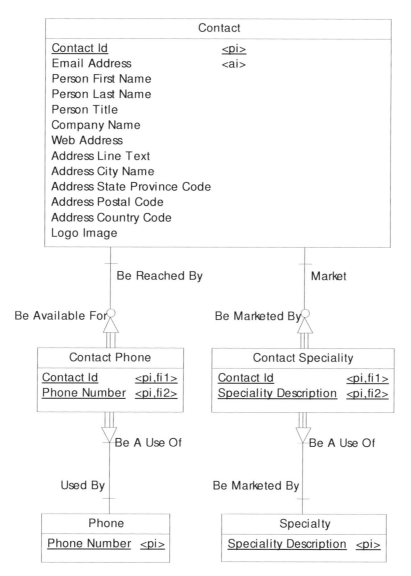

Create two new entities, called **Person** and **Company**, and move the following attributes from **Contact:**

Person First Name	to entity **Person**
Person Last Name	to entity **Person**
Person Title	to entity **Person**
Company Name	to entity **Company**
Logo Image	to entity **Company**

Create an inheritance, making **Person** a subtype of **Contact**, and add an inheritance link from **Company** to the same inheritance.

Add the following optional relationship:

Each **Company** may *Employ* one or more **Person**

Each **Person** may *Be Employed By* at most one **Company**

The result should look like the model shown in Figure 16.32.

Figure 16.32 Contact model in 2NF updated with Person Company relationship

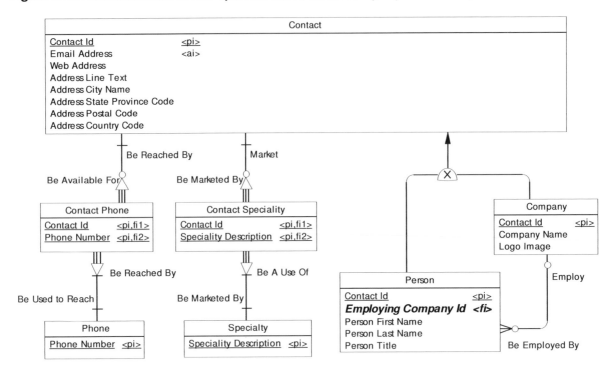

Third Normal Form

Create a new entity called **City**, and move the following attributes to it from **Contact**:

Address Postal Code	Address State Province Code
Address City Name	Address Country Code.

Remove the word 'Address' from all the attribute names, and add **Postal Code** to the primary identifier of **City**.

Add the following optional relationship:

Each **City** may *Be Location Of* one or more **Contact**

Each **Contact** may *Be Located In* at most one **City**

Abstraction

Convert the relationship from **Phone** to **Contact Phone** into an entity – PowerDesigner will call this new entity **Phone Used By Contact Phone**. Rename the entity as **Communication Medium**, and carry out whatever changes are required to make the model look like the model shown in Figure 16.33. Remember to add the values shown in Table 16.6 to the attribute **Communication Medium Type Code**, or to the associated domain, if you have chosen to create one.

The result should now look like the model shown in Figure 16.33. Save the model – you will need it in Exercise 21.

Figure 16.33 Contact data model with Communication Medium

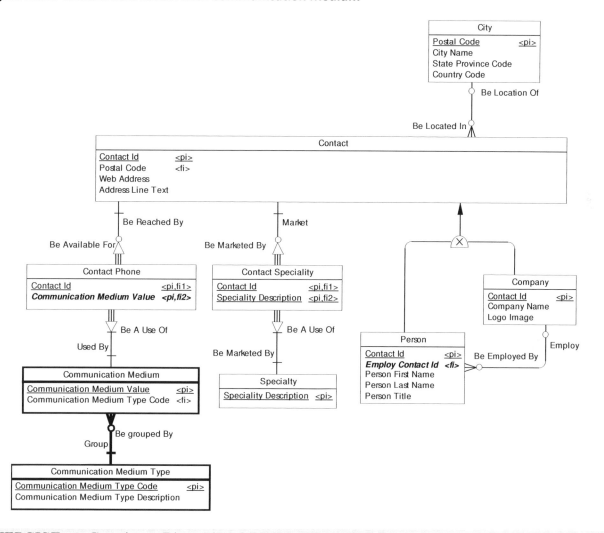

EXERCISE 19: Creating a Dimensional LDM in PowerDesigner

We're the first to admit that transforming a Relational LDM into a Dimensional LDM is not rocket science, but it is vital that you understand the process, so we have provided detailed instructions in this exercise. Some of the material is new, so please don't skip this!

Complete the Relational LDM

Open the Relational LDM you created in Exercise 11 in Chapter 13. Before transforming this into a Dimensional LDM, you need to complete it. First, create the domains shown in Table 16.8.

Table 16.8 Domains

Domain	Data Type	Length	Precision	List of Values
Color Code	Characters	1		b=blue g=green
Short Name	Characters	20		
Sugar or Wafer Indicator	Characters	1		S = Sugar W = Wafer
Height	Number	3		
Ice Cream Container UPC	Number	16		
Standard Identifier	Number	10		
Standard Date	Date			
Standard Large Value	Number	4	2	

Now complete the Attributes using the information shown in Table 16.9.

Table 16.9 Attributes

Entity	Attribute Name	Domain	Description
Color	Color Code	Color Code	The short name of one of the standard ice cream colors.
Color	Color Name	Short Name	The full name of one of the standard ice cream colors.
Ice Cream Cone	Ice Cream Cone Sugar or Wafer Indicator	Sugar or Wafer Indicator	Determines whether the ice cream cone is made of a sugar-based or wafer-based material.
Ice Cream Container	Ice Cream Container Height	Height	The height, in millimeters, of the container. Used by inventory to determine how many containers can fit on a storage shelf.
Ice Cream Container	Ice Cream Container Name	Short Name	The name our store employees use for communicating with consumers on what they would like to order.
Ice Cream Container	Ice Cream Container UPC	Ice Cream Container UPC	A numeric code used to identify a specific product across the ice cream industry.
Order	Order Number	Standard Identifier	The unique number assigned to each order placed by a consumer. It is a numeric sequence number that never repeats.
Order	Order Placed Date	Standard Date	The date the order was placed.
Order	Order Total Value	Standard Large Value	The total value of the order in the default national currency, including any applicable sales tax.

Now add the Entity descriptions shown in Table 16.10.

Table 16.10 Entity descriptions

Entity	Description
Color	A primary color within the spectrum of visible light.
Ice Cream Cone	An edible container which can hold one or more ice cream scoops.
Ice Cream Container	A holder of ice cream that is either edible, in the case of an ice cream cone, or recyclable, in the case of an ice cream cup.
Ice Cream Cup	A recyclable container which can hold one or more ice cream scoops.
Order	Also known as an ice cream sale, an order is when a consumer purchases one or more of our products in a single visit to our ice cream store.
Order Line	A product purchased during a single visit to our ice cream store.

Transform the Relational LDM into a Dimensional LDM

The next step is to transform the relational LDM in Figure 16.2 into the Dimensional LDM we saw in Figure 16.25, repeated below in Figure 16.34.

Figure 16.34 The target dimensional model

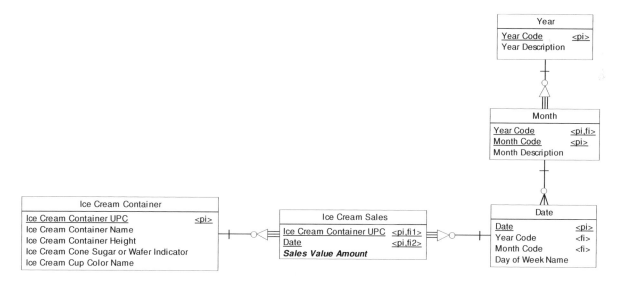

Using the `Tools` menu, generate a new LDM, called "Exercise 19". Make sure you save the generation dependencies.

The only entity we need to keep in the new model is **Ice Cream Container**, effectively merging it with the two subtypes, and with the **Color** entity. Drag the additional attributes (check Figure 16.34 to see which attributes) from the **Color** and **Ice Cream Cone** entities before you delete them. Delete all other entities, and the inheritance.

Create the new entities and relationships shown in Figure 16.34, along with supporting domains. Remove any domains that are no longer used. To find unused domains, create a *Dependency Matrix*. The rows should contain *Domains*, the columns should contain *Entity Attributes*, and the Dependency should be *Attributes*. Click the *Display Only Empty Rows* tool. The rows in the matrix will now show only unused domains.

To check that all your attributes reference domains, create another *Dependency Matrix*, with *Entity Attributes* in the rows, and *Domains* in the columns; the dependency should be *Domain*. Click the *Display Only Empty Rows* tool. The rows in the matrix will now show only those attributes that do not reference a domain.

Add Entity and Attribute Stereotypes

Now you need to add some annotation to the diagram to indicate the Dimensions, Grain, Meter, and Measure. The simplest way to do this is to use Stereotypes. You could just type them in for each object, but it is very easy to create drop-down lists of values in the model extension you created earlier. Just follow these steps.

1. Open the model extension *Local Extensions* via the Browser
2. Right-click the *Profile* entry, and select `Add Metaclasses`. In the *Metaclass Selection* window, select *Entity* and *Entity Attribute*. See Figure 16.35.

Figure 16.35 Adding metaclasses

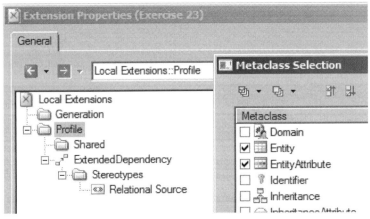

3. Two new entries will be created, called *Entity* and *Entity Attribute*. Now you can create the stereotypes for each one, as listed in Table 16.11. To create a stereotype, right-click one of the new entries, and select `New|Stereotype`. Change the name of the new stereotype. If you want to, you can create a category to group the dimensional stereotypes together. See Figure 16.36 for the final result.

Table 16.11 Stereotypes to be added to the extension

Entity	Attribute
Dimension	Dimensional Attribute
Meter	Grain
	Measure

Figure 16.36 The finished extension

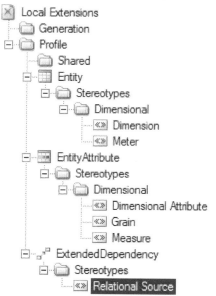

Have you spotted the other stereotype? The 'Relational Source' entry is the link type you added earlier. To add more link types, add more stereotypes under the *ExtendedDependency* entry (*Traceability Links* used to be called *Extended Dependencies*).

⊖ If you rename any stereotype in the model extension, PowerDesigner will **not** update any objects that use that stereotype. You can update them yourself using a list of objects, a list report, or an Excel import.

You can save the model extension to a file or to the repository, so that it is available for re-use in other models.

It's been a long, complex exercise, but the last task is finally here. Update the stereotype for entities and attributes (list reports and lists of objects are good for this) according to Table 16.12.

Table 16.12 Entity and attribute stereotypes

Entity	Attribute	Stereotype
Date		**Dimension**
Date	Year Code	Dimensional Attribute
Date	Month Code	Dimensional Attribute
Date	Day of Week Name	Dimensional Attribute
Ice Cream Container		**Dimension**
Ice Cream Container	Ice Cream Container Name	Dimensional Attribute
Ice Cream Container	Ice Cream Container Height	Dimensional Attribute
Ice Cream Container	Ice Cream Cone Sugar or Wafer Indicator	Dimensional Attribute
Ice Cream Container	Ice Cream Cup Color Name	Dimensional Attribute
Ice Cream Sales		**Meter**
Ice Cream Sales	Ice Cream Container UPC	Grain
Ice Cream Sales	Date	Grain
Ice Cream Sales	Sales Value Amount	Measure
Month		**Dimension**
Month	Month Description	Dimensional Attribute
Year		**Dimension**
Year	Year Description	Dimensional Attribute

Adjust the Display Preferences for your diagram, to display the stereotype for both entities and attributes. Your diagram should look something like Figure 16.26. To be sure that you haven't missed something essential, run the model check, making sure you select all the checks.

Key Points

- A logical data model (LDM) represents a detailed business solution.

- A relational logical model represents how the business works. A dimensional logical model represents what the business is monitoring.

- Normalizing is a formal process of asking business questions. Normalization ensures that every data element is a fact about the key (1NF), the whole key (2NF), and nothing but the key (3NF).

- Abstraction brings flexibility to your logical data models by redefining and combining some of the data elements, entities, and relationships within the model into more generic terms.

- There are a number of important terms unique to dimensional modeling, including factless facts and conforming dimensions.

- Dimensional modeling requires having mandatory cardinality on relationship lines and not relating dimensions to each other.

- Relationships in a Dimensional model do not have to mimic their relational counterparts.

- The LDM is the most appropriate type of model for a Logical Data Model in PowerDesigner.

- Make sure how you present the LDM to your audience(s) is appropriate for what you're trying to accomplish.

- Use the PowerDesigner repository and portal to provide comprehensive impact analysis.

Let's get Physical
Consider environment
Time to make it real

The highlighted row in Table 17.1 shows the focus of this chapter, which is the physical data model.

Table 17.1 The Physical Data Model is the focus of this chapter

	Relational	Dimensional
Subject Area Model (SAM)	'One-pager' on how something works	'One-pager' on what is monitored
Logical Data Model	Detailed business solution on how something works	Detailed business solution on what is monitored
Physical Data Model	**Detailed technical solution on how something works**	**Detailed technical solution on what is monitored**

A physical data model (PDM) takes the business solution defined on a logical data model to the next level of a technical solution. That is, once you solve the problem independent of software and hardware concerns, you can then make adjustments for software and hardware. This chapter will explain the most popular techniques for making adjustments to a business solution to create an efficient technical solution. I will explain the PDM and then discuss the techniques of denormalization, views, indexing, and partitioning. Although these techniques apply to both relational and dimensional models, their names may differ depending on which type of model they are applied to. I will explain these terminology differences in this chapter, as well. I will conclude with a discussion on how to adjust your physical data model to accommodate data value changes, and introduce the concept of a slowly changing dimension.

As in the previous chapter, PowerDesigner notes intrude as little as possible in this discussion. At the end of the chapter we describe the specific techniques introduced in the PowerDesigner PDM.

Physical Data Model Explained

The physical data model (PDM) is the logical data model modified for specific software or hardware. On the SAM, we might learn what the terms, business rules, and scope would be for a new order entry system. After understanding the need for an order entry system, we create a LDM representing the business solution. It contains all of the data elements and business rules needed to deliver the system. For example, the subject area model will show that a Customer places many Orders. The LDM will capture all of the details behind Customer and Order, such as the customer's name, their address, and the order number. After understanding the business solution, we move on to the technical solution and build the PDM.

While building the PDM, we address the issues that have to do with specific hardware or software such as:

- How can we retrieve this information in fewer than 5 seconds?
- How can we make this information secure?
- There is a lot of information here. What is the best way to manage storage space?

Note that in the early days of data modeling, when storage space was expensive and computers were slow, there were major modifications made to the PDM to make it work efficiently. In some cases, the PDM looked like it was for an entirely different application than the LDM. As technology improved, the PDM started looking more like the LDM. Faster and cheaper processors, cheaper and more generous disc space and system memory, and also specialized hardware, have all played their part. We should continue to see this trend as better hardware and software lead to fewer compromises on the PDM, resulting in a PDM that looks more like its LDM.

Denormalization Explained

Denormalization is the process of selectively violating normalization rules and reintroducing redundancy into the model (and therefore, the database). This extra redundancy can reduce data retrieval time, which is the primary reason for denormalizing. We can also denormalize to create a more user-friendly model. For example, we might decide to denormalize company information into an entity containing employee information, because usually when employee information is retrieved, company information is also retrieved.

The faster retrieval and user-friendliness, however, come with the price of extra redundancy on the model, which could in turn:

- Cause update, delete, and insert performance to suffer
- Introduce data quality problems
- Take up more space
- Stunt growth of the application.

There are five denormalization techniques:

- Standard
- FUBES
- Repeating groups
- Repeating data elements
- Summarization.

We will apply each of these five techniques to the Contact logical data model from the previous chapter, repeated here in Figure 17.1.

Figure 17.1 Contact logical data model

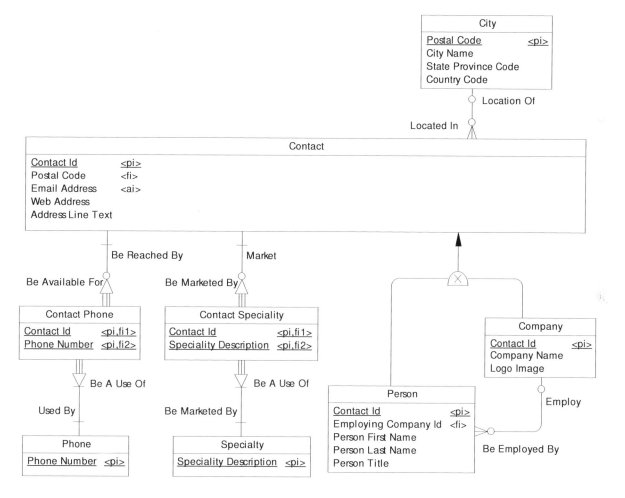

Standard

The standard method is the most common of the five denormalization techniques. The parent entity in the relationship disappears, and all of the parent's data elements and relationships are moved down to the child entity. You'll recall that the child entity is on the many side of the relationship and contains a foreign key back to the parent entity, which appears on the one side of the relationship.

Although the standard technique is traditionally applied to a one-to-many relationship, we can illustrate the standard technique using the subtyping structure from Figure 17.1. The subtyping structure must be resolved on the physical data model, as there is no subtyping relationship defined in a relational database. There are three ways of resolving the subtyping symbol on the physical data model: identity, rolling down, and rolling up.

Identity is the closest to subtyping, itself, because the subtyping symbol is replaced with a one-to-one relationship for each supertype/subtype combination. The main advantage of identity is that all of the business rules at the supertype level and at the subtype level remain the same as in the logical model. That is, we can continue to enforce relationships at the supertype or subtype levels, as well as enforce that certain data elements be required at the supertype or subtype levels. The main disadvantage of identity is that it can take more time to retrieve data, as it requires navigating multiple tables to access both the supertype and subtype information. Identity is not a form of denormalization, but it is shown in Figure 17.2 for completeness.

Figure 17.2 Identity method of resolving subtyping

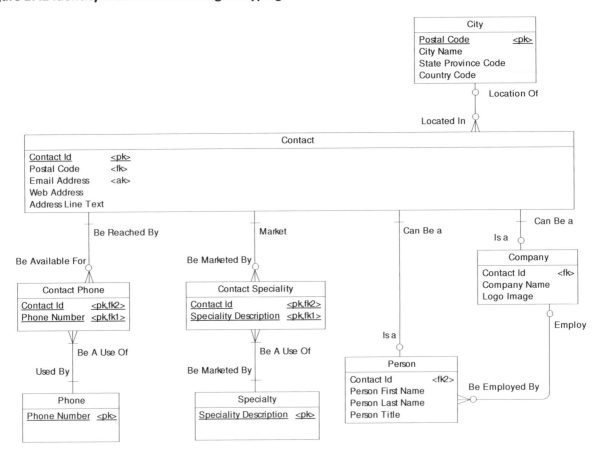

In this example, we can continue to enforce certain rules at the supertype level, such as a Contact can have only one City and must have one **Email Address**. We can also enforce rules at the subtype level, such as a Person can work for one Company, and **Person Last Name** is a required data element that must always contain a value.

In Figure 17.2, note the difference in the notation for dependent references (relationships). I'm sure you remember that, in the Logical Data Model, the triangle on the relationship indicates dependency, as shown below:

In the Physical Data Model, there is no notation to represent dependency. Here is the equivalent reference:

In Figure 17.2, the table and column names include spaces, but this is not a software bug, nor is it a problem when generating the database. Remember that PowerDesigner draws a distinction between the Name and the Code of an object, and allows you to determine how Codes are derived from Names, or vice versa. It is the Code of an object, not the name, that is generated in the database. The columns in the **Contact Phone** table below illustrate default code names, which are suitable for use in a relational database.

You can choose to display object codes in symbols, rather than their names.

Another standard denormalization method is to eliminate table joins by merging tables. If you merge a parent table into a child table, it's referred to as rolling down. Merging child tables into a parent table is referred to as rolling up.

The 'Collapse Tables' feature allows you to roll up or roll down tables.

In our example model, rolling down is when the supertype is 'rolled down' into each subtype, moving all of the data elements and relationships from the supertype into each subtype, then removing the supertype from the data model. Rolling down can produce a more user-friendly structure than identity or rolling up, because subtypes are often more concrete concepts than supertypes, making it easier for the users of the data model to relate to the subtypes. For example, users of our Contact model would probably feel more comfortable with the concepts of Person and Company, rather than the concept of Contact. However, we are repeating relationships and data elements, which could reduce any user-friendliness gained from removing the supertype. In addition, the rolling down technique enforces only those rules present in the subtypes. This could lead to a less flexible data model, as we can no longer easily accommodate new subtypes without modifying the data model. See Figure 17.3 for what rolling down would look like in our Contact example.

Figure 17.3 Rolling down method of resolving subtyping

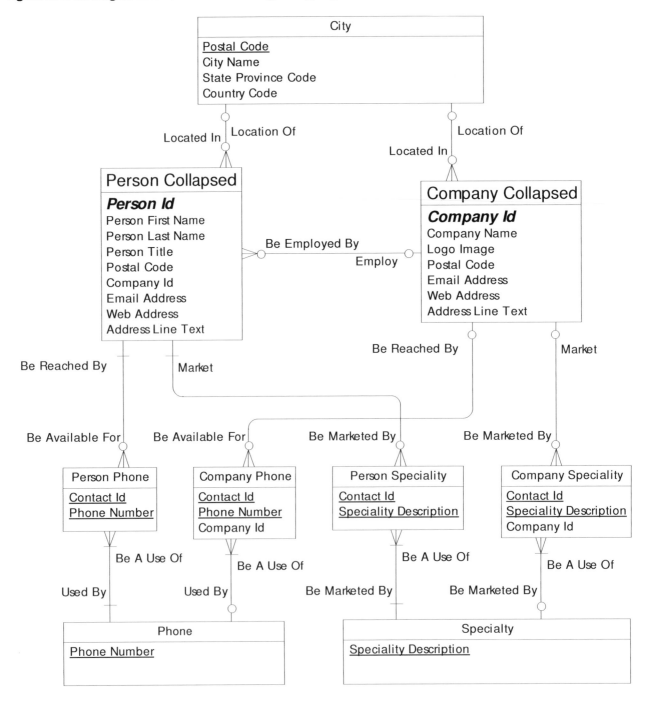

In the rolling down technique, we no longer have the Contact concept, and everything at the supertype level has been copied down into each subtype. Notice that although we have the user friendly concepts of Person and Company, we also have the redundancy of extra relationships to Phone, Specialty, and City, as well as repeating **Email Address**, **Web Address**, and address information for each subtype.

In Figure 17.3, two of the table names include the word 'Collapsed' – these tables were created by PowerDesigner during the de-normalization process. For the time being, I have retained the original **Contact**, **Person,** and **Company** tables in the model, though they don't appear in the diagram. The Rolling Down technique can be driven from the LDM, by unchecking the 'Generate parent' option in the inheritance property sheet, and selecting 'Generate children'.

Rolling up is when each subtype is 'rolled up' into the supertype, moving the data elements and relationships from each subtype into the supertype. The subtypes disappear and all data elements and relationships only exist at the supertype level. Rolling up adds flexibility to the data model because new types of the supertype can be added, often with no model changes. However, rolling up can also produce a more obscure model, as the audience for the model may not relate to the supertype as well as they would to the subtypes. In addition, we can only enforce business rules at the supertype level, not the subtype level. See Figure 17.4 for rolling up in our Contact example.

When we roll up, we need a way to distinguish the original subtypes from each other. Therefore, we add a data element that distinguishes people from companies, in this case **Contact Type Code**. Two of the values of **Contact Type Code** would represent 'Person' and 'Company'.

Using rolling up, we still retain the business rules for Contact, yet lose the rules that were only enforced for Person or Company. For example, we cannot make **Company Name** a mandatory data element in Contact because a Person does not have a **Company Name** and may not be assigned to a Company.

The Rolling Up technique can be driven from the LDM, by unchecking the 'Generate children' option in the inheritance property sheet, and selecting 'Generate parent'. This causes all the attributes from sub-types to be migrated to the super-type entity.

In addition to choosing denormalization because of the need for faster retrieval time or for more user friendly structures, the standard way of denormalizing can be chosen in the following situations:

- **When you need to maintain the flexibility of the normalized model.** Folding the data elements and relationships together using the standard approach still allows one-to-one and one-to-many relationships to exist. In Figure 17.4 for example, we did not lose the flexibility that a Contact can be a Person or Company (it is just harder to see and enforce).

• **When you want to reduce development time and complexity.** Often there is a direct relationship between the number of tables and relationships on a model, and the amount of effort it will take to develop the application. A developer will need to write code that jumps from one table to another to collect certain data elements, and this can take time and add complexity. Denormalizing into fewer tables using the standard method means the data elements and relationships from different entities now exist in the same entity. In Figure 17.4, for example, if the developer needs to retrieve both the person and company name, they can easily do so from the same entity, Contact.

 Use the 'Table Collapsing' feature to apply standard denormalization

---

Figure 17.4 Rolling up method of resolving subtyping

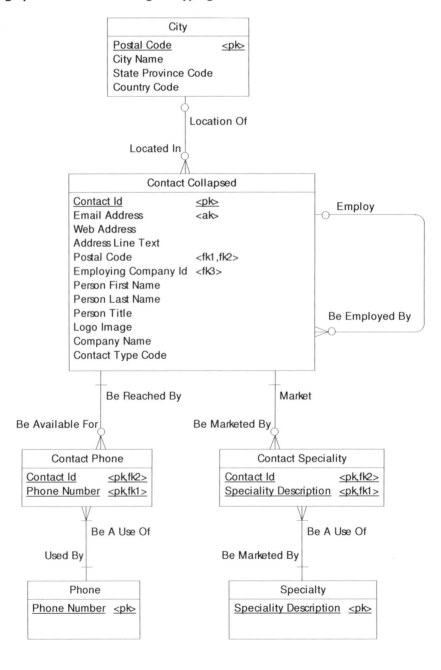

FUBES

FUBES (Fold Up But Easily Separate) is an acronym I made up for a technique that uses the standard method of denormalizing while also allowing access to just the data elements from the parent side of a one-to-many relationship. There is an additional data element that contains a level code and additional instances for each of the parents. In Figure 17.5, for example, we have a subset of the logical data model for Calendar.

Figure 17.5 Subset of the Calendar logical data model

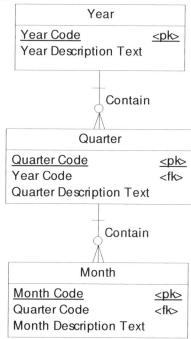

Table 17.2 contains sample values for each of these entities.

Table 17.2 Sample values for Figure 17.5

Year

Year Code	Year Description Text
2007	Two Thousand Seven
2008	Two Thousand Eight
2009	Two Thousand Nine

Quarter

Quarter Code	Year Code	Quarter Description Text
Q12009	2009	First Quarter Two Thousand Nine
Q22009	2009	Second Quarter Two Thousand Nine
Q32009	2009	Third Quarter Two Thousand Nine

Month

Month Code	Quarter Code	Month Description Text
Jan2009	Q12009	January Two Thousand Nine
Feb2009	Q12009	February Two Thousand Nine
Mar2009	Q12009	March Two Thousand Nine

If we decide to denormalize these three entities using the FUBES option, we would have the one entity in Figure 17.6.

Figure 17.6 FUBES being applied to Calendar

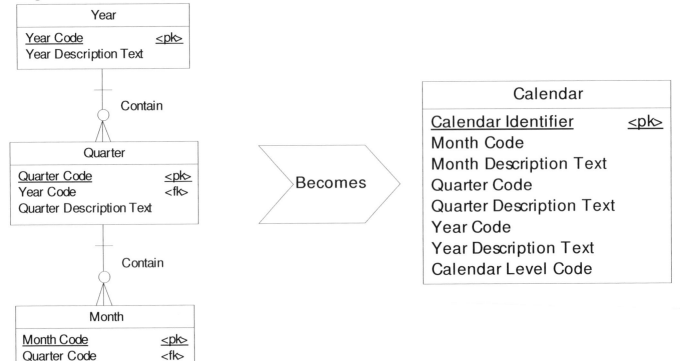

Table 17.3 contains sample values for this table.

You may be wondering what value FUBES provides. After all, we are adding a substantial amount of redundancy when using FUBES: we have all of the redundancy of the standard option, plus we are repeating each parent for the child, and repeating all of the parents for that parent. That is, repeating each quarter in our example, plus repeating the year for each quarter.

FUBES should be chosen when there is value in denormalizing, but there is still a need to access parent instances. Having an instance for each parent allows us to achieve better report performance, as we can directly tie to parent levels without having to roll up from the child. We can store sales at a year level, for example, and save the time of summarizing monthly level sales up into a year level. The value is that results can be retrieved extremely fast if we are doing reporting at the parent levels, in this example at the quarter and year level. For example, see Figure 17.7.

Table 17.3 Sample values for Figure 17.6

Cal Id	Mo Code	Mo Desc	Qtr Code	Qtr Desc	Yr Cd	Yr Desc	Level Cd
1					2007	Two Thousand Seven	Year
2					2008	Two Thousand Eight	Year
3					2009	Two Thousand Nine	Year
4			Q12009	First Quarter Two Thousand Nine	2009	Two Thousand Nine	Quarter
5			Q22009	Second Quarter Two Thousand Nine	2009	Two Thousand Nine	Quarter
6			Q32009	Third Quarter Two Thousand Nine	2009	Two Thousand Nine	Quarter
7	Jan2009	January Two Thousand Nine	Q12009	First Quarter Two Thousand Nine	2009	Two Thousand Nine	Month
8	Feb2009	February Two Thousand Nine	Q12009	First Quarter Two Thousand Nine	2009	Two Thousand Nine	Month
9	Mar2009	March Two Thousand Nine	Q12009	First Quarter Two Thousand Nine	2009	Two Thousand Nine	Month

Figure 17.7 Sales reporting with the Calendar FUBES structure

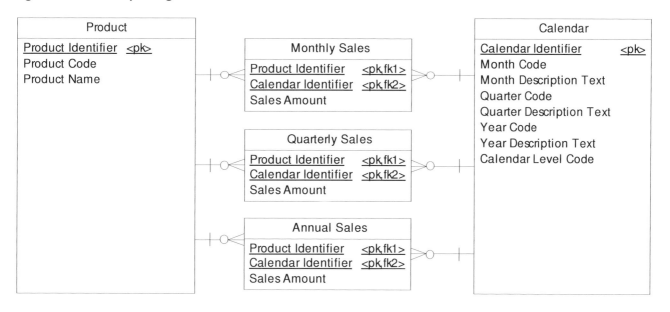

In Figure 17.7 we are summing and loading sales data at the month, quarter, and year levels. If there is a need to retrieve Annual sales for 2011, we can quickly find this number because we are storing the **Sales Value Amount** for 2011 in Annual Sales, which references the Calendar instance where **Calendar Level Code** equals 'Year' and **Year Code** equals '2011'.

> To apply FUBES, use the 'Column Denormalization' feature. Alternatively, replicate columns with the standard replication feature, although this will not appear in the list of model transformations.

Repeating Groups

In the repeating-groups technique, the same data element or group of data elements is repeated two or more times in the same entity. Also known as an *array*, a repeating group requires making the number of times something can occur static. Recall that in 1NF we removed repeating groups. Well, here it is, being reintroduced again. An example of a repeating group appears in Figure 17.8.

Figure 17.8 Repeating groups in our Contact example

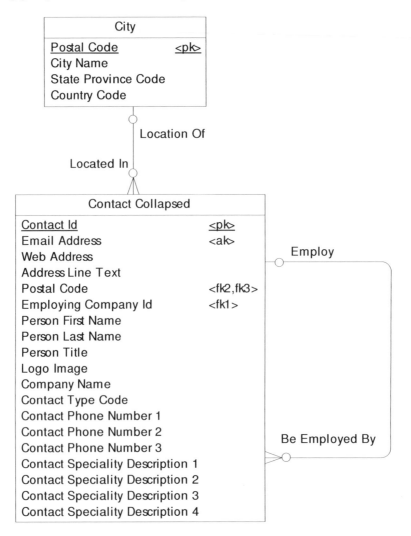

In this example, we can have up to three phone numbers for a Contact and up to four specialties. In addition to choosing denormalization because of the need for faster retrieval time or for more user friendly structures, repeating groups may be chosen in the following situations:

- **When it makes more sense to keep the parent entity instead of the child entity.** When the parent entity is going to be used more frequently than the child entity, or if there are rules and data elements to preserve in the parent entity format, it makes more sense to keep the parent entity. For example, in Figure 17.8, if Contact is going to be accessed frequently, and when Contact is accessed, **Phone Number** and **Specialty Description** are also occasionally accessed.
- **When an entity instance will never exceed the fixed number of data elements added.** In Figure 17.8, we are only allowing up to three phone numbers for a contact, for example. If we have four phone numbers for Bob the Contact, how would we handle this? Right now, we would have to pick which three of them to store.
- **When you need a spreadsheet.** A common use is to represent a report that needs to be displayed in a spreadsheet format. For example, if a user is expecting to see a sales report in which sales is reported by month for the last 12 months, an example of a repeating group containing this information is shown in Figure 17.9. At the end of a given month, the oldest value is removed and a new value is added. This is called a *rolling 12 months*. Faster performance and a more user-friendly structure lead us to add repeating groups in this example and purposely violate 1NF.

Figure 17.9 Sales-report entity with repeating group

Sales Summary Report	
Product Identifier	<pk>
Month Code	<pk>
Year Code	<pk>
Current Month - 1 Total Sales Amount	
Current Month - 2 Total Sales Amount	
Current Month - 3 Total Sales Amount	
Current Month - 4 Total Sales Amount	
Current Month - 5 Total Sales Amount	
Current Month - 6 Total Sales Amount	
Current Month - 7 Total Sales Amount	
Current Month - 8 Total Sales Amount	
Current Month - 9 Total Sales Amount	
Current Month - 10 Total Sales Amount	
Current Month - 11 Total Sales Amount	
Current Month - 12 Total Sales Amount	

To apply the repeating groups technique, replicate columns with the standard replication feature – this will not appear in the list of model transformations.

Repeating Data Elements

Repeating data elements is a technique in which you copy one or more data elements from one entity into one or more other entities. It is done primarily for performance because by repeating data elements across entities, we can reduce the amount of time it takes to return results. If we copy **Customer Last Name** from the Customer entity to the Order entity, for example, we avoid navigating back to Customer whenever just **Customer Last Name** is needed for display with order information.

Repeating data elements differs from repeating groups because the repeating groups technique replaces one or more entities and relationships, while the repeating data elements technique retains the existing entities and relationships and just copies over the data elements that are needed. For example, to apply the repeating groups technique to Customer and Order, we'd need to determine the maximum number of orders a customer can place, then remove the Order entity and its relationship to Customer and repeat three or four or however many times all of the order data elements within Customer. The repeating data elements technique would just involve copying over the data elements we need and keeping everything else intact.

See Figure 17.10 for an example of this technique using our Contact example. In this example, there was a need to view the country along with contact information. Therefore, only the **Country Code** data element needed to be copied to Contact, while the City entity and its relationship remains intact.

> In PowerDesigner, you should use the 'Column Denormalization' feature to copy columns to child tables. The new column is a managed, read-only copy of the original – any changes made to the original column are automatically made to the denormalized copy of it. In fact, you cannot alter the copy column.

In addition to choosing denormalization because of the need for faster retrieval time or for more user friendly structures, repeating data elements can be chosen in the following situations:

- **When the repeated data element or elements are accessed often and experience few or no changes over time.** If, for example, **Country Code** changed frequently, we would be required to update this value on City and for each of the contacts related to City. This takes time to update and could introduce data quality issues if not all updates were performed correctly, completely, or on a timely basis.
- **When the standard denormalization option is preferred, but space is an issue.** There might be too huge an impact on storage space if the entire parent entity was folded up into the child and repeated for each child value. Therefore, only repeat those parent data elements that will be used frequently with the child.
- **When there is a need to enforce the business rules from the LDM.** With the repeating data elements technique, the relationships still remain intact. Therefore, the business rules from the logical data model can be enforced on the physical data model. In Figure 17.10 for example, we can still enforce that a Contact live in a valid City.

Figure 17.10 Repeating data elements in our Contact example

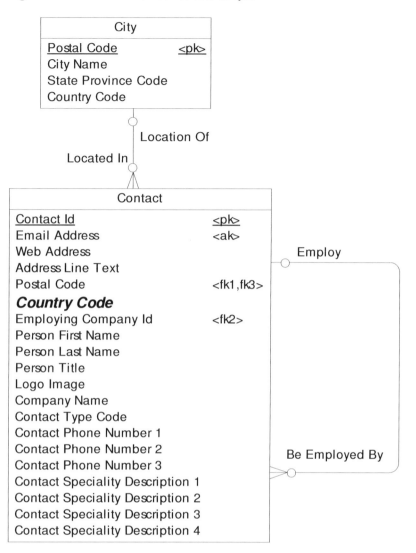

To apply the repeating data elements technique, use the column denormalization feature.

Summarization

Summarization is when tables are created with less detail than what is available in the business. Monthly Sales, Quarterly Sales, and Annual Sales from Figure 17.7 are all summary tables derived from the actual order transactions.

In addition to choosing denormalization because of the need for faster retrieval time or for more user friendly structures, summarization can be chosen when there is a need to report on higher levels of granularity than what is captured on the logical data model. Annual Sales for example, provides high level summary data for the user, and therefore the user (or reporting tool) does not have to spend time figuring out how to produce annual sales from detailed tables. The response time is much quicker because time does not need to be spent summarizing data when it is requested by a user; it is already at the needed summarization level, ready to be queried.

> To apply the summarization technique, create a new summary table. To create similar tables, either copy or replicate the original. In Figure 17.7, for example, the **Quarterly Sales** and **Annual Sales** could be replicas of **Monthly Sales**. Any changes made to **Monthly Sales** (e.g. new columns) would also be made to the replicas. If you need the tables to have more independence, you can break the replication link at any time.

Star Schema

Denormalization is a term that is applied exclusively to relational physical models, because you can't denormalize something unless it has already been normalized. However, denormalization techniques can be applied to dimensional models, as well - you just can't use the term 'denormalization'. So all of the techniques from the standard method through summarization can be used in dimensional modeling, just use a term such as 'flattening', instead of 'denormalization'.

A star schema is the most common dimensional physical data model structure. The term 'meter' from the dimensional logical data model, is replaced with the term 'fact table' on the dimensional physical data model. A star schema results when each set of tables that make up a dimension is flattened into a single table. The fact table is in the center of the model, and each of the dimensions relate to the fact table at the lowest level of detail. A star schema is relatively easy to create and implement, and visually appears elegant and simplistic to both IT and the business.

Recall the dimensional logical modeling example from the previous chapter, copied here as Figure 17.11.

Figure 17.11 Dimensional logical data model of ice cream

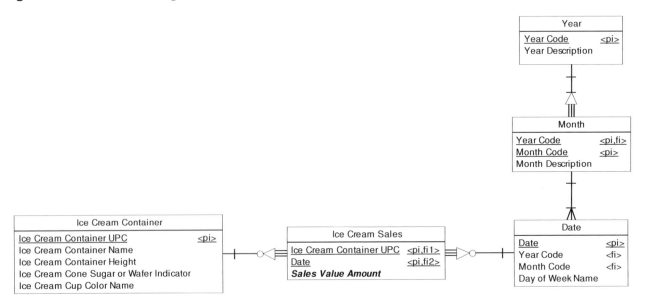

A star schema of this model would involve folding Year into Month and Month into Date, and then renaming Date with a concept inclusive of Month and Year, such as 'Time' or 'Calendar'. See Figure 17.12 for the star schema for this example.

Figure 17.12 Ice cream star schema

> 🐝 To create a star schema, use a combination of new tables and columns, and the FUBES and repeating data element techniques described above.

> 🐝 In Figure 17.12, I populated the *Dimensional Type* property on the 'General' tab for each Table. PowerDesigner automatically displays the icons in the top left corner of the table symbols. These tell you that **Ice Cream Sales** is a 'Fact' table, and that the other two tables are 'Dimensions'. PowerDesigner also allows you to create special 'Multidimensional' diagrams, where Facts and Dimensions are objects in their own right, not just specialized tables. 🔖

❓ "Building Multidimensional Diagrams"

Views Explained

A view is a virtual table. It is a dynamic "view" or window into one or more tables (or other views) where the actual data is stored. A view is defined by a query that specifies how to collate data from its underlying tables to form an object that looks and acts like a table, but doesn't physically contain data. A query is a request that a user (or reporting tool) makes of the database, such as "Bring me back all **Customer Ids** where the Customer is 90 days or more behind in their bill payments." The difference between a query and a view, however, is that the instructions in a view are already prepared for the user (or reporting tool) and stored in the database as the definition of the view, whereas a query is not stored in the database and may need to be written each time a question is asked.

Returning to our Contact example, let's assume that the users continuously ask the question, "Who are the people that live in New Jersey?" We can answer this question in a view. Figure 17.13 contains the model from Figure 17.10 with the addition of a view to answer this question.

In many tools, a view is shown as a dotted box; PowerDesigner uses solid lines and rounded corners, instead. In this model, it is called **Person In New Jersey**. This view needs to bring together information from the entity City and from the entity Contact to answer the business question.

Figure 17.13 View added to answer business question

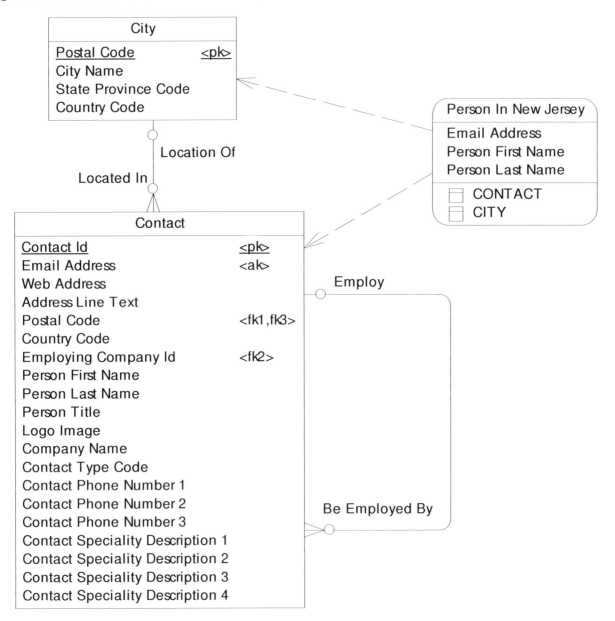

PowerDesigner records the interdependencies between the view and the tables, but doesn't automatically create lines to illustrate those dependencies. In Figure 17.13, the dashed lines connecting the view to the table were added manually, as 'traceability links'. This feature allows you to visually document any dependencies that matter to you.

The instructions to answer this business question are written in a query language a database can understand, usually in the language SQL (pronounced 'sequel'). SQL is powerful for the same reason that data modeling is powerful: with a handful of symbols, one can communicate a lot. In English, the SQL statement in Figure 17.14 is saying "Give me the last name, first name, and email address of the Contact(s) whose postal code matches a postal code in the City table that has a state code of 'NJ', where the Contact is a person (and not a company)".

Figure 17.14 SQL language to answer question "Who are my Contacts that live in New Jersey?"

```
select

    CONTACT.EMAIL_ADDRESS,

    CONTACT.PERSON_FIRST_NAME,

    CONTACT.PERSON_LAST_NAME

from

    CONTACT,

    CITY

WHERE (CITY.POSTAL_CODE=CONTACT.POSTAL_CODE)

AND (CITY.STATE_PROVINCE_CODE='NJ')

AND (CONTACT.CONTACT_TYPE_CODE = 'PRSN');
```

> PowerDesigner allows you to define and preview the SQL for the query in the property sheet for the View, in the 'SQL Query' tab. It is also visible in the 'Preview' tab. PowerDesigner creates dependencies between the view and the objects that it accesses, based upon the SQL statements.

There are different types of views. Typically, execution of the view (i.e. the SQL statement) to retrieve data takes place only when a data element in the view is requested. It can take quite a bit of time to retrieve data, depending on the complexity of the request and the data volume. However, other types of views can match and sometimes even beat retrieval speed from actual tables, because their instructions are run at a predetermined time, with the results stored in the database, similar to a database table.

Views are a popular choice for assisting with security and user-friendliness. If there are sensitive data elements within a database table that only certain people in the company should have access to, then views are a great way to hide these sensitive data elements from the common user. Views can also take some of the complexities out of joining tables for the user or reporting tool.

In fact, we can use views in almost all situations where we are using denormalization. At times, views can offer all of the benefits of denormalization *without the drawbacks associated with data redundancy and loss of referential integrity*. A view can provide user-friendly structures over a normalized structure, thereby preserving flexibility and referential integrity. A view will keep the underlying normalized model intact, and at the same time present a denormalized or flattened view of the world to the business.

Indexing Explained

An index is a pointer to something that needs to be retrieved. An analogy often used is the card catalog, which in the library, points you to the book you want. The card catalog will point you to the place where the actual book is on the shelf, a process that is much quicker than looking through each book in the library until you find the one you need. Indexing works the same way with data. The index points directly to the place on the disk where the data is stored, thus reducing retrieval time. Indexes work best on data elements whose values are requested frequently, but are rarely updated.

Primary keys, foreign keys, and alternate keys are automatically indexed just because they are keys. A non-unique index, also known as a secondary key, is an index based on one or more non-key data elements that is added to improve retrieval performance. When to add a non-unique index depends on the types of queries being performed against the table. For example, recall Figure 17.12, repeated here as Figure 17.15.

Figure 17.15 Ice cream star schema

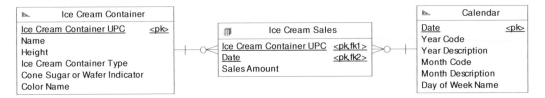

Assume that an often-asked question of this dimensional model is "What are my sales by Container Type?" Or in more business speak, "What are my sales by Ice Cream Cup versus Ice Cream Cone?" Because this query involves the data element Ice Cream Container Type, and because Ice Cream Container Type is most likely a stable data element which does not experience many value updates, Ice Cream Container Type would be a good candidate for a secondary index.

Keys and Indexes in the PDM

In the PDM, an index is a data structure associated with a table, logically ordered by the values of a key. It improves database performance and access speed.

You normally create indexes for columns that you access regularly, and where response time is important. Indexes are most effective when used on columns that contain mostly unique values.

When you generate a PDM, PowerDesigner automatically creates indexes for keys. If you create keys manually in the PDM, you must create the indexes yourself. Creating an index is a simple task, as is linking the index to a key.

Partitioning Explained

In general, a partition is a structure that divides or separates. Specific to the physical design, partitioning is used to break a table into rows, columns, or both. An attribute or value of an attribute drives how the records in a table are divided among the partitions. There are two types of partitioning - vertical and horizontal. To understand the difference between these two types, visualize a physical entity in a spreadsheet format where the data elements are the columns in the spreadsheet and the entity instances are the rows. Vertical means up and down. So vertical partitioning means separating the columns (the data elements) into separate tables. Horizontal means side to side. So horizontal partitioning means separating rows (the entity instances) into separate tables.

An example of horizontal partitioning appears in Figure 17.16. This is our data model from Figure 17.10, modified for horizontal partitioning. In this example, we are horizontally partitioning by **Contact Last Name**. If a contact's last name starts with a letter from 'A', up to and including 'H', then the contact would appear as an instance of the entity Contact A Through H. If a contact's last name starts with a letter from 'I', up to and including 'Z', then the contact would appear as an instance of the entity Contact I Through Z.

Figure 17.16 Horizontal partitioning in our contact example

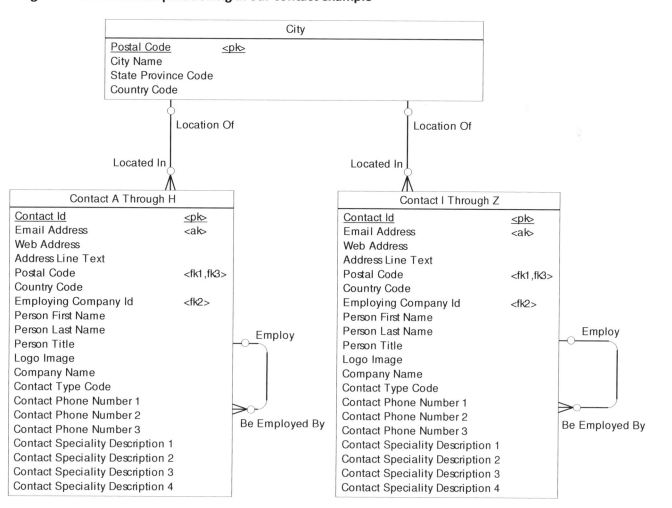

An example of vertical partitioning appears in Figure 17.17. Also based on the example from Figure 17.10, we have vertically partitioned the phone numbers into a separate table and the specialties into a separate table. This might have been done for space or user access reasons.

Figure 17.17 Vertical partitioning in our contact example

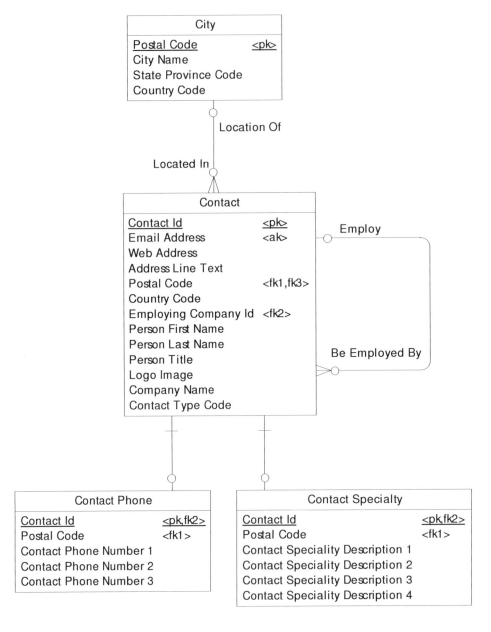

Snowflake

In dimensional modeling, there are two main types of physical designs: the star schema and snowflake. We mentioned earlier that the star schema is when each dimension has been flattened into a single table. The snowflake is when there are one or more tables for each dimension. Sometimes the snowflake structure is equivalent to the dimensional logical model, where each level in a dimension hierarchy exists as its own table. Sometimes in a snowflake, however, there can be even more tables than exist on the dimensional logical model. This is because vertical partitioning is applied to the dimensional model.

For example, Figure 17.18 is based on our ice cream dimensional model from Figure 17.11. This is a snowflake. Not only does the calendar dimension exist in separate tables (one for year, one for month, one for date), but we have vertically partitioned the **Ice Cream Cone Sugar Or Wafer Indicator** into the Ice Cream Cone entity, and vertically partitioned the **Ice Cream Cup Color Name** into the Ice Cream Cup entity. Notice that in this example, vertical partitioning is equivalent to the Identity method of resolving a subtype. Another way of saying this is that Identity is a type of vertical partitioning.

Figure 17.18 Ice cream snowflake

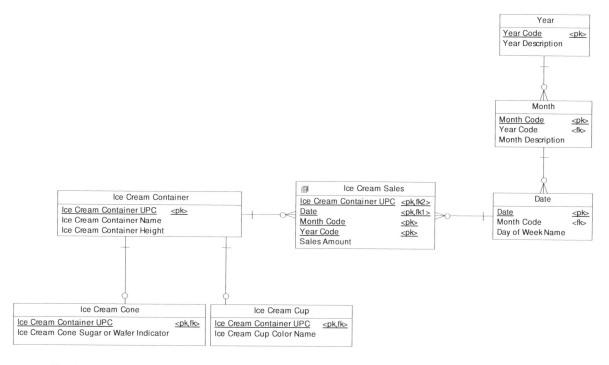

Almost all dimensional logical data models become star schemas in the physical world. Therefore, it is rare to see a snowflake design. However, it does occur from time to time for the two main reasons of data volatility and the need for higher level access.

Figure 17.18 was simple to create in PowerDesigner by applying Vertical Partitioning to the **Ice Cream Container** table, and adjusting the **Month** and **Date** tables, deleting unwanted columns, and altering the primary keys. You can also generate this scenario when generating the PDM from the LDM, by opting to generate both parent and child tables for the inheritance.

Data volatility means that values are updated frequently. If we have a four level product hierarchy on a dimensional model, for example, and all four levels are relatively stable except for the second level, which experiences almost daily changes, vertically partitioning to keep this second level separate can reduce database complexity and improve database efficiencies.

In dimensional modeling, users often want to query across data marts, so dimensions need to be built consistently across them. One data mart might need to see facts at different grains than another data mart. For example, one data mart might need **Gross Sales Value Amount** at a date level, and another data mart might only require **Gross Sales Value Amount** at a year level. Keeping the calendar structure as on the dimensional logical model with separate tables for Date, Month, and Year would allow each data mart to connect to the level they need. Another option is to use the FUBES techniques discussed previously. This would allow the modeler to use a star schema design, storing all calendar data elements in one table and accessing different levels using the **Calendar Level Code** data element.

When Reference Data Values Change

Transaction data elements are those that capture data on the events that take place in our organizations, while reference data elements are those that capture the context around these events. For example, an order is placed for '5'. The order itself is a transaction, and data elements such as **Order Number** and **Order Quantity** are transaction data elements. However '5', does not provide any value unless we give it context. Product information, Customer information, Calendar information, etc., provides the context for '5' – all of these data elements are reference data. *Bob ordered 5 Widgets on April 15th, 2011.* 'Bob' is the customer reference data, 'Widgets' is the product reference data, and 'April 15th, 2011' is the calendar reference data.

Transaction data and reference data behave very differently from each other in terms of value updates. Transaction data occurs very frequently and usually once they occur they are not updated (e.g. once an order has been delivered you can no longer change its properties, such as **Order Quantity**). Reference data, on the other hand, is much less voluminous but values can change more often (e.g. people move to different addresses, product names change, and sales departments have reorganizations).

Reference entity instances will therefore experience changes over time, such as a person moving to a new address, or product name changing, or an account description being updated. There are three ways of modeling to support changes to data values:

- **Design the model to contain only the most current information**. When values are updated, store only the new values. For example, if Bob the customer moves to a new address, store just his new address, and do not store any previous addresses.
- **Design the model to contain the most current information, along with all history**. When values are updated, store the new values along with any previous values. If Bob the customer moves to a new address, store his new address along with all previous addresses. New entity instances are created when values are updated and previous entity instances remain intact.
- **Design the model to contain the most current information, and some history**. When values are updated, store the new values along with some of the previous values. If Bob the customer moves to a new address, store his new address along with only his most recent previous address. New data elements are added to store the changes.

These three ways of handling changing values can be applied to both relational and dimensional models. On dimensional models, there is a special term that describes how to handle changing values: Slowly Changing Dimension (SCD). An SCD of Type 1 means only the most current information will be stored. An SCD of Type 2 means the most current along with all history will be stored. And an SCD of Type 3 means the most current and some history will be stored.

Using the Contact table from Figure 17.18 as an example, Figure 17.19 shows all three types of SCDs.

Figure 17.19 The three types of SCDs

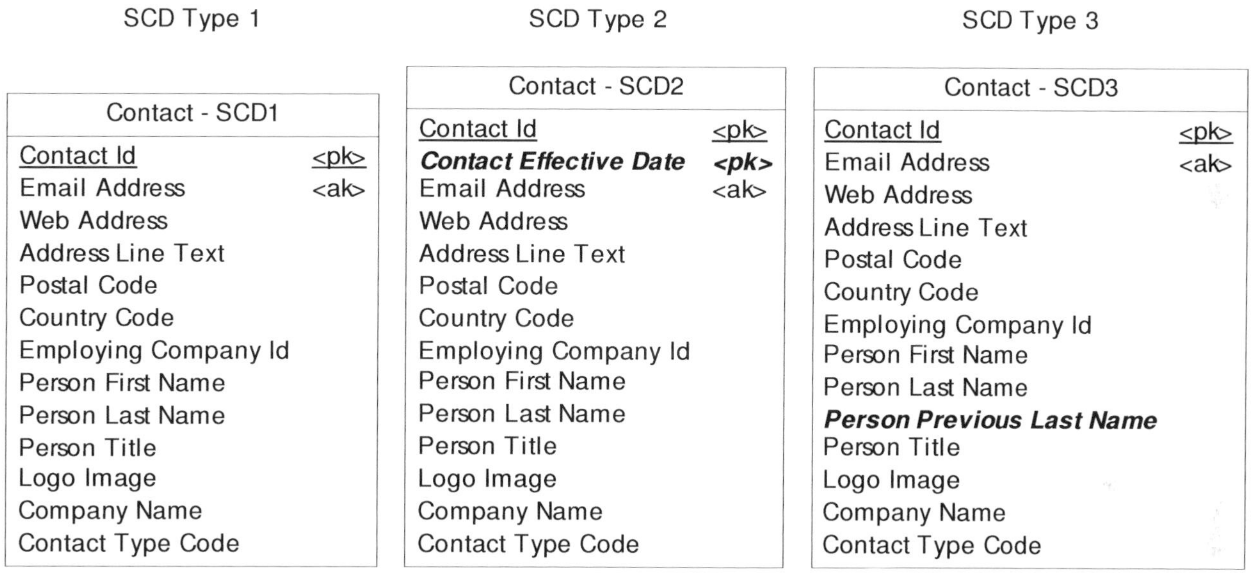

SCD Type 1 | SCD Type 2 | SCD Type 3

Contact - SCD1		Contact - SCD2		Contact - SCD3	
Contact Id	<pk>	Contact Id	<pk>	Contact Id	<pk>
Email Address	<ak>	*Contact Effective Date*	*<pk>*	Email Address	<ak>
Web Address		Email Address	<ak>	Web Address	
Address Line Text		Web Address		Address Line Text	
Postal Code		Address Line Text		Postal Code	
Country Code		Postal Code		Country Code	
Employing Company Id		Country Code		Employing Company Id	
Person First Name		Employing Company Id		Person First Name	
Person Last Name		Person First Name		Person Last Name	
Person Title		Person Last Name		*Person Previous Last Name*	
Logo Image		Person Title		Person Title	
Company Name		Logo Image		Logo Image	
Contact Type Code		Company Name		Company Name	
		Contact Type Code		Contact Type Code	

The SCD Type 1 is just a current view of Contact. If there are any updates to a Contact, the updates will overlay the original information. The SCD Type 2 contains the most current data as well as a full historical view of Contact. If a Contact instance experiences a change, the original Contact instance remains intact, and a new instance is created with the most current information. The SCD Type 3 includes only a current view of Contact, with the exception of the person's last name, where we have a requirement to also see the person's previous last name. So if Bob changes his last name five times, the SCD Type 1 will just store his current last name, the SCD Type 2 will store all five last names, and the SCD Type 3 will store the current last name, along with the most recent previous last name.

Physical Data Models in PowerDesigner

Creating and managing a PowerDesigner PDM is essentially the same as creating and managing any other type of model, so this section will focus on the differences. It is in the technology-specific artifacts that the differences arise. Please remember that this book includes the words 'Made Simple' in the title, so we focus on the basic information needed to manage a

PDM. To find out more about defining references, indexes, keys, and other objects, refer to the PowerDesigner documentation, and then have a good time experimenting.

If you have worked through the earlier chapters, you have already tried most of the PowerDesigner techniques you need to create a Physical Data Model:

Chapter 10   **General 'how-to' knowledge**
Chapter 11   **Creating Entities**
Chapter 12   **Creating Data Elements**
Chapter 13   **Creating Relationships**
Chapter 14   **Creating Keys**
Chapter 15   **Creating Subject Area Models**
Chapter 16   **Creating Logical Data Models**

 PDM Settings

Before you add content to your model, we suggest that you set the options listed in Table 17.4. Remember to click on <Set As Default> within the model options and display preferences.

Table 17.4 PDM settings

Category	Settings
Model Options – Model Settings	Choose the notation required by your modeling standards. Enable links to requirements (if you intend to create a Requirements model).
Model Options – Naming Convention	Enable Glossary for auto completion and compliance checking (if you use a Glossary). Display – select 'Code', if you prefer to see object codes rather than their names (this applies to symbols, diagram tabs, and the Browser).
Display Preferences – General Settings	Enable the following: Show Bridges at Intersections Auto Link Routing Snap to Grid Enable Word Wrapping. If you have a preference for the color of lines and symbol fill, or for the use of symbol shadows, set them here.
Database Menu - Default Physical Options	Each DBMS definition includes default physical options for each type of object in the model. You can override these settings for individual objects.

The Database Menu

The `Database` menu is specific to the PDM. When you create a PDM, you choose the DBMS you want the model to support. The `Database` menu allows you to change to a different DBMS, alter the DBMS properties, configure default physical options, and connect to a live database. I'm sure you can see the breadth of the options, they're in Figure 17.20.

Figure 17.20 The Database menu

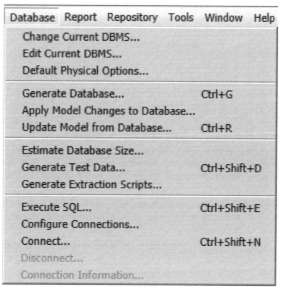

When you choose a different DBMS, the model will be altered to conform with the new DBMS, as follows:

- All data types specified in your model will be converted to their equivalents in the new DBMS
- Any objects not supported by the new DBMS will be deleted
- Certain objects, whose behavior is heavily DBMS-dependent, may lose their values.

The Tools Menu

The `Tools` menu for the PDM is considerably bigger than that for the CDM and LDM. Figure 17.21 shows the central part of the menu; everything above and below this point is shared with the other models.

You can generate five different types of models from a PDM; for the XML model, you have a choice of two mechanisms.

There is a wizard for creating Views, which we'll show you shortly. The `Rebuild` options enable to you make sure your indexes, primary keys, references, procedures, and packages are correct. The `Denormalization` options enable you to transform your model to improve performance. You can connect to a database to update the database statistics in the model. You can import or export test data profiles, for use when generating test data (see the `Database` menu). The `Multidimension` options allow you to convert a standard PDM into a data warehouse PDM, and rebuild Cubes 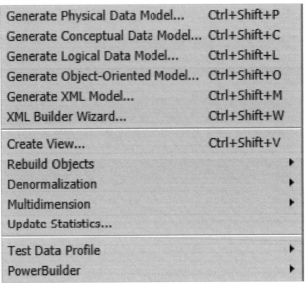. Finally, you can communicate with `PowerBuilder` to exchange metadata, which enables you to refactor existing PowerBuilder applications within PowerDesigner.

Most of the preceding topics are beyond the 'made simple' label of this book.

Figure 17.21 The PDM tools menu

Generate Physical Data Model...	Ctrl+Shift+P
Generate Conceptual Data Model...	Ctrl+Shift+C
Generate Logical Data Model...	Ctrl+Shift+L
Generate Object-Oriented Model...	Ctrl+Shift+O
Generate XML Model...	Ctrl+Shift+M
XML Builder Wizard...	Ctrl+Shift+W
Create View...	Ctrl+Shift+V
Rebuild Objects	▶
Denormalization	▶
Multidimension	▶
Update Statistics...	
Test Data Profile	▶
PowerBuilder	▶

Approaches for Creating a PDM

You can use a variety of techniques to create a PDM in PowerDesigner. Which approach is appropriate for you will depend on the models and information you have available.

- Create from scratch
- Generate a PDM from a SAM (CDM) or another PDM
- Generate a PDM from a LDM
- Copy or replicate tables, etc. from other PDMs, including reference models held in the Library
- Use the Excel Import facility to create or update objects in your PDM

The Physical Diagram Palette

Figure 17.22 shows the Toolbox dedicated to physical diagram symbols. The tools on this palette allow you to create or select (from left to right):

Packages
Tables
Views
References
Procedures
Files

Figure 17.22 The physical diagram palette

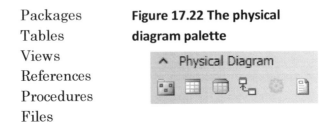

The *procedures* tool is unavailable in this palette, because the current DBMS does not support procedures.

Creating a Reference from the Palette

A reference in the PDM is drawn in the opposite direction from what you are used to in the CDM and LDM. To draw a reference, click on the reference tool in the palette, click on the *child* table first, then click on the *parent*. Think of it as drawing a line from one table to another table that it references, or needs data from.

Reference Optionality & Cardinalities

In the CDM and LDM, you adjust the relationship optionality and cardinalities in one place, the relationship's 'Cardinalities' tab.

In the PDM, you change the optionality of the parent table in a reference by adjusting the optionality of the foreign key column in the child table. The child cardinalities are adjusted via the 'Integrity' tab on the reference property sheet.

The reference name is not the same as the name of the foreign key constraint; this is on the reference's 'Integrity' tab.

❷ "Reference Properties" (Data Modeling)

 Creating a View

There are several ways to create a view. Here is the simplest and quickest way:

1. In the Browser or diagram, select the tables, views, and references that the new view needs to include.
2. Select `Tools|Create View` menu to create the view.
   a. PowerDesigner will automatically create the required SQL, including WHERE clauses (if you selected the necessary references).
   b. The 'Columns' tab on the view property sheet shows a list of all the table columns and view columns in the query.
   c. This list cannot be edited – edit the query (on the 'SQL Query' tab), instead.
   d. Dependencies are automatically created between the view and the tables, and between the view columns and table columns. These can be seen on the object 'Dependencies' tabs.
3. Tailor the SQL to remove unwanted columns and refine the logic.
4. On the diagram, draw traceability links to show dependencies.

For example, I selected the tables and reference in Figure 17.23, and the 'create view' wizard automatically created the view called **View_1**. PowerDesigner will not create any diagrammatic links between the tables and the view; you can add these yourself if you want.

Figure 17.23 A wizard view

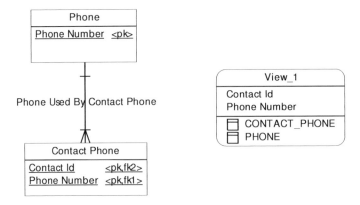

Figure 17.24 shows the SQL Query generated by PowerDesigner.

Figure 17.24 The SQL query

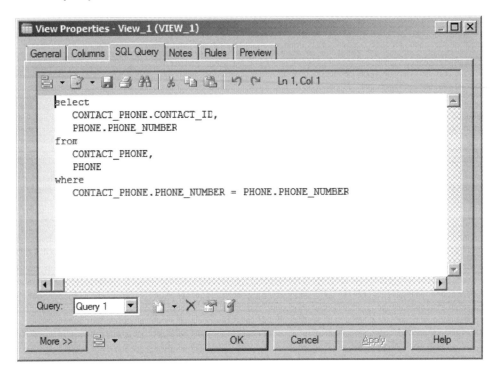

Using the tools in this tab, you can edit the Query using a built-in SQL editor or an external editor.

Display Preferences

The PDM Display Preferences are fundamentally the same as you have already seen, with a different list of object types.

SQL Preview

PowerDesigner allows you to preview the code that will be generated for an object, even for the whole PDM. Figure 17.25 shows the preview for a table. The tools on the toolbar allow you to choose the parts of the SQL to include.

Figure 17.25 SQL Preview

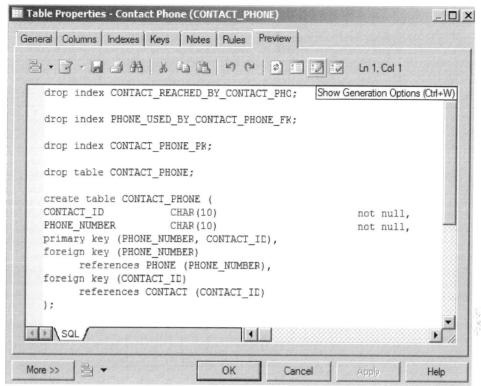

● "Previewing SQL Statements" (Data Modeling)

Viewing Data

Right-click a table in the Browser or diagram and select View Data. This allows you to connect to a database and look at the data in the table.

Denormalization in PowerDesigner

PowerDesigner supports all five of the denormalization techniques described in this chapter. Table 17.5 summarizes how that support is provided. In addition, PowerDesigner supports Horizontal and Vertical Partitioning of tables.

All of the denormalization techniques are available via the Tools menu, and also via the contextual menu for tables. When you run one of these processes, you have the option to retain the original tables. It is always advisable to do this, for several reasons:

- To preserve generation dependencies and other links in the original tables
- PowerDesigner links the original and new tables; these links are accessible via the 'Version Info' tab
- Some of the transformation definitions can be altered, allowing you to experiment with alternative design approaches
    - o For example, re-arranging the columns in a vertical partition
- The *Generate* property can be set to 'false' in the original tables, preventing them from being generated in future models or database schemas

Assuming the PDM was generated from another model, retaining the original tables improves the update process, should you update the PDM via the 'generation' feature.

Table 17.5 Denormalization in PowerDesigner

Technique	Approach
Standard	The 'Table Collapsing' feature.
FUBES	The 'Column Denormalization' feature. Alternatively, replicate columns with the standard replication feature, although this will not appear in the list of model transformations.
Repeating Groups	Replicate columns with the standard replication feature – this will not appear in the list of model transformations.
Repeating Data Elements	The 'Column Denormalization' feature.
Summarization	Create a new summary table. To create similar tables, either copy or replicate the original.
Star Schema	Combine the FUBES and Repeating Data Element Techniques.

The denormalization features work in pretty much identical fashion - you choose one or more tables to work with, then tell PowerDesigner what to do with them. You can experiment with this in Exercise 21. The results of each denormalization process are stored in the model as Transformations, and a list of them is available from the Model menu. See Figure 17.26.

Figure 17.26 List of transformations

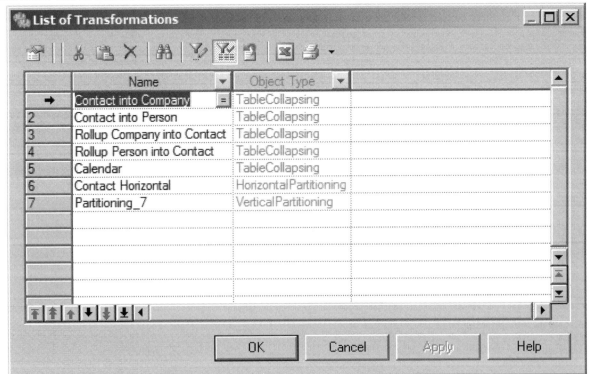

For example, assume that the column **ICE_CREAM_CONTAINER.HEIGHT** has been denormalized into the **ICE_CREAM_SALES** table. Figure 17.27 shows part of the 'version info' for the denormalized column. This allows you to access the details of the transformation (and hence the original object), and to break the link back to the original object.

Figure 17.27 Link back to the original

Figure 17.28 shows the impact analysis for the original column, with the link to the new column.

Figure 17.28 Link to the new column

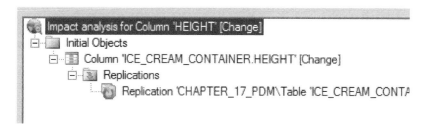

Collapsing Subtypes

There is one more way of denormalizing a model where the LDM has an inheritance structure. For example, consider the structure in Figure 16.1, reproduced here as Figure 17.29.

Figure 17.29 Simple subtypes

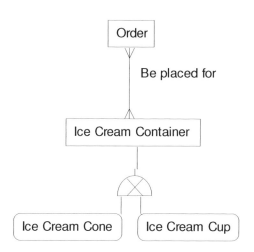

In the PDM, we may wish to collapse this structure, and migrate all of the columns in **Ice Cream Container** to the **Cone** and **Cup** tables. The best place to do this is in the LDM, via the 'Generation' tab in the Inheritance's property sheet – uncheck 'Generate parent', and ensure that 'Inherit all attributes' is selected. Now re-generate the PDM in update mode.

❷ "Denormalizing Tables and Columns" (Data Modeling)

Reverse-engineering Databases

The term 'reverse-engineering' refers to the creation of a new PDM by scanning the structure of a database schema or reading SQL scripts. To start the process, select `Reverse Engineer|Database` on the `File` menu, and the dialog shown in Figure 17.30 will appear. Type the name of the new model, choose your DBMS, choose any model extension required, and then click on <OK>.

Figure 17.30 Choosing the DBMS etc

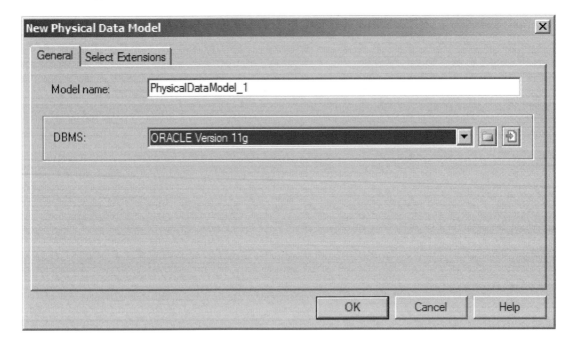

Now you have to tell PowerDesigner more about what you want it to do. Where will it find the database definition? Are there any data models open in the workspace representing databases linked to the one you're reverse-engineering? Provide some detailed options, such as whether or not you want diagram symbols created in the new model. In Figure 17.31, I want to create a PDM by reverse-engineering the structure of my PowerDesigner repository database.

PowerDesigner will read the source material and create the model for you. You can monitor progress in the PowerDesigner Output window.

Remember to save the model in a file, PowerDesigner leaves that up to you.

For some databases (e.g. Microsoft Access), you will need to check DBMS-specific help for detailed instructions on reverse-engineering.

"Reverse Engineering a Database into a PDM" (Data Modeling)

Figure 17.31 Reverse-engineering options

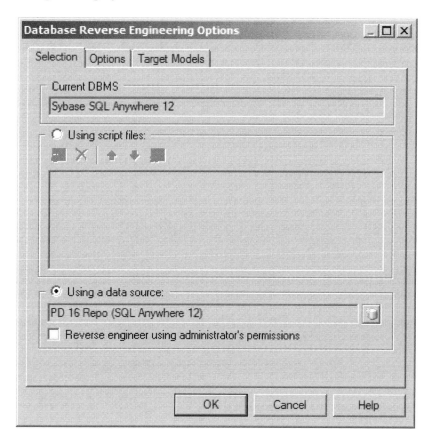

Now you have to choose the database objects that you want to reverse-engineer, using the dialog in Figure 17.32.

Figure 17.32 Choosing your objects

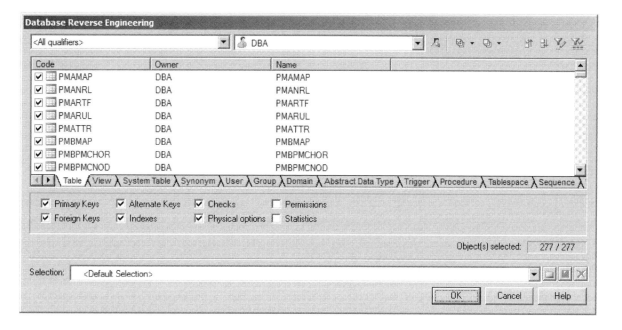

Keeping the Model and Database Synchronized

Okay, you have a database, and you have a PDM. How do you update one from the other? The answer lies in two commands on the `Database` menu:

`Update Model from Database`	This uses the same process we showed you for reverse-engineering a database; the model is updated to match the database. If you need to compare a PDM to the current database, compare it with a new PDM you create by reverse-engineering the database.
`Generate Database`	Allows you to update a database from a model, either by generating SQL scripts, or by a live connection. Just complete the options listed in Figure 17.33, and click <OK>.

Figure 17.33 Database generation options

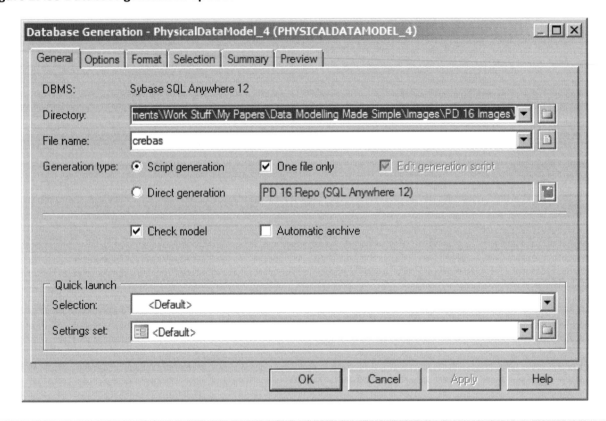

EXERCISE 20: Getting Physical with Subtypes in PowerDesigner

Subtyping is a powerful communication tool on the logical data model, because it allows the modeler to represent the similarities that exist between distinct business concepts to improve integration and data quality. As an example, refer to Figure 17.34, where the supertype **Course** contains the common data elements and relationships for the **Lecture** and **Workshop** subtypes.

Figure 17.34 Course subtyping structure

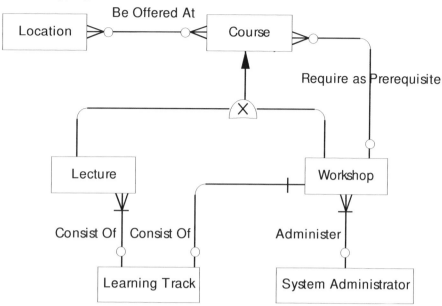

Briefly walking through this model, we learn that each Course, such as "Data Modeling 101", can be either a Lecture or a Workshop. Each Course must be taught at many Locations. Each Learning Track, such as the Data Track, must consist of one or many Lectures, yet only one Workshop. Each Workshop, such as the Advanced Design Workshop, can require certain Courses as a prerequisite, such as Data Modeling 101 and Data Modeling 101 Workshop. Each System Administrator must administer one or many Workshops.

Assume this is a logical data model (with data elements hidden to keep this example manageable). On the physical data model, we can replace this subtype symbol in one of three ways:

- **Rolling down**. Remove the supertype entity and copy all of the data elements and relationships from the supertype to each of the subtypes.
- **Rolling up**. Remove the subtypes and copy all of the data elements and relationships from each subtype to the supertype. Also add a type code to distinguish the subtypes.
- **Identity**. Convert the subtype symbol into a series of one-to-one relationships, connecting the supertype to each of the subtypes.

For this Challenge, using the Course structure from Figure 17.34, build all three options.

In PowerDesigner, create a new project for the exercise, then create an initial LDM. Now generate three LDMs from the initial LDM, using the default options. You'll find the Generate Logical Data Model command on the Tools menu. Use the phrases 'IDENTITY', 'ROLLING DOWN', and 'ROLLING UP' in the model names. Remember that denormalizing subtype structures can only be done in the LDM.

Generate a PDM from each LDM using your choice of DBMS; use the generic 'ODBC' option if you like. In each model, carry out the appropriate denormalization manually. See the Appendix for my answers.

EXERCISE 21: Denormalizing a PDM in PowerDesigner

Open the LDM you created in Exercise 18, illustrated in Figure 17.35. Your task is to denormalize this model several different ways, using the techniques described earlier in this chapter. I know we haven't provided much information about how to run the denormalization features - that is intentional. It's time for you to do some investigation of the Tools menu. Select the tables you need to denormalize, then select Denormalization on the Tools menu, and select the required technique.

Generate three different PDMs from the LDM, and denormalize them to produce the target models listed in Table 17.6.

Table 17.6 Your tasks

Model Name	Target Model
Exercise 21 – Identity	See Figure 17.2
Exercise 21 – Rolling Down	See Figure 17.3
Exercise 21 – Rolling Up	See Figure 17.4

Use the phrases 'IDENTITY', 'ROLLING DOWN', and 'ROLLING UP' in the model names.

Figure 17.35 Contact data model with Communication Medium

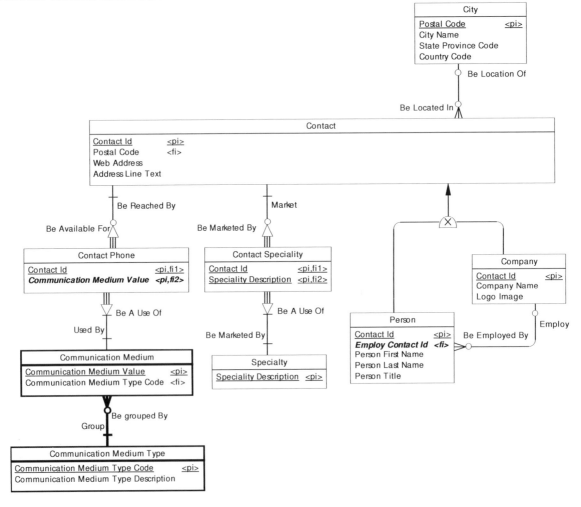

Key Points

- The physical data model builds upon the logical data model to produce a technical solution.

- Denormalization is the process of selectively violating normalization rules and reintroducing redundancy into the model.

- There are five denormalization techniques: standard, repeating groups, repeating data elements, FUBES, and summarization.

- A star schema is when each set of tables that make up a dimension is flattened into a single table.

- A view is a virtual table.

- An index is a pointer to something that needs to be retrieved.

- Partitioning is breaking up a table into rows, columns, or both. If a table is broken up into columns, the partitioning is vertical. If a table is broken into rows, the partitioning is horizontal.

- Snowflaking is when vertical partitioning is performed on a dimensional model, often due to data volatility or frequent user access to higher levels in a hierarchy.

- Data values change over time. We have the option of storing only the new information (Type 1), storing all of the new information plus all of the historical information (Type 2), or storing the new information plus some of the historical information (Type 3).

- PowerDesigner does not use object names when generating a database – it uses the object 'codes'.

- When denormalizing, keep the original tables, and uncheck 'generate'.

- The 'Dependencies' tab tells you everything about how a column is used.

Tie them together
With traceability and
Generation links

The ability to create and manage links between models, and between objects in models, is a key strength of PowerDesigner. There are several types of links, but the key links for data modelers are the generation dependencies created when we generate one model from another. The best way to create models as you move up or down the data model pyramid described in Section IV is to generate each model, in turn. As a reminder, take a look at the model chain illustrated in Figure 18.1, which you may remember from Chapter 9.

Figure 18.1 Generation dependency chain

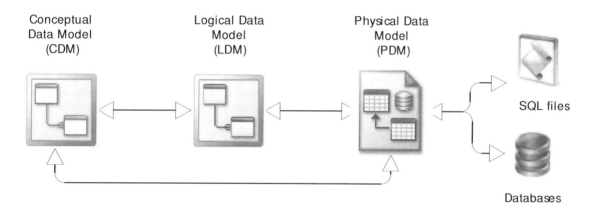

PowerDesigner manages each link in the chain by storing linkage information in all the affected objects. In fact, this is how PowerDesigner manages all such model-to-model and object-to-object links – they refer to it as 'Link and Sync'. Links are visible on the property sheets for affected objects – generally on one or more of the following tabs:

Dependencies   *Traceability Links*   *Version Info.*

You can see a list of the models your current model is connected to via the list of Target Models on the `Model` menu. Through the `Tools` menu, you can start up the Mapping Editor, or view Generation Links.

In addition to generation dependencies, you can create shortcuts to objects, link objects to related diagrams in any model, create replicas of objects and sub-objects, create mappings between models, and create traceability links. You can also create dependency matrices to view or edit links. Project diagrams map out the connections between models.

In addition, there are dedicated methods for linking models, such as mapping data models to data objects in business process models.

Using impact and lineage analysis, you can view the links in the chain, varying the rules to suit your purposes. Via the repository, you can extend the impact analysis beyond the models that you're aware of, to models you didn't even know existed in the repository.

Depending on the complexity of your modeling environment, all of these capabilities can give you an administration issue. If you allow every modeler to invent their own strategy for linking models to each other, that will lead to complex and inconsistent model linkages, which will complicate an analysis of the impact of a change. Planning and setting standards is essential.

In this book, we merely scratch the surface of the subject of linking models. In this chapter, we'll help you to get the best out of the links that we've covered.

Generating Models

As you build a pyramid of data models, you will need to create new models and propagate changes through your chain of models. Figure 18.2 illustrates the potential creation and update tasks in a chain of four models. In PowerDesigner, all of these tasks are carried out using model generation. The bold links represent the generation of new models, and the remainder represent the update of one model based on changes made to the other.

Figure 18.2 Model creation and update tasks

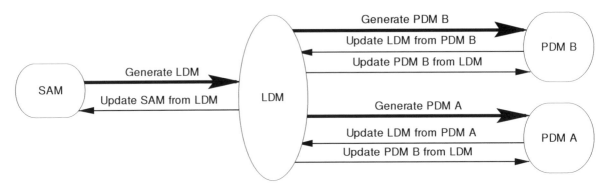

Remember, updates are only applied in one direction. Two-way synchronization requires two updates.

The remainder of this section is a summary of the process you go through when creating or updating a model via the generation feature.

Step 1

Launch the required generation tool via the Tools menu, and choose between creating a new model, or updating an existing one. If there are existing generation dependencies, PowerDesigner will default to the 'update' option, as in Figure 18.3, and the drop-down list will include all of the models of that type that were previously generated from the current model. The ellipsis tool (circled in Figure 18.3) opens a list of all the models of that type (see Figure

18.4) in the current workspace, allowing you to choose a previously unlinked model to update. If you want to generate a new model, select the 'generate' option in Figure 18.3, and type in a name for the model.

Figure 18.3 Update or create?

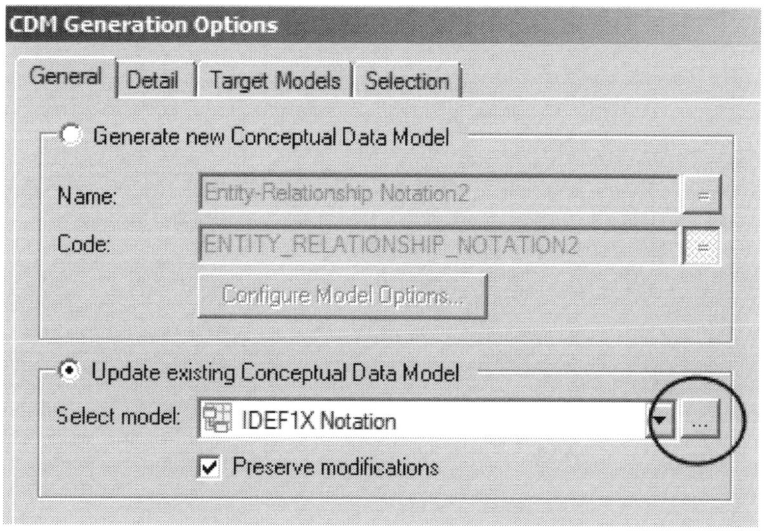

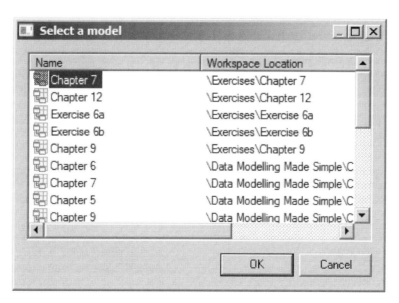

Figure 18.4 Select a model

The 'preserve modifications' option is vital during an update. If you uncheck this option, PowerDesigner will ignore changes made to previously-generated objects in the target model and overwrite them with the generated version.

Step 2

Look at the remaining tabs (we'll skip the 'Target Models' tab – the documentation will tell you what this is for). The 'Detail' tab is shown in Figure 18.5.

Figure 18.5 The 'Detail' tab

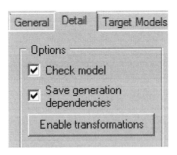

The 'Check model' option will run the standard model checks before generating; any errors will stop the process in its tracks.

The 'Save generation dependencies' option will do just what it says – it will create or update generation dependencies to keep a record of how the two models are related.

Figure 18.6 shows the 'Selection' tab. By default, all of the objects in the model (where 'generate' = True) are selected here, but you can change the selection and save it for future use, if you want to.

Figure 18.6 Your selection

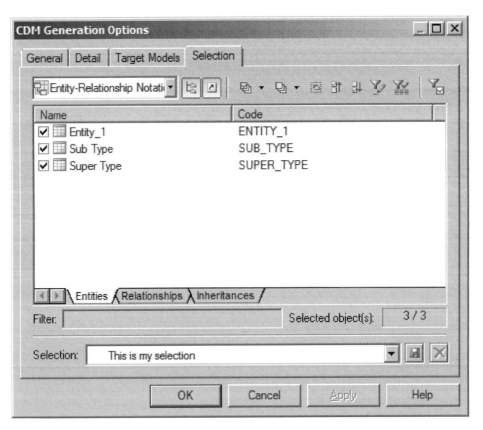

This is a variation on the selection window you've seen before – previously, selection windows have only listed one type of object. In Figure 18.6, we have three types of object to choose from, Entities, Relationships, and Inheritances, each with their own tab. We saw the selection window toolbar in Chapter 11. Here we have an additional tool, the *Use filter for selection* tool  on the right. This tool applies the filter conditions defined in the 'Customize Columns and Filter' dialog to select all objects meeting the criteria from the list. This selection by criteria is persistent for as long as the tool is applied.

When you've finished here, just click <OK> to continue.

If you see the message shown in Figure 18.7, the model check has found some errors, and the generation process has been halted. The errors are listed in the output window. To carry on with the generation, correct the errors first, or re-run the process with the 'Check model' option unchecked.

Figure 18.7 Errors found

The generation has been cancelled because errors have been found by the check model.

Since this is an update process, the next step is to examine the differences between the two models and decide what to do with them. Take a look at Figure 18.8, which has been filtered to show just the things that are different. This is the standard 'model merge' dialog, which we will describe in Chapter 23.

Figure 18.8 What shall we change?

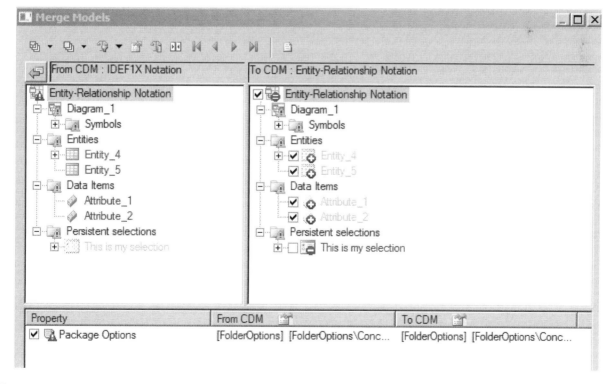

"Generating Models and Model Objects" (Core Features Guide)

Generating Model Objects

You can extend the inter-model generation capabilities provided by PowerDesigner by defining your own object generation commands. You can define as many commands as you want, and generate any of your model's objects as any kind of objects in any other model. The generated objects are linked to the original objects and can be resynchronized at any time.

This feature is available by selecting `Generate Objects` on the `Tools` menu. It's useful for ad-hoc generation of objects, but you should make sure there isn't another way of achieving the same objective before you use it.

❷ "Generating Model Objects" (Core Features Guide)

Traceability Links

You can use traceability links to show any kind of relationship between two model objects (including between objects in different models)

Traceability links are under your control. You can add them in an object's property sheet (via the 'Traceability Links' tab), draw them on a diagram (using the *Link/Traceability Link* tool 🔗), or create them via a dependency matrix. You can categorize links by creating your own link types.

For example, let's suppose that we decide to add traceability links from a Dimensional model back to the original Relational model. Rather than using an unclassified link, we will create a new type of link specifically for this task.

To create the new Link Type, open the property sheet for an attribute; on the 'Traceability Links' tab, click the *Types and Grouping* tool, and then select 'New Link Type'. Type in 'Relational Source' and click <OK>.

The new Link Type will be created within a new model extension called Local Extensions, which you can see in the Browser.

Staying in the 'Traceability Links' tab, click on the '*Types and Grouping*' tool and select 'Group By Link Type'. A new sub-tab will appear, called 'Relational Source'. Now click on the '*Add Objects*' tool 🔲, and the 'Add Objects' window will appear. In the 'Model' selection box, select the model you want to link to, and then select an object or sub-object. Click on <OK> twice.

Congratulations, you have created a traceability link, and also created a model extension.

Figure 18.9 shows such a link, and the view of the same link from the Relational attribute, shown in the 'Dependencies' tab.

Figure 18.9 A traceability link

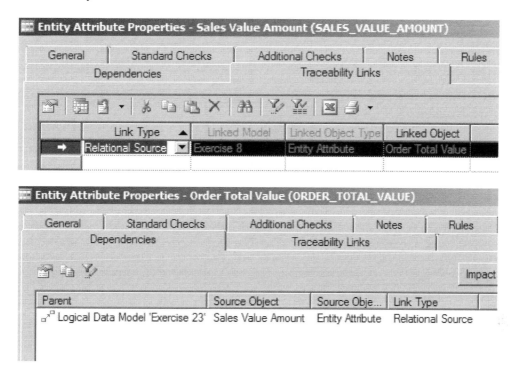

The list of columns has been customized in both of these property sheets, to include information that helps us understand the link. Refer back to "Object Lists" in Chapter 10. The *Link Type* property was included, to provide a drop-down list in the 'Traceability' tab. If you double-click an entry in either list, you will open the property window for the linked object.

Traceability Links have direction – each link has an outgoing connection and an incoming connection, illustrated in Figure 18.10.

Figure 18.10 Incoming and outgoing traceability links

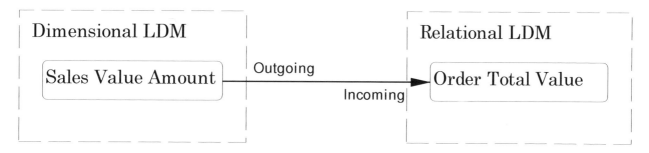

You will need to understand this distinction when creating reports or dependency matrices that contain traceability links. The link can be viewed from both ends, but it can only be created, edited or deleted in the object that has the outgoing connection, such as **Sales Value Amount** in the example above. You will need to bear this in mind when working out how best to manage traceability – you can't expect an analyst to create an outgoing connection in a model they can't update.

⊘ "Creating Traceability Links" (Core Features Guide)

The Mapping Editor

In PowerDesigner, mappings are designed to document the transfer of data between the database represented by two PDMs. In reality, they can be used to link any two data models to each other. Mappings between PDMs can be transformed into a data movement model.

The Mapping Editor is available on the Tools menu. You need to supply a name for the mapping, and choose a model to map from – this model will be treated as the source model in the mapping. You can create mappings via the 'Mapping' tab on an object, if you prefer, but the Mapping Editor gives you a visual display of the mappings. It also allows you to create a set of default mappings simply by finding objects in the two models that have the same name, and then linking them to each other. A sample Mapping Editor view is shown in Figure 18.11.

Figure 18.11 Sample Mapping Editor window

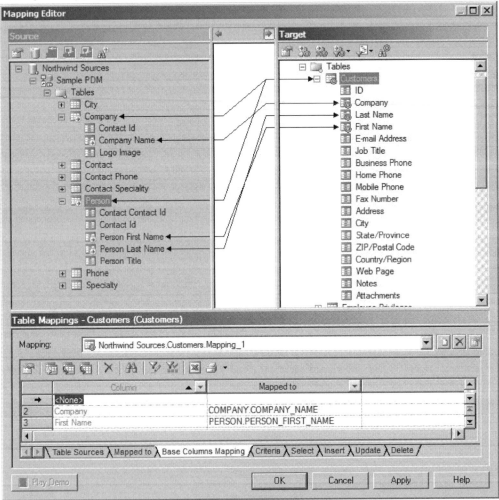

❷ "Linking and Synchronizing Models" (Core Features Guide)

❷ "Object Mappings (Core Features Guide)

Key Points

- Linking models and objects to each other is a key strength of PowerDesigner.

- Generation dependencies are key for data modelers.

- Model generation also includes model updates.

- Don't forget to preserve modifications during an update.

- Save the generation dependencies.

- Traceability links are under your control.

- Mappings can be complex things.

We have covered a lot of material so far. Assuming you have completed all of the Exercises and 'Your Turn' material, you have already rehearsed the PowerDesigner skills you need.

In Chapter 19, we describe a coordinated set of tasks – complete these tasks, and you will have rehearsed it all again, this time in a more coordinated fashion. You will have built your own data model pyramid.

Practice, and practice
Create, generate, export
Follow all the steps

In this chapter there is a set of tasks for you to follow – complete these tasks, and you will have built your own data model pyramid. Please remember that this chapter is intended to provide practice using PowerDesigner, it is not a lesson in database design!

Your Tasks

You will start from a blank canvas, and create four models and two files of SQL. Figure 19.1 shows the steps you will take to create the models. Each solid line represents a use of the model generation feature to create or update a model.

Figure 19.1 Steps

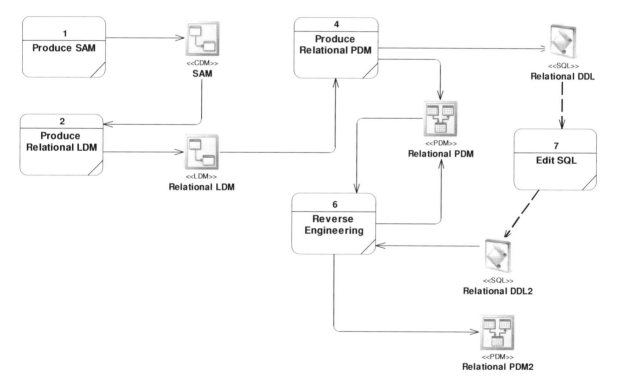

In this chapter, we describe what you need to do, we do not tell you how to do it. We suggest you create a special project, but that is up to you. We also suggest that you attach the following model extensions to all your models:

- Excel Import
- Relationship Assertion with Plural Entity Names.

To completely match the appearance of the target models, you will need to adjust model options and display preferences.

Produce Subject Area Model

Figure 19.2 is your objective, a simple Subject Area Model with six entities, two of which are subtypes of **Contact**.

Figure 19.2 Your subject area model

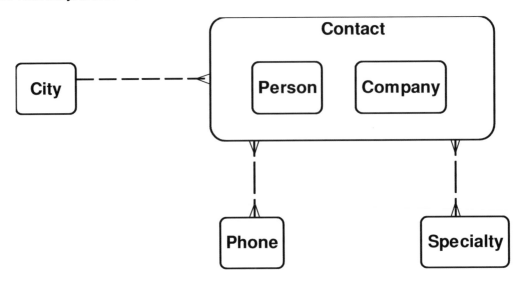

Describe the entities yourself, and create some basic documentation from the model in the form of a report. When you create the report, use the 'Standard Conceptual report' template.

Produce Relational LDM

Generate the LDM from your Subject Area Model, making sure you keep the generation dependencies. Add domains, attributes, and identifiers, and convert the many-to-many relationships into entities. Make sure you describe all the entities and attributes.

Figure 19.3 shows your target model, split across two separate images. The images are from the same PowerDesigner diagram – note the use of graphical synonyms for the **Contact** entity, allowing us to separate the inheritance hierarchy from the rest of the model.

Table 19.1 contains details of the domains you need to complete – copy these into an Excel spreadsheet, and import them into your model.

Use a dependency matrix to link attributes to domains.

Create a second diagram with an alternative view of the model. Use the display preferences and auto-layout feature to mimic the diagram shown in Figure 19.4.

Figure 19.3 The relational LDM

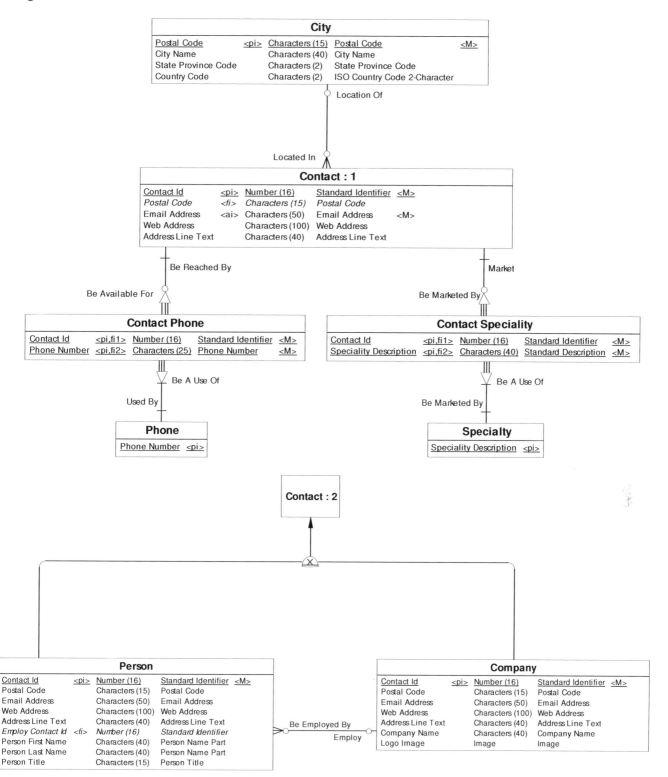

Table 19.1 LDM Domains

Name	Data Type	Length
Address Line Text	Characters (40)	40
City Name	Characters (40)	40
Company Name	Characters (40)	40
Email Address	Characters (50)	50
Image	Image	
ISO Country Code 2-Character	Characters (2)	2
Person Name Part	Characters (40)	40
Person Title	Characters (15)	15
Phone Number	Characters (25)	25
Postal Code	Characters (15)	15
Standard Description	Characters (40)	40
Standard Identifier	Number (16)	16
State Province Code	Characters (2)	2
Web Address	Characters (100)	100

Figure 19.4 An alternative view

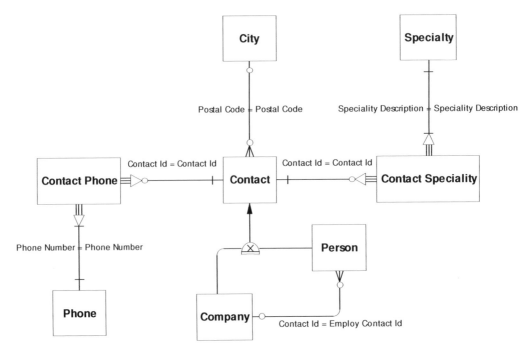

Produce Relational PDM

There will be two iterations in this process. For the first iteration, create the model shown in Figure 19.5. Take a close look at Figure 19.5 before you generate the PDM, as you will need to adjust the generation options in the LDM.

Generate the PDM from your LDM, making sure you keep the generation dependencies.

Figure 19.5 Target PDM – 1ˢᵗ iteration

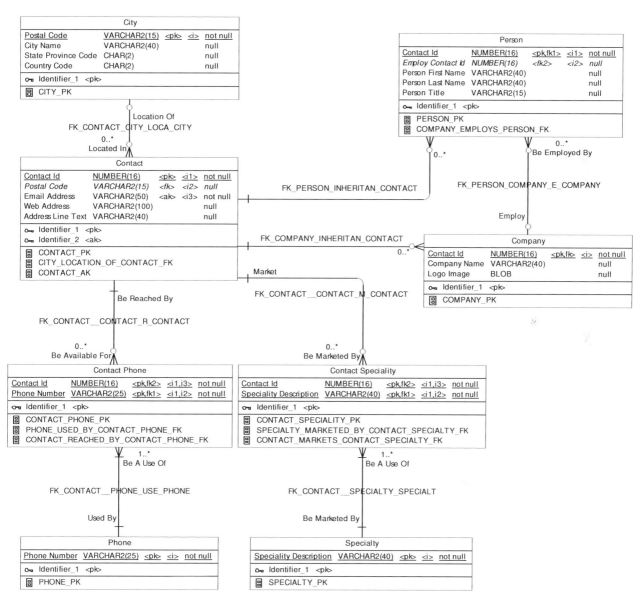

In the second iteration, adjust the generation options for the inheritance in the LDM, then re-generate the PDM. Figure 19.6 shows the required results for the supertype and subtypes this time.

Figure 19.6 2nd iteration – where the differences lie

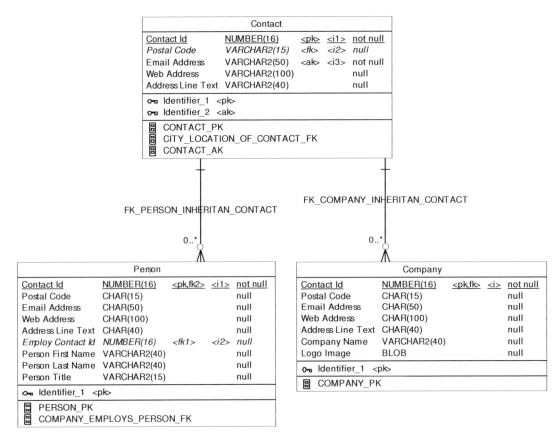

Create a new diagram containing the tables shown in Figure 19.7, and then create the view that is also shown in the diagram, using the wizard on the `Tools` menu. Create the dashed lines shown on Figure 19.7 by drawing traceability links from the view to each table.

Figure 19.7 The view

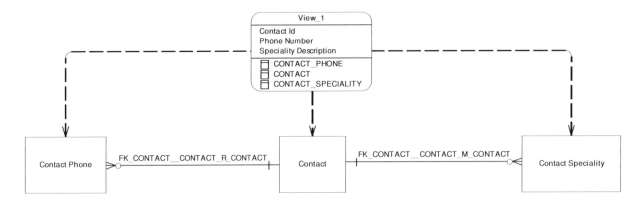

Now it's time to do some denormalization. Collapse the **Person** and **Company** tables into **Contact**, making sure to keep the original tables. Set the *Generate* property to 'False' in the original tables, and delete the references that connect the original tables to the rest of the model. Use column denormalization to replicate the columns shown in the diagram in **bold** type. There are also other changes you need to make – check the diagram carefully.

Figure 19.8 The denormalized model

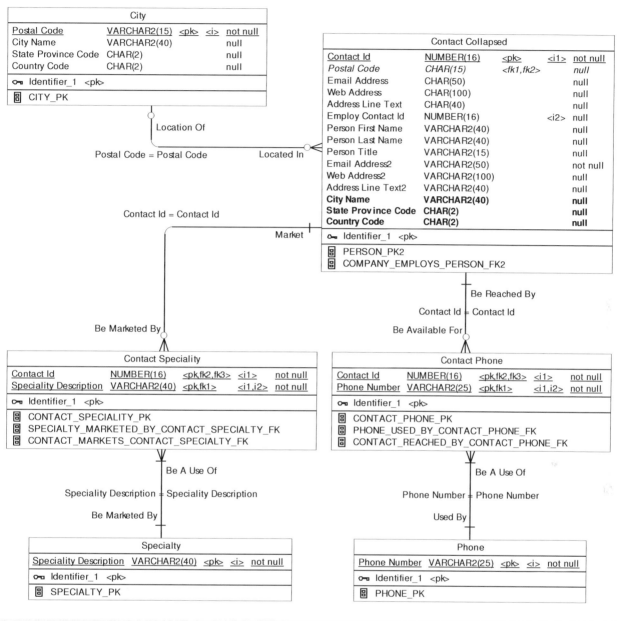

Generate a SQL File

Generate a single file of SQL from the PDM.

Reverse Engineering

Create a new PDM by reverse-engineering from the SQL file. Make some changes to the new model, then save the model and compare it to the original PDM. Your new model will look something like Figure 19.8. How closely it matches will depend on the changes you made to the SQL.

A good way to visualize the similarities and differences is to run the Mapping Editor, If you create the default mappings, the result will be similar to Figure 19.9. Make sure you keep the mappings.

Figure 19.9 Really close mappings

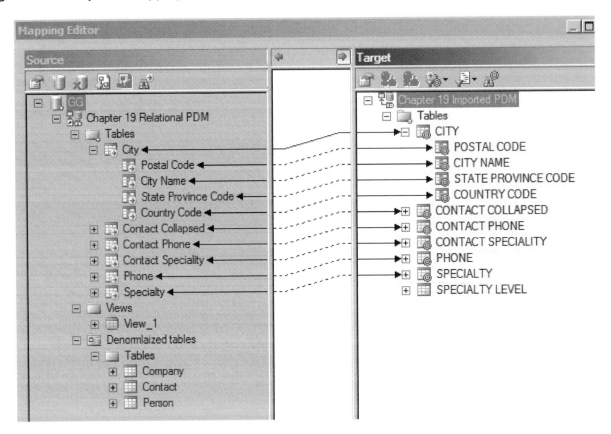

You've reached the end of this exercise, but not the end of the book.

Take time to flesh out the models with descriptions, use the Excel Import to provide comments for your tables and columns, and create list reports and matrices. Practice, and then practice some more.

Key Points

- The chapter leads you through a top-down approach. You're likely to use a combination of top-down and bottom-up in the real world.

- Dependency matrices and Excel Imports can reduce the time it takes to create a model.

- Use different diagrams to present to different audiences.

- Use graphical synonyms to your advantage.

By now, you know the important role data modeling plays in application development, you know the components of a data model, and you know the six different types of data models. Now that we have all this data modeling knowledge, how can we improve the quality of our data modeling deliverables? Section VI focuses on additional PowerDesigner features (some of which have already been introduced) that improve life for data modelers.

Chapter 20 describes some tasty treats for the discerning data modeler, and discusses the lineage of data elements.

Chapter 21 covers straight forward methods for importing and exporting metadata.

Chapter 22 provides an overview of the Data Model Scorecard and cross-references it to key PowerDesigner features.

Chapter 23 discusses general PowerDesigner features that are useful to data modelers for collaboration and standardization, linking with Business Analysis, and Impact and Lineage Analysis.

Manage the whole chain
Glossary and Library
Names and Codes matter

In earlier chapters, we described the core data modeling features of PowerDesigner. In this chapter, we tempt you with features for the mature, discerning, modeler.

Distribution of Reference Models

A common issue in any organization is the creation and distribution of reference models, the models we want everybody to take notice of, such as a data dictionary, a PDM containing standard domains, or any model containing objects to share, reference, or reuse. They don't even have to be PowerDesigner models, you can also share standard spreadsheets and document templates.

The PowerDesigner Library gives you a means of distributing those models. If you have a repository, you can deploy an enterprise library containing reference models, which are pushed to repository users, and appear in a special folder in the Browser's 'Local' tab. The Library models are held locally, and automatically updated whenever users connect to the repository. By default, the Library appears at the top of your workspace as a folder named '.Library'. The Library shown in Figure 20.1 includes three models and an Excel file.

Figure 20.1 The library

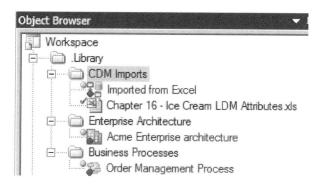

The models can be used in the same way as any other model, though update access is managed via the repository. If the Library contains models that your license doesn't support, you won't even see them.

You can rename your local library folder, move it in the Browser tree, or detach it from your workspace. To ensure that you have the very latest version of library models, select `Repository|Synchronize Library`. This will also add the Library to a workspace if it is not visible.

❷ "The Library" (Core Features Guide)

Deploying an Enterprise Glossary

We introduced you to the Glossary in Chapter 12, where we showed you how Terms in the Glossary can impact the names of objects. Terms aren't the only objects the Glossary can hold. Each of the Glossary objects are described in Table 20.1.

Table 20.1 Glossary Objects

Category	A container for grouping Terms, Rules, and other Categories. Categories allow you to construct a hierarchical structure for managing Terms and Rules. See sample hierarchy in Figure 20.2.
Term	A word or phrase that forms part of a controlled vocabulary. If auto-completion of object names is enabled in a model, Terms are suggested from the Glossary as you type the name of an Object.
Synonym	A word or phrase that means the same as a Term, but is not approved for use. If auto-completion of object names is enabled in a model, when you type a synonym into an object name the relevant Term is suggested, instead.
Business Rule	The Glossary allows you to share common business rules across all models.
Reports	The standard Report Editor is used to create reports to extract information from the Glossary.
Extensions	If you add your own properties to objects in the Glossary, they are stored as an Extension.
Excel Imports	If you use the Excel Import feature to import into your Glossary, the details of the import are recorded in the Glossary, allowing you to re-run the import in the future, and also providing a path to the source of definitions.

The Glossary appears in its own pane in the Browser window, and has two views. The *Filter* view lets you dynamically filter a flat list of Glossary terms, and the *Category* view allows you to construct or display a hierarchy of Categories, together with all other Glossary objects. A sample *Category* view is shown in Figure 20.2.

In this Glossary, we have one high-level Category 'Business Terms', which has three child Categories, and one grand-child Category. There are a number of Terms within the Categories, and two of them (**Division** and **Cone**) have synonyms.

We also have two Business Rules, a Glossary Report, and an Extension. The presence of the Extension implies that we have customized the properties of at least one Glossary object type.

Behind the scenes here, we also have relationships between Terms, between Terms and Business Rules, and between Categories and Business Rules. The best way to see these relationships is to generate a report to a web browser, or to use the Repository Portal.

Figure 20.2 Glossary category view

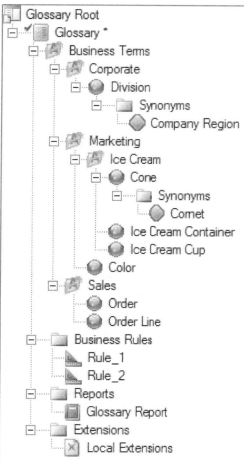

You can create a new Glossary very quickly by importing Terms, etc. from existing models. If you right-click the name of the Glossary in the Browser (or press <F4>), you can check the contents using the standard model check feature.

Just like any other type of object, you can run impact and lineage analysis for objects in the Glossary.

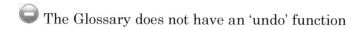 The Glossary does not have an 'undo' function

Creating a Glossary From Existing Documentation

Right-click the Glossary entry in the Browser, and you'll see several options for loading a Glossary from existing documentation, which could be an existing model, an Excel file, or a Glossary in another repository. (See Figure 20.3.)

Figure 20.3 Glossary import options

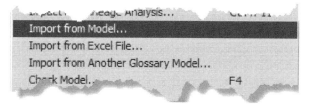

If you choose to import from an existing PowerDesigner model, you can select the kind of object whose names you want to import as glossary terms and, optionally, a property of the object to specify the category of the imported term.

Creating an Object in the Glossary

You create objects in the Glossary using all the standard techniques, bar one – you cannot open a list of objects from the Model menu, because there is no Model menu. Instead, open a list of objects by right-clicking the Glossary entry in the Browser, select List Of, and then the required object type.

How can we use the Glossary?

The words used in the names of Business Rules are just as likely to be used in the names of Entities and Attributes. It is important to be consistent in your terminology: avoid the use of synonyms, and direct modelers to the correct words to use in names. There should be a great deal of commonality in the vocabulary used in object names; the question is, how can we manage that vocabulary?

The PowerDesigner Glossary allows you to document your enterprise vocabulary: you can limit it to critical common terminology, or define all the words modelers can use in their object names. Realistically, most of us would aim for somewhere in between.

You could use the Glossary as a simple dictionary of terms and synonyms, and allow non-modelers to update it using the 'Composer' license. However, the power of the Glossary really comes into play when you use it as part of your name management process, which we demonstrated in Chapter 12.

Linking the Glossary to Existing Objects

There are only two ways to link existing objects to terms in the Glossary:

- Add a traceability link to each object, via the 'Traceability' tab or via dependency matrix
- Manually rename each object – this will cause PowerDesigner to suggest terms from the Glossary.

Managing Names and Codes

We first talked about object names and codes in Chapter 10. As you generate a chain of data models, the object names are passed from object to object. In each model, the code is derived from the name, according to the rules set in the naming conventions. You access the naming conventions via the 'Model Options'. You can set conventions for the whole model, as well as for individual types of objects. Change the conventions here, click <OK>, and object names and codes are automatically changed to reflect the changes you've made on all of the tabs. PowerDesigner refers to this as 'mirroring'.

Use the 'Naming Template' options to save settings in a file, or to import previously saved settings. You can save settings in a template model, which modelers use when creating new models. You can also create and share user profiles containing standard model options.

There are four tabs for Naming Conventions, but we only need to show you two tabs to explain them to you. The 'Name' and 'Code' tabs are identical, and allow you to set the convention for the format of names and codes.

Figure 20.4 The 'Name' tab

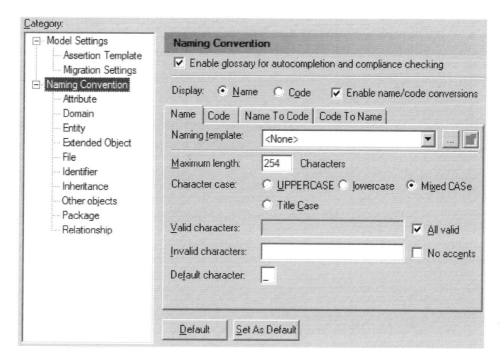

Figure 20.4 shows the 'Name' tab, and the common options above the four tabs. You have seen some of these common options before. They allow you to enable Glossary checking, and choose what to display (names or codes) on diagram symbols. There is also a vital check box that tells PowerDesigner to apply whatever conversions you specify in the 'Name To Code' and 'Code To Name' tabs.

The 'Name' tab provides straightforward options for the format of object names.

The 'Name To Code' tab, shown in Figure 20.5, allows you to control how codes are derived from names. The default conversion script shown will replace spaces with underscores. You can alter the script to carry out more complex transformations, including adding prefixes or suffixes to codes. If your naming standards require you to replace specific strings encountered in the name when you derive the code, then you can specify a conversion table to use. For example, you may wish to replace the word 'Customer' with 'Cust'. In Figure 20.5, we have chosen to use the names and codes in the Glossary as our conversion table.

If you change the conversion script or conversion table settings and want to apply them immediately, you must select 'Enable name/code conversions' and 'Apply name to code conversion'. The radio buttons allow you to ignore objects where you have deliberately desynchronized the name-code mirroring, perhaps by typing in your own code, or to apply the rules to all objects.

Figure 20.5 The Name To Code tab

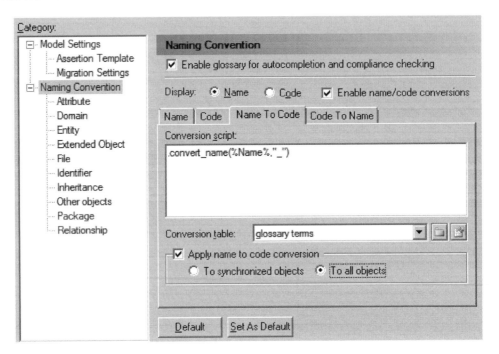

The 'Code To Name' tab is almost the same. It's useful when you reverse-engineer a database into a PDM, and you want to convert the object codes back into 'real names', by applying abbreviation standards in reverse. This can only be run against all objects in your new model.

Model Generation

When you generate a new model, you can alter the model options before the new model is created – this is the best time to set the model's naming standards.

The Lineage of Data Elements

When you create a chain of data models, data elements are transferred from model to model. The names and codes of the data elements are automatically subjected to the naming conventions in each model. In addition, you need to define standards for the 'content' of data elements. Those standards will be an integral part of your approach to managing domains, data items, and data elements. In this section, we describe one possible approach, and use it to illustrate the potential impact on object names.

The following three figures illustrate some sample data elements, showing how they would be integrated, where they may reference other objects, and the Glossary Terms required to completely support the names.

First, Figure 20.6 shows six Domains that are referenced by a total of 10 Data Items in a CDM. One of the Data Items also references a Business Rule, which may be held locally in the model, or held in the Glossary.

There are three categories of domain in use here; which ones you use in your organization will depend on your local standards. The first three, **Date**, **Email Address,** and **Identifier**, fall into the first category, simple format domains that can apply to many attributes in many entities. **Order Line Status Code** and **Order Status Code** fall into the second category - domains that can only be referenced by one Data Item because they are used to manage the allowed values for that Data Item. They may, of course, be referenced by copies of the Data Item in other data models, or by Attributes and Columns. The remaining Domain, **Person Name**, is a combination of the two. Its purpose is to define the format of names, but only those names that describe a Person.

Figure 20.6 Domains and business rules referenced by data items

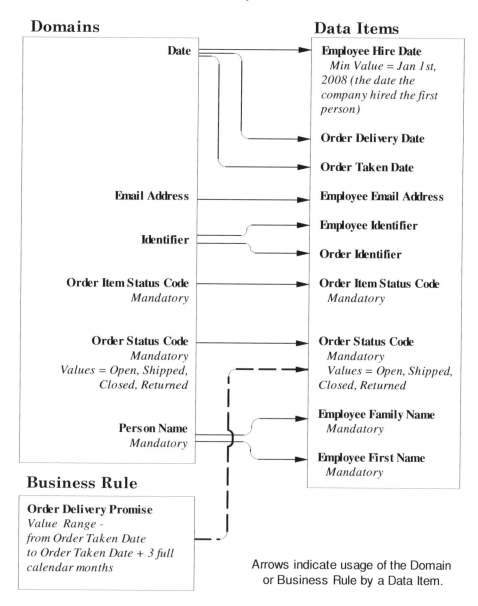

Arrows indicate usage of the Domain or Business Rule by a Data Item.

Figure 20.7 takes the lineage of the first of our Data Items, **Employee Hire Date**, further; it shows the CDM Attribute that references the Data Item, and the LDM Attribute and Column that have been generated from the CDM Attribute. Notice that the names of the LDM Attribute and Column, while they obviously have the same meaning, are not identical to the name of the Data Item.

Figure 20.7 The lineage of a column

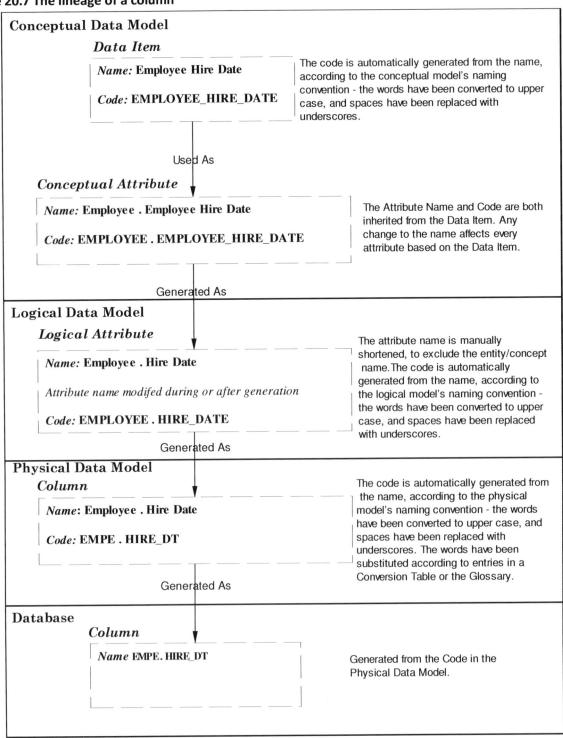

We do not need to include the word 'Employee' in the name of our LDM attribute; we know that it applies to an Employee because it is an Attribute of the Employee Entity – it helps us to describe an Employee. The same logic is true for the column in the database table. In the LDM, we had to manually change the name of the Attribute; you could probably write a script to handle most of this conversion, stripping the entity name from the start of each attribute name.

Figure 20.7 demonstrates the name-code mirroring – as the name changes, so does the code. It is only in the PDM where the mirroring process has used a conversion table to replace words. You could also apply this conversion table in higher level models, which has the advantage of making the database names (in the form of codes) more visible in higher-level models. It does require more effort to ensure consistency – you need to distribute the conversion table to more modelers and make sure they apply the same version to all models. The easiest way to do this is to use the Glossary. To manage the names of all the Data Elements in our sample, we would need to define the Terms shown in Figure 20.8.

Figure 20.8 Glossary terms required

Business Vocabulary
    Key Concepts
       • Address
       • Client
          Synonym - Customer
       • Employee
       • Order
       • Promise
 	
    Key Actions
       • Delivery
       • Employee Hire
          Synonym - Employee Start
	Naming Approach
	    Class Words
	       • Code
	       • Count
	       • Date
	       • Identifier
	       • Name
	       • Quantity
	       • Value
	
	    Information Words
	       • State
	       • Status

In this example, we have two broad categories of Terms, 'Business Vocabulary' and 'Naming Approach'; each is used for a different reason, and will have different ownership. The business vocabulary will be defined by data owners, and the words used in the naming approach will form part of the organization's data modeling standards.

Test Data

So you have a PDM and a development database, and you need to populate the database with test data – a common scenario. PowerDesigner can generate data into the database for you by using data it generates, data read from another database, or data specified by you in PowerDesigner or an external file.

To make use of this feature, you need to create Test Data Profiles and link them to domains (on the 'General' tab) or database columns (on the 'Detail' tab).

On the `Database` menu, choose `Generate Test Data`. Here you can specify more options, then generate data in the database.

Multidimensional Diagrams

A multidimensional data diagram provides a graphical view of your data mart or data warehouse database, and helps you identify its facts, cubes, and dimensions.

❷ "Multidimensional Diagrams" (Data Modeling)

Generating Extraction Scripts

You can model operational and data warehouse data structures in PDMs, and specify mappings between the operational data sources and the data warehouse to generate extraction scripts to populate the data warehouse with operational data.

In the Physical Diagram, select `Database|Generate Extraction Script` to open the Extraction Script Generation dialog box.

❷ "Generating Extraction Scripts" (Data Modeling)

Data Movement Modeling

A data movement model (DMM) provides a global view of the movement of information in your organization. You can analyze and document where your data originates, where it moves to, and how it is transformed on the way, including replications and ETL. Depending on the technology you use, you may also be able to generate and reverse-engineer data replications. If you have defined mappings between PDMs, you can use the `Convert Mappings to ETL Wizard` on the `Tools` menu, to create data movements in the model.

Key Points

- Distribute reference models via the Library.

- Use the Glossary to standardize your vocabulary and share business rules.

- The Glossary is the best name conversion table you can have.

- Naming conventions apply to whole models, and can be overridden for selected object types.

- Generate Test Data directly into a database.

- Convert your PDM-PDM mappings into a Data Movement Model.

CHAPTER 21

How do we get information in and out of PowerDesigner?

Information In
Models, Communication
Information Out

Integration with associated activities is key to the success of data modeling. This integration is achieved within PowerDesigner by the broad range of modeling techniques supported, which reduces the need for integration with external tools. The integration features are summarized in Table 21.1.

Table 21.1 PowerDesigner integration features

Capability	Supported by
Importing from Spreadsheets	Excel Import Extension - *See this chapter*
Exporting to Spreadsheets	*See this chapter*
Exporting via the Clipboard	*See this chapter*
Exporting Diagram Images	*See Chapter 11*
Reverse-engineering external artifacts	Reverse Engineering - *see Chapter 18* Model comparison - *see Chapter 23* Excel Import Extension – *see this chapter*
Generating external artifacts	Model Generation - *see Chapter 18* Model comparison - *see Chapter 23*
Importing from Word Documents	Creating Requirements Model from a Word document - *See this chapter*
Importing from existing data models	Model import – *See this chapter*
Exporting models in other formats	Supported by third-party tool interfaces – see 'Model Import', below
Generating test data	*See Chapter 20*
Publication via Microsoft Office format documents	Reporting - *See this chapter*
Publication via HTML extracts	Reporting - *See this chapter*
Web access to repository	Repository Portal - *See Chapter 23*

See Figure 25.1 for an alternative view of PowerDesigner's external dependencies, and some of the internal links.

The straightforward methods for importing and exporting content are described below.

Model Import

PowerDesigner can import models from a number of other tools. None of these imports require the original tool to be installed, and they all create new PowerDesigner models. The following types of models are supported:

CA ERwin (.erx or .xml)	*Data Models*
XML Metadata Interchange (XMI)	*Object-oriented models*
IBM Rational Rose	*Object-oriented models*
SIMUL8	*Process simulation*
Legacy PowerDesigner models	*Various*

You'll find the import options under `Import,` on the `File` menu.

An ERwin XML format file can contain a Logical Data Model and/or a Physical Data Model; during the import, you can choose to create a CDM, LDM, and/or a PDM. You can even import several ERwin files at the same time, following the same approach.

If you're not an ERwin user, the best approach is to use your existing tool to save your models in PowerDesigner or ERwin XML format. If you have a lot of models to migrate, or you have to maintain two or more tools concurrently, you should investigate the 'point-to-point' tool interfaces supplied by Reischmann Informatik[10]. Some of their interfaces also transform models, such as converting UML class models into PowerDesigner Conceptual or Logical data models.

   "Migrating from ERwin to PowerDesigner" (Data Modeling)

XMI format files can be imported, but implementation of the XMI standard[11] is notoriously inconsistent, so it may or may not work for you.

---

[10] See http://www.reischmann.com

[11] The XML Metadata Interchange standard designed to assist with integrating tools, repositories, applications, and data warehouses – see http://www.omg.org/spec/XMI/.

Importing Requirements

PowerDesigner can import the structure and contents of a Word document into a Requirements model. You can use a Requirements model to represent any structured document (e.g. functional specification, test plan, business goals, etc.) and import and export hierarchies of requirements as Microsoft Word documents. Take a look under `Import` on the `File` menu.

Once you have agreed on your requirements, take them one stage further by generating other objects (such as conceptual entities) from them.

Excel Export

PowerDesigner allows you to export parts of your models into Microsoft Excel format files. Just click on the *Export to Excel* tool ▣, available within several PowerDesigner features:

- Object Lists
- Property Sheets
- List reports
- Dependency Matrices

Excel Import

The Excel Import extension allows you to launch a wizard that guides you through mapping tables of objects to be modeled from Excel files (v2003 and higher) to PowerDesigner objects and properties, and to import the contents of the files into your model.

You can import any number of different types of objects from a single Excel file, so long as they can all be imported into a single type of model. Each worksheet of the Excel file must contain only one type of object. Each row in a table represents one object to import, and each column represents one property (an attribute or collection of associated objects) of the object.

You can create a new model by importing objects from an Excel file, or import your objects into an existing model.

To create a new model from an Excel file, select `File|Import|Excel File`. Specify the kind of model you want to create in the New Model dialog, and then click <OK>. Now follow the steps in the wizard. The first step is shown in Figure 21.1.

To import objects into an existing model, you must have the Excel Import extension in your model. Instructions for doing this are in "Attaching Extensions to an Existing Model", in Chapter 23).

Once the model has the extension attached, you just need to right-click the model in the Browser and select `Import Excel File`. Now follow the steps in the Wizard.

Figure 21.1 Excel import wizard step 1

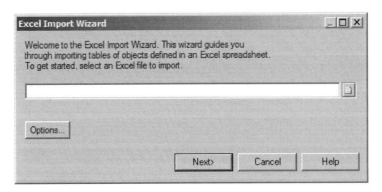

The specification for the Excel Import will be saved as an object in your model, with the same name as the Excel import file, and can be copied to or generated for another model of the same type. Like any other object, an Excel Import object has a contextual menu that allows you to rerun the import, change the mappings, or change the options. If the structure of the Excel file has changed since the last import, you will need to change the mappings.

To reference a sub-object or composite object in an Excel Import, you need to provide a qualified name so that PowerDesigner can locate the object you're referring to, or provide the name of the parent object in a separate column. Table 21.2 provides some examples. This approach is also useful in another way – if you have a spreadsheet containing attributes, the Excel Import will create new entities if you qualify the attributes, as in the first example in Table 21.2.

Table 21.2 Examples of qualified names

Object Type	Example
Entity.Attribute	`Class.Class Full Name`

Package (referenced by any object)	▢ HR
	  ▢ Benefits
	    ▢ Pension
	      ▢ Pension Subject Area ERD
	      ▢ Entities
	        ▢ Pension Type
	
	The entity *Pension Type* is owned by the *Pension* package, which is owned by the *Benefits* package, which is owned, in turn, by the *HR* package, so the full reference for the entity is:
	
	        `"HR.Benefits.Pension.Pension Type"`
	
	The full reference for the *Pension Type Code* attribute for this entity would be:
	
	    `"HR.Benefits.Pension.Pension Type.Pension Type Code"`

The default separator for qualified names is '**.**'. You can change this within the *Options* for the Excel import.

- "Importing Objects from Excel Files" (Core Features Guide)
- "Preparing Your Excel File for Import" (Core Features Guide)

Exporting and Importing Lists of Values

Data items, domains, attributes, and columns all have a *List of Values* property, where you specify the allowed values for the data. This property may look like a list of sub-objects, but values are not sub-objects, so you cannot export and import values in the way you might think.

You cannot display the *List of Values* property in a list of objects or a list report, but you can export the property one object at a time, via the *Export to Excel* tool ⊠ in the *List of Values* property. The only other way to export them is via a report.

There are two ways of importing values:

1. Pasting values and labels from the Windows clipboard.
2. Importing values (but not labels) via the Excel Import wizard – all the values have to be in a single cell, as illustrated in Figure 21.2. To create a new line inside a cell, press <Alt+Enter>.

Figure 21.2 Formatting Excel values

Parent	Name	List of Values
Color	Color Code	01
		02
		03
		04

Using Excel Import to Create Surrogate Keys

By default, tables in the PDM have the same primary key as the equivalent entities in the LDM. If you want to replace some or all of these with surrogate keys, here's a simple guide:

1. Using a list of Keys (from the Model menu), remove the *primary* designation of the existing keys. If you have many Keys to change, select all the rows you want to change, then click on the 'P' column for any entry. Every row will then change. When you change the *primary* designation, the underlying Index will also change, and the constraint name will be updated.
2. Create an Excel spreadsheet containing the new columns, and set the *Primary* property to 'True'. When you import this using the Excel Import Wizard, PowerDesigner will automatically create the required Keys and Indexes. Use the format shown in Figure 21.3 to import the new columns and keys.

Figure 21.3 Importing new identifiers

Table	Column Name	Mandatory
Color	Color Key	X
Ice Cream Container	Ice Cream Container Key	X
Order	Order Key	X

▸ ▸| Table.Column / Table.Key / ⊠

Figure 21 Surrogate keys.xlsx:1

B	C	D
Identifier Name	**Primary**	**Columns**
Color Primary	X	Color.Color Key
Ice Cream Container Primary	X	Ice Cream Container.Ice Cream Container Key
Order Primary	X	Order.Order Number,Order.Order Placed Key

◂ ▸ ▸| Table.Key / ⊠

Exporting via the Clipboard

The Edit menu and keyboard shortcuts allow you to copy symbols to the Windows Clipboard. If you paste the Clipboard contents into an external application such as a word processor, spreadsheet, or image editor, you are effectively exporting part of the contents of the model.

🌐 "Copying and Pasting Objects" (Core Features Guide)

Reporting

PowerDesigner provides three ways of creating report definitions, which you can use to provide documentation from your models in various output formats.

Report

Reports document the contents of a model, listing all or a selection of its objects, and showing how they are associated with one another. Reports are listed in the Browser within the Reports folder beneath their parent model, and saved with the model.

To create a Report, right-click the model name in the Browser, select New, and then Report. Give your report a name, choose the language you want for the headings, etc., and the template you want to use, if any. The Report Editor opens as a new tab in the model, and gives you complete control over the content and format of your report.

Figure 21.4 shows the Report Editor, containing a report based upon the 'Full LDM Report' template.

You can also create a blank report from the List of Reports, open it in the Report Editor, and build it using Report Items.

To change the content of the report title page and set the RTF or HTML layout preferences, open the property sheet for the model. If you need to add extra sections to the report, do that here as well.

The output of reports can be generated as HTML or RTF files. Once a report has been created, you can generate it by right-clicking the report name in the Browser; you don't need to open the Report Editor.

You can save a report as a template so that it can be used by other modelers. You can also copy reports between models of the same type.

Figure 21.4 The report editor

List Report

A List Report is very similar to a list of objects – it documents a single object type within a model, and is displayed as a customizable list with columns and rows that you can filter, as necessary. What makes a List Report different is that it is saved in the model, and can be exchanged between models of the same type. They are listed in the Browser within the 'List Reports' folder.

You can create snapshots (called result sets) of a List Report to keep a history of its execution in your model. In effect, they are snapshots of your model. Result sets are listed in the Browser beneath their parent List Report, and are saved with the model. Result sets can contain information about objects that no longer exist in the model.

The content of a List Report can be exported in various formats: CSV, RTF, HTML, or XML. Launch the List Report Wizard by selecting `Report|List Report Wizard`, and select the type of object for which you want to create the report.

You can create List Reports for objects and sub-objects, such as attributes.

To create a List Report, right-click the model name in the Browser, select 'New', and 'List Report'. Figure 21.5 shows the content of a List Report containing the description and generation origin of all of the entities in a model.

You can see that the 'Content' tab looks like a customized List of Objects, but you can have many List Reports showing different entities, and you can save the results as result sets. List Reports are objects in a model, so you can copy them (including any existing result sets) between models of the same type.

Figure 21.5 A List Report

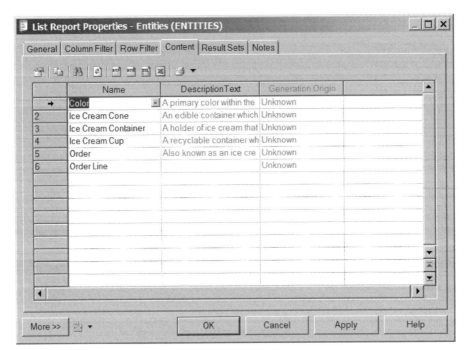

You can edit and access the objects in the List Report in the same ways as you can in a List of Objects.

☻ "Creating a List Report" (Custom Features Guide)

Multi-Model Report

A Multi-Model Report documents one or more models, and can help you to see, for example, the links from tables in a physical data model (PDM) to entities in a conceptual data model (CDM). The report is treated like a model, shown in the Browser as a top-level object, and saved as a file with the suffix ".mmr".

To create a Multi-Model Report, click on the 'New Model' button on the Main toolbar. For a 'normal' report, choose the language and template, and also choose one of the currently open models for content. The Report Editor is essentially the same as that of the standard single model report.

To change the content of the report title page and set the RTF or HTML layout preferences, open the property sheet for the model. If you need to add extra sections to the report, you can do that here, as well. To add a new model to a Multi-Model Report, create a new section via the property sheet.

"Reports" (Core Features Guide)

Exercise 22: Importing from Excel

Find the Excel file you created in Exercise 9 in Chapter 11. Use the Excel Import wizard to create a new Conceptual Data Model from the spreadsheet, call this model 'Exercise 22'. Compare the model to the model you created in Exercise 9.

Notes for the Excel Import:

- You can't import the *Modification Date* property
- The 'G' column can be imported as the *Generate* property

Exercise 23: Creating a List Report

In your 'Exercises' workspace, open one of your Logical Data Models. Create at least two List Reports containing entities, and one containing attributes. Sort the Entity Reports by the entity name, and the Attribute Report by a combination of the entity name and the attribute name. Note that the property containing the attribute name is just called 'Name'.

In at least one of your List Reports, filter the report to select objects where the Description is empty.

Key Points

- Import complete models using `File|Import` or reverse engineering.

- Import existing information from Microsoft Word documents (as a Requirements model) or from Microsoft Excel worksheets (as new models or updates to existing models).

- Third-party interfaces can be used to extend PowerDesigner's capabilities.

- Configure reports to suit your audience.

- Utilize the web portal – it provides direct access to models in your repository via a web browser.

Quality, correct
Requirements, complete and right
Take all into account

In this chapter, we will discuss the factors that influence the quality of your data models, and identify the ways in which PowerDesigner can help you to achieve and maintain the quality of your models. The PowerDesigner features we refer to are all explained elsewhere; we will guide you to the other parts of the book that are relevant.

A frequently overlooked aspect of data quality management is that of data model quality. We often build data models quickly, in the midst of a development project, and with the singular goal of database design. Yet the implications of those models are far-reaching and long-lasting. They affect the structure of implemented data, the ability to adapt to change, understanding of and communication about data, definition of data quality rules, and much more. In many ways, high-quality data begins with high-quality data models. A good data model can lead to a good application, and similarly, a bad data model can lead to a bad application.

There are three reasons why sound data design is a requirement for application success:

- **Leverage**. All application development, including interfaces, extracts, screen designs, and functionality are built upon the database design. The database design is built from the data model. Therefore, the data model can make or break an entire application. Once an application is built based on a good data model, it becomes easier to support and expand, leading to a long and stable application life.
- **Data quality**. The data model can enforce many rules that can dramatically improve data quality and catch many data errors before they are loaded into the application. There are other areas where the model can help with data quality, such as the definitions. Clear and concise definitions can help people make better decisions and identify issues before development begins.
- **'Big picture'**. Although a data model is usually built to support a particular application, the terminology and structures in the model need to have a level of consistency across the enterprise. This broader view is easier to achieve with sound modeling practices, such as using generic structures and consistent naming standards.

Data Model Scorecard

After reviewing hundreds of data models, Steve formalized the criteria he had been using into the Data Model Scorecard®. The Scorecard provides an objective way of measuring what is good or bad about a data model, using ten assessment categories. For data models in your organization to consistently achieve high scores; you will need more than good luck or a competent modeler. The quality of your data models will be influenced greatly by the level of business knowledge of your data modelers (and the people supporting the modelers), the presence and application of modeling standards of various types, the functionality and flexibility provided by your data modeling tools, and how the modeling processes integrate with other analysis, design, and development activities.

For a very detailed examination of the Data Model Scorecard, see Steve's Modeling Master Class Training Manual (Hoberman, 2011).

Scorecard Categories

In this section, we describe each of the Data Model Scorecard categories, and identify the support provided by PowerDesigner. Look in the index to track down further information.

- **Category 1 – How well do the characteristics of the model support the type of model?**

This category ensures that the type of model (subject area, logical, or physical – and then either relational or dimensional) has the appropriate level of detail. In general terms, the subject area model should contain a well-defined scope, the logical data model should be application-independent and represent a business solution, and the physical data model should be tuned for performance, security, and take into consideration hardware and software. The physical data model should represent a technical solution; a dimensional model is built when there is a need to play with numbers, while a relational model is built for everything else. PowerDesigner support for this category is shown in Table 22.1.

Table 22.1 PowerDesigner support for Data Model Scorecard Category 1

PowerDesigner Support
Full support for all 6 types of data models
Full support for over 60 database platforms and 3 XML Schema standards
Automated creation of associative entities to resolve many-to-many relationships.
Drag and drop to move or copy objects and sub-objects.
Ability to extend the types of information we can record against a model.
Denormalization capabilities in PDM.
Domains and Data Items

- **Category 2 – How well does the model capture the requirements?**

This is the "correctness" category. That is, we need to understand the content of what is being modeled. This can be the most difficult of all 10 categories to grade because we really need to understand how the business works and what they want from their application(s). If we are modeling a sales data mart, for example, we need to understand both how the invoicing process works in our company, and what reports and queries will be needed to answer key sales questions from the business.

We need to ensure that our model represents the data requirements, as the costs can be devastating if there is even a slight difference between what was required and what was delivered. Besides not delivering what was expected, there is the potential for the IT/business relationship to suffer. The model must support business expectations. PowerDesigner support for this category is shown in Table 22.2.

Table 22.2 PowerDesigner support for Data Model Scorecard Category 2

PowerDesigner Support
Full support for all 6 types of data model
Import of Requirements documents and linking to data models.
Import of analysis material from Excel directly into • Data Models • Glossary • Data Items
Reporting and web portal
Documenting Business Rules
Alternate Identifiers and Keys
Ability to extend the types of information we can record against a model.
Matrix Editor – e.g. show requirements not satisfied by entities
Mapping Editor
Export to Excel for editing and review
Cross-reference to Business Process Models

- **Category 3 – How complete is the model?**

This is the "completeness" category. This category checks for data model components that are not in the requirements, or requirements that are not represented on the model. If the scope of the model is greater than the requirements, we have a situation known as "scope creep", where we are planning on delivering more than what was originally required. This may not necessarily be a bad thing, as long as this additional scope has been factored into the project plan. If the model scope is less than the requirements, we will be leaving information out of the resulting application, usually leading to an enhancement or "Phase II" shortly after the application is in production. For completeness, we need to make sure the scope of the project and model match. PowerDesigner support for this category is shown in Table 22.3.

Table 22.3 PowerDesigner support for Data Model Scorecard Category 3

PowerDesigner Support
Model Checking
Matrix Editor – e.g. show requirements not satisfied by entities, or entities not mapped to requirements
List Reports - Ensure that all the necessary data model descriptive information is provided
Export to Excel for editing and review
List Reports – e.g. unreferenced Business Rules, or attributes using default format
Ability to extend the types of information we can record against a model.
Reporting and Portal
Model Comparison
Reverse Engineering

- **Category 4 – How structurally sound is the model?**

This is the "structure" category. This category validates the design practices employed in building the model to ensure we can eventually build a database from our data model. Good design practices include avoiding design errors such as having two data elements with the same exact name in the same entity, a null data element in a primary key, and/or partial key relationships[12]. Traditionally, when we review a data model, the violations we catch fall into this category, because we don't need to understand the content of the model to score this category. Even if the reviewer knows nothing about the industry or subject matter represented by the model, it can still be graded accurately in this category. PowerDesigner support for this category is shown in Table 22.4.

---

[12] A partial key relationship is when only part of the parent entity's primary key is brought over to the child entity as a foreign key. Good design practice ensures that when a relationship is created between two entities, the entire primary key from the parent entity on the 'one side' of the relationship line is copied over to the child entity on the 'many side' of the relationship line. A partial key relationship is when a subset of those data elements in the primary key are copied, instead of all of the data elements in the primary key.

Table 22.4 PowerDesigner support for Data Model Scorecard Category 4

PowerDesigner Support
Domains and Data Items
Model Checking
Model Generation options and tailoring
Auto-creation of Associative entities
Converting relationships into entities

- **Category 5 – How well does the model leverage generic structures?**

This is the "abstraction" category. In this category we confirm an appropriate use of generic structures on the model. One of the most powerful tools a data modeler has at her disposal is abstraction, the ability to increase the types of information a design can accommodate using generic concepts. Recall our earlier discussion on abstraction in Chapter 16. Going from **Customer Location** to a more generic **Location**, for example, allows the design to handle other types of locations, such as warehouses and distribution centers, more easily. Abstraction can be properly applied (or abused!) at the entity, relationship, and data element levels. PowerDesigner support for this category is shown in Table 22.5.

Table 22.5 PowerDesigner support for Data Model Scorecard Category 5

PowerDesigner Support
Reference Models
Mapping Editor – map generic models to less generic models
Subtypes
Denormalization and Normalization in the PDM
Business Rules

- **Category 6 – How well does the model follow naming standards?**

This is the "standards" category. Correct and consistent naming standards are extremely helpful for knowledge transfer and integration. New team members who are familiar with similar naming conventions on other projects will not need to take time to learn a new set of naming standards. Efforts to bring together information from multiple systems will be less painful if the data elements are named consistently across projects. This category focuses on naming standard structure, terms, and syntax. PowerDesigner support for this category is shown in Table 22.6. See Chapter 6 for a more detailed discussion of the importance of names and definitions.

Table 22.6 PowerDesigner support for Data Model Scorecard Category 6

PowerDesigner Support
Name to code conversion
Naming Conventions
Glossary
Naming Templates
PDM Naming Conventions
Domains and Data Items
Model Checking
List Reports
Excel Import
Ability to extend the types of information we can record against a model.

- **Category 7 – How well has the model been arranged for readability?**

In this category, we check whether the model is visually easy to follow. This question is definitely the least important category, as it is solely concerned with presentation. However, if your entities, data elements, and relationships are difficult to read, you may not accurately address the more important categories on the Scorecard. PowerDesigner support for this category is shown in Table 22.7.

Table 22.7 PowerDesigner support for Data Model Scorecard Category 7

PowerDesigner Support
Auto Layout
User Profiles
Display Preferences
Multiple Diagrams
Packages
Embellishing your diagrams
Resequencing attributes and columns
Aligning Symbols
Ability to extend the types of information we can record against a model.

- **Category 8 – How good are the definitions?**

This category deals with whether definitions are clear, complete, and correct.

- Clear – a reader can understand the meaning of a term by reading the definition only once.
- Complete – it is at the appropriate level of detail, and includes all the necessary components, such as derivations and examples.
- Correct – a definition that totally matches what the term means, and is consistent with the rest of the business.

PowerDesigner support for this category is shown in Table 22.8. See Chapter 6 for a more detailed discussion of the importance of names and definitions.

Table 22.8 PowerDesigner support for Data Model Scorecard Category 8

PowerDesigner Support
Accessing data from a database
Reporting and Portal
Export to Excel for review and revision

- **Category 9 – How consistent is the model with the enterprise?**

This is the "consistency" category. Does this model complement the "big picture"? This category ensures that the information is presented in a broad and consistent context, so that the organization uses one set of terminology and rules. The structures that appear in a data model should be consistent in terminology and usage with structures that appear in related data models, and ideally, with the enterprise data model, if one exists. In this way there will be consistency across projects.

An enterprise data model is a subject-oriented and integrated data model containing all of the data produced and consumed across an entire organization. Subject-oriented means that the concepts on a data model fit together as the CEO sees the company, as opposed to how individual functional or department heads see the company. There is one Customer entity, one Order entity, etc. Integration goes hand-in-hand with subject-orientation. Integration means that all of the data and rules in an organization are depicted once and fit together seamlessly. PowerDesigner support for this category is shown in Table 22.9.

Table 22.9 PowerDesigner support for Data Model Scorecard Category 9

PowerDesigner Support
Glossary
Reference Models
Mapping Editor
Model Generation
Excel Import
Model Compare and Merge
Ability to extend the types of information we can record against a model.

- **Category 10 – How well does the meta data match the data?**

This criterion ensures that the model and the actual data that will be stored within the resulting database or documents are consistent with each other; this reduces the risk of surprises during software development.

This might be very difficult to do early in a project's life cycle, but the earlier the better so you can avoid later surprises, which can be much more costly. PowerDesigner support for this category is shown in Table 22.10.

Table 22.10 PowerDesigner support for Data Model Scorecard Category 10

PowerDesigner Support
Displaying data from a database
Ability to extend the types of information we can record against a model.
Excel Import
Excel Export

Key Points

- The Data Model Scorecard® is a collection of ten categories for verifying the quality of a data model.

- Applying the Scorecard early in the modeling process saves rework later and increases the chances that your comments on the model will be incorporated.

- The Scorecard can be customized for a particular organization. Categories and point scores can be changed to make it work for you.

- The simplest techniques can provide invaluable support.

CHAPTER 23
What other components in PowerDesigner
can be leveraged by data modelers?

Repository
Portal, check, compare and merge
Assess the Impact

By any measure, the data modeling features in PowerDesigner are comprehensive - the data model pyramid is fully supported. Along the way, we have fully described some features, and briefly mentioned others. The purpose of this chapter is to provide more information about some of the latter group of features.

Collaboration and Standardization

Very few data modelers work in isolation, although sometimes it may feel like it. How many times have you wanted to replicate a colleague's diagram style, or share validation rules or other options, and felt that your modeling tool was part of the problem?

We all agree that we should establish and follow 'best practices'. To do that, we have to make it easier to follow 'best practices' than not. That means we should push facilities out to modelers, so they don't have to ask for them. In this section, we briefly describe how PowerDesigner helps.

Repository

If more than one person needs access to a model, then a repository is necessary. The repository provides a common location to store documents, models, and other files. The repository eliminates the necessity to locate the individual who might have a model locked, or who might have implemented some changes.

A repository supports collaborative modeling by managing versions of models, making them available for viewing, for comparison, and for impact analysis. A database administrator may need to implement a change in a physical model, but at the same time, a modeler needs to implement a change in the same model. Both people can extract a copy of the model from the repository, make changes, and then put the model back into the repository. Upon storing the model back into the repository, the differences are presented to the modeler consolidating the changes, through the standard PowerDesigner comparison feature (see later in this chapter).

The repository administrator can define users, groups, roles, and rights to manage access permissions for folders, projects, models, and packages in the repository. Depending on their rights, individual users can browse models in the repository and portal (see below), and check models in and out. They can also compare local and repository models, compare model versions, and carry out repository-based impact analysis. Via the web portal, users can carry out many of the same actions. Using the 'Composer' license, non-modelers can submit changes to certain text properties via the portal. Figure 23.1 shows a sample of the content of the repository as viewed in the Browser – note the Library and Glossary at the top of the list. The content of one model has been expanded in the same way as the content of local models can be expanded in the Browser.

Figure 23.1 Sample repository content

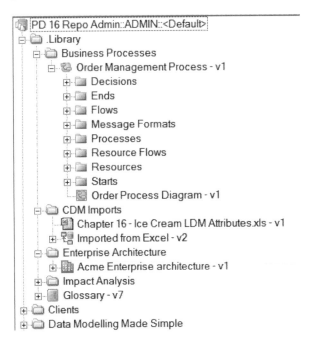

Sharing Resources

One of PowerDesigner's secret weapons is the concept of a resource file. There are several types of resource files, each of which has the ability to tailor PowerDesigner capabilities in a particular fashion. Via the `Tools` menu, you have access to all the shared resource files. Figure 23.2 shows you just how many different types of resource file are available. Each of the options shown takes you to a list of the resources available, where you can modify or delete them, or create your own. For example, Figure 23.3 shows the list of extensions available for PDMs.

Figure 23.2 Resource files available

Figure 23.3 DBMS list

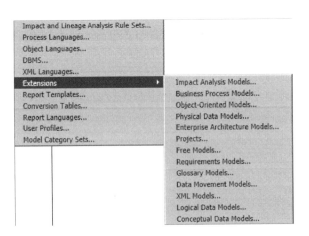

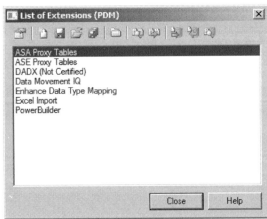

Some of the default actions taken when checking models into the repository can be changed. See the `Repository` section in `Tools|General Options`.

Deploying Shared Resource Files

You can store PowerDesigner resource files in the repository and automate their deployment to your team. Resource file sharing helps you ensure that all your teams are using the same DBMS or other target with any appropriate extensions.

❷ "Deploying Shared Resource Files" (Core Features Guide)

User Profiles

When setting your organization's modeling standards, you'll want to advise or enforce the use of general options, model options, display preferences, and various other options. In PowerDesigner, user profiles help you to standardize the look and feel of your models and to support standards. Profiles allow you to group options and preferences together for sharing and reuse across your organization. Various profiles are provided with PowerDesigner, or you can create your own.

User profiles can contain default values for:

- Display Preferences – to control the color, shape, size, etc. of your diagram symbols and the information that is displayed on them.
- Model Options – to control naming conventions, case sensitivity, notation, default values, etc.
- General Options – to control dialog preferences, environment variables, fonts, etc.
- Check Model options – to control which checks are applied, and which are errors, warnings, etc.
- Other options – such as the layout of toolbars and windows, favorite property tabs, default columns for object lists, etc.

To load a new profile, select `Tools|Apply User Profile`. The defaults, preferences, and options contained within the profile will overwrite the existing values for those defaults, preferences, and options, while leaving all others unchanged. Note that while general options take effect immediately, model options and display preferences only take effect when you create a new model. An administrator can prepare customized preference profiles, available to users on their first connection to the repository.

❷ "User Profiles" (Core Features Guide)

Project and Model Templates

You can save a project as a template. If you choose to apply this template when you create a new project, the new project will be a carbon copy of the original. This is useful if you want to provide a default folder structure or distribute standard models (the Library is an alternative). Where it really shines is when the project contains a modeling framework.

A framework can be used to provide guidance regarding modeling tasks to be undertaken in a project, and to provide shortcuts to models (and parts of models) that have been created. They also allow you to define standard actions, such as creating or editing a list of subject areas, or generating the next model in the chain. It's a simple workflow mechanism.

For example, Figure 23.4 shows the Federal Enterprise Architecture Framework (FEAF) framework supplied with PowerDesigner. The FEAF promotes shared development for US federal processes, interoperability, and sharing of information among US federal agencies and other governmental entities.

Figure 23.4 FEAF framework

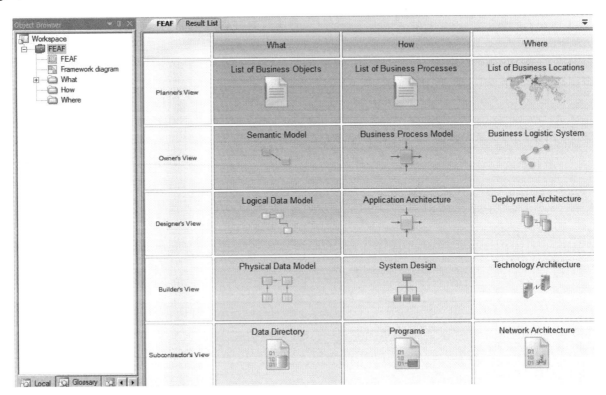

Model Templates

You can create model templates with predefined targets, extensions, and first diagrams to help guide users through model creation. You can organize these templates in categories and share them with your team, supplementing, or even replacing the default New Model dialog with these categories.

The simplest way to create a model template is to save a model in the default template folder.

❷ "Creating a Model Category Set" (Core Features Guide)

Linking with Business Analysis

Capturing Requirements

PowerDesigner has a model dedicated to capturing requirements – the requirements model. You can import requirements from the headings or table rows in a Microsoft Word document (see `Import|Word Document` on the `File` menu), and keep the document and the model synchronized. You can then link objects in other models back to the requirements in your model, and also generate new model objects from requirements. For example, you could generate business rules or conceptual entities from requirements. If your requirements change, you can examine the impact on your other models, and even re-generate some of the objects you created.

❷ "Enable links to requirements" (Core Features Guide)

Business Rules in PowerDesigner

Business Rules are available in every type of model, and can also be shared via the Glossary. Any object or sub-object can link to any number of business rules, regardless of the model in which the rules are defined (subject to your license and access rights). This may sound open-ended, but it is deliberately so. Business Rules provide a flexible mechanism for defining rules that can be linked to the objects they impact and the objects designed to implement the rules.

To find out more about business rules in general, we suggest that you read the 'Business Rules' chapter in (Ross, 2009).

❷ "Business Rules" (Core Features Guide)

Checking Spelling

The spelling checker is a PowerDesigner add-in that needs to be enabled.

1. Select `Tools|General Options` to open the General Options dialog box.
2. Click the 'Add-Ins' node in the Category view, and select the 'Spell Checker' checkbox.
3. Click <OK> to return to the model diagram.
4. Select `Tools|Spell Checking Options` to open the `Spell Checking Options` dialog box.

You can use the spelling checker at any time.

1. Right-click an object or model node in the Browser, or a diagram symbol, and then select `Spell Check` in the contextual menu.
   Spell checking starts. If an error is found, the Spell Checking dialog box opens.
2. For each error, you can:
   - Click <Change> to accept the suggested replacement word, or
   - Type your own replacement and click <Change>, or
   - Click <Change All> to apply the change to the entire object or model, or

- Click <Add> to add the word to your custom dictionary
- Click <Options...> to change the language, and include or exclude standard object properties.

To check the spelling in the whole model, right-click the diagram background and select `Spell Check`.

📖 "Spell Checking" (Core Features Guide)

Repository Portal

The Portal is effectively a gateway into the repository, allowing users (who do not need PowerDesigner licenses) to browse, search, and compare models, and carry out impact analysis. Coupled with the 'composer' license introduced in Version 16, selected non-modelers can edit comments, descriptions, and annotations.

When models are checked in to the repository, you have the option to make the diagrams available in the portal. By default, this is disabled, but you can change this behavior via `Tools|General|Options|Repository`.

📖 "The PowerDesigner Portal" (Core Features Guide)

Automation and Simplification of Common Tasks

Compare and Merge

The ability to compare models, and to update a model with selected changes, is key to the management of our data model pyramid. There are several scenarios where such a comparison is required:

- Generating into an existing model
- Checking an updated model into the repository
- Comparing versions of a model
- Comparing two models of the same type
- Merging two models of the same type.

A single comparison engine in PowerDesigner supports all of these scenarios. Figure 23.5 shows a sample dialog – in this case, it was invoked by updating a PDM from a LDM using `Generate Physical Data Model` on the `Tools` menu.

The Toolbar in Figure 23.5 is almost the same as you would see when comparing models – the compare toolbar does not have the two icons on the left, which allow you to select or de-select changes to apply.

The merge and compare dialogs show three panes. The top two panes show you the content of each model, which can be filtered (see below). The bottom pane shows the changes to the properties of a selected object. In Figure 23.5, there has been a change to the code of an object. The display has been filtered to show objects that exist in both models but are not the same. PowerDesigner uses the icons on the objects and the color of each entry to indicate the type of change.

Right-click any of the headings or objects in the right-hand pane to choose types of actions to select or de-select. Alternatively, use the selection tools on the Toolbar.

Choose the objects and properties you want to compare using the '*Comparison Options*' tool, which displays the dialog shown in Figure 23.6. Filter the display using the '*Change Filter*' tool, which displays the selections shown in Figure 23.7.

Figure 23.5 Merge model view

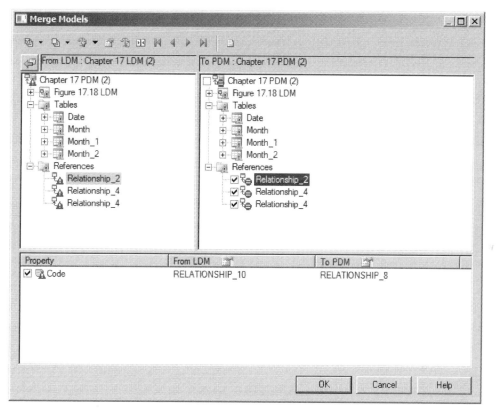

● "Comparing and Merging Models" (Core Features Guide)

● "Synchronizing Objects Manually" (Core Features Guide)

● "Analyzing Differences in the Merge Models Window" (Core Features Guide)

Figure 23.6 Filter options   **Figure 23.7 Comparison options**

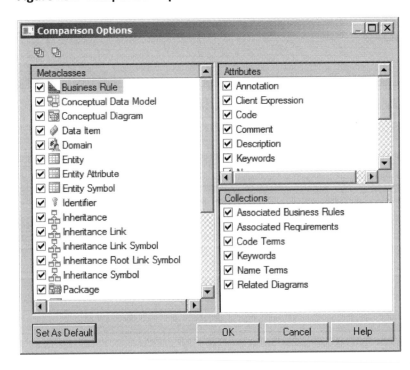

Checking a Model

Another standard feature is the ability to check the validity and completeness of a model. Each model has a standard set of checks, each of which will result in either a warning or a result. If you run the model check as part of model generation, errors will result in the generation being abandoned.

Initiate the model check by pressing <F4>, or selecting `Tools|Check Model`. The first thing you see is the Check Model Parameters window, shown in Figure 23.8. This is where you choose the checks you want to run. The icon next to each check indicates whether it produces a warning or an error; you can change this using the Toolbar. Some problems can be automatically fixed by PowerDesigner, which the *Automatic Correction* tool on the toolbar allows you to enable. For example, in Figure 23.8, I have chosen to allow PowerDesigner to correct any issues with non-unique table names.

Click <OK> to run the model check, and watch the progress messages in the output window, then have a look at the results in the Result List. Figure 23.9 shows the result of the model check initiated in Figure 23.8. There are two errors visible; the remaining entries are warnings. Double-click one of the entries in the list to open the object properties. If you right-click an entry, you are presented with various options to help you deal with the problem – in Figure 23.9, the contextual menu refers to the highlighted Domain warning.

Figure 23.8 Check Model Parameters

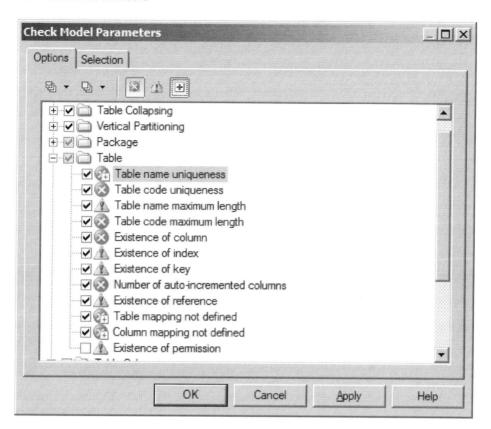

Figure 23.9 Model check results

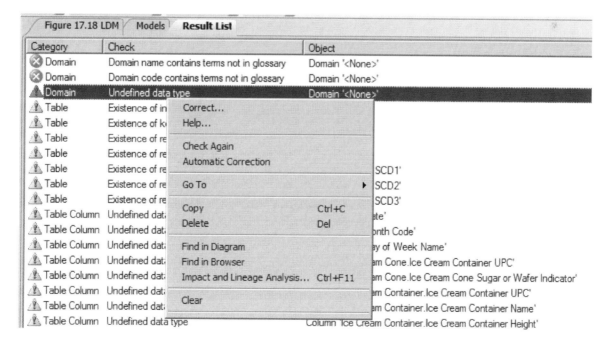

Impact and Lineage Analysis

Impact analysis, or the ability to understand the consequences of a model change, needs to be a function of the modeling tool. As part of the impact analysis, a modeler needs to be able to understand the object's lineage (objects that form the basis for a particular object). Impact analysis includes more than just understanding where an object is used. It is also a requirement for proper impact analysis to be able to understand what has happened to an object since it was generated. Was a CDM entity's attribute generated into the LDM? Was it then generated into a PDM? Was the data type changed by the DBA when working on that PDM? Did a modeler generate a set of classes from the LDM so that the developers would be able to start building applications? It is useful to be able to store these analyses for later review, as well as creating version documentation. It is a better use of resources to intelligently discuss the proposed change with the stakeholders, rather than make a change in the LDM, propagate it to the PDM and database, only to find that the application now fails.

PowerDesigner has true and extensive impact analysis. An object's lineage is stored with the object. When models and documents are stored in the repository, the impact analysis becomes more extensive. While viewing an object's properties, clicking the 'Impact and Lineage Analysis' button will bring up a window similar to the one in Figure 23.10. The analysis results depend on the analysis rule sets you use. Rule sets allow you to tailor the impact analysis, determining the types of objects that are traversed in the impact analysis, and the properties that are displayed. There are several rule sets supplied, or you can create your own, if you need them, and share them via the repository.

Not only is impact analysis available for the data modeling functionality, but it is core to the tool, and is available in all modeling modules.

By default, impact and lineage analysis only examines local models that are open, which could limit the scope of the analysis more than you would like. Just select the 'Use Repository' option, and PowerDesigner will extend the analysis into the repository. Figure 23.10 shows the impact and lineage analysis for the **City** entity. Note the wealth of additional information shown, and the inclusion of links to requirements, business rules, and classes. Entries with the small database symbol on their icon were retrieved from the repository.

Each of the entries provides a shortcut to the actual definition in a local model, and to a summary of the information held in the repository. Generate a diagram from this analysis, and you will be able to view this hierarchy in the Browser.

PowerDesigner stores lineage and impact analysis information at both 'ends' of the relationship. For example, the LDM stores details of generated tables, and the PDM stores details of the entities that tables were generated from.

Figure 23.10 PowerDesigner impact and lineage analysis

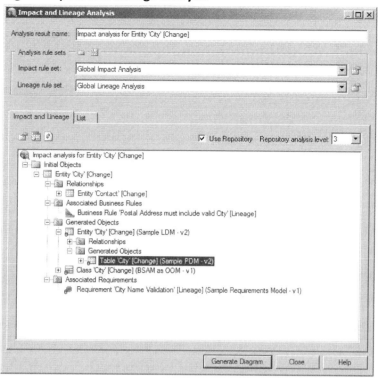

Impact Analysis Model

The best way to fully appreciate the depth and breadth of the impact analysis capabilities of PowerDesigner is to generate an impact analysis diagram. Did you notice the 'Generate Diagram' button in Figure 23.10? If you click on that button, PowerDesigner will generate a diagram illustrating the results of the analysis. The diagram can be saved, providing point-in-time snapshots throughout the development life cycle. Remember, you can choose between different analysis rule sets, which will produce different results and, therefore, different diagrams. Right-click any object in the analysis results to change the paths you want to analyze (e.g. to ignore subtypes or add links to data objects in process models), and the analysis is re-run. Figure 23.11 shows the Impact Analysis Objects for a CDM entity.

Figure 23.11 Impact analysis selection

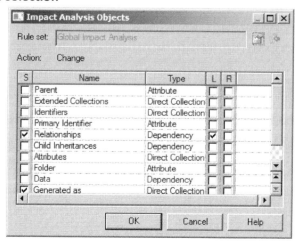

Figure 23.12 shows such a diagram, generated using the 'conceptual impact analysis' rule set and no lineage rules, resulting in a much smaller set of impacted objects. The left-hand entry is the **City** entity. Double-clicking a symbol will open the properties of that object.

Figure 23.12 PowerDesigner impact and lineage analysis diagram

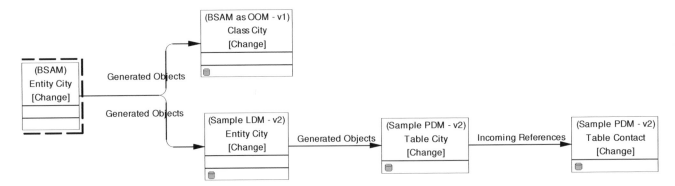

Figure 23.13 shows the entries in the Browser for the Impact Analysis model shown above. This information can be saved as a model. If you have more than one Impact Analysis Model, you can compare them to see how the impact has changed over time.

Figure 23.13 PowerDesigner impact analysis model in Browser

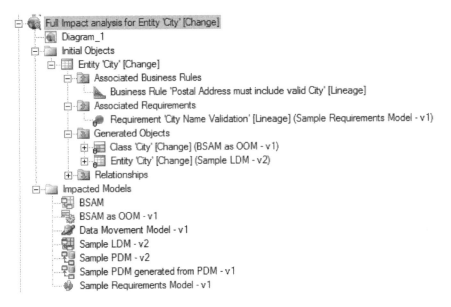

To PowerDesigner, the Impact Analysis Model is like any other model – it keeps a record of the fact that the entity is present in the model, which you can see in the object's 'Dependencies' tab, shown in Figure 23.14.

Besides changing the analysis parameters in the original analysis, you can also change them via the Impact Analysis diagram or in the Browser. Just right-click the symbol or Browser entry.

Figure 23.14 Impact analysis Dependencies

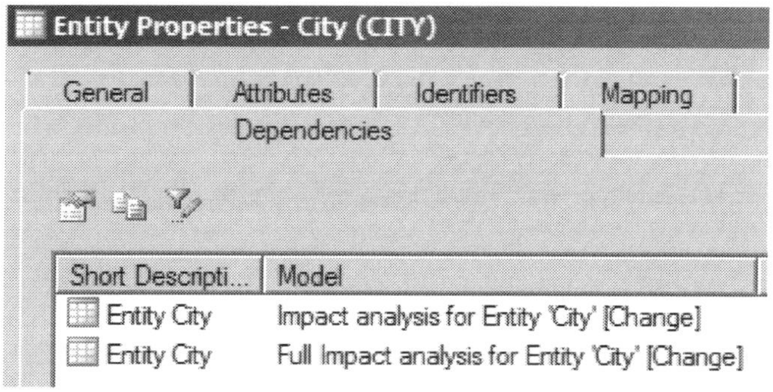

Customization and Extension

Extend the Scope of Model Information

Here's where data modeling gets really abstract. Imagine the Logical Data Model that describes the objects supported by PowerDesigner. It would include entities like:

Model, Diagram, Entity, Attribute, Relationship, Column, Domain.

We refer to that data model as PowerDesigner's 'metamodel'. The metamodel is very rich, but we can always find reasons to extend it, such as adding a *Plural Name* property to entities, or stereotype values for tables. We make these changes to the metamodel using 'model extensions'.

You have already seen an extension in Chapter 16, when adding stereotype values.

You can attach a model extension to your model at the time of creation of the model by clicking the <Select Extensions> button on the New Model dialog. You can subsequently attach an extension to your model at any time from the List of Extensions.

Each extension is valid for a single type of model, although some of them have been defined for multiple types of models. If, for example, the LDM supports the *Plural Name* property on entities, and the PDM supports the same property on tables, PowerDesigner will transfer the values of plural names between tables and entities during model generation.

You can extend the metamodel in the following ways:

1. Add or sub-classify new kinds of objects:

- Metaclasses – drawn from the metamodel as a basis for extension
- Stereotypes – to sub-classify objects
- Criteria – to evaluate conditions to sub-classify objects
- Extended objects, sub-objects, and links – to create new kinds of objects

9. Provide new ways of viewing connections between objects:

- Dependency matrices – to show connections between two types of objects

- Extended collections and compositions – to enable manual linking between objects
- Calculated collections – to automate linking between objects

10. Add new properties to objects and display them:

- Extended attributes – to provide extra metadata
- Forms – to display custom property tabs or dialog boxes
- Custom symbols – to help you visually distinguish objects

11. Add constraints and validation rules to objects:

- Custom checks – to provide data testing
- Event handlers – to invoke methods when triggered by an event

12. Execute commands on objects:

- Methods – to be invoked by other profile extensions such as menus and form buttons (written in VBScript)
- Menus – to customize PowerDesigner menus

13. Generate objects in new ways:

- Templates and generated files – to customize generation
- Transformations and Transformation profiles – to automate changes to objects at generation or on demand.

❷ "Extension Files" (Customizing and Extending PowerDesigner)

Automatically Attaching Extensions to New Models

Extensions are just one example of common resources available to PowerDesigner. Like other resources, they're available on the `Tools` menu, under `Resources|Extensions`.

In Chapter 10 we showed you how to add an extension to a model. If you have standard extensions that you need to apply to every new model of a given type, you can do that. One of the properties of an extension is *Auto Attach*; if this is enabled, the extension will always be included automatically whenever you create a new model of that type. The menu path required to access CDM extensions is shown in Figure 23.15.

Figure 23.16 shows the extensions available for CDMs (the active model was a Requirements model). The tools on the Toolbar allow you to open the property sheet for an extension, check extensions in and out of the repository, merge extensions, and compare them with the repository version.

Figure 23.15 Accessing available CDM extensions

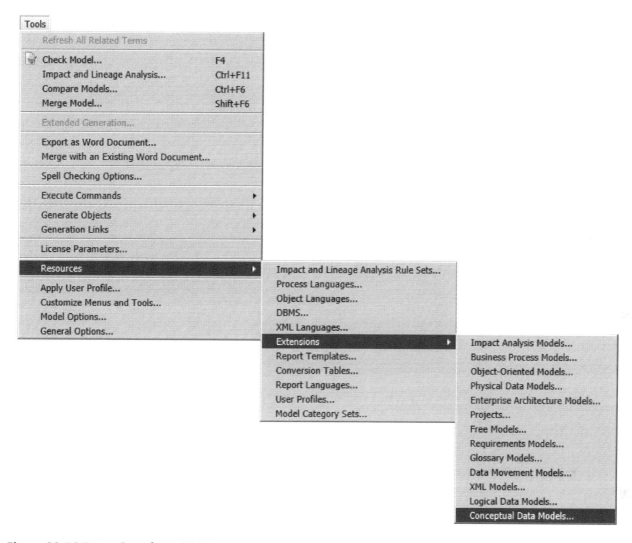

Figure 23.16 Extensions for a CDM

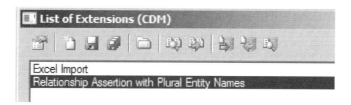

Double-click an extension to open the property sheet. Figure 23.17 shows the property sheet for **Relationship Assertion with Plural Entity Names**.

Figure 23.17 Relationship Assertion with Plural Entity Names

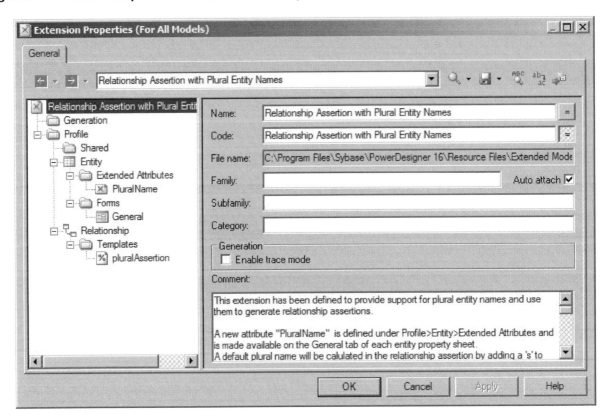

The browser-like panel on the left shows the contents of the extension; we don't need to know how it works to guess that it adds *Plural Name* to entities via a form called *General* (this form replaces the default 'General' tab), and that it adds some form of template to relationships.

The Toolbar at the top allows you to, among other things, save the extension in a new file – useful if you want to base a new extension on an existing one, or share the extension with other modelers.

The main property of interest in Figure 23.17 is *Auto Attach*; select this property to ensure that the extension is automatically added to all new models of this type.

Customizing Menus, Toolbars, and Toolboxes

To customize PowerDesigner menus, toolbars, and toolboxes, select `Tools|Customize Menus and Tools`.

❷ "Customizing Menus, Toolbars, and Toolboxes" (Core Features Guide)

Modifying DBMS Support

PowerDesigner supports the peculiarities of different RDBMS's via DBMS Definition Files, which are similar to extensions. To enable a new, unsupported, DBMS, or to add DBMS features that PowerDesigner does not currently support, you can create your own definition file and attach it to your PDMs. Use a copy of one of the definition files supplied with PowerDesigner to give you some help. See `Tools|Resources|DBMS`.

❷ "DBMS Definition File Structure" (Customizing and Extending PowerDesigner)

Role-based UI

An administrator can create profiles in the repository to customize and simplify the PowerDesigner interface for users by hiding types of models, objects, and object properties, by reconfiguring menus, toolbars, and toolboxes, and by setting appropriate defaults for options and preferences. You can define multiple profiles to customize the interface in different ways for different kinds of users, and apply them as appropriate, to individual user accounts or to repository groups.

❷ "Using Profiles to Control the PowerDesigner Interface" (Core Features Guide)

Scripting

If you are prepared to indulge in some programming, you can alter or extend PowerDesigner behavior with scripts.

❷ "Scripting PowerDesigner" (Customizing and Extending PowerDesigner)

Key Points

- Use the 'composer' license to share responsibility.

- Share resources and best practices.

- Standard approach? Develop a framework.

- Save your Impact Analysis Model for great tracking abilities.

- Automatically attach useful extensions to new models.

Section VII contains the final two chapters, which discuss PowerDesigner topics beyond data modeling.

Chapter 24 describes the fundamental differences between the XML models and other Physical Data Models

Chapter 25 describes the other types of PowerDesigner models that may be available to you.

What's different about the XML Physical Data Model?

Is hierarchical
Visualization, tags
Are metadata

Extensible Markup Language (XML) is a specification for storing information, and for describing the structure of that information. The data in a file of XML is in a hierarchical format using human-readable tags to name the data, allowing both people and software applications to easily exchange and share information. XML is useful and powerful for the same reasons any data model is useful and powerful: the structure is easy to understand (assuming you can visualize the hierarchy), can be technology-independent, and represents complex problems with simple syntax.

XML rules are represented through XML schemas, which specify the structural rules for XML documents in much the same way as a Physical Data Model specifies the rules for the data in a database structure. XML data structures can be visualized in PowerDesigner in a similar way to visualizing database tables.

There is a fundamentally different approach to the creation of XML message structures, compared to designing a database – designing XML Message structures is process modeling, not data modeling. What we're doing is expanding a message or data flow on a process flow diagram.

Figure 24.1 contains an XML document based on an example from Wikipedia.

Figure 24.1 Recipe XML document

```
<Recipe Name = "bread" PrepTime="5 mins" CookTime="3 hours">
<Title>Basic bread</Title>
<Ingredient Amount="8" Unit="cup">Flour</Ingredient>
<Ingredient Amount="10" Unit="grams">Yeast</Ingredient>
<Ingredient Amount="4" Unit="cup" State="warm">Water</Ingredient>
<Ingredient Amount="1" Unit="teaspoon">Salt</Ingredient>
<Instructions>
  <Step>Mix all ingredients together.</Step>
  <Step>Knead thoroughly.</Step>
  <Step>Cover with a cloth, and leave for one hour.</Step>
  <Step>Knead again.</Step>
  <Step>Place in a bread baking tin.</Step>
  <Step>Cover with a cloth, and leave for one hour.</Step>
  <Step>Bake at 180 degrees Celsius for 30 minutes.</Step>
</Instructions>
</Recipe>
```

The terms such as '<Step>' are called 'tags'. The data within each pair of tags is called a 'value'. So the value for the tag pair <Title>and </Title> is 'Basic bread'. This represents the name of the recipe; it's part of the data in the XML document.

Figure 24.2 shows the hierarchical structure of this XML document in PowerDesigner.

Figure 24.2 The XML hierarchy in PowerDesigner

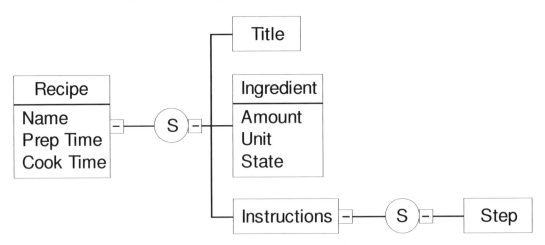

Along with the schema for this XML document, we can learn quite a bit about the actual data. For example, we know that a Recipe can contain Ingredients, and Instructions can contain Steps. Because XML is hierarchy-based, however, the rules only go one way. That is, we know a Recipe can contain Ingredients, but can an Ingredient belong to more than one Recipe? I email out monthly Design Challenges (add your email address at www.stevehoberman.com), and in a recent Design Challenge, Norman Daoust, business analysis consultant and trainer, summarized this: "XML documents frequently only indicate the cardinality of relationships on one end of the relationship, not both ends."

Therefore, we can take this XML document and schema, and by asking additional business questions, derive a logical data model such as that in Figure 24.3. Notice how the LDM object names reflect the original XML tag names. PowerDesigner ensures that traceability is maintained, enabling you to ensure that your relational and hierarchical data designs all align with common data standards.

Take note of all of the business questions that would need to be answered to arrive at this model; a small sample includes:

- Can the recipe have more than one long name (i.e. title)?
- Is Recipe Short Name really the natural key for Recipe?
- Is Ingredient Name really the natural key for Ingredient?
- Can an Ingredient belong to more than one Recipe?
- Can a Recipe Step require more than one Recipe Ingredient?

Figure 24.3 Recipe logical data model

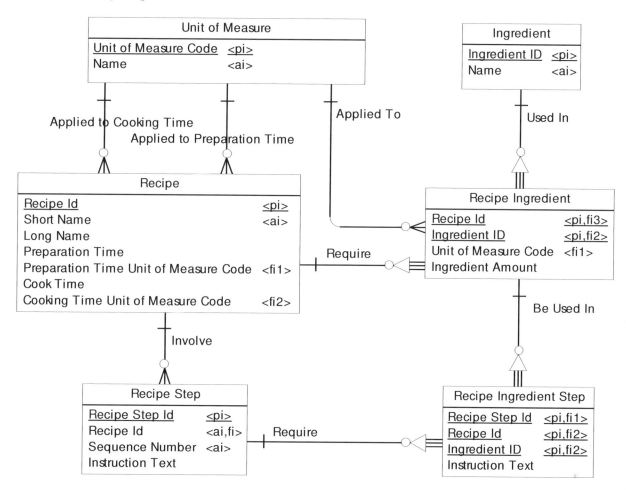

The use of XML is widespread, so the advantage the analyst or modeler can gain from it is a better understanding of a business area and building a more accurate data model. This is especially true when modeling industry standards. Many industries have created formalized XML-based standards so that they can exchange information. One example is ePub, an XML standard for exchanging publishing information between organizations within the publishing industry. Standards that use industry-wide terminology and rules can help to build more accurate enterprise data models and applications that are more useful.

Key Points

- The structure of an XML document is hierarchical.

- XML document design is not data modeling, it's process modeling.

- You can work bottom-up, deriving a Logical Data Model from an XML model, but you will need to ask business questions to provide missing detail.

Interconnected
Process, Data, other stuff
PowerDesigner

The richness of the PowerDesigner modeling environment enables you to model interconnected systems and view them in many different ways. Figure 25.1 illustrates the capabilities of the modeling environment, including the eleven types of models that are available, except the Free Model, which can represent anything you want it to.

Figure 25.1 PowerDesigner's Capabilities

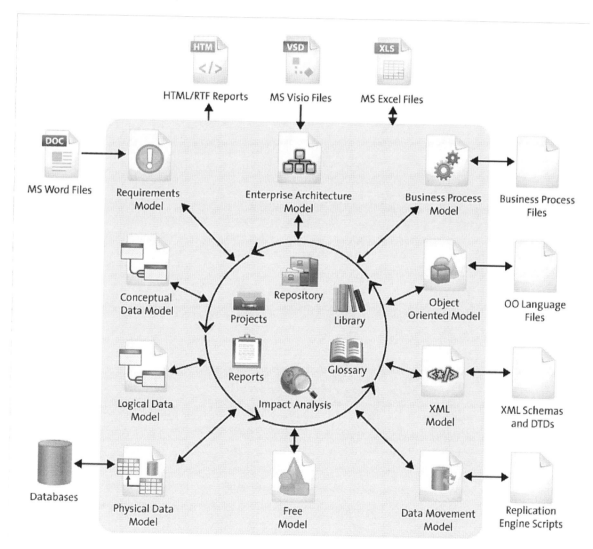

Which models are available to you depends on the PowerDesigner edition you have licensed. PowerDesigner provides several ways of integrating these models; see Chapter 10 and Chapter

18 to read about the ways in which you can integrate your data models with the other models that are available.

In Chapter 9 we described the CDM, LDM and PDM. Table 25.1 describes the remaining types of models that are available.

Table 25.1 Eleven Types of Models

Model Icon, Name, and File Type	Usage
Business Process Model (BPM)	A *Business Process Model (BPM)* helps you identify, describe, and decompose business processes. You can analyze your system at various levels of detail, and focus on control flow (the sequence of execution) or data flow (the exchange of data). You can choose from a number of process languages, including BPEL and BPMN.
Data Movement Model (DMM)	A *Data Movement Model (DMM)* provides a global view of the movement of information in your organization. You can analyze and document where your data originates, where it moves to, and how it is transformed along the way, including replications and ETL. Using a Data Movement Model, you can generate SQL scripts to replicate data via a Replication Server. You can create a data movement model from the mappings between PDMs. Prior to PowerDesigner 15.3, the Data Movement Model was called the Information Liquidity Model (ILM).
Enterprise Architecture Model (EAM)	An *Enterprise Architecture Model (EAM)* helps you analyze and document your organization and its business functions, along with the applications and systems that support them, and the physical architecture on which they are implemented.
Free Model (FEM)	A *Free Model (FEM)* provides a context-free environment for modeling any kind of objects or systems. It is generally associated with a set of extensions that allow you to define your own concepts and graphical symbols.

Model Icon, Name, and File Type	Usage
Impact and Lineage Model (IAM)	An *Impact And Lineage Model* (IAM) is a permanent graphical record of dependencies between model objects. When you perform an action on a model object, you can use: Impact Analysis – to analyze the effect of the action on the objects that depend on the initial object Lineage Analysis – to identify the objects that influence the initial object The use of analysis rule sets allows you to tailor the information that is presented for model objects.
Multimodel Report (MMR)	A *Multimodel Report (MMR)* is a PowerDesigner report that can document any number of models together and show the links between them. To create such a report, you must have at least one model open in the workspace, and you can add additional models at any time.
Object-Oriented Model (OOM)	An *Object-Oriented Model (OOM)* helps you analyze an information system through use cases, structural and behavioral analyses, and in terms of deployment, using the Unified Modeling Language (UML). You can reverse-engineer, model, and generate for XML, Java, .NET and other languages.
Requirements Model (RQM)	A *Requirements Model (RQM)* helps you analyze any kind of written requirements and link them to the users and groups who will implement them, and with analysis and design objects in other models. You can use an RQM to represent any structured document (e.g. functional specification, test plan, business goals, etc.) and import and export hierarchies of requirements as MS Word documents. You can import objects from other types of models as requirements, and also generate different objects, such as entities, from requirements into other types of models.
XML Model (XSM)	An *XML Model (XSM)* helps you analyze an XML Schema Definition (.XSD), Document Type Definition (.DTD), or XML-Data Reduced (.XDR) file. You can model, reverse-engineer, and generate each of these file formats.

DAMA International. (2008). *The DAMA Dictionary of Data Management.* New Jersey: Technics Publications, LLC.

Hay, D. (2011). *Enterprise Model Patterns: Describing the World.* New Jersey: Technics Publications LLC.

Hoberman, S. (2011). *Data Modeling Master Class Training Manual.* New Jersey: Technics Publications.

Maydanchik, A. (2007). *Data Quality Assessment.* Technics Publications, LLC.

Ross, R. G., & Lam, G. S. (2011). *Business Analysis with Business Rules - Building Business Solutions.*

Ross, R. G. (2009). *Business Rule Concepts* (3rd edition ed.). -: Business Rule Solutions LLC.

Silverston, L. Agnew, P. 2009. *The Data Model Resource Book,* Volume 3, Universal Patterns for Data Modeling. New York: John Wiley & Sons, Inc.

Simsion, G., Witt, G. (2005). *Data Modeling Essentials,* Third Edition. San Francisco: Morgan Kaufmann Publishers.

"Answers" is a strong word. It implies that I know *the* answer, as opposed to knowing *an* answer, which is closer to the truth. In other words, you may have different and possibly better answers than I, and that would be a very a good thing!

You will not find answers to the PowerDesigner exercises here – as the exercises describe your objectives.

EXERCISE 1: Educating Your Neighbor

I find the analogy that I use most frequently is comparing the data model to a blueprint. Most non-technical friends, family, and neighbors understand this analogy. "Just like you need a blueprint to ensure a sound building structure, you need a data model to ensure a sound application." Sometimes I also explain to people that a data model is nothing more than a fancy spreadsheet that contains not just the spreadsheet columns, but also the business rules binding these columns. If both the blueprint and spreadsheet analogies fail, I quickly change the subject to the other person and ask what they do (and hope that they never ask me again!).

EXERCISE 4: Assigning Domains

Here are the domains for each of the following three data elements.

Email Address

Based upon information from Wikipedia:

An e-mail address is a string of a subset of characters separated into 2 parts by an "@", a "local-part" and a domain, that is, local-part@domain. The local-part of an e-mail address may be up to 64 characters long and the domain name may have a maximum of 255 characters. However, the maximum length of the entire e-mail address is 254 characters.

The local-part of the e-mail address may use any of these characters:

- *Uppercase and lowercase English letters (a-z, A-Z)*
- *Digits 0 through 9*
- *Characters ! # $ % & ' * + - / = ? ^ _ ` { | } ~*
- *Character . (dot, period, full stop) provided that it is not the first or last character, and also provided that it does not appear two or more times consecutively.*
- *Additionally, quoted-strings (e.g.: "John Doe"@example.com) are permitted, thus allowing characters that would otherwise be prohibited, however they do not appear in common practice.*

Gross Sales Value Amount

A format domain of Decimal(15,4). Both negative and positive numbers are acceptable.

Country Code

As part of the ISO 3166-1993 standard, Country Code is two characters in length, and is a list domain consisting of over 200 values. Here is a partial list:

Code	Definition and Explanation
AD	Andorra
AE	United Arab Emirates
AF	Afghanistan
AG	Antigua & Barbuda
AI	Anguilla
AL	Albania
AM	Armenia
AN	Netherlands Antilles
AO	Angola
AQ	Antarctica
AR	Argentina
AS	American Samoa
AT	Austria
AU	Australia
AW	Aruba
AZ	Azerbaijan
ZM	Zambia
ZR	Zaire
ZW	Zimbabwe
ZZ	Unknown or unspecified country

Just the codes beginning with 'A' or 'Z' are shown. 'ZZ' is an interesting country, and illustrates how easy it is to circumvent a business rule. That is, if we don't know the country and Country Code is required, we can always assign a 'ZZ', for 'Unknown'.

EXERCISE 5: Reading a Model

Recall the model on the facing page:

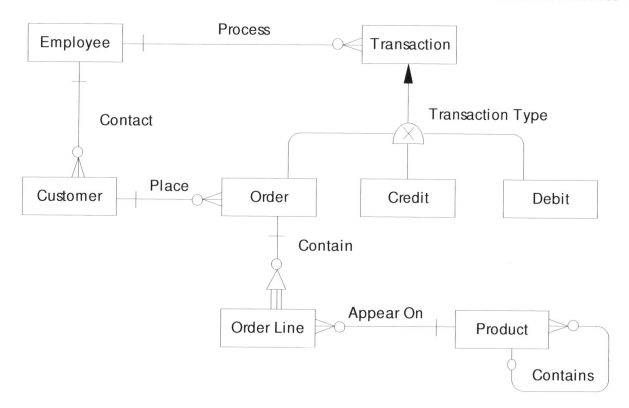

The following statements can be made about the business rules, based on the role names specified in the relationships in PowerDesigner. The role names are shown *in italics*.

Each Employee may *process* one or more Transactions.
Each Transaction must *be processed by* one and only one Employee.
Each Transaction must be either an Order, a Credit, or a Debit.
Each Order is a Transaction.
Each Credit is a Transaction.
Each Debit is a Transaction.
Each Employee may *contact* one or more Customers.
Each Customer must *be contacted by* one and only one Employee.
Each Customer may *place* one or more Orders.
Each Order must *be placed by* one and only one Customer.
Each Order may *contain* one or more Order Lines.
Each Order Line must *belong to* one and only one Order.
Each Product may *appear on* one or more Order Lines.
Each Order Line must *reference* one and only one Product.
Each Product may *contain* one or more Products.
Each Product may *belong to* at most one other Product.

The following diagram is an alternative view of the same model, hiding the relationship names, and displaying the role names instead.

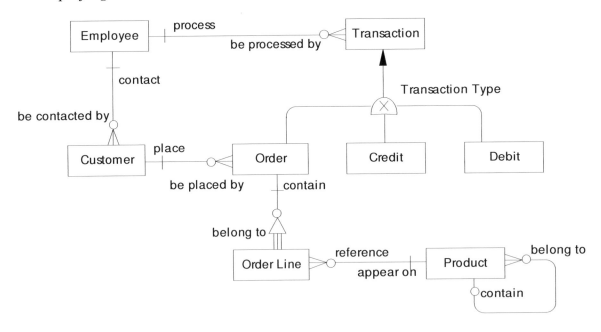

EXERCISE 6: Clarifying Customer Id

There are three terms within this definition that require an explanation: *'unique'*, *'identifier'*, and *'Customer'*.

Document Uniqueness Properties

The term 'unique' is ambiguous and could easily be interpreted differently by readers of this definition. To maintain clarity and correctness, these questions should be answered within the definition:

- Are identifier values ever reused?
- What is the scope of uniqueness?
- How is the identifier validated?

Document the Characteristics of the Identifier

We can describe the actual identifier in more detail by addressing these areas:

- **Purpose.** For example, perhaps the identifier is needed because there are multiple source systems for Customer data, each with their own Id. To enable a common set of data to be held about them, this identifier needed to be created to facilitate integration and guarantee uniqueness across all customers.
- **Business or surrogate key.** Document whether the identifier is meaningful to the business (i.e. the business or natural key) or whether it is a meaningless integer counter (i.e. the surrogate key).
- **Assignment.** Document how a new customer identifier is assigned. The party that is responsible for creating new identifiers should also be mentioned.

Define the Customer

Because definitions should stand on their own, we also can define a customer within this definition. We can reference the subject area definition of customer.

EXERCISE 8: Creating your own Workspace, Project, and Models

In this exercise, you had a great of control over the content and style of the diagrams, so we can only show you an example of what you might have achieved.

Here's the CDM diagram:

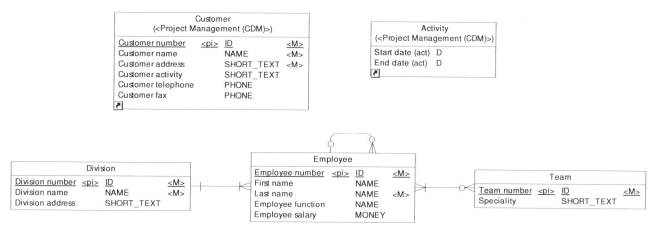

Here's the Project Diagram:

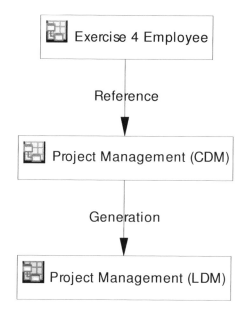

EXERCISE 12: Naming an Associative Entity

Firstly, what name should we give the new entity? We could just concatenate the two original entity names and call it **Person Project** or **Project Person**, but those names are not descriptive enough. We need to say more about the real meaning of the entity. We know from the role names that each instance of the entity represents the assignment of one person to a project, so let's call the entity **Project Assignment**.

The original relationship used the role names 'Assigned To' and 'Worked on By'. There is no reason to believe that these are incorrect, so we should use them for two of the role names in the two new relationships. Looking at the remaining two role names, it seems reasonable to say that a **Project Assignment** can 'apply to' a **Person**, and 'be assigned to' a **Project**. This results in the following:

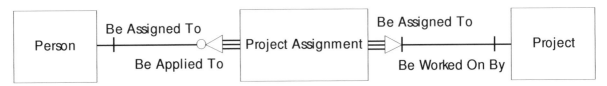

If your organization uses a particular term to refer to a person assigned to a Project, that would be a prime candidate to replace the role name 'Be Applied To'.

EXERCISE 17: Modifying a Logical Data Model

There are two ways to model this situation. What you hopefully spotted in the question was the new business rule relating to employees and offices; only Managers can have offices, so we need to revise our thinking on relationships in the model. The key point with this challenge is to use subtyping and keep Office First Occupied Date in the subtype as mandatory (not null), because every Manager has an office.

Option 1

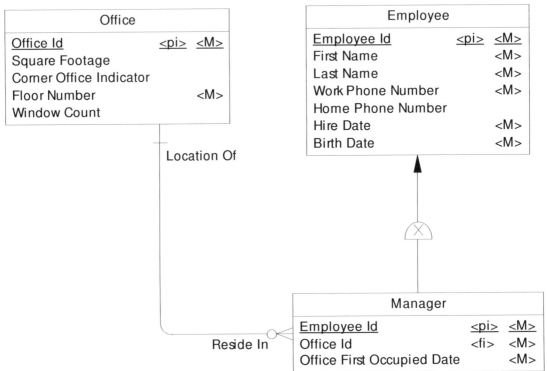

In this model, we subtyped Manager as a type of Employee. All of the data elements and relationships that are specific to a Manager are moved to the Manager entity. Therefore, the business rule that each Manager must reside in one and only one Office and each Office may contain one or many Managers is represented. In addition, the Office First Occupied Date is now a mandatory field in the Manager entity, whereas in the Employee entity it would have to be null.

Option 2 (a bit more abstract)

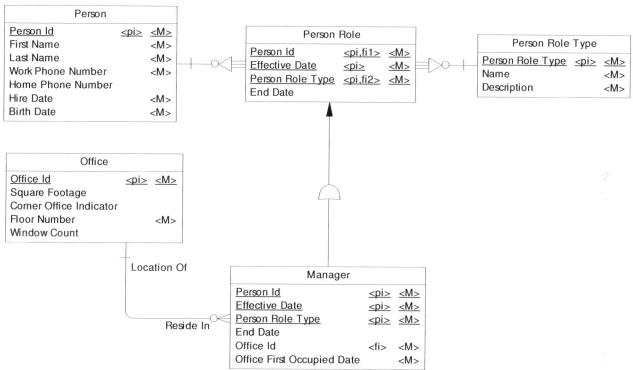

Thinking in more generic terms, we have allowed for the fact that a Person can play many Roles. One of these Roles is a Manager. The Manager subtype has the additional relationship and mandatory Office First Occupied Date that we saw in the previous model. This type of model works out well where application longevity and stability is the goal, such as in a data warehouse or integration hub.

EXERCISE 20: Getting Physical with Subtypes in PowerDesigner

The following are the three different ways this subtyping structure can be represented on the physical data model.

Identity

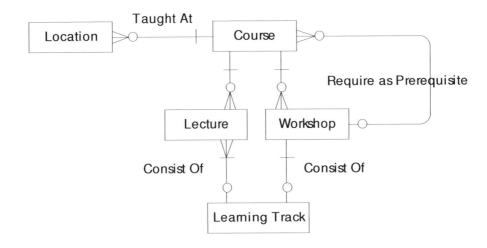

Rolling Down

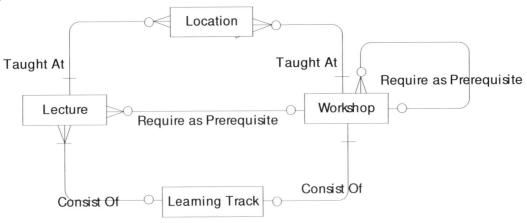

Rolling Up

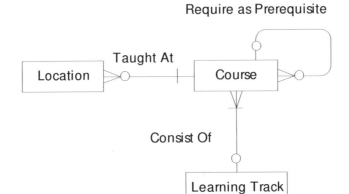

Conceptual Data Model (CDM)	helps you identify the principal entities of importance to the business, their attributes, and the relationships between them.
Logical Data Model (LDM)	helps you analyze the structure of an information system, with consideration for a relational storage structure, while remaining independent of any specific physical database implementation.
Physical Data Model (PDM)	helps you to analyze the tables, views, and other objects in a database, including specific support for a selected variant of a relational database management system (RDBMS).

Memory Joggers

- *Model Options* and *Display Preferences*
- Model menu gives access to many object lists
- The content of menus depends upon your current diagram
- The 'Dependencies' and 'Version Info' tabs will show you where an object is used

One model per file	Three models means three files
Creating a PDM from a CDM or LDM	Nothing automatic – generate the new model via the Tools menu. Merge model updates using the same tool. Control what is generated via the *Generate* property.
Merge / Compare	only works on models of the same type – compare models of different types using model generation
Adding existing symbols to a diagram	Use Complete Links or Show Symbols

Standard Generation Options

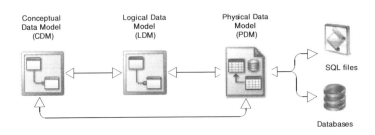

Shortcuts

Object manipulation

DEL	Delete object (with confirmation)
Shift + DEL	Delete object (no confirmation)
Alt + ENTER	Open property sheet of selected object
Ctrl + K	Paste as shortcut
Ctrl + H	On selected link: link is horizontal
Ctrl + L	On selected link: link is vertical
Ctrl + *Resize* (dragging a symbol handle)	Resize object keeping object center
Ctrl + Shift + *Resize*	Resize object keeping object center and proportions
Ctrl + right-click on name	Rename object

Palette

Double click Pointer or Ctrl + A	Select all symbols in diagram
Double click Delete tool	Delete all selected symbols (with confirmation)
Double click Grabber	Display global view
Double click Object tool	Select all symbols of same type
Shift + Double click Object tool	Keep previous selection and add all symbols of same type
Right click	Release current tool and select pointer

Drag & drop

Shift + move item	Move symbol
Ctrl + move item	Copy symbol
Ctrl + Shift + move item	Create shortcut
Alt + move item	Create replica
Click item + Right click drag & drop	Open menu to choose an action

Browser

***** **(Num pad)**	Expand all nodes in active Browser
+ (Num pad)	Expand sub nodes in active Browser
- (Num pad)	Collapse sub nodes in active Browser
F2	Rename
Ctrl + Shift + F	Find selected object in diagram

Wildcard syntax. This syntax is used in the Filter and Find functions.

*	¨ Wildcard for any string
?	¨ Wildcard for any character
* or \?	¨ * or ? is a normal character

Keys & accelerators

F4	Check model
F5	Actual size
F6	Zoom in
F7	Zoom out
F8	Global view (whole diagram)
F9	Previous view
F10	Display used pages
Shift + F5	Redisplay
Shift + F9	Next view
Shift + Click item	Select contiguous items
Alt + 0	Show/Hide Browser tree view
Alt + 1	Show/Hide Output window
Alt + 2	Show/Hide Result list
Alt + 3	Display Welcome Page
Alt + F6	Switch between active windows
Ctrl + Double click or Ctrl + '+' key	Open package diagram
Ctrl + tab	Insert tab in text or Change the page in property sheets
Ctrl + Page up/down	Change the tab inside property sheet pages
Ctrl + B	Find selected object in Browser
Ctrl + D	Select diagram
Ctrl + E	Open list of reports
Ctrl + F	Find objects
Ctrl + J	Adjust to text in object symbol
Ctrl + F4	Close current diagram
Ctrl + Alt + F4	Close model
Ctrl + F5	Run `Complete Links`
Ctrl + F6	Switch between open property sheets
Ctrl + Shift + F6	Switch backwards in property sheets
Ctrl + Q	Toggle symbol style in Project Diagram
Ctrl + U	Go to parent diagram
Shift + F2	Open workspace
Shift + F3	Save workspace
Shift + F4	Close workspace
mouse wheel scroll	Scroll diagram up/down
Ctrl + *mouse wheel scroll*	Zoom in/out
Shift + *mouse wheel scroll*	Scroll diagram left/right

Accelerators in lists

F2	Select text for edit
F4	Select cell to add text
Ctrl + Shift + Spacebar	Select line
Ctrl + A	Select all
Ctrl + Shift + A	Deselect all
Ctrl + N or Ctrl + I	Insert line
Ctrl + D	Delete line

How to find out more about PowerDesigner, or get help from others

The easiest place to find general information about PowerDesigner is the Sybase web site[13]. The first port of call when using the product is the online help, which you can access by pressing the <F1> key, clicking on 'Help' buttons, or via the 'Help' menu. Generally speaking, the help system will open at a page relevant to the PowerDesigner feature you are using.

If you have specific questions, there are several places you can turn to for help [14].

Resource	Link
Info Advisors Discussion Group	http://wb.itboards.com/wb/?boardid=powerdesigner
Google Group	http://groups.google.com/group/sybase.public.powerdesigner.general *Google account needed*
Linked In group	http://www.linkedin.com/groups?gid=689287 *Membership may need to be approved by group owner*
Power Designer Blogs etc	Jay Stevens - http://powerdesignerplus.com/ Richard Kier - http://rkkier.wordpress.com/ George McGeachie - http://metadatajunkie.wordpress.com/
Sybase Code Exchange	http://www.sybase.com/developer/codexchange *Requires registration with Sybase support web site*
Sybase Community Forums	http://www.sybase.com:80/support/community-forums
Sybase International User Group	http://www.isug.com/
Sybase Newsgroup	http://www.sybase.com/detail?id=203814
Sybase Online Documentation	If you have the product installed, you can find a copy of the documentation at *C:\Program Files\Sybase\PowerDesigner 15\Documentation\index.htm*. The path is slightly different if your computer is running 64-bit Windows.
Sybooks online	http://sybooks.sybase.com/nav/summary.do?prod=9392&lang=en&prodName=PowerDesigner
YouTube Channel	http://www.youtube.com/user/SybaseInc

---

[13] http://www.sybase.com//powerdesigner

[14] These were all available when we went to press, but we cannot guarantee they'll be there when you need them

Data Modeling Terms

abstraction   Abstraction is the removal of details in such a way as to broaden applicability to a wider class of situations, while preserving the important properties and essential nature of concepts or subjects. By removing these details, we remove differences and, therefore, change the way we view these concepts or subjects, including seeing similarities that were not apparent or even existent before. For example, we may abstract Employee and Consumer into the more generic concept of Person. A Person can play many Roles, two of which are Employee and Consumer.

alternate key   An alternate key is a candidate key that although unique, was not chosen as the primary key, but still can be used to find specific entity instances.

architect   An experienced and skilled designer responsible for system and/or data architecture supporting a broad scope of requirements over time, beyond the scope of a single project. The term implies a higher level of professional experience and expertise than an analyst, designer, or developer.*

associative entity   An entity or table that resolves a many-to-many relationship between two other related entities or tables.*

business analyst   An IT or business professional responsible for understanding the business processes and the information needs of an organization, for serving as a liaison between IT and business units, and acting as a facilitator of organizational and cultural change.*

candidate key   A candidate key is one or more data elements that uniquely identify an entity instance. Sometimes a single data element identifies an entity instance, such as ISBN for a book, or **Account Code** for an account. Sometimes it takes more than one data element to uniquely identify an entity instance. For example, both a **Promotion Code** and **Promotion Start Date** are necessary to identify a promotion.

cardinality   Cardinality defines the number of instances of each entity that can participate in a relationship. It is represented by the symbols that appear on both ends of a relationship line. It is through cardinality that the data rules are specified and enforced. Without cardinality, the most we can say about a relationship is that two entities are connected in some way through a rule. For example, where we know that **Person** and **Company** have some kind of relationship, but we don't know much more than this.

class word   A class word is the last term in a data element name, such as Amount, Code, and Name. Class words allow for the assignment of common domains.

conformed dimension	A conformed dimension is one that is shared across the business intelligence environment. Customer, Account, Employee, Product, Time, and Geography are examples of conformed dimensions. Ralph Kimball made the term popular. It requires the modeler to design the conformed dimension with a much broader perspective than just the requirements for a single data mart.
data element	A data element is a property of importance to the business. Its values contribute to identifying, describing, or measuring instances of an entity. The data element **Claim Number** identifies each claim. The data element **Student Last Name** describes the last name of each student. The data element **Gross Sales Value Amount** measures the monetary value of a transaction.
data model	A data model is a wayfinding tool for both business and IT professionals, which uses a set of symbols and text to precisely explain a subset of real information to improve communication within the organization, thereby leading to a more flexible and stable application environment.
data modeler	A business systems analyst who identifies data requirements, defines data, and develops and maintains data models.*
data modeling	Data modeling is the process of building a data model. More specifically, data modeling is the set of techniques and activities that enable us to capture the data to support the structure and operations of an organization, as well as a proposed information solution that will enable the organization to achieve its goals. The process requires many skills, such as listening ability, courage to ask lots of questions, and even patience.
database administrator (DBA)	The IT professional role responsible for database administration, the function of managing the physical aspects of data resources, including database design and integrity, backup and recovery, performance and tuning.*
denormalization	Denormalization is the process of selectively violating normalization rules and reintroducing redundancy into the model (and therefore, the database). This extra redundancy can reduce data retrieval time, which is the primary reason for denormalizing. We can also denormalize to create a more user-friendly model. For example, we might decide to denormalize company information into an entity containing employee information, because usually when employee information is retrieved, company information is also retrieved.
developer	A person who designs, codes and/or tests software. Synonymous with software developer, systems developer, application developer, software engineer, and application engineer.*
dimension	A dimension is reference information whose purpose is to add meaning to the measures. All of the different ways of filtering, sorting, and summing measures make use of dimensions. Dimensions are often, but not exclusively, hierarchies.

dimensional model	A dimensional model focuses on capturing and aggregating the metrics from daily operations that enable the business to evaluate how well it is doing by manipulating the numbers. For example, examining the measure **Gross Sales Value Amount** at a day level and then, after getting the answer, looking at **Gross Sales Value Amount** at a month or year level, or at a product or brand level, or a city or country level. The dimensional model is all about playing with numbers.
domain	A domain is the complete set of all possible values that a data element may be assigned. A domain is a set of validation criteria that can be applied to more than one data element. For example, the domain 'Date', which contains all possible valid dates, can be assigned to any of these data elements:
	Employee Hire Date
	Order Entry Date
	Claim Submit Date
	Course Start Date
enterprise data model	An Enterprise Data Model (EDM) is a subject-oriented and integrated data model containing all of the data produced and consumed across an entire organization. Subject-oriented means that the concepts on a data model fit together as the CEO sees the company, rather than how any individual functional or department heads see their view of the company. There is one Customer entity, one Order entity, etc. Integration goes hand in hand with subject-orientation. Integration means that all of the data and rules in an organization are depicted once and fit together seamlessly. Every data element has a single definition and name. Integration implies that with this single version of the truth comes a mapping back to the chaotic real world.
entity	An entity represents a collection of information about something that the business deems important and worthy of capture. A noun or noun phrase identifies a specific entity. It fits into one of several categories - who, what, when, where, why, or how.
entity instance	Entity instances are the occurrences or values of a particular entity. Think of a spreadsheet as being an entity, with the column headings representing the pieces of information about the entity. Each spreadsheet row containing the actual values represents an entity instance. The entity Customer may have multiple customer instances with names Bob, Joe, Jane, and so forth. The entity Account can have instances of Bob's checking account, Bob's savings account, Joe's brokerage account, and so on.
Extensible Markup Language (XML)	Extensible Markup Language (XML) is a specification for storing information, and for describing the structure of that information. XML is both useful and powerful for the same reasons any data model is useful and powerful: it is easy to understand, can be technology-independent, and enables representing complex problems with simple syntax. Similar to distinguishing subject area models from logical data models from physical data models, XML distinguishes the data content about formatting (e.g. blue, Arial, 15 point font) from rules.

factless fact

A fact table that does not contain any facts (i.e. measures) is called a factless fact. Factless facts count events by summing relationship occurrences between the dimensions. For example, a fact table called Attendance contains no measures. It links to the Student, Course, and Semester dimensions with the goal of counting relationship occurrences of how many students take a particular course in a particular semester.

foreign key

A foreign key is a data element that provides a link to another entity. A foreign key allows a database management system to navigate from one entity to another. For example, we need to know who owns an Account, so we would want to include the identifier of the customer to whom it belongs in the entity. The Customer Id in Account is the primary key of that Customer in the Customer entity. Using this foreign key back to Customer enables the database management system to navigate from a particular account or accounts, to the customer or customers that own each account. Likewise, the database can navigate from a particular customer or customers, to find all of their accounts.

grain

The grain is the meter's lowest level of detail. It should be low enough that the answers to all of the business questions within the scope of the dimensional model are derivable. It is generally a good practice to define the measures and grain as early as possible in the requirements process. In the ice cream model in this book, the grain is Ice Cream Container and Day.

index

An index is a pointer to something that needs to be retrieved. An analogy often used is the card catalog, which in the library, points you to the book you need. The card catalog will point you to the place where the actual book is on the shelf, a process that is much quicker than looking through each book in the library until you find the one you need. Indexing works the same way with data. The index points directly to the place on the disk where the data is stored, thus reducing retrieval time. Indexes work best on data elements whose values are requested frequently but rarely updated.

key

There is often a need to find specific entity instances using one or more data elements. Those data element(s) that allow us to find specific entity instances are known as keys. The Library of Congress assigns an ISBN (International Standard Book Number) to every book. A particular tax identifier can help us find an organization. The key **Account Code** can help us find a particular account.

logical data model (LDM)

A logical data model (LDM) is a business solution to a business problem. It is how the modeler captures the business requirements without complicating the model with implementation concerns such as software and hardware.

measure

A measure is a data element that may be manipulated in or is the result of a calculation (e.g., sum, count, average, minimum, and maximum).

metadata   Metadata is text, voice, or image that describes what the audience wants or needs to see or experience. The audience could be a person, group, or software program. Metadata is important because it aids in clarifying and finding the actual data.

A particular context or usage can turn what we traditionally consider data into metadata. For example, search engines allow users to enter keywords to retrieve web pages. These keywords are traditionally data, but in the context of search engines they play the role of metadata. In much the same way that a particular person can be an Employee in one role and a Customer in another role, text, voice, or image can play different roles - sometimes playing 'data' and sometimes playing 'metadata', depending on what is important to a particular subject or activity.

meter   A meter is an entity containing a related set of measures. It is not a person, place, event, or thing, as we find on the relational model. Instead, it is a bucket of common measures. As a group, common measures address a business concern, such as Profitability, Employee Satisfaction, or Sales. The meter is so important to the dimensional model that the name of the meter is often the name of the application.

natural key   A natural key is what the business sees as the unique identifier for an entity.

normalization   Normalization is the process of applying a set of rules with the goal of organizing *something*. With respect to data elements, normalization ensures that every data element is single-valued and provides a fact completely and only about its primary key. 'Single-valued' means a data element must contain only one piece of information. If **Consumer Name** contains **Consumer First Name** and **Consumer Last Name,** for example, we must split **Consumer Name** into two data elements - **Consumer First Name** and **Consumer Last Name**. 'Provides a fact' means that a given primary key value will always return no more than one of every data element that is identified by this key. If a **Customer Identifier** value of '123' for example, returns three customer last names ('Smith', 'Jones', and 'Roberts'), this violates the dependency definition. 'Completely' means that the minimal set of data elements that uniquely identify an instance of the entity is present in the primary key. If, for example, there are two data elements in an entity's primary key, but only one is needed for uniqueness, the data element that is not needed for uniqueness should be removed from the primary key. 'Only' means that each data element must provide a fact about the primary key and nothing else. That is, there can be no hidden dependencies.

object   In an object-oriented design, synonymous with a class; an entity that combines descriptions of the common behavior of like instances along with their common data attributes. Objects may be business objects, interface objects, or control objects.*

ontology   An ontology is a formal way of organizing information. It includes putting 'things' into categories and relating these categories with each other. The most quoted definition of an ontology is Tom Gruber's definition: "Explicit specification of a conceptualization." In other words, an ontology is a model – a model being a simplification of something complex in our environment using a standard set of symbols.

partition

In general, a partition is a structure that divides or separates. Specific to the physical design, partitioning is used to break a table into rows, columns or both. There are two types of partitioning - vertical and horizontal. To understand the difference between these two types, visualize a physical entity in a spreadsheet format where the data elements are the columns in the spreadsheet and the entity instances are the rows. Vertical means up and down. So vertical partitioning means separating the columns (the data elements) into separate tables. Horizontal means side to side. So horizontal partitioning means separating rows (the entity instances) into separate tables.

physical data model (PDM)

The Physical Data Model (PDM) is the Logical Data Model modified for a specific set of software or hardware. The PDM often gives up perfection for practicality, factoring in real concerns such as speed, space, and security.

primary key

A primary key is a candidate key that has been chosen to be *the* unique identifier for an entity.

program

A program is a large, centrally organized initiative that contains multiple projects. It has a start date and, if successful, no end date. Programs can be very complex and require long-term modeling assignments. Examples include a data warehouse, operational data store, and a customer relationship management system.

project

A project is a plan to complete a software development effort, often defined by a set of deliverables with due dates. Examples include a sales data mart, broker trading application, reservations system, and an enhancement to an existing application.

project manager

A person who manages project resources and activities in order to deliver the agreed-upon project outputs.*

recursive relationship

A relationship between instances of the same entity. For instance, one organization can report to another organization.*

Note: PowerDesigner refers to these as 'reflexive' relationships

relational model

A relational model captures how the business works and contains business rules, such as "A Customer must have at least one Account", or "A Product must have a **Product Short Name**."

relationship

Rules are captured on our data model through relationships. A relationship is displayed as a line connecting two entities. If the two entities are Employee and Department, the relationship may capture the rules "Each Employee must work for one Department" and "Each Department may contain many Employees."

semi-structured data

Semi-structured data is equivalent to structured data with one minor exception: Semi-structured data requires looking at the data itself to determine structure, as opposed to structured data which only requires examining the data element name. Semi-structured data is one processing step away from structured data.

♦ = See "Data Modeling Glossary"

slowly changing dimension (SCD)
Reference entity instances will experience changes over time, such as a person moving to a new address, or product name changing, or an account description being updated. On dimensional models, there is a special term that describes how to handle changing values: Slowly Changing Dimension (SCD). An SCD of Type 1 means only the most current information will be stored. An SCD of Type 2 means the most current along with all history will be stored. And an SCD of Type 3 means the most current and some history will be stored.

snowflake
A snowflake occurs when there are one or more tables for each dimension. Sometimes the snowflake structure is equivalent to the dimensional logical model, where each level in a dimension hierarchy exists as its own table. Sometimes, in a snowflake there can be even more tables than exist on the dimensional logical model. This is because vertical partitioning is applied to the dimensional model.

spreadsheet
A spreadsheet is a representation of a paper worksheet, containing a grid defined by rows and columns, where each cell in the grid can contain text or numbers.

stakeholder
A stakeholder is a person who has an interest in the successful completion of a project. Examples of stakeholders are project sponsors, business users, and team leads.

star schema
A star schema is the most common dimensional physical data model structure. A star schema results when each set of tables that make up a dimension is flattened into a single table. The fact table is in the center of the model and each of the dimensions relate to the fact table at the lowest level of detail. A star schema is relatively easy to create and implement, and visually appears elegant and simplistic to both IT and the business.

structured data
Structured data is any data named with a simple class word. 'Simple' means if data can be broken down, it can only be broken down further through normalization.

Examples:

Order Entry Date

Customer Name

Gross Sales Value Amount

subject area model (SAM)
A Subject Area Model is a set of symbols and text representing the key concepts and rules binding these key concepts for a specific business or application scope, for a particular audience, that fits neatly on one page. It could be an 8 ½ x 11, 8 ½ x 14, or similar sized paper, but it cannot be a plotter-sized piece of paper. Limiting the subject area model to one page is important because it forces the modeler and participants to select only key concepts.

subject matter expert (SME)
A person with significant experience and knowledge of a given topic or function.*

surrogate key   A surrogate key is a primary key that substitutes for a natural key, which is what the business sees as the unique identifier for an entity. It has no embedded intelligence and is used by IT (and not the business) for integration or performance reasons. Surrogate keys are useful for integration, which is an effort to create a single, consistent version of the data. Applications such as data warehouses often house data from more than one application or system. Surrogate keys enable us to bring together information about the same entity instance that is identified differently in each source system. Surrogate keys are also efficient. You've seen that a primary key may be composed of one or more attributes of the entity. A single surrogate key is more efficient to use than having to specify three or four (or five or six) attributes to locate the single record you're looking for.

taxonomy   A taxonomy is an ontology in the form of a tree. A tree is when a child only has a single parent and a parent can contain one or more children. If a child can have more than one parent, than the child is typically repeated for each parent. Examples of kinds of taxonomies are product categorizations, supertype/subtype relationships on a relational data model, and dimensional hierarchies on a dimensional data model.

use case   In object-oriented analysis, a work flow scenario defined in order to identify objects, their data, and their methods (process steps). *

user   A person who enters information into an application or queries the application to answer business questions and produce reports.

view   A view is a virtual table. It is a dynamic "view" or window into one or more tables (or other views) where the actual data is stored. A view is defined by a query that specifies how to collate data from its underlying table(s) to form an object that looks and acts like a table but doesn't physically contain data. A query is a request that a user (or reporting tool) makes of the database, such as "Bring me back all **Customer Ids** where the Customer is 90 days or more behind in their bill payments." The difference between a query and a view, however, is that the instructions in a view are already prepared for the user (or reporting tool) and stored in the database as the definition of the view, whereas a query is not stored in the database and may need to be written each time a question is asked.

wayfinding   Wayfinding encompasses all of the techniques and tools used by people and animals to find their way from one site to another. If travelers navigate by the stars, for example, the stars are their wayfinding tools. Maps and compasses are also wayfinding tools. All models are wayfinding tools. A model is a set of symbols and text used to make a complex concept easier to grasp. The world around us is full of obstacles that can overwhelm our senses and make it very challenging to focus only on the relevant information needed to make intelligent decisions. A map helps a visitor navigate a city. An organization chart helps an employee understand reporting relationships. A blueprint helps an architect communicate building plans.

♦ = See "Data Modeling Glossary"

PowerDesigner Terms

The following terms have specific meanings within PowerDesigner, which may differ from their usage in data modeling or more generally. Words in italics refer to other entries in this Glossary.

attribute (1)   An Attribute within an entity in a data model.

attribute (2)   A type of property available on an *Object* or *Sub-object* in PowerDesigner, where the property can have a single value. For example, every type of *Object* has a *Name* property. You may see a list of these attributes when configuring Display Preferences.

collection   A type of property available on an *Object* or *Sub-object* in PowerDesigner, where the property can form a link to one or more other *Objects* or *Sub-objects*. For example, every type of *Object* has a collection that lists related Business Rules. You may see a list of collections when configuring Display Preferences.

composer   A special PowerDesigner license with limited privileges, that allows non-modelers to edit the comments, descriptions, and annotations of objects directly in the PowerDesigner Portal.

composite object   Any object that has a collection of sub-objects. For example, an entity can have a collection of attributes, a business process can have a collection of sub-processes.

conversion table   A table containing a list of strings that may appear in object names, matched with equivalent (generally shorter) strings with which to replace them when generating object codes.

data item   An elementary piece of information, which represents a fact or a definition in an information system, and which may or may not have any eventual existence as a modeled object. Data Items are an integral part of the Conceptual Data Model.

dependency   A link between any two 'things' in PowerDesigner. A 'thing' can be a diagram, *object*, or *sub-object*. These links can be created manually by the modeler, but the majority are created when you *generate* a model, add symbols to diagrams, populate *collections*, or create *shortcuts* or *replicas*. See also *internal dependency* and *external dependency*.

dependency matrix   You can create *dependency* matrices to review and create links between any kind of objects. You can create an individual matrix from the Browser or define a matrix in a *resource file*, for reuse.

document   A generic term for any model or file referenced by the PowerDesigner Browser or the repository.

entity attribute   See *Attribute (1)*

Term used in drop-down lists of *object* types, such as when selecting *objects* for a list report or *dependency matrix*

extended attribute	An *attribute* that has been added to PowerDesigner via an *extension*.
extended collection	A *collection* that has been added to PowerDesigner via an *extension*.
extended dependency	See *Traceability Link*.
extended objects / sub-objects / links	User-defined *objects, sub-objects,* and *dependencies*. Extended objects and extended links are available by default in the free model, and can be added to any other type of model through the Profile category in the model's *resource file* or in an *extension* file. In the Free Model, these objects and links can represent anything you want them to, using the *stereotype* property to categorize them.
extension	A type of *resource file* that allows you to extend the properties of objects and sub-objects in a model, and also to create *extended objects* and links.
external dependency	A *dependency* between two models, or between objects in two models.
framework	A standard feature of a *project* which provides the ability to direct how your project must be modeled and lists the documents that are needed. It can also contain default content for new projects, and define actions, providing some simple automation capabilities, such as building or editing a set of subject areas.
generate	The act of creating a new model by transferring and converting the content of an existing model. The term also refers to updating a model using the same mechanism. By default, generating a model will create a *dependency* between an *object* or *sub-object* in the original model, and the corresponding *object* or *sub-object* in the generated model.
glossary	The Glossary feature allows you to share a common vocabulary and business rules. The vocabulary is expressed as a hierarchy of Terms; a Term is a word or phrase that forms part of a controlled vocabulary.
grid editor	A standard editing technique in PowerDesigner, where lists of objects or sub-objects can be edited, sorted, and filtered in a consistent way. For example, list reports, lists of *objects, collections,* and lists of *sub-objects*.
identifier	The PowerDesigner term for key♦ in the CDM and LDM.
impact and lineage analysis	The standard PowerDesigner feature that analyzes *dependencies* to visualize the context of an *object* or *sub-object*.
inheritance	The PowerDesigner term for a grouping of subtype entities.
inheritance link	The PowerDesigner term for the link between a subtype entity and an *inheritance*.

♦ = See "Data Modeling Glossary"

internal dependency	A *dependency* between two *objects* or *sub-objects* in the same model.
library	A repository-based feature that allows the organization to share *reference models* and other shared material with all users with a repository connection.
link and sync	The generic term for the ability of PowerDesigner to create, manage, and review *dependencies*.
metamodel	The data model that describes the objects supported by PowerDesigner.
naming template	A set of characteristics of object names, such as 'mixed case', maximum 256 characters, no accent characters permitted'.
object	The key building blocks of PowerDesigner models. All the objects in a model are listed as items in the Browser and they may also appear as symbols in your diagrams.
object property sheet	The standard mechanism in PowerDesigner for editing the properties (see *property*) of *object*s, which present object properties on tabs. The content and layout of the tabs can be customized.
	You can open an object property sheet in any of the following ways:
	• In the Browser, double-click the object symbol or its entry.
	• Right-click the object symbol or its Browser entry, and select 'Properties'.
	• Select the object from an object list or in the property sheet of its parent object, and click the *'Properties'* tool.
	• Select an object symbol and press <Alt+Enter>.
project	A 'container' for managing related models and external files. A project can be checked in to the repository as an object in its own right. The *dependencies* between models in a project can be illustrated in a *project diagram*.
project diagram	A project diagram allows you to display documents in a project, and the dependencies between them.
property	A discrete item of information that can be captured about an *Object* or *Sub-object* in PowerDesigner. See also *collection* and *attribute (2)*.
property sheet	See *Object Property Sheet*
reference model	A model that is automatically shared with all users of the PowerDesigner repository via the *Library*, such as a data dictionary, a PDM containing standard domains, or any model containing objects to share or reference.
reflexive relationship	The PowerDesigner term for a recursive♦ relationship.

replica Something in a model that is a managed copy of an *object* or *sub-object*. Replicas can be edited, and therefore differ from the original object, subject to the limitations imposed in the associated Replication, which maintains the link between the replica and the original *object*. Replications can be viewed by selecting `Model|Replications`. Shortcuts can be viewed by selecting `Model|Shortcuts`.

See also *shortcut*.

resource file A file used to define customizations to PowerDesigner, such as additional objects and processes, or the methods for handling a given DBMS. Resource files can be shared via the repository.

shortcut A reference to an object defined elsewhere, such as in another model or package. Unlike a *replica*, a shortcut is not an object in its own right.

stereotype A categorization of a type of object or sub-object. The simplest form of stereotype is a text label on a diagram. At the other extreme, applying a stereotype to an object can completely change the way the object is treated in PowerDesigner. For example, the object could have its own Browser folder, symbol, and properties.

sub-object A special type of object that can only exist within another object, such as an attribute within an entity.

traceability link A user-defined link between two model objects (including between objects in different models) via the 'Traceability Links' tab of the object's property sheet. These links are used for documentation purposes only, and are not interpreted or checked by PowerDesigner. They can be included in Impact Analysis.

workspace A working set of folders, projects, and models in the 'Local' tab of the Browser. Only one workspace can be open at a time.

♦ = See "Data Modeling Glossary"

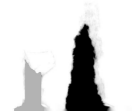

23983594R00285

Made in the USA
Lexington, KY
01 July 2013